Understanding China

The series will provide you with in-depth information on China's social, cultural and economic aspects. It covers a broad variety of topics, from economics and history to law, philosophy, cultural geography and regional politics, and offers a wealth of materials for researchers, doctoral students, and experienced practitioners.

Changsheng Chen • Guangpu Yang •
Chengjian Li

From Poverty to Prosperity

The A-C Theory to Explain China's Growth Miracle and Its International Applicability

Springer

Changsheng Chen
Macroeconomic Research Department
Development Research Center of the State
Council, China
Beijing, China

Guangpu Yang
Macroeconomic Research Department
Development Research Center of the State
Council, China
Beijing, China

Chengjian Li
Macroeconomic Research Department
Development Research Center of the State
Council, China
Beijing, China

ISSN 2196-3134 ISSN 2196-3142 (electronic)
Understanding China
ISBN 978-981-95-7170-3 ISBN 978-981-95-7171-0 (eBook)
https://doi.org/10.1007/978-981-95-7171-0

Jointly published with The Commercial Press, Ltd.

Translation from the Chinese Simplified language edition: "从贫穷走向繁荣: 解释中国增长奇迹的A-C理论及其国际适用性" by Changsheng Chen et al., © The Commercial Press, Ltd. 2021. Published by The Commercial Press, Ltd.. All Rights Reserved.

This Springer imprint is published by the registered company Springer Nature Singapore Pte Ltd.
The registered company address is: 152 Beach Road, #21-01/04 Gateway East, Singapore 189721, Singapore

Preface

There must be great stories behind great practices.

China's rapid rise from poverty to prosperity over the past half-century is undoubtedly one of the greatest achievements of humankind. How to explain the miracle of China's development, why China has been able to continue to get it "right," and whether there is a "China model" have long been debated both at home and abroad, especially since the financial crisis of 2008.

However, when interpreting the "China story," there are often two extreme tendencies internationally. One is to use Western standards as a yardstick to measure and evaluate China's development model, and the other is to try to make a fuss about the particularity or heterogeneity of China's economic development.

From the first tendency, the discussion of China's story turns into the question of whether China's development conforms to the Western model, which can be called the "Chinese student theory." This argument believes that there is no such thing as a China model, and that China's economic development achievements are the result of China's learning from the West to engage in a market economy and its reforms in accordance with the Washington Consensus, so there is nothing new and the so-called "Beijing Consensus" does not exist. If China succeeds, that is the Washington Consensus and the success of the Western development model; if China does not succeed, that means China's learning is not in place—learning the art of incompetence, to be improved—and hence this does not prove the failure of the Western development model. Some people even put forward the "China collapse theory" accordingly. They believe that so far all truly successful developed countries are Western-style or quasi-Western-style democracies, without exception. It is thus concluded that it is impossible for non-Western democracies to achieve sustained economic prosperity. China's system is very different from the so-called Western democracy, and even if "state capitalism" were to gain a short period of development, the inherent lack of self-consistency and inconsistency between China's own system and the market economy would be transformed into maladaptation and internal contradictions and would ultimately lead to collapse.

From this second tendency, the discussion of the China story often turns into a question of the opposition between Eastern and Western models. First, it takes the form of what is referred to as "Chinese exceptionalism," which holds that China's success is the result of a unique combination of history and culture, as well as a special political system and a market economy, which has produced a special and unexpected development performance—factors that no other country can possibly possess. Other countries cannot learn from it because the so-called "China model" is only an extremely special Eastern exception or even a lucky coincidence, and it has no significance for other countries in terms of popularization and reference. Based on this logic, the China Threat Theory and China-West Confrontation Theory have been proposed, arguing that China's development model is a combination of state capitalism and socialism, a combination of market economy and authoritarian system, which is inconsistent with Western traditions and breaks Western rules. If it continues to develop, it will inevitably challenge the Western standard model and threaten the so-called mainstream system in the West. "Those who are not of my race must have different hearts," as a Chinese proverb goes. In the name of maintaining the so-called Western order and international rules, the "Chinese exception" must be suppressed and contained.

As an ordinary Chinese, and as a member of the vast number of Chinese people whose destiny has been changed by the founding of new China and especially by the reform and opening up, it is difficult for me to accept the two views, both emotionally and rationally.

Emotionally, the pursuit of a better life is the common aspiration and the natural right of all human beings. Developed countries in the West have lived a rich life, and developing countries, including China, should be allowed to live a rich life, and "all roads lead to Rome." The Chinese have always believed in harmony and difference, and in order to reach the other side of the river, while the West had rowed across the river, the Chinese should also be allowed to build a bridge across the river. As to why the Chinese did not choose to row, that was determined by China's own reality and the freedom of the Chinese people. And what is wrong with providing a new possibility for "crossing the river"? History has never ended and will never end.[1] The world is more beautiful with diversity.

Rationally, the Western development model and China's development miracle are not antagonistic and incompatible, and there could be more essential factors hidden behind the two seemingly different systems. This is the central question of this book. As early as 2010, a team from the Development Research Center of the State Council conducted a study on the nature of China's economic slowdown, the core of which was to answer the question of whether the slowdown is cyclical or trending, whether the period of high-speed growth is coming to an end, and whether China will fall into the middle-income trap. Fortunately, I have been deeply involved in this study from the very beginning, and I have been responsible for summarizing the experiences and lessons learned by countries that experienced high growth and

[1]At one point in the twentieth century, with the collapse of the Soviet Union, Fukuyama (2003) claimed in *The End of History and the Last Man* that history would end with liberal democracy; that is to say, that there was no alternative to such a notion as Western liberal democracy as a universal principle of political legitimacy. This view has since proven to be bankrupt.

then fell into the middle-income trap. In the course of the study, in order to overcome the limitations of the existing theoretical framework, I spent a great deal of time reading and organizing historical documents, as well as, in particular, combing through the economic history of Europe, the United States, Latin America, the Soviet Union, and East Asia. The more one gets into the details and facts of history, the stronger the feeling becomes that, while there may seem to be a great deal of diversity among countries with different cultures, systems, and histories, there are in fact some common factors and conditions behind economic development, especially sustained economic development.

And of these conditions, two are the most fundamental, or the most important. The first is the stability of the state order and the ability of society as a whole to reach a consensus and take concerted actions; the second is the ease with which all types of members of society and economic factors can participate in the process of economic activity. If both are present, the economy is likely to take off and grow rapidly, regardless of the color of the people behind it, the religion it professes, or the system it adopts.

On this basis, I propose an analytical framework of economic accessibility and political cohesion, henceforth referred to as the A-C theory.[2] Its core argument emphasizes that the combination of cohesive political governance and access to an open economic system is the institutional basis for driving a country's economy on the road to prosperity—from poverty to wealth. In this context, cohesive political governance is usually political governance that creates a peaceful and stable social order, effectively builds a consensus, and promotes collective action, as opposed to conflictual political governance. An open-access economic system is one that guarantees people the opportunity to participate voluntarily in economic activities, as opposed to a restricted-access economic system. And according to the number of dominant political groups, political governance can be categorized into multi-peak governance and single-peak governance, which in turn leads to the formation of four forms of political governance: multi-peak conciliatory, multi-peak conflictual, single-peak unbiased, and single-peak biased. From the results, multi-peak conciliatory governance and single-peak unbiased governance, both of which are cohesive types of political governance, are in a position to realize sustainable economic development. In contrast, under multi-peak conflictual governance or single-peak biased governance, economic accessibility is often limited, and it is difficult to achieve sustained economic development and prosperity. In terms of actual development performance, whether or not an economy can achieve sustained growth and whether or not people's lives can be improved in a sustained manner have nothing to do with whether the form of political governance is multi-peak or single-peak and have nothing to do with whether or not it is a Western democratic political system.

If this framework is used to explain China's development history, it is the shift from conflict-based political governance to cohesive political governance, from

---

[2] For a nuanced discussion of economic accessibility and political cohesion (A-C theory), see Chap. 1 of this book.

access to a restricted economy to access to an open economy, and the formation of a benign interaction between single-peak unbiased political governance and access to an open economy, which has resulted in more than 40 years of rapid growth and has pushed China gradually from poverty to prosperity. Even when expanding the time to the period since the 1911 Xinhai Revolution, consistent conclusions can be drawn. Later, I used this framework to explain China's economic growth in several academic forums and visiting lectures abroad and sought advice from many experts and scholars, receiving many positive comments and responses.

Inspired by this, I began to try to use this framework to analyze the economic development of more countries, especially catch-up countries, and often gained brand-new inspiration. However, the information to be collected, the data to be mined, and the historical documents to be organized for this study were massive, and the workload was so heavy that the work was not progressing well. After 2015, with the gradual involvement of several young PhD students, including Chengjian Li, Guangpu Yang, Xing Xin, and Xiaoxiao Chen, in this work, the research progress was able to be accelerated somewhat, especially via the processing of a large amount of historical data and the refinement of theoretical models.[3] In retrospect, from the beginning of the research framework, the publication of working papers, and the continuous exchange of discussions and revisions, it took 12 years to the present time for the work to be presented to you, the readers, in the form of a monograph.

In terms of content presentation, in addition to proposing the framework of the A-C theory and using it to explain the miracle of China's economic development, we also applied this framework to analyze the country's technological catch-up process, local government competition, infrastructure construction, industrial park development, elimination of absolute poverty, growth of the middle-income population, attitudes toward new innovations, and China's economic decision-making process.[4] These are closely related to China's growth miracle and are also the areas where its development experience has attracted widespread attention from the international community. In addition, in order to explore the international applicability of this framework, we tested the A-C theory with development data from 209 countries or regions around the world and conducted long-term case studies on typical countries, such as Singapore, South Korea, Brazil, and Argentina, summarizing some lessons from falling into the middle-income trap and identifying important conditions for achieving sustained economic catch-up. For ease of reading, we took out a lot of the relatively boring technical derivations and mathematical models from the manuscript.

---

[3] In 2018, we published publicly the core theoretical results of the study for the first time as a working paper at the Institute of Development Studies at the University of Sussex, UK (Chen et al. 2018).

[4] The original manuscript of this book had a chapter devoted to the economic decision-making process and characteristics of China's central government, which are among the reasons why China was able to move from poverty to prosperity. The chapter was not made public at the time of the manuscript's official publication because the content involved some internal procedures.

Of course, the rise of China is the most important variable affecting the so-called "world pattern" in the twenty-first century. Coupled with China's own mega-scalability, this process from poverty to prosperity is in fact a complex, giant system of historical change. We dare not hope that our framework has truly deciphered the code behind China's development miracle. But as the Nobel-Prize-winning economist John Coase said, "The struggle of the Chinese is the struggle of the world." In 2020, the population of the developed world will be about 1.3 billion, while that of China will be 1.4 billion. Over the past three centuries, the two populations of comparable size have at different times made great explorations of how to move from poverty to prosperity and how to achieve industrialization and then modernization. The success of the former cannot simply be used to negate the latter, nor can the former be denied because the latter's path to success is different; when viewed in the broader context of human development, the two should be in harmony but different, and together they expand the cognitive boundaries of human life for the betterment of mankind.

The year 2021 will mark the 100th anniversary of the founding of the Communist Party of China. Under the leadership of the world's largest political party, the Chinese people are confidently embarking on a new journey of modernization by comprehensively eradicating absolute poverty, overcoming the new coronavirus epidemic, and holding high the banners of globalization and multilateralism.

Facts themselves tell stories. We firmly believe that when China becomes a truly developed country, when the Chinese people truly live a life of high income and common prosperity, and when the great rejuvenation of the Chinese nation is realized, the facts of China's success will surely be the best and most powerful explanation of the "China story," and the global value of China's development experience will also be better recognized.

And it would be our greatest honor if this preliminary research, spanning 12 years, could be a kind of commentary on this great story.

Beijing, China
Summer 2021

Changsheng Chen

References

Chen CS, Yang GP, Li CJ, Xin X (2018) From poverty to prosperity: explaining China's growth. IDS Working Paper 514, Institute of Development Studies

Fukuyama F (2003) The end of history and the last man (trans: Huang SQ). China Social Science Press, Beijing

Acknowledgments

Faced with China's prosperity today, sometimes people have an "illusion" that our lives have always been like this, especially some young people born in the twenty-first century. In fact, China has only been out of poverty for a short time, and those days of lack of food and clothing are still the childhood memories of many people. For most Chinese people, the process from poverty to prosperity is a new Long March, going through thousands of mountains and rivers.

For Chinese scholars engaged in economic research, conducting in-depth research on the logic behind China's growth miracle is not only a great fortune but also a due responsibility and a difficult practice. Why can China achieve sustained high-speed growth and long-term social stability? There is only one successful practice, but there are many possible explanations. We joined the ranks of "telling the Chinese story well" with enthusiasm and courage. But after the ambitious start, what followed was a torment of difficulties. From the start of research to the final meeting of this book with readers, it took a full 12 years.

The reason why it took so long is that, objectively, the time span involved in our research topic is relatively long. We needed to sort out the political and economic development history of China since the Xinhai Revolution and also sort out the political and economic development history of representative countries in the world, the earliest of which dates back to the fifteenth century. This is one reason. Second, data collection is very difficult. It took a lot of effort to sort out China's economic growth data since 1911 into a usable sequence, and we sorted out data from 209 countries or regions around the world, of which 41 countries' data were traced back to 1900 as much as possible. Subjectively, our research ability is still insufficient. It seems that we only discussed the issue of economic growth, but because the framework of the theory that we tried to establish had to be developed in both political governance and economic systems—especially in the field of political governance, which we were not familiar with—it was very difficult to handle and grasp. When writing, there are often countless "frustrating things" behind an exciting point, and I thought about giving up halfway many times. Fortunately, in this difficult process, we received help and encouragement from many leaders, friends, and colleagues, which enabled us to persevere.

Here, we would like to express our sincere gratitude to the leadership of the Development Research Center of the State Council, including He Liu, Mengkui Wang, Yutai Zhang, Wei Li, Jiantang Ma, Anshun Wang, Jun Han, Jiange Li, Shijin Liu, Junkuo Zhang, Laiming Zhang, Guoqiang Long, Yiming Wang, Bin Yu, and other leaders for their strong support at different stages of the research. We would also like to thank Adrian Wood, Richard Jolly, Ngaire Woods, Thomas Sargent, Minsoo Lee, Soohong Chew, Jonathan Wolff, Thomas Hale, Craig Holmes, Wen Hai, Min Liao, Zhiren Lin, Jing Huang, Junsen Zhang, Fan Zhang, Shuanglin Lin, Yong Wang, Shiji Gao, Sen Gong, Yi Liu, Wanda Guo, Geng Xiao, Yasheng Huang, Ying Ren, Xiaopu Zhang, Peilin Liu, Baoqun Fan, Shaojia Liu, Jing Gu, Benye Shi, Ting Zeng, Yukun Shi, Ning Zhang, Lu Xing, Anwen Zhang, and other experts and scholars for their comments and discussions on this book. We would also like to thank Jing Huang, Guoping Huang, Yuezhou Cai, Shuyi Yu, Xing Xin, Xiao Chen, Xiao Luo, Hang Yu, and others for their efforts and contributions to the research for the background report. We would like to thank the participants of the 2017 State Council Development Research Center–Harvard Forum for their valuable comments on this book. We would also like to thank the Blavatnik School of Government at Oxford University, the Institute of Development Studies at the University of Sussex, the Adam Smith Business School at the University of Glasgow, the National School of Development at Peking University, the Peking University HSBC Business School (Shenzhen), the Peking University HSBC Business School (Oxford), the School of Economics at Peking University, the School of Economics at Jilin University, and the School of Economics and Management at Southwestern University of Finance and Economics for hosting seminars on this book. We would also like to thank the scholars and policymakers for their feedback during our visits to Japan, Laos, Cambodia, Ethiopia, and Tanzania. We would also like to thank the China International Knowledge Center for Development (CIKD) and the Center for Emerging Countries and Global Development (CRPD) of DFID for their strong support. We would also like to thank the Central Propaganda Department for its "Four Batches" Talent Research Fund.

We would also like to thank our parents and our families for their tolerance and support. We would like to thank the Commercial Press for its strong support and the editors for their meticulous work. We would like to thank Ms. Xinyi Zhou for her careful proofreading. There are many people who have provided support and help for this research. We cannot name them one by one. We would like to express our sincere gratitude to all those who have helped us. Of course, all the opinions in this book are the responsibility of the authors and have nothing to do with the authors' unit.

We know that this research still has many shortcomings and flaws, which need further scrutiny and improvement and need to continue to be "polished." We welcome the criticism and correction of experts and readers. However, we firmly believe that by adhering to the combination of single-peak unbiased political governance and entering an open economy, China will surely move toward greater success and stronger and richer prosperity, and other developing countries can also find experience worth learning from it.

Competing Interests The authors have no competing interests to declare that are relevant to the content of this manuscript.

Contents

Chapter 1
Explaining Economic Growth: A New Framework

In the theory of economic growth, there is a long-standing and perplexing dilemma: why are some countries able to move towards affluence, while others find it difficult to escape from the quagmire of poverty? The developed economies, represented by the United Kingdom and the United States, have followed the classic Western economic development model, and it has taken more than two centuries for them to move from poverty to prosperity, creating a rich life for more than 1 billion people[1]; in contrast, the African continent, which is also home to more than 1 billion people, has had an extraordinarily arduous and tortuous path from poverty to prosperity. However, when we look at East Asia, we find a different story of growth unfolding in this part of the world. In addition to Japan, South Korea, Singapore, and a handful of other countries that succeeded in joining the ranks of the developed world, most East Asian countries are on the road from poverty to prosperity. Of course, the most notable success story is China. After more than 40 years of sustained efforts, this country of 1.4 billion people cumulatively succeeded in lifting 700 million people out of poverty, with GDP per capita of more than US $10,000 and GDP per capita in terms of purchasing power parity of more than US $17,000, and the people's standard of living already achieved an overall moderate affluence that is expected to reach the level of middle-developed countries by 2035.

So, what is it that has created this situation? Why do different countries have such different paths to development? Why is it that some countries are unable to escape the poverty trap? Are some countries really doomed to be "countries without hope", as some scholars have said? What should poor countries do in order to get rid of poverty and move towards prosperity? While the rapid development experiences of developed countries, catching-up economies, and China appear to be very different, are there any common factors behind them, and are there any common experiences that can be drawn on for the development of all countries?

---

[1] At the end of 2018, the total population of all member countries of the Organization for Economic Cooperation and Development (OECD), known as the "Club of Developed Countries," was 1.301 billion.

C. Chen et al., *From Poverty to Prosperity*, Understanding China,
https://doi.org/10.1007/978-981-95-7171-0_1

With these questions in mind, we conducted an in-depth comparative study of the development experiences of economies around the globe, on the basis of which we propose a new analytical framework for explaining a country's economic growth by revealing the more essential factors behind economic growth in terms of the dimensions of economic and political systems. We argue that a country's economic development depends on its economic accessibility and political cohesion, as well as the positive interaction between the two. If poor countries want to move out of poverty and into prosperity, they need to push their political governance as far as possible towards cohesion and continuously improve their economic accessibility. We call this theoretical framework the "A-C theory", based on the terms "accessibility" and "cohesion". In this chapter, we discuss the logical basis of our theoretical framework and its core ideas.

1.1 Origins of Problem: Searching for Common Factors Behind Different Development Models

There is a consensus in economics that institutions are a key determinant of economic development. As we comb through the relevant literature, we find that more and more researchers and policymakers have come to realize that the role of political and economic systems is crucial to economic growth. However, there is no consensus on, or even an answer to, some fundamental questions. For example, as most of the world's developed economies have adopted Western-style democracies, is this type of system a prerequisite for prosperity? If so, why do some democratic economies still struggle with poverty, while others achieve rapid long-term growth even under different institutional arrangements? Are there more fundamental factors other than political institutions that affect economic performance? If so, what are they, and how do they interact with economic development?

The initial major focus of research in the field of political economy was to explore the impact of economic performance on the political system. The dominating theories focused on the deterministic role of the economy in politics, and the research by scholars in the 1990s typified this theory. In his book *The Third Wave: Democratization in the Late Twentieth Century*, Huntington (1991) made an in-depth analysis of the causes of democratization, suggesting that economic development and cultural traditions have a strong relationship with political democratization. Although Huntington himself recognized that economic development is not a sufficient condition for democratization, there is a correlation between the degree of economic development and democracy. Represented by this "economic determinism", the field of modern political economy generally believes that the development of democracy is closely linked to the level of economic development and that the higher the level of economic development, the greater the likelihood of democratization. Seymour Martin Lipset, in his book *The Political Man: The Social Bas*es of Politics, stated that growing industrialization, urbanization, total wealth, and education levels are conducive to the establishment of democracy (Lipset 1997). Robert A. Dahl also argued that "market-capitalism has typically led to economic growth; and economic growth is favorable to democracy (Dahl 1999, p. 167)." The central idea of this view is that economic growth promotes the expansion of the middle class and that "the middle classes are the natural allies of democratic ideas and institutions (p. 168)". Djankov et al. (2003) argued that the growth of per capita income resulting from higher levels of human capital leads to the development of institutions. Glaeser et al. (2004) also emphasized that a country tends to emerge from poverty through the accumulation of both human and physical capital, and that it is only on this premise, once the country becomes rich, that it has the opportunity to improve the level of its institutions. Democracy is therefore likely to be a consequence rather than a cause of economic growth (Barro 2000). The above economic determinism views emphasize the fundamental role of economic growth and argue that economic development will provide a better foundation and context for the emergence and development of democratic political systems, but this does not manage to answer the theme of how the economy achieves prosperity and does not really answer the central questions of what determines sustained economic development and why there are large differences in economic performance across countries.

In order to solve the problems of how to achieve economic prosperity and sustained development under certain factor endowments, more and more people have begun to pay attention to the role of institutions, which has led to the formation of the influential so-called "institutional determinism". The core of institutional determinism is to emphasize the importance of institutions for economic growth. Scholars who hold this view believe that institutional change plays a decisive role in the process of economic growth and argue that it is the central factor in explaining economic growth and economic decline. In *The Rise of the Western World*, North and Thomas (1976) used the theory of institutional change to explain the economic history of Europe. They argued that the establishment of property rights and their incentives for production were key factors in initiating modern economic growth in Europe, and that the key to institutional incentives was to align the private rate of return on one's economic endeavors with the corresponding social rate of return. This view clarified for the first time the ambiguous attribute of "institution". Another representative of institutional determinism introduced econometric tools and game theory models into the study of political economy, and the differences in economic performance under different institutions were deeply examined. Acemoglu et al. (2001) looked at the seventeenth-century European colonies and argued that the huge differences in the present economic level of countries that were part of the European colonies are due to the different types of institutions and policies that the colonizers transplanted to these countries in the seventeenth to nineteenth centuries. Based on this, Acemoglu et al. (2002) further expanded the study sample and argued that political institutions have a significant impact on per capita income in former colonies. In order to prove the universality of political institutional determinism, Acemoglu et al. (2005) shifted the perspective to the examination of the reasons for the rise of Western European countries after the sixteenth century and, through a large number of statistics and empirical tests, proposed that there is an important relationship between the rise of Western European countries and the institutional changes brought about by the Atlantic trade. Regarding the mechanism of influence of institutional determinism, Acemoglu and Robinson (2000, 2006) suggested that different political regimes have different impacts on economic growth by influencing the incentives for technology introduction. Kaplan (2000) empirically analyzed countries with regime change and found that improvements in economic efficiency occurred after a change from a non-democratic to a democratic state. Rodrik and Wacziarg (2005) argued that the core of the ability of democratic societies to achieve economic growth lies in their ability to achieve better protection of private property rights and lower market entry costs. In 2012, Acemoglu and Robinson, in their important book *Why Nations Fail*, elaborated on the relevant research on institutional determinism in recent years and theoretically improved and integrated institutional determinism. Their main points are that economic and political systems have an important impact on economic growth, inclusive political systems and inclusive economic systems can promote economic growth, and predatory political systems cannot maintain an inclusive economic system in the long run, and thus are unable to maintain rapid economic growth.

In contrast to economic determinism, institutional determinism attempts to answer the proposition of what influences economic growth, but it fails to answer the question of why different institutions emerge. Acemoglu and Robinson (2012), in *Why Nation Fail*, proposed the theory of "institutional drift", which explains the formation of initial institutions as an exogenous and random process. Whether it is the theory of property rights or the theory of the impact of political and economic systems, for scholars from North to Acemoglu, the core of their systems all fall into democratic politics. They believe that the Western-style democratic political system can better match the market economy, thus improving the efficiency of resource utilization and allocation efficiency and bringing positive incentives to promote capital accumulation and technological progress.

In reality, however, Latin American countries with Western-style democracies, such as Argentina and Brazil, have experienced weak economic performance in recent years and have fallen deep into the trap of economic growth. Entering the twenty-first century, Iraq and other Middle Eastern countries established democratic systems after the war. After the Jasmine Revolution, Arab countries, such as Tunisia, Egypt, and Libya, overthrew their original regimes and established democratically elected governments. However, these countries have since been mired in political struggles, government corruption, armed conflicts, and terrorist attacks. The Western-style democratic system has not brought economic prosperity to the local area. In contrast, East Asia has seen the emergence of many non-Western democracies that maintain rapid growth. Historically, the rapid development of the Japanese economy began with the imperial edict of the Meiji Emperor, but there was no real democratic system when the South Korean economy took off. There was no real "presidential" election during the period of rapid economic growth in Taiwan Province, China, and the takeoff of the Singaporean economy happened to be the period when its government was dominated by the People's Action Party led by Prime Minister Lee Kuan Yew. At the stage of rapid economic development, these economies did not implement the so-called Western democratic system. In the nearly 100 years before the end of World War II, there was no fundamental change in Japan's political system while its economy maintained rapid development; Singapore's political system has likewise been maintained up to the present day. What is more noteworthy is that since 1978, China, the world's most populous country, has maintained high growth for more than 40 years under its current political system, even though it has not implemented a Western-style democratic political system. The fact that these cases, which differ from Western-style democratic political systems, have also resulted in high rates of growth over time suggests that there may be other, more fundamental, mechanisms for the role of institutions in the economy outside of the Western-style democratic framework, which has a more fundamental impact on economic growth.

In order to explore the role of institutions in an economy from a deeper perspective, many researchers have begun to explore the more essential causes. In this regard, North (1981) argued that social access systems have a significant impact on a country's economy. He distinguished between the concepts of limited access under a "natural state" and open-access order under an "open power society" and proposed three conditions required for the transition to open-access order: rule of law for elites; permanent public or private business organizations, including the state; and unified political control over the military. There is also a view that the political order has an important impact on the economy. Huntington (1991) believed that political stability and political order are important backgrounds for economic and political development. North (1989) further proposed the concept of an "effective state" on this basis, believing that on the basis of political stability, an "effective economic organization is the key to growth, and the emergence of an effective economic organization has led to the rise of the West."

Fukuyama (2011) also held this view. His early main view is that liberal democracy may be "the end point of human ideological development" and "the last form of human rule", and thus constitutes the "end of history" theory. However, in recent years, Fukuyama himself has begun to recognize the importance of an "effective state", where real political development means maintaining a balance between state-building, the rule of law, and democracy: the state promotes economic growth through its monopoly on violence and achieves neutrality and autonomy through the bureaucratic system. He argues that the lack of development in African countries and the debt crises in various countries, such as Italy and Egypt, among other issues, are vitally related to the lack of state-building and national capacity. Of course, while wars, political reforms, and national identity can all contribute to nation-building, it is not the case where the more dominant the state is, the better the country will develop, with fascism being a classic counterexample (Boduszyski and Pickard 2013).

These views go beyond the discussion of the democratic system itself and explore the role of the political system on the economy from a deeper level of social access and political stability. However, these theories do not answer the question of how different institutions dynamically transform and interact with each other, and they have not yet provided a sufficiently credible explanation of the path through which an institutional change affects the economy.

Taking China as an example, we can see that the political system has a very profound and essential impact on the economy, which is far from being explained by a simple democratic system. China has the largest population in the world and the second largest economy in the world, and it has achieved high economic growth for more than 40 years, with a GDP per capita of more than US $10,000 in 2020, under a non-Western democratic political system. As a result, research on the Chinese model has been enriched, and more and more attention has been paid to finding explanations for China's high economic growth from the institutional perspective. However, there are currently two very different voices regarding the relationship between institutions and economic development in China. Among them, Acemoglu and Robinson (2012) believed that there are currently two common interpretations of China's economic miracle: one is that this success relies on free markets and neoclassical economics, and the other is that it relies on wise state intervention. Both are unconvincing. They considered the institutional basis to be a key factor in understanding economic development and growth. They defined China's political system as a "grabbing political system" and argued that it was difficult to achieve sustained long-term economic growth under such a system. Huang Yasheng (2008) argued that the so-called "China model" does not exist, that China's development has benefited from the direction of market economy reforms, and that a government--led economic model is not sustainable. Fukuyama (2011) argued that China's state capacity is important to support economic development, but there are deficiencies in the rule of law and democracy.

In contrast to the optimistic view of the Chinese economy, Lin Yifu (2003, 2008) suggested that a country's development strategy determines its institutional arrangements, and these institutional arrangements ultimately determine economic performance. Yao Yang (2009) proposed the concept of a "selfless government" to explain the Chinese model, arguing that such a government is broadly representative and does not serve only specific groups of the population but prioritizes the long-term welfare of society as a whole and can therefore reject the short-term needs of certain groups. Yao Yang attributed the "neutrality" of this government to social equality, an assumption that is increasingly challenged in light of China's rising social inequality, and his framework does not address the mechanisms by which government institutions interact with economic development. Huang Shao'an (2000) suggested that China's marketization direction is consistent with the government's goals, and thus China has achieved a comprehensive transformation of its market system under the government's strong impetus. Furthermore, Zhou Li'an (2007) argued that the reason why China's economy has been able to maintain its rapid development in the long run is related to the tournament-style selection system of Chinese officials, under which incentives are provided to increase the motivation of officials to carry out economic construction, thus promoting economic growth. While these perspectives provide a number of insights at the institutional level, none of them have been able to clarify the relationship between government decision-making behavior, national strategic behavior, and institutions, and they have similarly failed to elaborate on how such institutions are formed and changed.

In order to fill the research gap in the literature on common factors behind different development models, we took a deeper look at the mechanisms surrounding the impact of institutions on economic development.

In our view, institutions affect economic growth in two main ways: first, through the ability of a society to reach a consensus and act in a coherent manner, and second, through the ability of various types of economic actors to smoothly participate in various economic activities and access markets. In order to ensure the smoothness of these two pathways, we further distinguish between types of political and economic institutions and define the conditions that need to be met by "good" institutions, which are the core factors affecting the performance of economic growth, namely, cohesive political governance and access to an open economic system, which we will discuss in the next section.

1.2 A-C Theory: Analytical Framework Based on Institutional Perspective

On the basis of an in-depth comparative study of the development experiences of global economies,[2] we put forward a brand-new theoretical framework based on the dimensions of economic and political systems to explain a country's economic growth, namely, the "accessibility-cohesion theory" (abbreviated as the A-C theory). In this framework, the development of a country's economy mainly depends on its political cohesion and economic accessibility, as well as the positive interaction between the two. In this context, political governance refers to the structure of the distribution of political power and operational mechanisms in the operation of a state, the core content of which is the allocation of power in the design, formulation, and implementation of state policies.[3] An economic system mainly is referred to as a series of institutional arrangements that determine the actions and incentives of economic entities. The core is the possibility and convenience of people's voluntary participation in economic opportunities.

Specifically, we can divide political governance into conflict-type political governance and cohesive political governance based on whether a peaceful and stable social order can be formed, a consensus can be effectively reached, and collective action can be achieved. We can divide economic systems into open-access economy

[2] Later in the book, a special section is devoted to our in-depth comparative study of the development experiences of economies around the globe, as well as the explanatory power and applicability of the A-C theory.

[3] Besley and Persson (2009, 2010, 2011) and others have conducted in-depth and detailed research on the concept of "state capacity" with a similar meaning. These studies focused on results brought about by state capacity and the mechanisms by which it works. The concept of political governance we propose in this book is broader and more fundamental.

and restricted-access economy based on whether different groups of people can participate in the economic process conveniently and fairly. Based on these two dimensions, we can broadly categorize most countries in the world into these four types, falling into the four quadrants of Fig. 1.1. Cohesive governance, as well as access to an open economic system, are conducive to economic development, and countries with such political governance and economic systems are more likely to be rich. In other words, if poor countries want to move towards affluence, they need to push political governance as far as possible towards sticking together and continuously improving economic accessibility.

1.2.1 *Different Types of Political Governance and Their Evolution*

1.2.1.1 Characteristics of the Two Types of Political Governance

Cohesive political governance refers to a form of political governance that is capable of maintaining social stability and order, facilitating social compromise and consensus, and effectively promoting collective action under a particular political power distribution structure. It is mainly characterized by some or all of the following features: (1) despite differences or conflicts among interest groups within the country, effective ways and mechanisms can be found to reach a consensus or reconciliation, and effective collective action can be formed; (2) there is no obvious deprivation and exploitation between different social groups; (3) the government can effectively implement rules and policies and has strong resource-mobilization capabilities; (4) the government attaches importance to development, has incentives to create and accumulate new wealth, and has relatively clear and consistent medium- and long-term development goals; and (5) the government is a legitimate monopolist of violence, and public power can generally be used fairly.

Conflict-based political governance refers to a form of political governance in which social order is not guaranteed under a given political power distribution structure and in which it is difficult to promote social compromise, consensus, and collective action. It is characterized by some or all of the following features: (1) there are obvious conflicts between different interest groups within the country and it is difficult for social organizations based on them to reach a consensus and take joint actions; (2) there is a tendency for one group to exploit or deprive another group; (3)

Open access economy	II	I
Restricted access economy	III	IV
	Conflict political governance	Cohesive political governance

Fig. 1.1 A-C theory: Analytical framework based on institutional perspective

the government's execution capacity is insufficient and its ability to mobilize resources is weak; (4) the government focuses on distributing existing wealth and income but does not attach importance to creating and accumulating new wealth and does not have clear and consistent medium- and long-term development goals; and (5) the government is not a legitimate monopolist of violence, or public power is often abused.

1.2.1.2 Evolution of Types of Political Governance and Their Varieties

Political governance is the result of the evolution of organized social structures. The most basic form of organization is an interest group, which can be organized by different groups, such as political parties, religions, ethnic groups, regions, cultures, occupations, and so on, and is an organized crowd. Political games, conflicts, compromises, adjustments, and the rise and fall of interest groups through certain political procedures form the basis of the basic governance structure of a society. In the process of conflict and competition among interest groups, four subtypes comprising multi-peak reconciliatory governance, multi-peak conflictual governance, single-peak unbiased governance, and single-peak biased governance are often formed, as shown in Fig. 1.2. Multi-peak reconciliatory governance and single-peak unbiased governance belong to the cohesive type of political governance, while multi-peak conflictual governance and single-peak biased governance belong to the conflictual type of political governance.

Multi-peak political governance refers to a mode of political governance in which a small number of interest groups win at the end of the process of competition among many interest groups, but none of them are able to form an overwhelming advantage, and a balance is temporarily struck between the interest groups in terms of their ability and power, which can also be referred to as pluralistic political governance. In multi-peak political governance, there are two different states of affairs. One is compromised multi-peak political governance. In this state of affairs, the two or more winning interest groups can find an effective mechanism for reconciliation and negotiation (e g, a presidential or parliamentary system, etc.) and are able to reach a short-term consensus that allows for effective collective action and implementation in situations that do not clearly oppress a particular interest group. The second is conflicting multi-peak political governance. In this state of affairs, the two or more interest groups that win have difficulty in reaching reconciliation or a consensus and are in a state of long-term confrontation and conflict. Even after acquiring the power to execute on behalf of the government in the short term through elections or forcible suppression, etc., they adopt annihilative policy arrangements, such as suppression and extraction of competing interest groups. Interest groups may take turns to gain short-term relative advantage and take turns to take measures of deprivation and extraction against relatively disadvantaged interest groups, sowing the seeds for the next round of conflict in a continuous feedback loop.

Single-peak political governance refers to the fact that in the process of competition among many interest groups, only one interest group wins at the end and forms

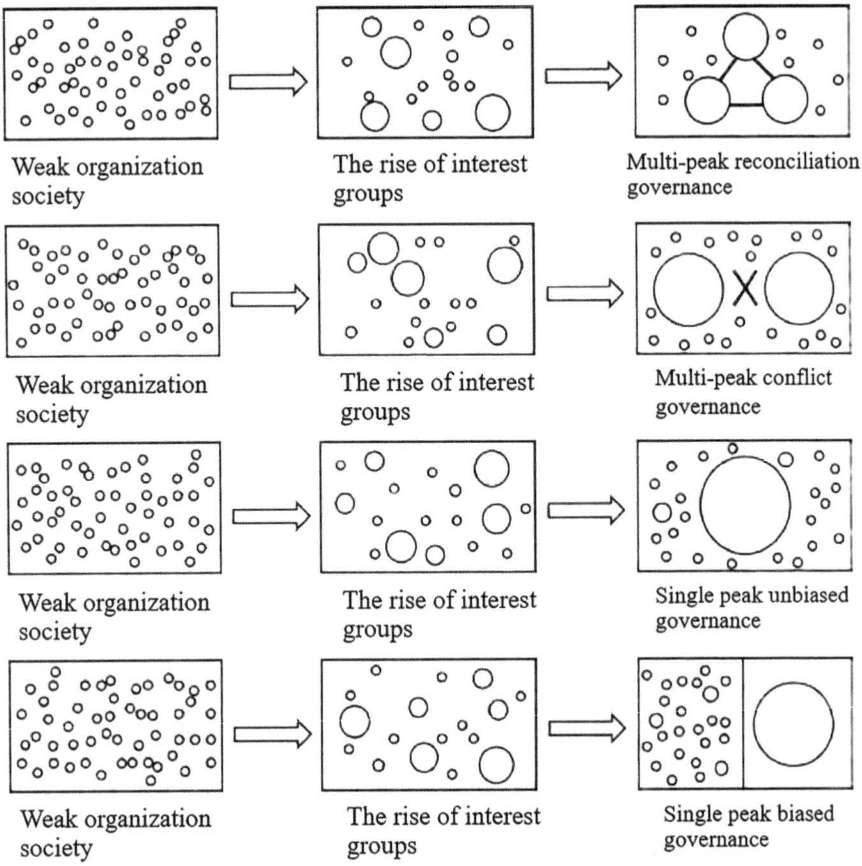

Fig. 1.2 Evolution of political governance and its four forms

an overwhelming advantage over the others, where it is impossible for other interest groups to form a counterbalance in terms of organizational capabilities, thus forming monolithic or single-peak political governance. After the single-peak organization gains control of state power, it adopts different behaviors and benefit distribution mechanisms, which in turn creates two completely different states of governance. The first is single-peak unbiased political governance. In this state of governance, the interest group that gains absolute dominance adopts a tolerant attitude towards interest groups that once competed and conflicted with it, abandons the narrow interest group view and short-term self-interest maximization, and instead focuses on medium- and long-term perspectives, balances the interests of other interest groups, strives to improve economic development performance so as to obtain more interest groups and longer-term support, and adopts an open policy towards other interest groups. In the implementation of government policies, there is no obvious bias towards interest groups, but governance proceeds from the interests of the majority of the population. In an unbiased way, it bridges the divisions and conflicts between interest groups, thereby further enhancing its absolute advantage in social support and the legitimacy of its governance. The second is single-peak biased political governance. In this state of governance, the interest group that gains absolute advantage will take an attitude of revenge or retaliation against interest groups that once competed or conflicted with it. Based on its narrow interest group view, the group will take unfair deprivation and exploitation against other interest groups, adopt a deprivation-style redistribution of social wealth and the wealth of other interest groups, and even take repressive and annihilative actions against other organizations. Instead of bridging the differences between interest groups, it may increase the differences and conflicts or just suppress such conflicts through temporary absolute advantages.

1.2.1.3 Cohesion: Key to Achieving Quality Political Governance

Whether a country forms multi-peak or single-peak political governance is essentially the result of a combination of the specific social structure formed in its history and a long process of social evolution with a certain degree of contingency, which we can regard as an exogenous decision. And will multi-peak political governance eventually evolve into multi-peak conciliatory political governance or multi-peak conflictual political governance? Will single-peak political governance eventually evolve into single-peak unbiased political governance or single-peak biased political governance? Or will multi-peak political governance and single-peak political governance transform into each other? These changes are the result of the initiative and self-selection of political groups (among themselves) in the governance process. This directly involves political legitimacy and support, discounting the long-term interests of political groups, and many other issues.

In the Western political arena, the legitimacy of the state and the legitimacy of those who implement power are commonly used as an important measure of a country's political system. Legitimacy, however, underpinned by the social contract and the theory of sovereignty over the people, emphasizes voter support. Governments and political governance that enjoy the support of the majority of voters are legitimate and legal, while the opposite is not. This is the most direct manifestation of the equation of the "majority principle" with "legitimacy" in Western democracies, which emphasizes procedural legitimacy. Accordingly, this criterion is often used to deny the legitimacy of "single-peaked political governance", especially when the summit organization wins not by the ballot, which is seen as illegitimate.

In reality, the long-term stability of governance often comes from the support of multi-dimensional legitimacy, and with only nested procedural legitimacy as its fundamental governance criterion, the governance process and policy settings are often passive, static, and fixed. First, at the institutional level, the overemphasis on procedural justice has essentially subverted the authorization-authorization relationship in democratic politics from the government-voter-government cycle, and the concept of governing legitimacy has been weakened into formalism and dogmatism. Second, the policy nesting of procedural legitimacy has its limitations, the fundamental problem being that overreaching procedural justice can slow down governing efficiency. The pandemic of the novel coronavirus in the West and the failure of governments to prevent and control the outbreak is a true reflection of policy lags caused by over-reliance on procedural legitimacy to deal with major public crises. In addition, the manipulation of voters' will to elect political elites will ultimately lead to the uneven distribution of political power and the solidification of classes. Thus, a government that rules with an overemphasis on procedural legitimacy is naturally unstable.

Typically, at the beginning of a government's existence, the population has a partially native political trust in the government based on the recognition of a value model. This trust incorporates their expectations for political performance, social order, and the long-term stable development of the country, thus conferring legitimacy on the government. However, this legitimacy conferred by ideology and native political trust is dynamic, and the government needs to utilize its promise of performance fulfillment and the organic cohesion of ideology to the realities of the country to maintain the government's long-term stability. For example, Newton and Norris (1997) introduced a government performance model to explain an important source of political trust in Western countries. Hetherington's (2005) study pointed out that the level of government trust depends on whether people believe that government performance meets their expectations. Based on cultural and institutional perspectives, Nye et al. (2015) in *Why People Don't Trust Government* included various factors, such as performance and the decline of the overall economy, as the main reasons for the decline in trust in the U.S. government. Based on the political economist Weber's (Bendix 1962) understanding of the source of state legitimacy, Zhao Dingxin (2016) incorporated the two characteristics of orthogonality and completeness and proposes that performance legitimacy is one of the ways of political legitimacy sources under the ideal type of system. Generally speaking, quantitative assessments based on rational choice are the basis for the explanation of government performance, i.e., the public will increase or decrease political trust based on the dynamics of its own interests. In addition, political entities that continue to benefit the public tend to be endowed with more long-term and stable political trust.

The emphasis on the mainstay of performance legitimacy is, to some extent, a contemporary reflection of the essence of the Confucian thought system. As the German philosopher Jaspers (De Rosa 1985) emphasized, China belongs to the imperial civilization system of the "world pattern". Compared with the institutional construction of Western countries, China has explored a national governance system paradigm that is suitable for its own situation, rooted in a social and cultural system, and has historical correctness in its thousands of years of development. As an important part of the world's axis of civilization, China has not only produced splendid material and spiritual wealth but, more importantly, institutionalized Confucianism has constructed a political system and ideological orientation for China's social order and value system that is different from the Western political ideology and value system, and that serves the value orientation of the Chinese society and the public.

In contrast to the West's procedural legitimacy, constructed on the basis of procedures and elections, as well as contractual governance, in which the government and the public compromise with each other in order to reach some kind of a consensus to rule and be ruled, the Confucian school's paradigm of state governance emphasizes the legitimacy of state governance modeled on responsibility and morality. As Qian Mu (2011) argued, the political paradigm of ancient China was a duty-based politics of the ruler. The system of social order and responsibility emphasized in traditional Confucian political thought in China urged and guided the government, on an ideological basis, to take the development of the country, the prosperity of the economy, and the well-being of the people as the starting and ending point of the governing strategy.

In addition, institutionalized Confucianism also emphasizes the importance of policy and political cohesion at the national governance level. Tang Junyi (2005) believed that the Chinese cultural spirit emphasizes integration and unity, and Parsons et al. (1953) believes that the sociological concept of integration is social harmony and unity. It can be seen that the traditional Confucian culture regards the cohesion of policy and political governance, the mutual cooperation between the public and those in power, and the spirit of unity and solidarity, as the model of an idealized society. Therefore, the vitality of institutional Confucianism is dynamically linked and historically mapped to the development of contemporary China, as well as to the correct understanding and transformation of the actual national conditions.

Of course, emphasizing only performance legitimacy is not without its problems. According to the Weberian theoretical framework, a polity that uses performance as its main source of legitimacy needs to continually propose the fulfillment of its political promises to the public in order to maintain the basis of its long-term governance. This means that as economic development goals are sequentially accomplished, the public's expectations of its performance in power will continue to rise. If the government lacks the necessary institutional and ideological support, its medium- and long-term policy planning and the design process of the input side of policy settings will inevitably be biased. If the government relies too much on performance as the basis of governance, the medium- and long-term governance pressure and policy tolerance will be affected. According to Knight (2014), a developmental government that is mainly oriented towards political performance may give rise to a number of common, as well as stage-specific, problems.

Therefore, ideological influence also plays a significant role in the ability of a government to maintain and strengthen its legitimacy. In fact, the discussion of whether or not long-term legitimacy can be achieved is essentially an adjustment of the interrelationship between procedural legitimacy, performance legitimacy, and ideological legitimacy, and centers on whether or not society is stable and whether or not it can reach a consensus on its actions.

Based on the above discussion, we assume that the objective function of political groups in both multi-peak governance and single-peak governance is to gain greater legitimacy and more popular support, which in turn promotes concerted societal action and welfare improvement, but we also assume that the ways in which political groups achieve their objectives can differ.

Under multi-peak governance, a political group can obtain power through legal procedures by means of unrealistic promises, political alliances, or oppression of opponents, and then use its advantage in power to promote amendments to the constitution and political framework, or even use the state violence machinery to suppress competing political groups and implement policies that only benefit its own interest group, leading to intensified conflicts between interest groups, reduced social stability, lower economic accessibility, and affected economic development progress. In this way, there is an obvious conflict between procedural legitimacy and performance legitimacy. Another situation may be the opposite. If a political group wants to win power, it needs to win the support of more people or more votes as much as possible, win over middle-class voters, promote alliances among political groups, and respond to people's concerns. In order to gain legitimacy and support within the existing political framework, it should also strive to reach a reconciliation between competing groups during its term of office, adopt policies that are conducive to economic development, improve economic performance, and benefit the vast majority of people (including competing interest groups). In such cases, procedural legitimacy and performance legitimacy are generally consistent. Many of the Organization for Economic Cooperation and Development (OECD) countries are now in the latter situation.

In the case of political governance, the legitimacy of the administration is not determined by the number of votes, but rather by the actions of the organization, the tangible benefits it brings to more people, the improvement of their well-being, and the further support it wins from more people. This is a different kind of legitimacy, one based on the performance of political governance. The better things are done and the more people's welfare is improved, the more people's support will be won for their rule. Selfish ends do not have to be achieved through selfish acts; selfish ends can also be achieved through selfless acts. The single-peak interest group knows that if it acts selfishly and biasedly, and when this degree of deviation reaches a certain level and critical mass, other groups with competing interests may emerge in dissatisfaction and revolt, and then its own dominant position will be threatened. As the ancient Chinese philosopher Lao Tzu said in *Tao Te Ching*, "The heavens and the earth are eternal. The reason why the heavens and the earth are eternal and lasting is that they do not produce themselves, and so they can live forever. Therefore, the sage puts others before himself and yet is ahead of others; he puts himself outside of himself and yet survives. Is it not because he is selfless? Therefore, he can achieve his own goals" (Chap. 7).

However, an interest group is not a permanent group. In the process of economic and social development, some people succeed and some people fail, and some people become rich and some people become poor. Interest groups and representatives will adjust accordingly. As a dominant interest group seeks to maintain its dominant position, it also must take into account its adaptability to such changes. Therefore, under unimodal governance, if a dominant interest group has sufficient foresight and patience and takes into account the possibility of the emergence of other competitive groups, it will act impartially as much as possible and strive to improve development performance in order to win long-term support and performance legitimacy, while maintaining the openness of its own organization and allowing emerging elites and representatives of other interest groups to enter the dominant group or to express their own interests through the dominant group. If, under single-peak governance, the ruling group is impatient (the discount rate is very low) or does not have the confidence to stay in power for a long time, there is a high risk of slipping into biased governance, which in turn will resort the ruling group to grabbing or squeezing, depriving other groups of people of their benefits and sacrificing the country's long-term development potential in order to maximize short-term gains for its own interest groups. The price it pays, of course, is the rise of other competing interests and the gradual loss of the group's dominance in political governance, or its decline to a multi-peak conflictual type of state.

Therefore, whether the ruling group is elected by referendum, and whether multi-peak or single-peak political governance is practiced, are not decisive for economic development performance; the key is whether political governance is cohesive. Whether the governance is multi-peak conciliatory political governance determined by proportionality of votes, or single-peak unbiased political governance based on performance legitimacy and the implementation of an unbiased system, only when the governance facilitates consensus, promotes collective action, puts in place and implements policies conducive to economic development, and improves access to economic opportunities that it is ultimately possible to propel a country from poverty to prosperity. If a country's initial governance structure is multi-peak, it needs to work towards multi-peak reconciliatory governance; if a country's initial governance structure is single-peak, it needs to work towards and remain unbiased. In the interim, ideological legitimacy often needs to serve this transformation process.

1.2.2 *Different Economic Systems and Their Mechanisms*

1.2.2.1 The Two Economic Systems and Their Characteristics

In our framework, access to an open economy refers primarily to the voluntary and relatively easy participation of people in a wide range of economic opportunities under a set of institutional arrangements that determine the actions and incentives of economic agents. It is characterized primarily by all or some of the following features: (1) people can migrate freely and their choice of occupation is not restricted or rarely restricted by innate factors (ethnicity, gender, region, family, etc.); (2) in a unified domestic market, various economic factors, such as capital, goods, and labor, can flow freely and internal invisible barriers are basically eliminated, forming a relatively sound national transportation network; (3) it is relatively easy to establish a business, and people can enter high-growth fields relatively freely, with property rights and contracts relatively well protected; and (4) people can participate in the global division of labor and actively strive for international markets, and their access to international knowledge and technology remain open. In general, an open economy facilitates economic activity and incentivizes capital accumulation, market development, and investment in technology.

An access-constrained economy is characterized by the existence of significant institutional barriers to voluntary participation in economic opportunities under a range of institutional arrangements that determine the actions and incentives of economic agents. It is characterized mainly by all or some of the following features: (1) people have unequal opportunities to participate in the economy, with some groups excluded from economic activities or treated unfairly; (2) the domestic market is relatively segmented, the flow of factors is significantly hindered, and the national transportation network is not sound; (3) it is difficult, or opportunities are unequal, to establish a business, making it difficult for people to enter high-growth areas, and property rights and contract enforcement are not guaranteed; and (4) people are unable or unwilling to participate in the international division of labor and there are high barriers to international trade or capital flows. Overall, there are constraints and obstacles to the development of economic activities, insufficient intrinsic economic incentives, and insufficient capital accumulation and investment in technology.

1.2.2.2 Economic Accessibility and Its Mechanisms

Economic growth in the modern sense is closely linked to the process of the Industrial Revolution. The mechanisms underlying this growth have been debated at different stages of history, with an increasing number of scholars arguing that it is technological progress that drives productivity growth and hence economic growth (Kuznets 1966; Rosenberg 1982; Mokyr 1990). The neoclassical growth theory attributes growth mainly to capital accumulation (Solow 1956), which is affected by the law of diminishing marginal returns to capital: with the increase of capital intensity, the economic growth rate theoretically slows down gradually. However, this is inconsistent with the phenomenon of long-term high-speed growth experienced by developed countries, such as the United States and Germany (Romer 1986). To solve this problem, the new growth theory began to introduce human capital and knowledge stock into the model, where increasing returns to scale are achieved through various factors, such as the externalities of public knowledge, the spillovers of innovative knowledge, and human capital externalities. In this way, if an economy conducts more research and development (R&D), the larger its knowledge stock will be and the more human capital it will accumulate, resulting in lower costs of further R&D, better returns on R&D, and more drive for sustained economic growth (Romer 1990; Helpman et al. 2004).

However, a new issue arises: if the stock of knowledge and research inputs determines technological progress and hence economic growth, developed countries, despite leading the way in R&D inputs, still experience a decline in productivity growth, which is known as the R&D "crowding out" problem. The key factor causing the problem of R&D crowding out is the difference in the diffusion of technology. As Hall (2004) puts it, the contribution of innovation and new technologies to economic growth is largely determined by the speed and extent of technology diffusion. That is to say, the contribution of technological progress to economic growth is reflected both in the invention of new technologies and, more importantly, in the depth and breadth of the use and diffusion of technology; without sufficient diffusion, the contribution of new technological advances to growth is difficult to demonstrate.

The world's technological frontier is the result of the accumulation and joint expansion of knowledge in all countries of the world. In fact, developing countries invest less in R&D and benefit mainly from the technological innovation activities of developed countries. While developed countries have to innovate in order to promote technological progress, developing countries can contribute to productivity gains by catching up with new technologies (Helpman 2004; Caselli and Coleman 2000). Countries at different stages of development will thus face different opportunities for technological progress, and their rates of productivity growth will be markedly different. For most late-developing countries, a very advantageous condition is the existence of a large number of readily available technologies (old technologies) that can be assimilated and applied without the need to create new ones.

Affluence is sometimes an absolute concept, but more often it is a relative one. For an economy to make the transition from poverty to affluence, it must promote technological progress that takes the growth trajectory beyond the original low-growth path and sustains a sufficiently long period of relatively high economic growth. Ready-made technology is there, and whether it can be absorbed effectively and diffused rapidly will determine the difference in the development performance of latecomers. The role of economic accessibility is particularly critical in enabling technology absorption and diffusion to occur smoothly.

Access to an open economic system includes two main aspects: external accessibility and internal accessibility. External accessibility is mainly manifested in the opening of the economy to the outside world, where it is possible to learn and acquire advanced international technology, knowledge, and experience and to actively participate in the international division of labor and strive for international markets through trade, investment, and other channels. Internal accessibility is mainly manifested in people of all types having the opportunity to participate in economic development and to freely migrate, start a business, and choose a job, where the horizontal and vertical flows of people are open; in a domestic market, efforts are made to break down market segmentation through transportation networks, tax system arrangements, etc., to establish a national unified market so that all types of production factors can be freely allocated and all parts of the country and all types of people have the opportunity to enter the market.

Access to an open economic system has important implications for technology absorption and application, mainly affecting the scale costs, allocative efficiency, and accelerated diffusion effects of technology, as shown in Fig. 1.3. First, openness to the outside world allows poor, late-developing countries to imitate, learn, and buy new technologies directly from the international community at a lower cost. The ability to overcome the costs of imitating, learning, and purchasing new technologies, and to make technology absorption a cost-effective affair, requires that the

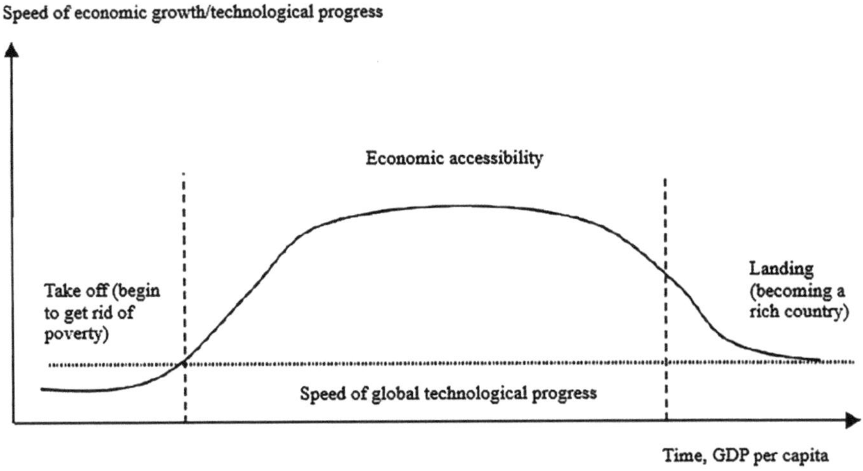

Fig. 1.3 Growth paths of economies from poverty to wealth

adoption and diffusion of technology reach a certain scale and that the cost of technology be diluted through the scale effect. A favorable condition for the late-developing countries is the natural existence of a large external market with more purchasing power than their own internal market. Opening up to the world means making full use of the ready purchasing power of international markets to make up for the shortcomings of the internal market in order to expand the scale of production of exports and then to provide financial support for the import of technology and the means of production containing new technology. Expanding the scale of foreign exports will provide opportunities for more people to participate in economic activities, which will in turn raise the income of domestic residents and promote the expansion of the size of the domestic market. In this way, with the expansion of the scale of exports, the strengthening of import capacity, and the expansion of the domestic market, the cost of technology diffusion and absorption will continue to decrease. There is ample evidence that international trade and the deepening of the division of labor have played an important role in accelerating the diffusion of new technologies, with the world's diffusion of technology three times as fast after 1925 as it had been before (Comin et al. 2008).

Second, expanding the scale of exports and imports will help to promote competition in the domestic market. Sectors and firms that can absorb new technologies more efficiently will reap higher profits. This allows the absorption and application of new technologies to take place in a competitive context, and the efficiency of resource allocation is thus enhanced. Moreover, under unified market conditions, all regions and all types of people have the opportunity to absorb and apply new technologies, and through interregional competition, more people have the possibility of being exposed to new technologies, which is conducive to the accelerated diffusion of technologies within the country. Under the pressure of competition, technology diffusion between enterprises and industries is accelerated through industrial linkages or upstream and downstream relationships.

In addition, through the opening up of the economy both externally and internally, and especially through the expansion of the scale of production in which new technologies are applied, more of the workforce has the opportunity to participate directly in the production activities of the sectors of new technology, accelerating the diffusion of technology beyond formal education through the mechanism of "learning by doing". More importantly, as the production scale of enterprises and industrial sectors applying new technologies expands, the labor force will show a more pronounced agglomeration effect, thus accelerating the process of urbanization in low-income countries. As cities expand, the rate of diffusion of knowledge and technology will also accelerate further.

As shown in Fig. 1.4, the most effective technological path for poor countries (latecomers) is not to develop unknown technologies, i.e., taking the 0→1 pathway, but to use known technologies to produce existing products and maximize cost advantages, i.e., choosing the 1→N pathway. The larger the scale of N, the lower the cost of absorbing and applying known technologies. The larger the scale of production of existing products, the more domestic resources can be absorbed and further allocated to sectors absorbing new technologies, attracting more labor to the new sectors, and contributing to overall domestic technological progress and the expansion of the size of the domestic market. This will promote a positive interaction between external and domestic entry and openness.

Entering into an open economic system is like a doorway to economic prosperity, and it is only when this door is opened that the story of economic development can be expected to take place. Creating the conditions for opening the door thus becomes an important prerequisite in the process of moving an economy from poverty to prosperity. This requires a key role for political governance and effective collective action under a given political governance to create the door that will gradually open

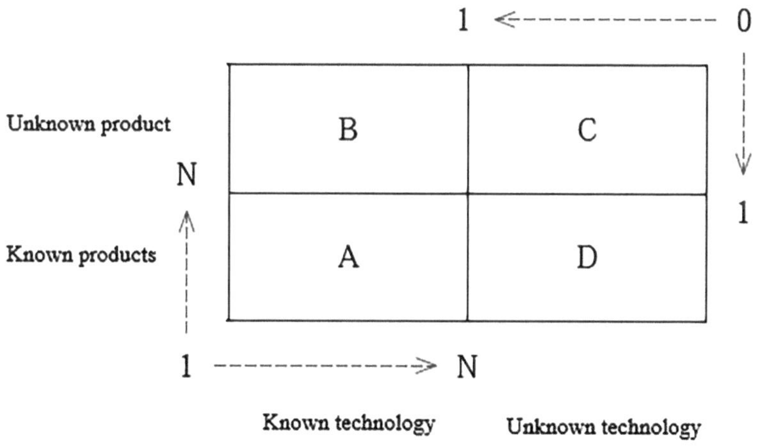

Fig. 1.4 Choice of technology pathways for poor countries to become rich

and unlock the process of economic growth. Typically, the process of opening the door of an economic system is gradual, not the wider the door is opened the better, as opening the door inevitably introduces risks and shocks, and the speed and extent of the opening of the door is predicated on continued reconciliatory political governance and stabilization of the social order. Achieving a certain level of economic development results after opening the door will facilitate further political consensus, reduce resistance to further opening the door, and seek to further expand economic accessibility. In general, the earlier and wider the doors of an economic system are opened to the internal market and made accessible to the population, the better the results will be. The doors to the external market should be opened in a gradual and orderly manner, which must be commensurate with the ability to cope with the risks of opening up. To summarize, the process of economic prosperity and the transformation of a country from poverty to wealth is a process of gradual evolution from a restricted economic system to an open-access economic system.

1.2.3 Interaction Between Political Governance and Economic System

In order to strive for long-term power and maximize the gains of interest groups, political groups will actively promote further liberalization of economic accessibility through legislation, policy adjustments, and other political actions. Increased economic accessibility will contribute to improved overall economic development performance, benefiting more people and, in turn, increasing the support of the incumbent ruling group and the likelihood of long-term power.

In a multi-peak governance model, in order to win more votes and stay in power longer, the incumbent group, while defending its own interests, will try to win over the middle voters (swing voters) to benefit more people and to ensure that its policies are supported by more people, which gives the incumbent itself an incentive to open up the economy to accessibility. Increased economic accessibility will promote competition in the marketplace and further lead to the polarization of different interest groups, with new interest groups needing new spokespersons to express their demands. Through competition among political parties, the demands of interest groups will be reflected in the political market, and the economic market will be linked to the political market, with multi-peak reconciliatory governance interacting with access to an open economic system.

If unbiased governance is to be achieved under the single-peak governance model, four conditions need to be met: the patience of the ruling group to govern for a long period of time, the potential pressure of the emergence of other interest groups, the popular demand for legitimacy of performance, and the group's openness, competitiveness, and self-innovation. If the ruling group has the patience and confidence to govern for a long time, the discount coefficient of future benefits will be relatively high; if there is the possibility of the emergence of other interest groups, the ruling group will not dare to implement overly biased governance, the people's demand for performance will prompt it to strive to maximize the overall interests in order to gain the support of the broadest population, the openness of the group will ensure that social elites and emerging interest groups can enter the ruling interest group or express their demands through effective mechanisms, and self-innovation will mean that the group has a self-correcting motivation and mechanism and can take corrective actions in time when there is a tendency to undermine impartiality. Therefore, under the single-peak unbiased governance model, through the openness and competitiveness of the ruling group itself, the interests of other groups can be expressed and reflected through internal mechanisms, thus harmonizing the political governance model with the openness and competitiveness of the economy.

Political competition under multi-peak reconciliatory is the externalization of competition in the political market, while group opening under single-peak unbiased governance is the internalization of competition in the political market. Which of the two types of competition, external or internal, is advantageous will depend on the cost of reaching political reconciliation and promoting concerted action. Whoever has lower costs is better placed to promote economic development.

Based on the framework of the A-C theory (Fig. 1.1), we can broadly categorize most of the world's countries into one of four types, i.e., one of four quadrants. Cohesive political governance and an open-access economy are more conducive to economic development, and countries with such political governance and an economic system are more likely to be rich. In order for a country to move from poverty to affluence, i.e., for its economy to achieve sustained development, the following important conditions need to be met:

1. In terms of the degree of organization, the conditions for sustained economic development are only available to a society that is effectively organized, and it is not possible to guarantee sustained economic development in a scattered or anarchic state.
2. In terms of political governance, an organized society should have the ability to reach reconciliation, form a peaceful and stable social order, and take collective action, thus forming cohesive political governance, in which both multi-peak reconciliatory governance and single-peak unbiased governance are cohesive and in which there are incentives to promote economic development.
3. In terms of the economic system, the country should adopt an entry-open economic system, or at least a gradual and orderly removal of barriers to the entry of economic factors and markets, with the sequence and pace of liberalization depending on the specific circumstances of each country.
4. In terms of the government-market relationship, as markets in poor countries are very imperfect and do not automatically improve themselves, the state should play a key role in creating markets, supporting their development, and maintaining market order. Markets and governments are not substitutes, nor do they simply make up for each other's failures; the larger the market and the more complex the transactions, the higher the demand for government capacity and the larger

the government. The government and the market are mutually reinforcing. Sustained economic growth requires developmental government and market-augmenting government.

5. In terms of the development path, due to the mutually reinforcing relationship between an economic system and political governance, giving priority to improving economic accessibility can create the economic foundation for improving the cohesion of political governance. Taking the "III→II→I" path is one option: giving priority to improving the cohesion of political governance and then promoting economic system reform and sustainable economic development. Taking the "III→IV→I" path is another option: promoting the coordinated advancement of establishing cohesive political governance and improving economic accessibility, hence evolving in mutual promotion and gradually moving towards the first type, which is taking the "III→II/IV→I" path.

1.3 Chapter Summary

To explore how a country or economy moves from poverty to prosperity, we propose a theoretical analytical framework based on an institutional perspective that reveals the more essential factors behind economic growth in terms of the dimensions of economic institutions and political governance. We argue that the combination of cohesive political governance and an open-access economy is the determining factor in moving a country from poverty to prosperity. If political governance can build a stable social order, reach a social consensus, form unified collective action, and promote efficient policy implementation, it is cohesive political governance; if under a series of institutional arrangements, various economic entities can voluntarily and relatively conveniently participate in various economic opportunities, it is an open economy. Furthermore, we categorize political governance patterns into two main types, which are multi-peak governance and single-peak governance, based on the number of political interest groups that prevail, and the patterns are further subdivided into four scenarios, which are multi-peak conciliatory governance, multi-peak conflictual governance, single-peak unbiased governance, and single-peak biased governance, based on the outcomes of the different governance patterns. Among them, multi-peak reconciliatory governance and single-peak unbiased governance belong to cohesive governance. In our framework, a political governance model being multi-peak or single-peak does not have a significant impact on sustained economic development; rather, the key lies in achieving cohesive governance. In other words, multi-peak conciliatory governance and single-peak unbiased governance can achieve cohesive political governance and promote sustained economic development, while multi-peak conflictual governance or single-peak biased governance will have difficulties achieving sustained economic prosperity.

References

Acemoglu D, Johnson S, Robinson J (2001) The colonial origins of comparative development: an empirical investigation. Am Econ Rev 91(5):1369–1401

Acemoglu D, Johnson S, Robinson J (2002) Reversal of fortune: geography and institutions in the making of the modern world income distribution. Q J Econ 117(4):1231–1294

Acemoglu D, Johnson S, Robinson J (2005) The rise of Europe: Atlantic trade, institutional change and economic growth. Am Econ Rev 95(3):546–579

Acemoglu D, Robinson J (2000) Political losers as a barrier to economic. Am Econ Rev 90(2):126–130

Acemoglu D, Robinson J (2006) Economic backwardness in political perspective. Am Polit Sci Rev 100(1):115–131

Acemoglu D, Robinson J (2012) Why nations fail: the origins of power, prosperity and poverty. Crown, New York

Barro RJ (2000) Inequality and growth in a panel of countries. J Econ Growth 5(1):1–31

Bendix R (1962) Max Weber: an intellectual portrait. Doubleday, New York

Besley T, Persson T (2009) The origins of state capacity: property rights, taxation, and politics. Am Econ Rev 99(4):1218–1244

Besley T, Persson T (2010) State capacity, conflict, and development. Econometrica 78(1):1–34

Besley T, Persson T (2011) The logic of political violence. Q J Econ 126(3):1411–1445

Boduszyski MP, Pickard D (2013) Libya starts from scratch. J Democr 24(4):86–96

Caselli F, Coleman WJ II (2000) The world technology Frontier. NBER working paper no. 7904

Comin D, Hobijn B, Rovito E (2008) A new approach to measuring technology with an application to the shape of the diffusion curves. J Technol Transf 33(2):187–207

Dahl RA (1999) On democracy. Yale University Press, New Haven

De Rosa R (1985) Der Neubeginn der Universität 1945, Karl Heinrich Bauer und Karl Jaspers. Springer, Berlin

Djankov S, Glaeser E, La Porta R et al (2003) The new comparative economics. J Comp Econ 31(4):595–619

Fukuyama F (2011) The origins of political order: from prehuman times to the French revolution. Farrar, Straus and Giroux, New York

Glaeser E, La Porta R, Lopez-de-Silanes F, Schleifer A (2004) Do institutions cause growth? J Econ Growth 9(3):271–303

Hall BH (2004) Exploring the patent explosion. J Technol Transf 30(1–2):35–48

Helpman E (2004) Trade, FDI, and the international organization of production. Conference Paper

Helpman E, Melitz MJ, Yeaple SR (2004) Export versus FDI with heterogeneous firms. Am Econ Rev 94(1):300–316

Hetherington MJ (2005) Why trust matters: declining political trust and the demise of American liberalism. Princeton University Press, Princeton

Huang SA (2000) Three hypotheses about institutional change and their verification. Soc Sci China 4:37–49+205

Huang Y (2008) Capitalism with Chinese characteristics, entrepreneurship and the state. Cambridge University Press, Cambridge

Huntington SP (1991) The third wave: democratization in the late twentieth century. University of Oklahoma Press, Oklahoma

Kaplan RD (2000) The nothing that is: a natural history of zero. Oxford University Press, Oxford

Knight JB (2014) China as a development state. World Econ 37(10):1335–1347

Kuznets S (1966) Modern economic growth: rate, structure, and spread. Yale University Press, New Haven

Lin YF (2003) Advantages and disadvantages of latecomers - a discussion with Professor Yang Xiaokai. China Econ Q 4:234–249

Lin YF (2008) Development and transformation: ideology, strategy, and self generating ability. Mon China 1:116–118
Lipset SM (1997) Political man: the social bases of politics (latest revised edition) (trans: Zhang CZ). Shanghai People's Publishing House, Beijing
Mokyr J (1990) Punctuated equilibria and technological progress. Am Econ Rev 80(2):350–354
Newton K, Norris P (1997) Confidence in public institutions: faith, culture, or performance? In: Rharr SJ, Putnam RD (eds) Disaffected democracies. Princeton University Press, Princeton
North D (1981) Structure and change in economic history. Norton, New York
North D (1989) Institutions and economic growth: an historical introduction. World Dev 17(9):1319–1332
North D, Thomas RP (1976) The rise of the western world. Cambridge University Press, Cambridge
Nye JS, Zeljko FD, King DC (eds) (2015) Why people don't trust government? (trans: Zhu FF). Commercial Press, Beijing
Parsons T et al (1953) Working papers in the theory of action. Free Press, London
Qian M (2011) Chinese cultural spirit. Jiuzhou Press, Beijing
Rodrik D, Wacziarg R (2005) Do democratic transitions produce bad economic outcomes? Am Econ Rev 95(2):50–55
Romer PM (1986) Increasing returns and long-run growth. J Polit Econ 94(5):1002–1037
Romer PM (1990) Endogenous technological change. J Polit Econ 98(5):71–102
Rosenberg N (1982) Inside the black box: technology and economics. Cambridge University Press, Cambridge
Solow RM (1956) A contribution to the theory of economic growth. Q J Econ 70(1):65–94
Tang JY (2005) The spiritual value of Chinese culture. Guangxi Normal University Press, Guilin
Yao Y (2009) Neutral government: an explanation for China's economic success during the transition period. Econ Rev 3:5–13
Zhao DX (2016) State legitimacy and state-society relations. Acad Mthly 48(8):166–178
Zhou LA (2007) A study on the promotion tournament model of local officials in China. Econ Res J 7:36–50

Chapter 2
Explanation of China's Development Miracle Based on A-C Theory

Since the founding of New China, there have been significant changes in the course of China's development. In particular, since the reform and opening up, its economy has entered a phase of rapid growth, China's economic strength and comprehensive national power have steadily increased, and the living standards of the people have realized an unprecedented improvement. Between 1978 and 2020, China's GDP increased from US $149.5 billion to US $14.7 trillion, and its total economic output accounted for more than 17% of the global total, placing it firmly in second place in the world. China's GDP per capita also increased from US $156 to more than US $10,000, resulting in more than 700 million poor people being lifted out of poverty in a comprehensive manner and people's lives going from subsistence to overall affluent well-being. The realization of such tremendous development in such a short period of time is unprecedented not only in the history of China but also in the history of the world, and China can be said to have created a miracle in the history of human development. The debate on China's development experience and model has never ceased. One of the topics that has aroused much debate is whether China's development experience and model of development are a special case compared with those of developed Western countries. Or are they essentially the same? Are there lessons to be learned from China's development experience and model for other less-developed countries? Some argue that China's success is no different from the path taken by developed Western countries and can be explained by all existing theories. There are also those who believe that China's development is the success of a new development model and that China has achieved results in many areas that cannot be explained by existing theories. It has even been pointed out that no one has yet been able to fully explain why China has been able to achieve so much development in such a short period of time.

Based on the framework of the A-C theory proposed above, we believe that whether the reason is the classical Western development model that developed economies follow to achieve their modern development achievements or the "Chinese model" that has guided more than one billion Chinese people from poverty to prosperity over the past 40 years, the fundamental determinants behind them

C. Chen et al., *From Poverty to Prosperity*, Understanding China,
https://doi.org/10.1007/978-981-95-7171-0_2

are the same, namely, political cohesion and economic accessibility. With specific reference to China's development experience, we believe that China's development has gone through a transformation from conflict-based political governance to cohesive political governance and from a restricted economy to an open economy, culminating in a combination of single-peak unbiased political governance and an open-access economy, which has led to China's high-speed growth in the past 40 years or so and pushed the country to progressively move from poverty to prosperity.

2.1 From Multi-Peak Conflictual to Single-Peak Impartial Governance

A wider historical perspective is needed to understand the evolution of political governance in China. Thousands of years of dynastic changes and a long political and cultural history have prompted the Chinese people to constantly explore the reasons for the rise and fall of nations. In the voluminous historical literature, *The Hundred Schools of Thought*, the positive histories, the wild theories, and the philosophical sayings of the scriptures have all engaged in profound thoughts and reflections on China's governance. Compared with the long dynastic history of a thousand years, 1911 was a watershed year in China's political governance. The Xinhai Revolution marked the complete disintegration of China's more than 2000 years of monarchical authoritarianism, and China, as the "First Republic of Asia," took the lead in Asia in an unprecedented attempt to establish a modern democratic system. China's political governance put an end to the "family world" model of the empire and opened the way to the search for a modernized model of democratic and republican political governance. However, it has been a magnificent journey of repeated exploration and trial-and-error correction in the midst of deep national humiliation, brutal political struggles, and profound historical lessons. Looking back at China's political governance model since 1911, two main lines can be clearly seen in the country's complicated historical changes: the continuous convergence from multi-peak to single-peak governance and the difficult trek from conflictual to cohesive governance. Under these two main lines, we categorize China's political governance model since 1911 into five stages, as discussed in the following subchapters.

2.1.1 Disintegration of Single-Peak Governance and Formation of Multi-Peak Conflictual Governance (1911–1916)

When the Qing army entered the country in 1644, China's political system basically followed the Ming system and established a monarchical centralized dynasty. The Kangxi period saw the complete liquidation of domestic clans and the recovery of

Taiwan, the improvement of the efficiency of centralized local control through the system of the inner court and the system of supervision, the opening up of the bureaucracy to Han Chinese scholars, and a series of further policies to promote economic development. Against this background, the traditional monarchy was formed and maintained smoothly until the Opium War. The First Opium War broke out in 1840, marked by the defeat of the Qing government and the signing of the Treaty of Nanjing. Foreign powers, such as the United Kingdom, actually began to enjoy extraterritoriality in China, and a semi-colonial society was forced to begin. China's national sovereignty and monarchical governance were unprecedentedly challenged. The Taiping Heavenly Kingdom movement, which began in 1851, further dealt a heavy blow to the rule of the Qing Dynasty. On the one hand, as an independent regime, the Taiping Heavenly Kingdom lasted for more than 10 years and had a wide range of influences. In its heyday, it occupied half of the Qing Dynasty and controlled the Yangtze River Basin, where the dynasty's food and taxes were plentiful, dealing a fierce blow to the autocratic dynasty. In order to pacify civil unrest, the Qing Dynasty allowed local powerful bureaucrats to carry out regimentation and prepare local armies on their own, which contributed to the strengthening of the privatization of the army and the serious weakening of the centralization of power. In the ensuing domestic and international wars, the economic, military, and political power of the bureaucratic factions continued to expand, resulting in the formation of such important and powerful bureaucrats as Zeng Guofan, Li Hongzhang, Zhang Zhidong, Zuo Zongtang, Yuan Shikai, etc. These powerful bureaucrats mastered the state railroads, shipping, iron and steel, coal, arms and machinery, navy and army, and other important departments, and the monarchical dictatorship and centralization of power continuously weakened. After the 1911 Xinhai Revolution, the Qing Emperor abdicated his throne, and after a brief period of division and conflict in China, a unified Republic of China was formed in the form of North-South peacemaking. At this time, although the Republic of China inherited the Qing Dynasty's territory, a large number of political factions and local warlords had already appeared. The social structure of the monarchical period basically disintegrated, and the embryo of multimodal governance was already in place. From 1911 to 1916, Yuan Shikai struggled to maintain the superficial unity of the Republic of China amid internal and external troubles. However, after the assassination of Kuomintang founder Song Jiaoren, many local battles, such as the Second Revolution and the National Protection Movement, broke out in China. The revolutionaries established the National Government in Nanjing and Guangzhou, and the formal unity of the Republic of China could no longer be sustained. In 1916, Yuan Shikai died, and the Beiyang warlords split into many factions, such as the Zhi, Feng, and Wan factions. The unified central government fell apart both formally and substantively, and the era of warlord conflagration ensued, marking the beginning of multi-peak conflictual governance in China's political landscape.

2.1.2 *Difficult Trek from Multi-Peak Conflictual to Multi-Peak Reconciliatory Governance (1916–1945)*

After Yuan Shikai's death in 1916, the Beiyang Warlords split. In the north and in the Yangtze River valley, the actual control of the Beiyang Warlords split into many warlords, such as the Zhi, Feng, and Wan factions, while Shanxi, Guizhou, and Yunnan were also controlled by local warlords. In the south, the Nationalist Party controlled Guangdong. There were constant conflicts between various interest groups, and their forms were not limited to political struggles but also local military conflicts. From 1916 to 1926, China presented a typical multi-peak conflictual social form. There were constant conflicts between different interest groups, and it was difficult to reach a consensus, let alone take collective action. The warlords in power did their utmost to suppress the opposition forces, which led to many political and military events. In the Beijing National Government, there was always a struggle between the pro-Japanese faction headed by Duan Qirui and the pro-American faction headed by Li Yuanhong. The two factions had different interests in many areas. On key issues, the interest groups within the Beijing government were diametrically opposed, and it was difficult to reach a joint decision. During this period, the Zhi-An War and the two Zhi-Feng Wars broke out in northern China. In Beijing, there were also major political disturbances, such as Zhang Xun's restoration, Cao Kun's bribery in elections, and Feng Yuxiang's Beijing coup. At the same time, southern China saw the Protectorate War, the two Protectorate Wars, and the battles between the Cantonese warlords and the Nationalist government in Guangzhou. Prior to the reorganized Kuomintang's Northern Expedition in 1926, the jockeying and clashes between multiple forces brought serious socio-economic harm, and conflicts under a multi-peak society were clearly characterized.

During this period, the workers and peasants represented by the Communist Party of China began to rise continuously. On the eve of the Northern Expedition, Sun Yat-sen proposed the New Three Principles of the People and promoted and implemented allying with Russia, allying with the Communist Party, and helping farmers and workers as an important part of the New Three Principles of the People. At the first Kuomintang Congress in 1924, the cooperation between the Kuomintang and the Communist Party was formally established. In 1926, the Nationalist government launched the Northern Expedition, which went smoothly. The Southern Revolutionary Army eliminated warlords, such as Sun Chuanfang and Wu Peifu in the South, within a year and established the National Government in Nanjing on April 18, 1927. In July 1927, Nanjing and Wuhan merged, and the Wuhan National Government and the Nanjing National Government were peacefully unified. In 1928, the National Revolutionary Army defeated the Fengtian warlords and controlled Beijing and Tianjin, and the Fengtian warlords retreated to the outside of the Great Wall. After the Huanggutun Incident, Fengtian leader Zhang Xueliang announced the "change of flag in the Northeast," accepting the Three Principles of the People and obeying the Kuomintang. In 1930, Shanxi warlord Yan Xishan and Northwest warlord Feng Yuxiang united to resist Chiang Kai-shek, the leader of the

Nationalist government, and the Central Plains War broke out. The war ended with Chiang Kai-shek's final victory, and his ruling position was established. At this point, the national government formally unified China. Although this unification did not substantially change the relative independence of local warlords, and thus the pattern of multi-peak governance was not broken, under the coordination of the Nanking Government, domestic interest groups had a channel for consultation. The actual mobilizing capacity of the National Government expanded to the national level, and the initial shape of multi-peak reconciliatory governance was formed for the time being.

Under multi-peak reconciliatory governance, China's economy and society achieved restorative development. From 1931 to 1936, China's industrial growth rate averaged 9.3% per year and the transportation industry flourished. In addition to telecommunications and postal services, more than 20,000 km of railways and more than 80,000 km of roads were newly built. From 1927 to 1937, civil aviation opened 12 routes with a total length of more than 15,000 km. Science and education flourished, with the number of elementary school students increasing by 86% and the number of university students by 94% between 1931 and 1937. During this period, the banking industry also showed rapid development: 23 new banks were established in Shanghai alone between 1928 and 1931. The total assets of the nation's 28 important banks grew from US $1391 million in 1926 to US $2569 million in 1931.[1] In 1935, the Nanjing government introduced a fundamental program of monetary reform, in which all grain tax payments, public and private payments, and commercial trade were to be made in fiat currency, and no more cash silver or silver dollars were to be used. From the time of the currency reform until the Lugouqiao Incident of 1937, domestic prices were stabilized, the money supply increased, the purchasing power of the people rose, the savings of the population increased, and the investment for industry and commerce increased considerably. The stabilization of the foreign exchange rate also promoted foreign trade, and with a rapid increase in the volume of exports and a rapid reduction in the foreign trade deficit, the whole national economy was thriving. During this phase, although many interest groups existed in the country, whether politically, militarily, or economically, the national government achieved collective action based on a certain degree of consensus, the economy performed well, and the state of conflict was greatly controlled. Chinese society showed a brief trend of evolution from multi-peak conflictual governance to multi-peak reconciliatory governance.

The outbreak of the Anti-Japanese War objectively had a significant impact on the formation of a consensus. Firstly, the Japanese army, which had not yet encountered serious challenges when moving southward from the northeast before entering the Yangtze River Basin, was destroying the power of local power factions wherever it passed through and objectively impacting the pattern of multi-peak society. Secondly, amid China's domestic clamor to resist foreign humiliation, especially with the establishment of the anti-Japanese national united front promoted by the

[1] Source of data: Feuerwerker (1983).

Communist Party of China (CPC), there was unprecedented unity among various classes and forces in the country, who were inspired by the call for salvation and survival. The Second Sino-Communist Cooperation, the United Front, and other forms of cooperation against external enemies continued to emerge, and although China was still in the midst of a war, it was moving towards reconciliation under a united domestic situation. In 1945, the CPC and the Kuomintang held negotiations in Chongqing, and following the signing of the Double Tenth Agreement, a coalition government was established. Thus, 30 years after the complete disintegration of single-peak society and the resulting multi-peak conflictual society in 1916, a multi-peak social structure of reconciliation finally emerged in China after the turbulence and war.

2.1.3 Re-Emergence of Single-Peak Governance and Efforts for Unbiased Governance (1945–1957)

However, China did not continue along the path of multi-peak reconciliatory governance; the Double Tenth Agreement was soon torn up by Chiang Kai-shek, and violent military clashes began in June 1946 in Henan and Hubei, followed by a full-scale civil war. The CPC-led People's Liberation Army, gradually shifting from strategic defense to strategic offense, won decisive victories in the world-renowned Three Battles, which led to the unification of mainland China. After the War of Liberation, the Communist regime was established on the mainland, China's pattern of multi-peak governance since the late Qing Dynasty came to an end, and the Central People's Government, which was unified and centralized in the true sense of the word, was established.

With the establishment of the Central People's Government of the People's Republic of China under the leadership of the CPC, the single-peak governance model became an important feature of China's political governance. After the founding of New China, the CPC developed a highly centralized model of governance for the party, government, and military, with the CPC setting up corresponding party organizations at the central and local levels of the government, the military, and other organizational bodies and centralizing the decision-making within the CPC through a democratic centralization system. The social structure at the grassroots level also underwent a major restructuring after the ensuing socialist transformation, with the unified mobilizing power of the CPC-led government reaching every village in the republic through the people's commune system, the production brigade, and grassroots party organizations. Thus, political governance with the CPC in absolute leadership authority was formed, and unimodal political governance was established.

In addition to the formation of single-peak governance, the CPC also made a rapid transition from biased to unbiased governance. At the beginning of its founding, the CPC was centered on workers and peasants and made its goal, with a distinctive revolutionary orientation, the overthrow of landlords and bourgeoisie regimes. As the domestic situation continued to change, the CPC's specific practices also constantly adjusted. For example, before the Long March, the program implemented in the revolutionary base areas in southern China was "fight the local tyrants and divide the land", while during the War of Liberation, the policy of "reducing rent and interest" was implemented for the landlord class. It can be seen that the CPC, in the process of constantly adapting to the new situation, adjusted its own development strategy, focusing on uniting the forces of all parties and coordinating their contradictions, as well as promoting the formation of a consensus in order to achieve its goals. The CPC also developed a strong mobilizing capacity through the establishment of branches, political commissars, and other means of transmitting its influence directly to the grassroots organizations. During this period, the CPC showed the characteristics of gradually transitioning to an impartial party. After the convening of the first National People's Political Consultative Conference in 1949, this impartiality became increasingly evident. Article 1 of the Common Program of the Chinese People's Political Consultative Conference stipulates: "The People's Republic of China is a new democratic state, that is, a people's democratic state. It practices the people's democratic dictatorship led by the working class, based on the worker-peasant alliance, and unites all democratic classes and nationalities in the country. It opposes imperialism, feudalism, and bureaucratic capitalism, and strives for China's independence, democracy, peace, unity, and prosperity." This provision fully reflects the vision of the CPC to build a China under unbiased governance.

After the stabilization of the new regime, China began to promote the *Three Major Reforms*, which reformed private ownership in agriculture, handicrafts, and capitalist industry and commerce. Through effective internal consultations and rational arrangements, the reforms were completed in just 3 years, using such mild transitional policies as agricultural cooperativization and asset redemption and relying on its strong mobilization capacity. The Eighth National Congress of the Communist Party of China in 1956 proposed: "After the socialist transformation of the private ownership of the means of production is basically completed, the main contradiction in the country is no longer the contradiction between the working class and the bourgeoisie, but the contradiction between the people's demand for the establishment of an advanced industrial country and the reality of a backward agricultural country, and the contradiction between the people's need for rapid economic and cultural development and the current situation where the economy and culture cannot meet the people's needs." Economic construction replaced class struggle and became the focus of the work of the party and the state. From 1957, with China's first *Five-Year Plan* completed ahead of schedule and a complete industrial system initially established, the national economy developed rapidly. At this point in time, China was politically inclusive with democratic consultation and democratic centralization, the ruling party had a strong mobilizing capacity, the government was actively involved in socio-economic construction with clear development plans and goals, and discrimination and deprivation among all segments of society had been eliminated. At this stage, the People's Republic of China, under the leadership of the CPC, basically formed the pattern of single-peak unbiased governance.

2.1.4 *Twists and Turns, and Challenges, in Development of Single-Peak Unbiased Governance (1957–1978)*

The development of China's unbiased political governance has not been smooth sailing. The Anti-Rightist struggle began in 1957 and soon became more extensive, and preventing the restoration of the bourgeoisie within the CPC gradually made "class struggle as the key link" the focus of political work. Leftist ideas and practices became more and more serious and eventually evolved into the later Cultural Revolution. According to the results of a comprehensive review conducted after the Third Plenary Session of the Eleventh Central Committee of the Communist Party of China, people branded as "rightists" throughout the country were subjected to all kinds of discrimination within their organizations; deprived of opportunities in many areas, such as education and employment; and even threatened with threats to the safety of their persons and property. Their relatives, friends, and children were also implicated. Against the backdrop of "class struggle being talked about every year, every month, and every day", the so-called "class origin" has become an important criterion for dividing the objects of struggle. Completely different policies are adopted towards the "people" and "class enemies". The country's legislative and judicial departments were severely impacted, the government was almost paralyzed, conflicts between different social groups were seriously magnified, and the unilateral and unbiased political governance encountered twists and turns. At this point, any consultative mechanism became weak and ineffective, and cohesive governance was seriously challenged. During the 10 years of civil strife, the number of cadres and people who suffered from crackdowns and persecution and were implicated reached more than 100 million throughout the country.[2]

"The Cultural Revolution wreaked havoc on national development and people's lives. The national economy was also seriously harmed," as Li Xiannian pointed out at the National Planning Conference. He said that during the 10 years of the Cultural Revolution, national income alone was lost by 500 billion yuan, a figure equivalent to 80% of all the capital investment made in the 30 years since the founding of New China, and more than the sum total of the country's fixed assets in the 30 years since the founding of New China.[3] According to Hua Guofeng's government work report at the first session of the Fifth National People's Congress, due to the destruction of

---

[2]At the closing ceremony of the Central Working Conference on December 13, 1978, Ye Jianying said, "Including those implicated, hundreds of millions of people have been victimized, accounting for one-ninth of the country's population. This lesson is extremely painful."

[3]Estimates cited by Li Xiannian in his speech at the December 1977 National Planning Conference.

the Cultural Revolution, from 1974 to 1976 alone, the country "lost a total industrial output value of 100 billion yuan, steel production of 28 million tons, and fiscal revenue of 40 billion yuan, and the entire national economy was almost on the verge of collapse." (Hua 1978). Since the founding of New China, the development process of the single-peak unbiased political governance model experienced twists and turns, as well as challenges.

2.1.5 *Improvement and Intensification of Single-Peak Unbiased Governance (1978–Present)*

In December 1978, the convening of the Third Plenary Session of the Eleventh Central Committee of the Communist Party of China marked the rapid development of China's single-peak unbiased governance after more than twenty years of setbacks. After the session, the CPC carried out a thorough correction on its ideological, political, and organizational lines, vindicated the unjust and false cases since the expansion of the Anti-Rightist movement, and shifted the center of gravity of the party and the country from class struggle to economic construction. After continuous reflection and analysis of the previous period, all sectors of society reached a consensus on the major problems of Chinese society, abandoning the deviation from unbiased governance brought about by factors, such as political discrimination and lack of consultation, and incorporating a wider range of social groups into the national development track.

First of all, judging from the historical changes in the number and composition of party members, it can be seen that the CPC generally developed along the two directions of more openness and broader representation. When the CPC was first founded in 1921, there were only 53 party members, which grew to 4,488,000 in 1949 when New China was founded (Sun 2009); by 2019, it had reached 91,914,000 members. In terms of composition, the early days of the CPC were dominated by workers; in 1927, of the 57,967 CPC members, workers accounted for 50.8%, while 18.7% were peasants, 19.1% were intellectuals, 3.1% were military personnel, 0.5% were owners of small- and medium-sized businesses, and other people accounted for 7.8%. However, with the failure of the Revolution in 1927, the center of gravity of the CPC shifted to the countryside, and the composition of party members during the Agrarian Revolution was dominated by peasants. When the Sixth CPC Congress was held in 1928, peasants accounted for 76.6% of the 40,000-odd members of the CPC, while workers' membership declined to 10% and, at one point in 1930, fell to a mere 1.6%. The farmer-dominated structure continued until the founding of New China. During the War of Resistance Against Japanese Aggression and the War of Liberation, members of the military developed into the second-largest group of party members, reaching 24% at one point in 1949. After the founding of New China, with socialist construction in full swing, the proportion of workers' party members began to rise gradually, reaching 8.8% in 1956. Since the reform and opening up, the composition of the CPC's membership became more diversified, with intellectuals, professional technicians, and private entrepreneurs being absorbed into the party in large numbers, as well as elites from some of the newly emerging economic and social organizations. According to the Organization Department of the Central Committee of the Communist Party of China (2020), as of December 31, 2019, of the 91,914,000 party members, workers accounted for 7.0%, while 27.8% were farmers, 26.7% were business owners and employees, 8.4% were party and government workers, 20.5% were retirees, and 9.7% were students and those in other occupations. Women accounted for 27.9% of party members, and ethnic minority members accounted for 7.4%. Of the 4,681,000 grass-roots party organizations, those established by non-publicly owned enterprises account for 41% of all party organizations, and more than 60% of non-publicly owned enterprises had established party organizations. It can be seen that the CPC gradually shifted from a political party that represented only a particular class and a particular group when it was first founded to one that represents the interests of a wide range of groups in society, and the unbiased character of political governance became increasingly evident.

Secondly, in terms of changes in the philosophy of governance, it is also clear that the CPC, which is at the center of single-peak governance, is gradually moving in the direction of unbiased efforts. Marked by the adoption of the 1981 Resolution on Several Historical Issues of the Party since the Founding of the State, the Chinese Government, under the leadership of the CPC, undertook a comprehensive correction of the problems of political governance during the Cultural Revolution. The 13th National Congress of the Communist Party of China, held in 1987, clarified the party's basic line for the primary stage of socialism, namely, "to lead and unite the people of all ethnic groups in the country, to focus on economic development, to adhere to the four basic principles, to persist in reform and opening up, to rely on our own efforts, to work hard, and to strive to build our country into a prosperous, democratic, civilized, modern socialist country." It further established the direction of governing towards unbiased development. In 1992, Deng Xiaoping proposed "Three Benefits" in his Southern Tour speech and took three benefits—whether it is beneficial to the development of the productive forces of socialist society, whether it is beneficial to strengthening the comprehensive national strength of the socialist country, and whether it is beneficial to improving people's living standards—as the judgment standard for people to measure the pros and cons of all work. The proposal of "Three Benefits" dispelled people's doubts about the question of capitalism vs. socialism, refocused society's attention on economic construction, and mobilized the entire society to invest more resources and strength in socialist construction. In 2000, President Jiang Zemin proposed the important thought of "Three Representatives" during his inspection tour in Guangdong Province, namely, the CPC must always represent the development requirements of China's advanced productive forces, the direction of China's advanced culture, and the fundamental interests of the vast majority of the Chinese people. The proposal of "Three Representatives" further expanded the representativeness of the CPC and united social forces on a broader scale. In 2003, Hu Jintao proposed the "Scientific Outlook on Development", which further set "comprehensive, coordinated, and sustainable" development as an important goal, placed "people-oriented" action at the core, and highlighted the CPC's concept of continuing to move towards unbiased governance. In 2012, CPC General Secretary Xi Jinping proposed the "Chinese Dream", defining it as "realizing the great rejuvenation of the Chinese nation is the greatest dream of the Chinese nation since modern times" and stating that "the Chinese Dream is first and foremost the common dream of the 1.4 billion Chinese people," further highlighting the central position of the people in national development.

The restructuring of its membership and governing philosophy since the reform and opening up demonstrates that the CPC is firmly moving towards a single-peak unbiased governance model and that unbiased governance has become an important foundation of its political governance and society. The rapid course of China's socio-economic development also confirmed the important role of the shift to an unbiased model of political governance. Through unbiased governance, the CPC incorporated more social forces and resource elements into the process of economic development, benefiting a wide range of groups from the reforms, which enabled the CPC-led Chinese government to gain the support of a wider range of the public, pushed society as a whole to reach a consensus in major decision-making, fostered collective action, and built up the strength to further deepen the reforms. In the more than 40 years of reform and opening up, the inclusiveness of Chinese society has continued to expand and government policies have benefited more and more people. With further socio-economic development, although conflicts of interest among different groups in the country still exist, under the current political system, the mechanism of consultation and reconciliation is able to play an important role smoothly and, with a strong and in-depth mobilizing capacity, the central government is able to efficiently promote consensus-building and joint action. With the continuous improvement of legislation and judicial work, the influence of internal party supervision, government supervision, and public opinion supervision is expanding, while dictatorship and oppression between different groups in society have been completely eliminated and the use of government power is increasingly regulated and constrained by law. With a GDP per capita of more than US $10,000 in 2020, or more than 17,000 international dollars as measured by purchasing power parity (PPP), China is on its way from a middle-income country to a high-income country.

Looking at the course of China's political governance over the past century, two veins can be clearly seen: first, the continuous evolution from multi-peak to single-peak governance and second, the difficult quest from conflictual to cohesive governance. Putting aside all the tedious details of the historical environment, China's evolutionary trend from multi-peak to single-peak governance may be significantly related to the 2000-year political and cultural traditions and national identity, as well as the profound yearning for great unity, which is engraved with distinctive national sentiments and homeland feelings. Undeniably, this vein has a strong oriental political civilization, which may vary from nation to nation and from country to country in the world. However, the quest from conflictual to cohesive governance has more to do with mankind's desire for stability and order, its expectation of communication, and its deep desire to transform the world and create a better life. This quest for a reconciliatory society shines with the light of humanism and should be a value common to different races, regions, and countries.

2.2 Economic System: From Restricted Economy to Open-Access Economy

In addition to the political shift from conflictual to cohesive governance, the economic system of China since 1911 is also characterized by a distinctive shift from a restricted economy to an open-access economy. China today has maintained a high rate of economic growth for decades, with an average annual growth rate of more than 9%, and this is closely related to economic accessibility. Looking at China's economic development over the past 100 years or so, we can clearly see how changes in economic accessibility affected China's economic performance.

2.2.1 Formation and Consolidation of Restricted Economy (1911–1949)

Since the Xinhai Revolution, China has experienced not only a dramatic transformation of its political structure but also a difficult transformation of its economic system. During the long period prior to the founding of New China, under the combined influence of a variety of complex factors at home and abroad, the Chinese economy gradually moved into an entry-restricted quagmire. Internally, during this period, the unified commodity market was severely fragmented, the development of enterprises was limited by the impact of war, the mobility of labor was interfered with by the military and war-related factors, and the capital market was poorly regulated, chaotic, and risky; externally, during this period, China's economy was passively opened up, but it was difficult to transform the dividends of opening up into economic dividends and the lives of the people were rarely improved. The status quo of limited internal and external accessibility was reinforced by the domestic and external environments during this period and became the basic face of China's struggling economy in the long period before the founding of New China.

2.2.1.1 Internal Accessibility Limited by Domestic Political and Economic Orders

First, the domestic commodity market was divided. After the Xinhai Revolution, the country went through a number of political struggles and military wars, and even though there was formal unification, it failed to substantively change the situation regarding the warlords, and the transportation of commodities between regions was difficult. In addition, in order to prevent the infiltration of the central government, some warlords deliberately created a variety of institutional and infrastructure barriers and adopted different regulations for infrastructure construction. For example, Shanxi warlord Yan Xishan used narrow-gauge trains to increase the cost of transportation and decreed that only locally issued provincial banknotes could be used for transactions within the province, while foreign banknotes were not recognized. Such barriers led to strong regional limitations in the production and distribution of commodities, making it difficult to form a unified national commodity market.

Second, the entry of labor into economic production was also restricted. There were a variety of factors that affected the entry of labor into economically productive activities during this period. From the demand side, the number of domestic enterprises during this period was limited and concentrated, and the demand for labor was low and concentrated in large cities. In 1912, the industrial output value of the Central China region alone accounted for 41.35% of the total national output value, most of which was concentrated in large cities, such as Wuhan and Changsha; in 1933, the number of people employed in all industrial enterprises nationwide was only 19.23 million and the scale of the demand for labor was limited, while in 1978, on the eve of reform and opening up, the number of people employed in industrial enterprises nationwide was 79.78 million (Guan et al. 2020). From the supply side, warlords around the world regarded population as an important military resource, and restrictions on out-migration and the conscription and expansion of the army were widespread everywhere, with some areas even experiencing forced conscription and "capturing the strongest men", and so a large number of school-age laborers did not enter the production chain. In addition, a large number of workers during this period had insufficient labor skills and basic knowledge, and the general labor force was mainly composed of bankrupt homesteaders or sharecroppers (Coble Jr., 1988), which made it difficult for them to enter the economically important productive sectors of the city. Under the combined influence of many factors, it is difficult for labor to enter the appropriate economic sectors smoothly and a large number of workers are excluded from socialized mass production for objective reasons.

Furthermore, the capital market was in disarray. Capital inefficiency in this period was mainly reflected in four aspects. The first is that the normal operation of financial institutions, mainly commercial banks, was subject to strong provincial government intervention; decisions depended to a large extent on the political games within provincial government authorities. The flow of capital was out of touch with the actual needs of the market, and the management of local banks was also largely affected by fluctuations in the local political situation. For example, when the warlord Wang Jialie took control of the Guizhou provincial government in September 1932, Ma Kongfan, the governor of the Guizhou Bank under the former political power, immediately left his post and was succeeded by Zheng Xianxin (Qian 1944). The governance of commercial banks actually became an extension of the warlords' power struggle. The second aspect is regional monopoly exploitation. The warlords set up regional financial institutions in their jurisdiction, issued regional bonds and provincial banknotes in the local absorption of reserves, and used a large amount of capital for the expansion of armaments. Debt defaults and currency depreciation were not uncommon (Zhang 1948). During the Beiyang period, warlords could issue regional bonds with a single order. Throughout the Beiyang period, local governments borrowed a total of 78 loans, amounting to more than 62 million silver dollars, rendering "forced borrowing and public debt more endless" (Xu 1962; Association of Chinese Historians, Institute of Modern History CASS 1990), and the funds were mainly used for military and government spending. Debt defaults and banknotes depreciation occurred frequently. During the period of the Nanjing National Government, many provinces on their own issued bonds in the name of their localities, the main purpose of which was to raise funds for military expenditures, and some provincial military governments even took the liberty of using the flag of the Republic of China, deliberately making their local bonds having the color of the central government's public bond.

The third aspect is the chaotic regulation of market entities. During the period of the Nationalist Government, the domestic capital market had many complex entities. Chartered banks, large commercial banks, and money houses located in Shanghai represented the government; foreign financial institutions in the Shanghai Concession and Hong Kong, independent and autonomous financial organizations in Tianjin and Beijing, and provincial and municipal commercial banks were directly controlled by local warlords; and financial institutions in the Soviet areas and liberated areas were under the leadership of the CPC. Different market entities had overlapping functions and inconsistent regulations, which were all exclusive to a certain extent, greatly affecting the efficiency of the financial market. The fourth aspect is that the market risk was huge due to social and economic instability. Regulations were not strict during this period, and the domestic financial market faced a large potential risk, such as the Bank of China's refusal to stop honoring exchange certificates in 1916, the silver tide in 1934, and other major risk events. Speculations prevailed, and there were a number of inflationary and even hyperinflationary events. It can be said that from the Xinhai Revolution until the founding of New China, China had not formed a real capital market, and it had always been difficult for capital to serve socio-economic development efficiently and smoothly.

To summarize, during this period, the commodity market, labor, and capital did not have good access to economic growth, and the economy's internal access restriction was very obvious.

2.2.1.2 Incompleteness of Economic Sovereignty Creating Distortions in External Accessibility

Under normal circumstances, opening up an economy to the outside world is an active choice when the economy reaches a certain stage of development. However, during the long historical period from 1911 to the founding of the People's Republic of China, China was in a state of passive opening up for a long time. The unequal treaties signed by the government under pressure from various parties that required opening up did objectively expand the scale of contact with international markets, but this kind of opening up, which was based on incomplete economic sovereignty, brought many disadvantages.

Firstly, there was a lack of voice in international trade. Even if competitive products emerged domestically, it was difficult for them to compete with other international brands on a truly equal footing. For example, during World War I, China took advantage of the war in Europe to rapidly expand the production of textiles and chemicals, among others, but after the end of World War I, the Chinese authorities abandoned their policy of supporting some of the national firms under the pressure of other victorious countries, and the development of the industries that had been expected to grow was interrupted.

Secondly, the industrial layout lost its initiative. Under passive liberalization, the country's choice of industries and industrial regions was weakened by foreign economies that, through treaty privileges, were heavily positioned in core industries, such as mining and railroads, and were squeezing domestic competitors and reaping high profits, making it difficult for the authorities to manage the industries effectively. The Kailuan Coal Mines, for example, were cheated by British occupiers. Yuan Shikai started the Luanzhou Mining Company with an initial capital of 2 million taels, but the rapid development of production, the establishment of the Luanzhou Mining Company, and the British occupation of the Kaiping Mines caused a direct threat. With the support of the British government and international financial groups, the Kaiping Mines used political and economic means to oppress the Luanzhou Mining Company, making it difficult for the mine to be maintained. In January 1912, the two sides reached an agreement and signed the Draft Joint Operation Contract to establish the Kailuan Mining Administration. However, since the management rights were in the hands of the British, the so-called joint operation was actually a merger.

Thirdly, it was difficult to translate the open-door policy into economic dividends. Although the entry of foreign companies during this period objectively increased employment, in the context of passive opening up, the government had little say during negotiations in areas such as resource protection, worker protection, and technology sharing. A large number of workers were engaged in low-level physical work with meager incomes, and it was difficult to spread production technology through corporate cooperation and employee training. The open-door policy could not benefit more groups, and economic dividends were difficult to reap. As a result, although this phase showed a pattern of superficial openness, it was difficult for this openness to be a real driver of economic growth, and it did not lead to a substantial increase in external accessibility, with the economy languishing at a low level.

Looking at the characteristics of China's economic growth in 1911–1949, we find that China's economy was obviously restricted both in terms of internal and external accessibility, and the basic pattern of China's entry-restricted economy gradually took shape and solidified, a feature that had an extremely profound impact on China's economic growth.

2.2.2 Improvements and Challenges to Economic Accessibility (1949–1978)

The significance of the founding of New China is not just a simple change of regime; the CPC adopted a series of innovative designs in the areas of political and economic systems that are different from those of other regimes. If we look at China's historical achievements from 1949 to 1978 from the perspective of economic construction, we will find that many new features of China's economic path emerged during this period. Domestically, through economic reforms and infrastructure development, the founding of New China broke down the regional economic barriers formed by the warlords in various parts of the country under the National Government, and, through strong social mobilization, it launched a series of social campaigns and economic programs that opened up a smoother path for labor and capital to enter the field of production. Externally, against the backdrop of the Cold War, China created a relatively stable diplomatic environment for itself through an active and proactive foreign policy at different times. Although the scale of its foreign economic exchanges was affected by domestic productivity and the international political situation, compared with the period before the founding of the People's Republic of China, China's foreign economic policies at this stage had greater autonomy, which paved the way for China's opening up to the outside world after the reform and opening up.

With regard to objective improvements in internal accessibility, the gradual formation of a strong and unified administrative organization at the national level after the founding of New China formed the basis for the rapid improvement in the internal accessibility of the Chinese economy during this period.

Firstly, the basic framework of a large domestic market was gradually established. In January 1950, the CPC Central Committee issued *Instructions on Establishing Land Reform Committees within People's Governments at All Levels and Organizing Farmers' Associations at All Levels to Directly Lead the Land Reform Movement* and began to prepare for the implementation of land reform in batches in newly liberated areas. By the end of 1952, including the old liberated areas, the agricultural population that had completed land reform accounted for more than 90% of the total agricultural population in the country. By the spring of 1953, land reform was universally implemented throughout the country, with the exception of minority areas, such as Xinjiang and Tibet, as well as the Taiwan Province. The land reform revolutionized the distribution of wealth in society, enabling more than 300 million peasants throughout the country to receive about 700 million *mu* of land and a large amount of means of production without compensation. The Three Major Reforms, carried out from the second half of 1952 to 1956, transformed the private ownership of the means of production into socialist public ownership, and redistribution of the means of production was realized in agriculture, handicrafts, and capitalist industries and commerce. Both the nationwide agrarian reform at the beginning of the founding of New China and the completion of the Three Major Reforms in 1956 introduced a unified economic organization to most of the country. As a result, workers of different regions, nationalities, and incomes had an equal starting point for income distribution and enjoyed equal opportunities for economic entry. In addition, the goals of the *First Five-Year Plan* (1953–1957) were achieved ahead of schedule. In those 5 years, 46 billion yuan of new fixed assets were added, equivalent to 1.9 times the original value of the national fixed assets at the end of 1952. In 1957, the total industrial and agricultural output value reached 124.1 billion yuan, an increase of 67.8% over 1952. Some industries that China did not have in the past, including aircraft, automobiles, power generation equipment, heavy machinery, new machine tools, precision instruments, electrolytic aluminum, seamless steel pipes, alloy steel, plastics, radio, etc., were built from scratch, thus transforming China's incomplete industry and increasing the strength of basic industries. The successful completion of the *First Five-Year Plan* strengthened infrastructure development throughout the country during this period and laid the foundation for subsequent industrial development. Although there was no real commodity market under the planned economy, infrastructure connectivity and regional coordination during this period objectively removed the hardware and cognitive barriers to a unified commodity market.

Secondly, the quality and quantity of labor had never been higher. For a long time, men in China were the main participants in social production, whereas the CPC, since its early days, has made women's emancipation an important task, stating that "women's emancipation must be accompanied by the emancipation of labor, and that only when the proletariat has gained power will women be truly emancipated."[4] After the founding of New China, the CPC promoted a nationwide women's liberation movement, in which women gained full political rights and their labor rights were safeguarded by the State in the form of legislation, and hence women entered the process of socialized production as an important source of labor. Also, a series of social movements carried out after the founding of New China rapidly raised the level of national education. In 1945, CPC Chairman Mao Zedong pointed out at the Seventh Congress of the Communist Party of China that "the elimination of illiteracy from 80% of the population is an important task for the new China." On May 24, 1952, China launched a large-scale literacy campaign. The policy of compulsory education, launched during this period, also improved the knowledge level of workers. The *Common Program*, promulgated in 1949, stipulated that "compulsory education should be universalized in a planned and step-by-step manner" throughout the country. The *National Agricultural Development Program (Draft)*, promulgated in 1956, stipulated that "compulsory primary education should be universalized within 5 or 7 years according to local conditions." The popularization of basic education raised the level of education of workers, and the increase in the literacy rate greatly reduced the cost of training for workers, enabling more workers to participate in the production process and laying an important foundation for the training of high-level human resources in the country. In addition, the

[4] In 1922, the Second National Congress of the Communist Party of China adopted the Resolution on the Women's Movement.

improvement in healthcare was important in improving the quality of the labor force. At the beginning of the founding of New China, the overall medical and health situation was poor, with life expectancy of less than 40 years, frequent infectious diseases, and high neonatal mortality rates. In 1950, the First National Health Work Conference was held to determine the guiding principles of "focusing on workers, peasants, and soldiers, prevention first, and unity of Chinese and Western medicine". It proposed that while ensuring production and national defense construction, healthcare work should be carried out in rural, industrial, and mining areas by relying on the masses. In 1965, Chairman Mao called for "the focus of medical and healthcare to be placed in the countryside". By this time, the national urban and rural healthcare network had basically been formed, and some diseases, such as smallpox, cholera, schistosomiasis, malaria, and bubonic plague, were either eradicated or effectively prevented and treated. Nationwide improvements in healthcare and increased life expectancy greatly improved the quality of our workforce, allowing a healthier workforce to enter into economically productive activities.

Thirdly, the state coordinated the flow of capital. During this period, there was no capital market in the true sense of the word in China, and the state became the main body of large-scale investment, with the direction of capital investment decided by the state in accordance with actual policy objectives. Under the unified decision-making of the state, capital market risks no longer appeared. Under the framework of the state-led capital investment direction, this period of state-centered concentration of efforts to do great things created remarkable economic construction results, including the initial establishment of the industrialization system, the "Two Bombs, One Star" nuclear weapon program, the Nanjing Yangtze River Bridge construction, and other remarkable achievements.

However, the improvement in the internal accessibility of the Chinese economy during this period was the objective result, rather than the subjective motive, of a specific political system and economic system. Under the framework of a planned economy, as the economic construction work continued to deepen during this period, the further development of internal economic accessibility encountered profound challenges. Although the Third Front Construction campaign, which began in the 1960s, promoted the construction of infrastructure and the formation of an industrial system across the country, it also objectively prompted the formation of a small but complete economic system in various places, which continued to evolve into a highly regional feudal economy. In addition, the quality and quantity of labor were affected by natural disasters and political movements in the country, and the persistence of the household registration system and the ticket system imprisoned the free movement of labor. Also, the policy of single national investment limited the vitality of capital, resulting in inefficient investment, an imbalance in the lightness of the industrial structure, and a slow improvement in people's standard of living. In summary, in the 30 years from the founding of the People's Republic of China to the reform and opening up, while China's internal economic accessibility did indeed improve, under the basic framework of the planned economy, the improvement was passive and objective. It was the result of the planned economy rather than a subjective effort to promote the development of the market economy. This doomed the improvement in economic accessibility during this period, making it difficult to be sustained in the long term. In addition, the domestic economic construction during this period experienced the influence of political movements, such as the Great Leap Forward campaign, the Anti-Rightist movement, and the Cultural Revolution, and the further development of internal accessibility was hindered and restricted.

With regard to the optimization of the environment for external accessibility, since the founding of New China, the external accessibility of the economy demonstrated new characteristics, which are focused on two levels. Firstly, New China's political independence gave it autonomy and independence in making decisions on foreign economic policy. Between the spring and summer of 1949, Chairman Mao successively proposed three diplomatic principles: "starting anew", "cleaning up the house before inviting guests", and "leaning to one side", which gradually formed China's basic policy of independent and peaceful diplomacy. With the abolition of unequal treaties and the withdrawal of other countries' economic privileges in China, China has thrown off the historical burden of international economic activities and fundamentally ensured that, centering on its own national interests, China can carry out economic activities with other countries. Secondly, China maintained economic ties with the outside world through a variety of means. At the beginning of the founding of New China, China joined the socialist camp through a one-sided approach to diplomacy, established good economic cooperation with the Soviet Union, rapidly built up trade and economic relations, and received strong financial and technological support from the Soviet Union at the level of national construction. China also actively maintained its relations with Third World countries, provided economic assistance and support to neighboring countries, and established a good image among Asian and African countries.

In addition, the Chinese government also adhered to an open mindset towards the outside world, paying more attention to exchanges with important economies, such as the U.S. and Japan, after the Sino-Soviet exchange. US President Nixon's visit to China in February 1972 marked the normalization of US-China relations, and the Chinese and Japanese governments issued the Sino-Japanese Joint Declaration in October 1972, which led to the establishment of formal diplomatic relations between China and Japan. Looking at China's foreign economy since the founding of New China and before the reform and opening up, even in the international context of the Cold War, the Chinese government had always centered on the fundamental interests of the country and maintained good relations with other economies, creating a favorable international environment for further foreign economic exchanges.

However, although this period saw the creation of as favorable a political and diplomatic environment as possible for the opening of the economy to the outside world, the actual situation of external economic development showed that China's ties with the rest of the world's economies were still weak. In 2006, China's total exports of goods and services as a share of GDP peaked at 36.03% in 2006, while in 1960, it was 4.31%; even on the eve of the reform and opening up in 1978, the share was only 4.56%.[5] This is a result of the specific context of the times, such as the founding of New China and the international situation of the Cold War, which dictated that China diplomatically joined the socialist camp "one way or the other"; the establishment of a socialist system in China determined that foreign economic exchanges are based on the basic framework of a planned economic system, with countries within the socialist camp as main partners; after the deterioration of Sino-Soviet relations, the external environment was difficult for a short period of time. In addition, the emergence of domestic political movements affected the Party's emphasis on economic construction and the deviation of the central work of national development in this period. Also, the developing and prospering Asian emerging economies seized the opportunity for the layout of the international division of labor in industries. These factors affected China's ability to translate favorable factors for external economic development into real economic growth and made it difficult for China to truly achieve an increase in the level of external economic accessibility.

From the above analysis, we can see that China's economy between 1949 and 1978 presented a distinctive feature relative to that before the founding of New China. On the one hand, the infrastructure was built at the level of both internal and external accessibility of the economy, and the internal and external environments objectively improved; on the other hand, none of this improvement could be smoothly transformed into a long-term sustained growth engine for the economy. However, it is undeniable that this period was one of the most important stages in the preparation for China's economic growth. Firstly, it was a period in which China made a radical leap forward in terms of its political and economic framework and built a tightly connected, independent, and unified structure of cohesive political governance; secondly, this phase of economic construction allowed China to rapidly develop the framework of a modern industrial system, which greatly improved the basic appearance of China's infrastructure; thirdly, large-scale social movements, such as the women's liberation movement, the literacy campaign, and the policy of compulsory education, rapidly increased the size and quality of the workforce; and fourthly, a favorable external environment was created for China through diplomatic efforts. These achievements, although not fully translated into high economic growth in the current period, laid the foundations for the increase in the level of economic accessibility in the next stage and created conditions for the rapid development of China's economy during the reform and opening up.

[5] Data source: World Bank Global Development Indicators 2020 (WDI 2020).

2.2.3 *Finalization of Model for Opening Up Economy to Accessibility (1978–Present)*

Following the reform and opening up, China's economic development entered a new stage, and with the support of a series of national domestic and foreign policies, the level of China's economic accessibility increased unprecedentedly compared with that of the previous stage, which, combined with the foundation of the previous economic construction, the relatively stable international environment, and good opportunities for the transfer of the global industrial chain, contributed to the sustained and rapid growth of the economy during this period. Among them, the following four reforms have been particularly crucial to the finalization of the institutional framework for economic accessibility.

2.2.3.1 From People's Commune System to Household Contract Responsibility System: Opening Up Economy to Peasants

Soon after the founding of New China, socialist reforms were carried out, following the example of the Soviet Union. In 1957 the collective economic system, in which the government and the community were united, was introduced. Under this system, there was a state monopoly on the purchase and sale of agricultural products, and farmers did not have any autonomy in production. There was no effective incentive mechanism between the work of the farmers and the remuneration for their work, and most places adopted a fixed work-point system. For laborers of similar age and gender, the same criteria are set for work points, typically "doing more or less of the same thing, doing well or doing badly of the same thing," and so farmers had no motivation and agricultural productivity was naturally difficult to improve. In addition, the people's commune system in fact contributed to the typical dual social structure, which divided urban and rural areas, and under the constraints of the household registration system, the food stamp system, and the food ration system, peasants practically lost the right to freely dispense their own property and labor altogether (Wu 2002). What, how much, and how to produce were all determined by the people's commune and the production team. Under these circumstances, economic accessibility was severely hampered, as peasants, being tightly bound to a specific commune and collective land, were not free to dispense their labor and choose their own productive activities. They also did not have the freedom of movement, needing letters of introduction to other cooperatives to go shopping in the city or even to go out to visit friends, all of which required the approval of village cadres and commune cadres.

In fact, when the people's commune system was first introduced, its shortcomings were already seen in many places, and in some rural areas, such as Zhejiang, Anhui, and Sichuan, certain practices, such as contracting production to households and remunerating farmers on the basis of agricultural output, emerged spontaneously. It was only in the course of the expansion of the Anti-Rightist movement that these spontaneous practices to liberate productive forces were stopped. Until the end of the Cultural Revolution in November 1978, farmers in some areas, such as the Xiaogang Village, Fengyang County, and Anhui Province, were forced to again take the risk of implementing the division of farmland into households and contracting production to households. The following year, the grain harvest was bountiful. Unlike in the past, especially after the Third Plenary Session of the Eleventh Central Committee of the Communist Party of China at the end of 1978, the political winds changed markedly, with enlightened leaders at the local and central levels adopting a supportive attitude towards the practice. Since then, the household contract responsibility system, commonly known as the "big package", became the basic economic system in rural China, eliminating the unified management and distribution of the production team: "Pay enough for the state, keep enough for the collective, and the rest is all for yourself." Through the reform of the rural economic system, the transition from the people's commune system to the household contract responsibility system was realized, which preserved the collective economy, while returning the freedom of production and movement to the peasants. This greatly released farmers' motivation, both in terms of increasing agricultural incomes—substantially raising agricultural productivity, improving farmers' livelihoods, and creating conditions for maintaining the overall stability of rural society—and in terms of releasing a large amount of surplus agricultural labor and preparing them to participate in non-agricultural work.

2.2.3.2 From "Class Exploitation" to Entrepreneurship: Opening Economy to Entrepreneurs

In order to ease the pressure of urban employment and to exercise revolutionary will in the vast countryside, during the Cultural Revolution, in response to Chairman Mao's call, a large number of young intellectuals from China's cities and towns went to the countryside to receive re-education from the poor and lower-middle peasants. As a result, the pressure for employment in the cities and towns dissipated into the vast countryside. After the end of the Cultural Revolution, a large number of educated youths who had gone to the countryside, totaling nearly 20 million people, returned to the cities. Cities without industrial support faced huge employment pressure, and the large number of unemployed young people had an impact on social stability. The government was forced to gradually liberalize individual businesses and private enterprises, allowing these young people to find their own way out and abandon the ridiculous dogma dug out from Marx's books that "employing more than eight people is exploitation," which allowed the market economy to begin to grow on the edge of the dominance of the state-owned economy and the collective economy. It was a group of young entrepreneurs, looked down upon and considered dishonorable at the beginning, who grew up to become the earliest group of entrepreneurs in China.

In addition, due to the implementation of the rural household contract responsibility system, the people's commune system was dissolved, and a large number of commune cadres chose the original community enterprises as a good place to settle down (Coase and Wang 2013), and township and village enterprises were birthed under the rural collective economic system. In 1978, more than 28 million peasants worked in social enterprises, accounting for 9.5% of the entire rural labor force. These township enterprises, transformed from social enterprises, have some inherent advantages over state-owned enterprises in that they do not receive enough attention from the government, have little intervention from government bureaucratic control, and are not included in the state's industrial production program. Township enterprises produce according to market needs from the outset and are able to make their own decisions and dispense their profits. Moreover, township and village enterprises, whose workers come from nearby farmers, especially the labor force released from household contracting, are very flexible in hiring and firing workers. Systems such as bonuses and piece-rate pay, which determine pay based on actual performance, have been used in township enterprises for a long time. In addition, because of the long-term implementation of the policy of emphasizing the development of heavy industry at the expense of light industry, the supply of light industry products had long been insufficient. Based on their own capital and technological level, township and village enterprises aimed at the huge gap in the light industry market from the outset and produced according to market demand. These factors contributed to the rapid growth of township and village enterprises, which at their peak in 1996 accounted for 26% of the gross domestic product, 56.1% of the total industrial output, and employed 135 million people (Naughton 2007).

As Comrade Deng Xiaoping said: "In the rural reform, the biggest gain we did not expect at all was the development of township and village enterprises, which suddenly sprang up to engage in a variety of trades and industries, to engage in the commodity economy, and to engage in a variety of small enterprises, which have risen to prominence. This is not the merit of our central government." (Deng 1993) And more than 80% of these township enterprises were later transformed into private economies. The unexpected rapid growth of the individual economy, the private economy, and township and village enterprises was not an intentional design of the Chinese government's institutional reforms, but the government's general attitude of observation and openness to this was in fact a license for such attempts to open up the economy to entry, and these unforeseen developments contributed to the return and growth of China's entrepreneurial spirit. In fact, it is precisely because of the tremendous vitality of private enterprises and township enterprises that China has further strengthened its determination and confidence to carry out economic accessibility reforms. The accompanying decentralization and profit-sharing reform of state-owned enterprises and the shift from employment plan allocation to free choice of employment for college and technical school students are all important measures to increase the accessibility of the economic system.

2.2.3.3 Transformation from Inward-Oriented to Outward-Oriented Economy: Opening of Economy to International Markets

After the end of the Cultural Revolution, the Cold War mentality was broken, and China gradually opened its long-closed doors. In 1978, China sent a number of high-level government delegations, including 13 cadres at the level of vice premier, on some 20 trips, visiting a total of nearly 50 countries and regions, including Eastern Europe, Japan, Hong Kong, and Western Europe, which greatly broadened the horizons of the Chinese people. Among them, the May 2 to June 6 mission to Western Europe, headed by Vice Premier Gu Mu, had the greatest impact. The report of the Gu Mu mission submitted to the central government put forward such important suggestions as introducing foreign technology and equipment on a larger scale with flexible payment methods, giving certain powers to localities and ministries in the foreign trade system, carrying out a science and technology-driven industrial revolution, and strengthening technological exchanges and sending as many foreign students as possible to study abroad. This study report was supported by veteran CPC officials, such as Ye Jianying, Nie Rongzhen, and other old comrades, as well as Deng Xiaoping. Vogel (2011) analogizes the historical status of the 1978 high-level visit of the Chinese government to the 1871 visit of the Iwakura Mission of Japan in the pre-Meiji Restoration period. The most important effect of these intensive foreign study tours is that they allow China's decision-makers to see the huge gap between China's development and that of the outside world, the huge potential for learning from the West's modernization and management, and the urgency of accelerating China's opening up. At the end of the Retreat on the Construction of the Four Systems, held in September 1978, the Chinese government declared that China could no longer maintain a closed economy and that it would make full use of the current favorable conditions to introduce foreign technology, equipment, capital, and management experience to speed up development and promote China's entry into a new period of opening up to the outside world. Subsequently, in January 1979, the State Council agreed to establish the Shekou Industrial Zone. In July, the Central Committee of the Communist Party of China and the State Council jointly issued a document formally approving the establishment of special economic zones. In August 1980, the 15th meeting of the Standing Committee of the National People's Congress approved the implementation of the Guangdong Province Special Economic Zone Regulations, and China's door to international markets quickly opened. The opening up to the outside world via the creation of special economic zones increased exports, attracted foreign investment, and realized the linkage between internationally available technologies and domestic factors of production and between domestic production and international markets. The production activity for broad international markets created more urban employment opportunities and absorbed the labor released from agriculture, leading to a further concentration of the population in towns and cities. Moreover, such exports are, to some extent, exports for the sake of imports, with large amounts of exports generating foreign exchange, making funds available to support the absorption of more advanced foreign technology. In terms of trade patterns, this often manifests itself in the export of low-end consumer goods, raw materials, and primary-processed goods, and the import of the means of production containing more advanced technology than that available domestically. The role of imports in productivity and technological progress is prominent in this process. In their study of the experiences of Japan, South Korea, and the United States, Diewert and Lawrence (1999) found similar situations.

In summary, this process of liberalization played five important roles: accelerating the absorption and diffusion of technology, maintaining an approximate balance of trade, learning from the experience and knowledge of participating in international markets, facilitating population agglomeration, and contributing to the growth of the domestic internal market. In addition, through the participation of entrepreneurs in internationalized production management, the participation of workers in the production process, and the mechanism of "learning by doing," China's entrepreneurship and modern industrial workers were able to grow rapidly.

2.2.3.4 From Segmented to Unified Markets: Opening Economy to Domestic Markets

In a planned economy, the overall situation is one of "one chessboard for the whole country", and economic operations are carried out in accordance with a unified national plan. However, due to incomplete information, the problem of inefficiency in centralized planning is very prominent, and the economy lacks efficiency due to over-regulation and rigidity. Therefore, even during the period of planned economy, the practices of centralization and decentralization in China were tried continuously, but often there is a dilemma that "once it is collected, it will be dead; once it is released, it will be chaotic". After the end of the Cultural Revolution, the Chinese government once again embarked on decentralized reforms by deeply reflecting on the shortcomings of a highly planned economy. There were two main dimensions: one was administrative decentralization, i.e., the decentralization of administrative decision-making to local governments, and the other was economic decentralization, i.e., the decentralization of decision-making on economic activities to production units or enterprises (Schurmann, 1966; Wu 1991). The decentralized orientation was indeed effective in mobilizing localities and enterprises and unleashing strong dynamism.

Based on the Third Front Construction from the 1960s to the 1970s, China formed a decentralized, relatively independent, and self-contained industrial base. In addition, during the reform, the government adopted various systems, such as the fiscal contracting system and the decentralization and profit-sharing of state-owned enterprises. In this series of decentralization processes, local protectionism began to grow and spread. By the mid-1980s, China's economic development was marked by regional blockades and market segmentation. Local governments exercised administrative protection over local enterprises and economic activities and set entry barriers for foreign enterprises and products by imposing additional licensing fees and extra taxes, thus forming the so-called feudal economy that seriously affected the formation of a unified national market.

In order to address the issue of market segmentation, the central government adopted a series of reforms, while making various strategic compromises in view of continuing to mobilize local initiatives. Representative institutional arrangements include the establishment of a nationally connected infrastructure network, the establishment of a fiscal system based on a tax-sharing system, and the formation of an appraisal system for the promotion of local officials, with economic development as the core indicator. As the Chinese people say, "If you want to get rich, you have to build roads first." At that time, the problem of China's transportation facilities was obvious: there was a wide variety of means of transportation, with automobiles, tractors, bicycles, animal-drawn carts, and pedestrians running around in a mixed manner along the highways through more towns and cities, densely populated, through the serious interference; highway and railroad intersections; transportation efficiency is low; traffic accidents are frequent; and so on. Against this backdrop, China put forward a strategy to develop highways in the 1980s and adopted a variety of financing innovations, such as franchising and build-operate-transfer contracting. In 1988, the Shanghai-Jiading Expressway was completed and opened to traffic, ending the history of no expressway in mainland China; in 1990, the "First Road in China", the entire Shenyang-Dalian Expressway, was completed and opened to traffic; in 1992, a national highway plan of "five longitudinal and seven transverse roads" was formulated and started to be implemented. By 2020, the total mileage of China's expressways exceeded 160,000 km. Over the past 30 years, China's expressway construction has achieved a tremendous transformation from nothing to something, from slow to fast, from point to network, and from weak to strong.

Other infrastructures in railroads, communications, and energy underwent a similar development process. A large number of research studies have shown that the construction of infrastructure and networks has a significant positive contribution to local economic growth, with obvious positive spillover effects (Liu and Zhou 2014; Zhang 2012), and has a significant direct contribution to reducing manufacturing costs. The tax-sharing reform maintained some of the vested interests of local governments through the tax rebate policy (for every 1% increase in VAT and consumption tax, the central government's tax rebate to localities increased by 0.3%), clarified the rules for transfer payments to win the acceptance of the relatively poorer provinces, and reached a convergence of interests between the central government and localities through the sharing of the main taxes (VAT and, later, corporate income tax). The tax-sharing reform not only greatly enhanced the central government's ability to centralize tax revenues and balance regional financial resources but also roughly clarified the responsibilities of the central government and the local governments in terms of financial and administrative rights, laid the foundation for cleaning up extrabudgetary revenues and standardizing local barrier fees, and further strengthened the mechanism of inter-regional competition. And in the promotion tournament for local officials (Zhou 2007), economic growth becomes the core basis for the central government's assessment, and government officials further compete in improving infrastructure and the business environment and attracting investment projects in order to develop the local economy. Through inter-local competitive learning and the promotion or transfer of officials, the experience of successfùl places is quickly passed on to other areas.

Through unified tax arrangements, spillover effects in local competition, and the authority of the central government, China broke through market segmentation, a unified market was gradually established, all regions were given the opportunity to participate in the economy, and the door to domestic market economy accessibility was opened. Admittedly, the formation of a unified market in China is a gradual process. While local protectionism still exists to a greater or lesser extent and the segmentation of the labor market and the financial market is still relatively obvious, there is still a great deal of potential and space for further promoting market unification.

The process of China's rapid economic growth is also the process of opening up the accessibility of China's economy. The liberalization of economic accessibility also shows a snowball effect, i.e., when the door to accessibility is opened a little, some people will benefit significantly, and then they will demand that it be opened further so that more people can benefit. In this way, the door to economic accessibility will be opened wider and wider. Among other things, the rule of law is further promoted in the process of opening the door to economic accessibility.[6] Further development brings more development problems, and the problems in development under cohesive governance push for deeper and deeper reforms, which will run through the whole process of China's economic transformation from poverty to affluence.

2.3 Interaction Between Single-Peak Unbiased Governance and Open Economy

It is not easy to see the fundamental factors behind China's development in the century or so since the Xinhai Revolution if one looks at it in just one dimension. However, when we put together the evolution of China's political governance over the past century, the opening up of its economic accessibility, and an economic indicator (namely, GDP per capita), the answer becomes clear: rapid economic growth is closely related to political cohesion and economic accessibility, as well as the positive interaction between the two, as shown in Fig. 2.1 (for details on the construction of each indicator and the data source, please refer to Appendix A). For example, from 1916 to 1926, China's economic accessibility was significantly

[6] A typical example is that in order to promote opening up to the outside world and actively attract foreign investment, China passed the "Law of the People's Republic of China on Sino-Foreign Joint Ventures" as early as the Second Session of the Fifth National People's Congress in 1979, while the "Company Law of the People's Republic of China" was not passed until the Fifth Session of the Standing Committee of the Eighth National People's Congress on December 29, 1993, and took effect on July 1, 1994.

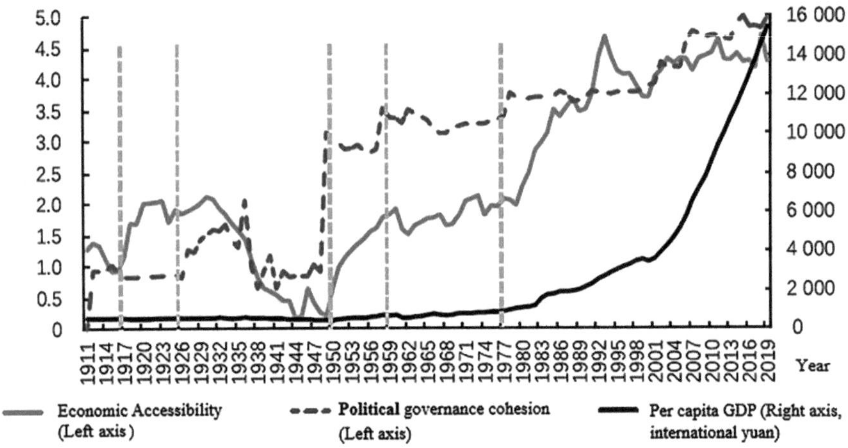

Fig. 2.1 China's economic accessibility index, political cohesion index, and GDP per capita since 1911 Revolution. Note: The data in the chart were compiled by the authors from multiple historical data sources; see Appendices A and B for details on indicator composition and raw data

higher, but the level of political cohesion during this period was relatively low due to the conflicts and chaos of the major warlords, and as a result, China's economy did not grow much during this period. Even worse than this decade was 1931–1949, when China's economic accessibility fell to its lowest level in history due to the continuous war, with a cumulative decline in GDP per capita of more than 20%. This contrasts with the 1949–1957 period and the period of reform and opening up, in which political cohesion and economic accessibility were both high compared with those of other periods, and both interacted relatively well with each other, ultimately translating into good development performance.

The rapid growth of China's economy over the past 40 years of reform and opening up has been regarded as a miracle in the history of human development. Although many scholars still have different views on this, the above review of the evolution of China's political governance patterns and economic accessibility in the framework of the A-C theory reveals that China's path from poverty to prosperity is not a smooth one, let alone an overnight one. China experienced a shift from conflictual to cohesive political governance, and from access to a restricted economy to access to an open economy, culminating in a combination of single-peak unbiased political governance and an open-access economy. It is this combination of positive interactions that has led to China's rapid growth for more than 40 years.

In the process of China's reforming and opening up, the central government's development strategies at different stages have always emphasized the need to deal with the relationship between development, reform, and stability and to maintain a balance among the three. While this may appear to be a mere political slogan, it in fact reflects an interactive relationship between China's political governance and economic system.

In the framework of the A-C theory, stabilization emphasizes maintaining social order, avoiding social unrest, and reaching a consensus wherever possible to advance collective action. Reforms emphasize lowering and removing barriers to economic and social development, opening up economic accessibility both internally and externally, giving more people opportunities, improving efficiency, and developing productive forces, and are essentially about solving problems. Development emphasizes greater incrementalism, increasing the size of the economy, lowering unit costs, promoting the diffusion of technology and knowledge, and enabling more people to access and share in the benefits of development, and the process of development is both a process of identifying and generating new problems, laying the groundwork for further reforms.

The Chinese government repeatedly reiterates that development is the first priority, reform is the fundamental way out, and stability is the foundation and prerequisite. The essence is that only by achieving development results and making the benefits of development available to more people will the ruling party win more support, facilitate the formation of a consensus on new policies and reforms, and further enhance its monolithic status. This is both a mechanism for legitimizing performance and a channel for achieving social reconciliation and a consensus on development solutions to development problems. Reforms, as the fundamental way out, emphasize the need to respond to new problems and expectations in development, and that only by breaking through obstacles of the system, creating more opportunities, and promoting more effective competition can society strive for greater development. The more open the economic accessibility, the greater the potential for economic development. Stability is the foundation and prerequisite; without a stable environment and social order, an effective social consensus cannot be reached, reforms cannot be advanced, and development will not take place; effective reforms and development, which result in improved benefits for the majority of the population, will further enhance social stability. In the process of development, it is precisely because of the efforts to realize the interaction and balance of these three that China's miracle of "always getting things right" has come about.

Not only that, there are also some distinctly Chinese features of the interaction between China's political governance and economic system that require special attention.

The first feature is China's mutually reinforcing government-market relationship. China's reform process began with a planned economy, but it was not true that reforms could be successful as soon as the government was decentralized during market-oriented reforms; in fact, the government plays a key role in the process of creating markets and facilitating their development, among others. The government and the market promote each other rather than complement each other, not simply that "the market cannot do what the government does, and the government cannot do what the market does". The government plays an important role in facilitating the transition from markets within the sphere of interpersonal relationships to markets outside the sphere of interpersonal relationships, and from small local markets to large national markets. The boundary between the government and the market has always been dynamically adjusted to the actual situation of economic and social development, rather than sticking to the government's size. On the one hand, the government constantly reduces its direct intervention in the market; on the other hand, with the complexity of market transactions, the government, in the process of regulation of the market, expands the functions of the government. There are advances and retreats in government functions throughout the process.

The second feature is the "two-track system" in the reforms of the system. There are three manifestations of the two-track system. The first is the progressive reforms, in which the stock market was left untouched and the increment was liberalized, and a marginal revolution was carried out, on the basis of which new institutions and organizations, such as the individual economy and township and village enterprises, continue to emerge and develop. The second is the special economic zones and industrial parks, which allow economic players in specific regions to enjoy different institutional policies. The third is the pilot reforms, in which reforms were first tried on a very small scale and then replicated if they succeeded or abandoned if they failed. The advantage of doing so is to minimize resistance to reform (both interest-based and ideological), keep risks to a small extent, and use local achievements and results to gain support for reform. This is a realistic strategy for reaching a consensus and forging collective action under single-peak governance. Incremental reforms and experiments in special economic zones make the benefits of the reforms visible, with the people at large and even those who oppose the reforms receiving tangible benefits, thus reaching a consensus and promoting further market-oriented reforms.

The third feature is the strength of the political parties, which reaches the grassroots, as well as the government's strong mobilization capacity. The CPC reaches into every village, village group, neighborhood committee, all kinds of organizations, and many enterprises, and has a strong mobilizing capacity; a directive from the central government can be cascaded down to every corner of the country in a very short period of time and be implemented through an efficient bureaucratic system. One of the major features of New China is that the mobilizing power of the state power exceeds that of any other dynasty in Chinese history, completely breaking the axiom of "imperial power does not go down to the counties" in Chinese history. Moreover, the government uses land, taxation, and the State-owned financial system to make full use of its savings mobilization capacity and to actively convert savings into investment.

Finally, the fourth feature is the strong central government and the competing local governments. Local government competition under central authority skillfully realizes the incentive compatibility of market unification and government competition, and it forms the mechanism of local championships. And in the competition, in order to attract funds and projects, local governments step up efforts to improve infrastructure and the business environment and enhance local connectivity to transportation arteries and hubs, which enhances the rapid spillover and dissemination of local management experience and objectively accelerates the process of building a unified market across the country.

2.4 Further Tests of Explanatory Power of A-C Theory for China's Economic Growth

To further verify the role of political cohesion and economic accessibility on China's economic growth, we sought to validate the findings above via relevant data from 1911 to 2019 and multiple linear regressions. In addition to the three indicators in Fig. 2.1, we calculated the GDP per capita growth rate and introduced a number of variables as control variables, which were political concentration, land area, and size of population.

The baseline model is constructed as follows:

$$GDPper_t = \beta_0 + \beta_1 access_t + \beta_2 cohesion_t + \beta_3 peak_t + X_t + \varepsilon_t \tag{2.1}$$

where $GDPper_t$ denotes the growth rate of GDP per capita in year t in constant 1990 dollars. Parameter $access_t$ denotes the indicator of economic accessibility in year t, while parameter $cohesion_t$ denotes the indicator of political cohesion in year t and parameter $peak_t$ denotes the indicator of political centralization in year t. Parameter X_t denotes other control variables for year t, such as territory size, domestic population, etc., and parameter ε_t is a random term for year t. The result of the ordinary least squares (OLS) estimation of the baseline model is shown in Table 2.1.

From Table 2.1, we found that the coefficients on economic accessibility and political cohesion are both significantly positive, while the coefficient on political concentration is not significant. This positive significance is equally robust with increasing control variables. From Model 3, we further found that each unit increase in economic accessibility increases the growth rate of GDP per capita by 3.14 percentage points, and each unit increase in political cohesion increases the growth rate of GDP per capita by 1.66 percentage points. Since both economic accessibility and political cohesion themselves undergo the same normalization process, we found that, across China's economic growth since the Xinhai Revolution, the contribution of economic accessibility is, on average, about twice as large as the contribution of political cohesion.

From the perspective of China's century-long economic development, the above results are generally intuitively consistent with historical facts. Since 1911, China's economic growth has been inextricably linked to its opening up to the outside world. Whether the opening up was active or passive, objectively, China did form a pattern of gradual opening up to the outside world over a long historical interval, and the expansion of the scale of opening up to the outside world improved the quality of accessibility indicators. Except for the more than 10 years of war from 1937 to 1949, the domestic regime and political forces attached importance to infrastructure construction and industrialization. Whether this emphasis was for the development of the economy or out of political needs and war preparation requirements, it objectively promoted the formation of the embryonic form of a domestic modern market, brought about an increase in internal accessibility, and thus improved the quality of accessibility indicators from another level. In contrast, China's central government

Table 2.1 OLS estimation results of baseline model

	GDP per capita growth rate		
Variable	Model (1)	Model (2)	Model (3)
Economic accessibility	1.929*** (0.343)	1.904*** (0.348)	3.143*** (0.430)
Political cohesion	0.676* (0.373)	0.820* (0.458)	1.657*** (0.464)
Political concentration	–0.222 (0.447)	–0.387 (0.541)	–0.364 (0.498)
Land area		√	√
Size of population			√
Constant term	–3.429** (1.680)	–7.546 (7.722)	–2.205 (7.223)
Observed value	104	104	104
R-squared	0.595	0.596	0.660

Note: * represents $p < 0.1$, ** represents $p < 0.05$, and *** represents $p < 0.01$

remained limited for a considerable period of time before 1949, making unified decision-making difficult and unified action hard to develop. With the formation of a central government with broad authority after the founding of New China, the contribution of political cohesion improved significantly.

Considering the complexity of China's political economy over the past century or so, and in order to understand more clearly the roles of economic accessibility, political cohesion, and political concentration on China's economic growth in different periods, we further analyzed data from different periods to verify the above conclusion.

Specifically, we divided Chinese history since the Xinhai Revolution into three periods: 1911–1949, 1949–1978, and 1978–present. The socio-economic environment in China during these three periods was markedly different, with no real peace or unification before 1949 and wars of various scales persisting at home. In 1949–1978, China's economy was under the planned economic system; after 1978, China reformed and opened up, and the socialist market economy continued to be established. From the regression result in Table 2.2, we can see that the coefficient of political concentration is insignificant in all periods (among them, the indicator of domestic political concentration is stable and unchanged from the start of the reform and opening up to the present, which is not shown in the empirical result), while economic accessibility and political cohesion show different contributions to the GDP per capita in different periods.

For the period of 1911–1949, the coefficient of economic accessibility is significantly positive at 1.93, while that of political cohesion is insignificant. This result is consistent with historical facts. During that period, both the Beiyang Government and the later Nanjing National Government were influenced by foreign unequal treaties or domestic political alliances, the domestic market was kept open, infrastructure was still being built, the process of industrialization continued to advance, and the increase in external accessibility and internal accessibility became the main

Table 2.2 OLS estimation result of staged validation

Variable	GDP per capita growth rate 1911–2019	1911–1949	1949–1978	1978–2019
Economic accessibility	1.931*** (0.344)	1.910** (0.794)	1.671 (1.441)	3.001*** (0.561)
Political cohesion	0.710* (0.376)	0.326 (0.588)	3.609** (1.725)	2.282** (0.872)
Political concentration	–0.209 (0.448)	–0.311 (0.554)	0.407 (2.145)	–
Control variable	√	√	√	√
Constant term	–3.536** (1.689)	–2.482 (2.132)	–11.81* (6.789)	–15.49*** (2.959)
Observed value	103	37	28	40
R-squared	0.596	0.173	0.323	0.687

Note: * represents $p < 0.1$, ** represents $p < 0.05$, and *** represents $p < 0.01$

driver of economic growth during that period. However, the ruling power of the domestic central government was limited, and the localities were still under the influence of warlord forces, which weakened the financial strength of the central government, as well as the implementation of related policies nationwide. Coupled with frequent wars in the country and the ruling structure of the government being repeatedly hit by wars, political cohesion did not show a significant contribution to economic growth during this period.

For the period of 1949–1978, the coefficient of political cohesion is significantly positive, while the economic accessibility indicator, although positive, is no longer significant. We can understand this result in the context of the actual economic construction of New China during this period. During this period, New China rapidly completed the Three Major Reforms, rapidly formed a planned economic system with public ownership as the mainstay, and concentrated its efforts on rapidly establishing the basis of a complete industrial system in the first *Five-Year Plan*. Under the planned economy, the country's working characteristic of concentrating resources to accomplish major tasks was very obvious. Whether in the field of economic construction or in the field of social movements, during this period, the country's strong mobilization capabilities showed extremely high work efficiency. Under such circumstances, higher political cohesion became an important driving force for economic growth. From the empirical result, the coefficient of political cohesion reached 3.61 during this time, which also indirectly proves this point of view. However, this phase was confronted with a complex international situation, with the gradual opening of the Cold War and China's "one-sidedness" affecting the level of openness of the Chinese economy, and with personnel management being represented by the household registration system and commodity management being represented by the regional ticket system, which reduced the internal accessibility of the economy. A combination of factors reduced the contribution of economic accessibility to economic growth during the period.

The results since the reform and opening up in 1978 show that the regression results for this period are characterized by two features. First, both the coefficients of economic accessibility and political cohesion are significantly positive, suggesting that the two main elements of this period played important roles in economic growth. Second, the coefficients of the two major indicators are close in size, with a coefficient of 3.00 for the economic accessibility indicator and a coefficient of 2.82 for the political cohesion indicator, suggesting that both had an outstanding contribution to China's economic growth during this period. Since the reform and opening up, China's social and economic fields have undergone major changes. As mentioned above, on the one hand, opening up to the outside world has accelerated China's integration into the global economic system, and economic accessibility has been improved through internal agricultural and rural reforms, social management system reforms, state-owned enterprise reforms, infrastructure construction, and the development of industrial parks. On the other hand, political cohesion has been improved by improving governance, optimizing decision-making processes, adjusting the tax system, and strengthening ideological and civilization construction. In addition, the performance of economic development has significantly improved people's lives, further enhancing people's support for political governance, and thus promoting the improvement of political cohesion. The combination of these two aspects led to an improvement in economic accessibility and economic bonding during this period, which in turn together contributed to the growth of the Chinese economy during this period.

To summarize, the above empirical tests provided us with at least the following two conclusions. On the one hand, we further confirmed that economic accessibility and political cohesion are important drivers of China's economic growth over the past century, once again validating the explanatory power of the A-C theory for China's growth experience. On the other hand, we found that economic accessibility and political cohesion played different roles at different stages of China's economic development, and their contributions to economic growth were closely and dynamically related to the socio-economic environment. These two conclusions not only deepen our understanding of China's development history but also provide insights into how China can continue its economic growth in the future.

References

Association of Chinese Historians, Institute of Modern History CASS (1990) The Beiyang warlords (1912–1928), vol 1. Wuhan Publishing House, Wuhan

Coase RH, Wang N (2013) How China became capitalist? (trans: Xu Y, Li ZM). CITIC Press Group, Beijing

Coble PM Jr (1988) In: The Shanghai capitalists and the nationalist government (trans: Yang XM, Wu LZ). China Social Science Academic Press, Beijing

Deng XP (1993) Selected works of Deng Xiaoping, vol 3. People's Publishing House, Beijing

Diewert WE, Lawrence D (1999) Measuring New Zealand's productivity. No. 99/05. https://econpapers.repec.org/paper/nztnztwps/99_2f05.htm

Feuerwerker A (1983) Economic trends, 1912–49. In: Fairbank J (ed) The Cambridge history of China. Cambridge University Press, Cambridge
Guan HH, Liu C, Xin X (2020) China's industrialization: past and present (1887-2017). China J Econ 7(3):202–238
Hua GF (1978) Government work report of the state council in 1978. State Council of PRC
Liu C, Zhou LA (2014) Highway construction and regional economic development: evidence from county-level level in China. Econ Sci 2:55–67
Naughton B (2007) The Chinese economy: transitions and growth. MIT Press, Cambridge
Organization Department of the Communist Party of China Central Committee (2020) 2019 Statistical communiqué of the communist party of China. Organization Department of the Communist Party of China Central Committee
Qian CQ (1944) Overview of Guizhou's financial industry. Guizhou Enterprise Q 2
Schurmann F (1966) Ideology and organization in communist China. University of California Press, Oakland
Sun YS (2009) The number and structure of members of the communist party of China and their development trends. J Beijing Admin Inst 5:28–32
Vogel EF (2011) Deng Xiaoping and the transformation of China. Bernhard, New York
World Bank (2020) World development indicators 2020. World Bank, Washington, DC
Wu JL (1991) Discussion on the relationship between planning and market and the orientation of China's economic system. Reform 1:19–29
Wu JL (2002) Transfer of rural surplus labor and the 'three rural issues'. Macroeconomics 6:6–9
Xu YS (ed) (1962) Statistical data on the history of China's modern foreign debt (1853-1927). Chung Hwa Book, Hong Kong
Zhang YF (1948) Local finance of our country since the Republic of China. In: Zhu SH (ed) Economic history of the Republic of China: bank weekly 30th anniversary commemorative issue. Bank Weekly
Zhang XL (2012) Does China's transportation infrastructure promote regional economic growth? On the spatial spillover effect of transportation infrastructure. Soc Sci China 3(60–77):206
Zhou LA (2007) A study on the promotion tournament model of local officials in China. Econ Res J 7:36–50

Chapter 3
Technological Catch-Up and Productivity Gains

In the framework of neoclassical growth theory, economic growth stems fundamentally from factor inputs and productivity improvements. As the level of development rises and the structure of the economy changes, the growth rate of factor inputs will slow down and their contribution to economic growth will naturally decline accordingly. Hence, sustained economic growth will depend more on sustained increases in productivity. In other words, it depends on making the best use of factors, as well as on sustained improvements in the efficiency of the use of factors of production, such as capital, land, and human resources, and in particular on a continuous increase in total factor productivity. The process of economic catch-up in low-income countries is, in part, characterized by technological catch-up to frontier countries and the filling of absolute productivity gaps. So, what are the trajectories and structural features of a country's productivity catch-up, as it moves from poverty to prosperity in the framework of the A-C theory? What is its relationship with political governance and economic system? These are questions that we sought to answer in this chapter. First, we will discuss the relationship between productivity, economic accessibility, and political cohesion from a theoretical perspective, and we will reinterpret the role of productivity in economic growth based on the A-C theory. Then, based on historical data from various countries, we will examine the theoretical relationship between productivity, economic accessibility, and political cohesion. On this basis, we will further discuss the reasons for the slowdown and differentiation in the growth rate of China's total factor productivity in recent years. Finally, based on the A-C theory, we will outline a path to promote the continuous improvement of China's total factor productivity.

C. Chen et al., *From Poverty to Prosperity*, Understanding China,
https://doi.org/10.1007/978-981-95-7171-0_3

3.1 Economic Accessibility, Political Cohesion, and Productivity

3.1.1 Meaning and Scope of Productivity

In layman's terms, the productivity of an economy is the efficiency with which factors of production are used throughout the economy: given a certain number of factor inputs, the more output there is, the more productive the economy is. In the case of a single-factor input and a single-product output, productivity can be directly expressed as the input-output ratio (output/input) of that factor. For example, labor productivity, the most commonly used and simplest productivity measure, actually uses labor as the only input factor. In reality, however, it is clear that there are more types of factor inputs than just labor, and the use of the input-output ratio of labor alone to measure the productivity of an economy is inevitably biased. In order to better measure productivity, it is necessary to measure the output efficiency of all observable combinations of factor inputs, hence the concept of total factor productivity (Hulten 2000; Coelli et al. 2005; Syverson 2011).

Following Solow's (1957) classic setting of an economy's production function, which introduces both the Hicks medium and constant returns to scale, we can treat an economy's output Y_t in year t as a function of capital stock K_t and the amount of labor L_t put into production at the beginning of that year:

$$Y_t = A_t \left(K_t\right) \alpha \left(L_t\right)^{1-\alpha} \tag{3.1}$$

where A_t represents other factors that are not measured, such as technological conditions, institutional environment, etc. In econometrics, the contribution of A_t to economic growth is also referred to as the Solow residual.

Based on this setting, we can define total factor productivity and single-factor productivity, including labor productivity and capital productivity.[1]

Productivity of labor (amount of output per unit of labor):

$$\frac{Y_t}{L_t} = A_t \left(\frac{K_t}{L_t}\right)^{\alpha} \tag{3.2}$$

Productivity of capital (amount of output per unit of capital):

$$\frac{Y_t}{K_t} = A_t \left(\frac{K_t}{L_t}\right)^{(\alpha-1)} \tag{3.3}$$

[1] The OECD (2001) provides a detailed description of the measurement of output, labor inputs, and capital inputs in separate sections.

Total factor productivity (TFP) is the productivity of factors that cannot be attributed to tangible factors of production,[2] i.e., A_t in the production function.

Not only that, we can also decompose the growth of an economy into the growth of labor factor inputs, the growth of capital factor inputs, and the growth of TFP:

$$\frac{\Delta Y_t}{Y_t} = \frac{\Delta A_t}{A_t} + \alpha \frac{\Delta K_t}{K_t} + (1-\alpha)\frac{\Delta L_t}{L_t} \tag{3.4}$$

Based on the setting of the production function and the definition of productivity above, there are a few points to highlight here.

First, in terms of ease of measurement, while labor productivity is the easiest to measure, labor productivity is not easily measured when labor is distinguished from quality. This is similar to the difficulty in measuring human capital. The measurement of the labor input is also much easier than that of the capital input. In order to accurately account for the capital input in economic production, it is necessary not only to measure the amount of stock capital but also to set how the production capacity of the stock capital in different years changes over time (i.e., the annual efficiency model). In addition, it is also necessary to set the retirement method of capital in different years and estimate the price of capital services.[3]

Second, TFP is not the productivity of all factors; the term "total" refers to part of the economic growth that cannot be attributed to observable factors of production. Due to the large number of unobservable or unidentifiable factors, conceptual differences, and measurement errors, direct comparisons of the numerical magnitude of TFP are not very meaningful. In practice, comparisons are usually made through the construction of TFP indices.

Third, the rate of growth of TFP—the residual of the rate of growth of output after deducting the rates of growth of capital factor inputs and labor factor inputs—can only be used to measure productivity growth excluding all observable factors of production. Since these unobservable factors usually include technological progress, institutional environment, etc., the growth rate of TFP is also commonly used to measure the extent of efficiency improvement and technological progress. Moreover, for the same economy, the more factor types that are put into the production function, the smaller the contribution of TFP growth to economic growth will appear.

Fourth, according to the definition of single-factor productivity above, increases in both labor and capital productivity are in fact the result of both technological progress and capital deepening, except that capital deepening contributes positively

[2] In earlier studies, TFP growth is very often equated with technological progress. It should be noted that while technological progress is indeed an important and direct source of TFP growth, it is by no means the only factor, as recognized in recent studies.

[3] In view of the importance of capital input in growth accounting and the complexity of the measurement process of capital services, the OECD (2009) specifically standardized the measurement of capital input in the form of a manual.

to increases in labor productivity and negatively to increases in capital productivity:

$$\frac{\Delta(Y_t / L_t)}{Y_t / L_t} = \frac{\Delta A_t}{A_t} + \alpha \frac{\Delta(K_t / L_t)}{K_t / L_t} \tag{3.5}$$

$$\frac{\Delta(Y_t / K_t)}{Y_t / K_t} = \frac{\Delta A_t}{A_t} - (1-\alpha) \frac{\Delta(K_t / L_t)}{K_t / L_t} \tag{3.6}$$

How, then, is an increase in TFP to be understood? We can answer this macro-level question at the micro level and at the industry level. From a micro-perspective, technological progress—producing more output with the same input or obtaining the same output with less input—is undoubtedly one of the main driving forces for improving the productivity level of micro entities (firms) or the growth of TFP, and the general technological progress of micro entities within the economy will undoubtedly bring about an increase in TFP at the macro level. At the industry level, in addition to general technological progress, industrial structural transformation can also lead to TFP gains. For example, directing factors, such as capital and labor, from sectors with lower levels of productivity to sectors with higher levels of productivity ultimately manifests itself at the macro level as an increase in the efficiency of inputs and outputs, i.e., an increase in TFP. Massell (1961) extended the Solow model and growth accounting to the industrial sector and further decomposed the macro-level TFP growth rate of an economy into the weighted TFP growth rate of each sector, the structural changes brought about by the flow of capital factors between sectors, and the structural changes brought about by the flow of labor factors between sectors. The first measures the overall technological progress of the economy and belongs to the technological effect, while the latter two measure the structural transformation within the economy and belong to the structural effect:

$$\frac{\Delta A_t}{A_t} = \underbrace{\varphi_1}_{\text{Technical effect}} + \underbrace{\varphi_2 + \varphi_3}_{\text{Structural effect}} \tag{3.7}$$

Parameter φ_1 roughly reflects the technological changes in each industry itself at the industry level and is the weighted value of technological progress in each industry within the economy, representing the technological effect of macro-level TFP growth. Parameters φ_2 and φ_3 reflect the flow of capital factors and the transfer of labor factors between industries, respectively, i.e., structural changes in the allocation of factor resources: a positive φ_2 indicates that a greater share of capital factors is allocated to industries with a relatively higher (or more efficient) marginal output, while a negative φ_2 indicates that a greater share of capital factors is allocated to industries with a relatively lower marginal output; similarly, a positive φ_3 indicates that a larger share of labor factors is allocated to sectors with a relatively high marginal output of labor, while a negative φ_3 indicates that a larger share of labor factors is allocated to sectors with a relatively low marginal output. Let's call φ_2 and φ_3 "capital factor structural effect" and "labor factor structural effect", respectively, where $\varphi_2 + \varphi_3$ represents the overall structural effect of macro-level TFP growth, which is the joint result of the reallocation of capital and labor factors.[4]

3.1.2 Relationship Between Economic Accessibility and Productivity

In the framework of the A-C theory, an increase in economic accessibility implies an increase in productivity, whether it is single-factor productivity or TFP.

First, increased economic accessibility can be expressed in terms of fewer barriers or restrictions to the movement of factors of production. By definition, increased economic accessibility tends to imply that there are fewer barriers to the movement of various types of factors of production and that resources of all types can move more quickly, easily, and at a lower cost. This will usually happen in one of two ways, one being that some factor resources that are restricted in their mobility may otherwise be idle, and that when their mobility restrictions are broken down, these idle resources can be utilized, implying in itself an increase in factor productivity; another situation is that some factor resources are unable to realize cross-region, cross-industry, and cross-enterprise mobility due to various barriers, and that when their mobility restrictions are broken down, the factors will naturally flow to regions, industries, or enterprises with higher productivity because higher productivity corresponds to higher factor rewards. Once this kind of resource redistribution becomes a reality, there will be an overall increase in productivity.

Second, increased economic accessibility means that markets will be more contestable or competitive, which in turn provides a better ground for innovation and technological progress. Competition is the soul of the market mechanism. Increased economic accessibility often means that the barriers to entering or exiting a market are lowered, that the market becomes more competitive, or that the market becomes more contestable. In fierce competition, it is difficult for enterprises to obtain excess profits; this means that, in order to continue to obtain excess profits, enterprises must achieve new competitive advantages through improved management, continuous innovation, and technological progress, either by lowering costs or by creating new technological thresholds to provide the market with cheaper, higher-quality, and more multi-functional products and services. If the accessibility of an economy continues to improve and the competition in the market continues to increase, market players in that economy will invest more and more in R&D and innovation, the stock of knowledge and the accumulation of human capital will increase, and the

[4] Massell (1961) disaggregated the U.S. economy into 19 industrial sectors and thus decomposed U.S. macro-level TFP growth in the 1950s; the results showed that technological effects contributed roughly 2/3 of the total and structural effects contributed roughly the remaining 1/3.

cost of carrying out further R&D will become lower and lower, thus promoting sustained economic growth.

Increased economic accessibility can also manifest itself in a faster rate of technology diffusion. Generally speaking, the contribution of technological progress to economic growth is reflected both in the invention of new technologies and, more importantly, in the depth and breadth to which technology is used and diffused. Without sufficient diffusion, the contribution of new technological advances to growth is difficult to demonstrate. In reality, in order to encourage innovation and technological progress, most countries protect the intellectual property rights of new technologies. However, at the macro level, if a new technology does not diffuse quickly in the marketplace, it is difficult to translate it into productivity gains for the industry as a whole. An ideal mechanism should be able to provide sufficient incentives to innovation agents, while enabling innovations, such as new technologies, to be transformed into higher productivity more quickly and efficiently. Of course, how to design such a mechanism to balance such micro-level incentives with macro-level technology diffusion is another topic. Increased market accessibility means that the uptake and application of new technologies can take place in a competitive context. Under unified market conditions, all regions and all types of people have the opportunity to absorb and apply new technologies, and through inter-regional competition, more people have the possibility of being exposed to new technologies, which is conducive to the accelerated diffusion of technologies within a country. Under the pressure of competition, the diffusion of technology among enterprises and industries is accelerated through industrial links or upstream and downstream relationships. Under open conditions, increased external accessibility means not only an increase in product diversity, but also that poorer and later-developing countries can imitate, learn, and buy new technologies directly from international sources at lower costs. In addition, the entry of capital is often accompanied by the transfer and spillover of large quantities of readily available technology and managerial experience, which is particularly valuable for less-developed countries.

Finally, increased economic accessibility, especially external accessibility, also implies increased market size. The experience of developed countries shows that for an economy to take off in terms of development, it must reach a certain market size and amortize various costs through scale effects. A favorable condition for latecomers is the natural existence of a large external market with more purchasing power than their own internal market. Improving the external accessibility of an economy means opening up to international markets and participating better in the international division of labor. By opening up to the outside world, an economy can give full play to its comparative advantages and resource endowments, make use of readily available international purchasing power to make up for the shortcomings of the internal market in order to expand the scale of production of exports, thereby providing more people with the opportunity to participate in economic activities, spurring the development of related industrial sectors, raising the incomes of the domestic population, and contributing to the expansion of the size of the domestic market. In this way, with the expansion of the scale of exports, the strengthening of import capacity, and the expansion of the size of the domestic market, the cost of technology diffusion and absorption will continue to be reduced and both single-factor productivity and total factor productivity will increase. More importantly, as the production scale of enterprises and industrial sectors applying new technologies expands, the labor force will show a more pronounced agglomeration effect, thus accelerating the urbanization process in low-income countries. In addition, expanding the scale of exports and imports will also help to promote competition in the domestic market.

3.1.3 Relationship Between Political Cohesion and Productivity

Similarly, in the framework of the A-C theory, higher political cohesion implies fewer frictions and lower institutional costs for economic operations, which contributes to increased TFP. According to the definition, at a higher degree of political cohesion, there are fewer disagreements or conflicts between different interest groups, it is less difficult to reach compromises and a consensus with each other, the social order is more stable, the transaction cost of the whole society is lower, the government can effectively implement rules and policies, and there is less friction, less waste, and fewer distortions in the operation of the economy, which is reflected in the efficiency in the form of a higher TFP. As various scholars, such as North, Huntington, and others, have pointed out, political stability and political order are important contexts for economic and political development. On the basis of political stability, effective economic organization is the key to growth, and the emergence of an effective economic organization led to the rise of the West. In a multi-peak reconciliatory form of political governance, a political group seeking to come to power needs to maximize the possibility of gaining the support of a larger number of people and, while in power, strives to achieve reconciliation between competing political groups, adopts policies that are conducive to economic development, and improves the performance of the economy in a way that benefits the vast majority of the population. In a single-peak unbiased political governance, the dominant interest group needs to be farsighted and patient enough to behave as unbiasedly as possible and to strive to improve development performance, with tangible benefits and improvements in the well-being of more people, in order to garner sustained support and increased legitimacy for their performance. It can be seen that, whether in the form of multi-peak governance or single-peak unbiased governance, political groups, in order to strive for long-term governance and maximize the gains of interest groups, will actively adopt economy-friendly actions or policies and will actively promote the improvement of economic accessibility through legislation, reforms, policy adjustments, and other political actions, which objectively are conducive to the improvement of TFP.

3.1.4 Productivity Evolution and Economic Growth in Framework of A-C Theory

In the above discussion, we have further deepened the A-C theory's explanation of economic growth by dissecting the theoretical relationships between economic accessibility, political cohesion, and productivity. In conjunction with the discussion of the A-C theory in Chap. 1, we use Fig. 3.1 to provide a small summary of this set of theoretical relationships.

Going further, we can also look at the relationship between economic accessibility, political cohesion, total factor productivity, and economic growth from a dynamic perspective. In a country with a closed economy and a disorganized political order, TFP is unlikely to grow more significantly and is likely to be lower than the world's average growth rate because of more frictions in the operation of the economy, higher institutional costs, less technological innovation, and slower capital accumulation. For one reason or another, if the country's economic accessibility or political cohesion (or both) begins to improve, we can expect the country's TFP growth rate and economic growth rate to rise as a result. An increase in TFP implies a rise in the level of wages and the rate of return on investment, which incentivizes sustained inputs of various factors, such as labor and capital, which, if economic accessibility can be sustained in this process, will facilitate the exercise of comparative advantage, the accumulation of capital, the diffusion of technology, and the expansion of the economy's size, thus further contributing to the increase in TFP. In addition, an increase in the cohesion of political governance implies a decrease in the transaction or institutional costs of economic operations, which will also be conducive to the optimal allocation of resources, ultimately manifesting itself in a sustained increase in TFP. Not only that, improved overall economic development performance will benefit more people, which in turn will increase the support of the incumbent ruling group and the likelihood of long-term rule, contributing to greater political cohesion. As long as this interaction is not broken, TFP growth can be

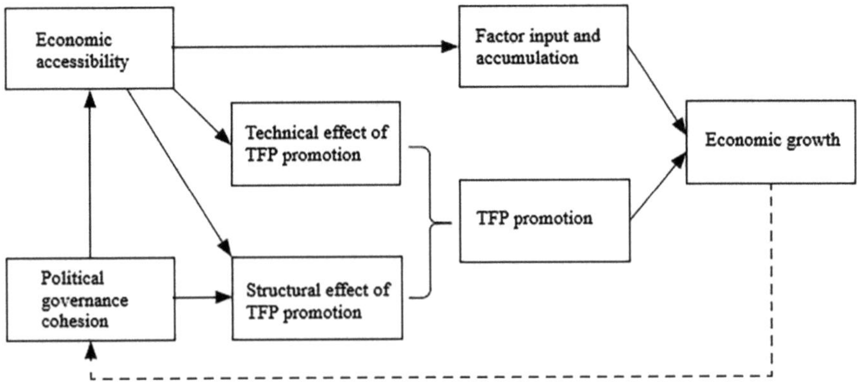

Fig. 3.1 Economic accessibility, political cohesion, TFP, and economic growth

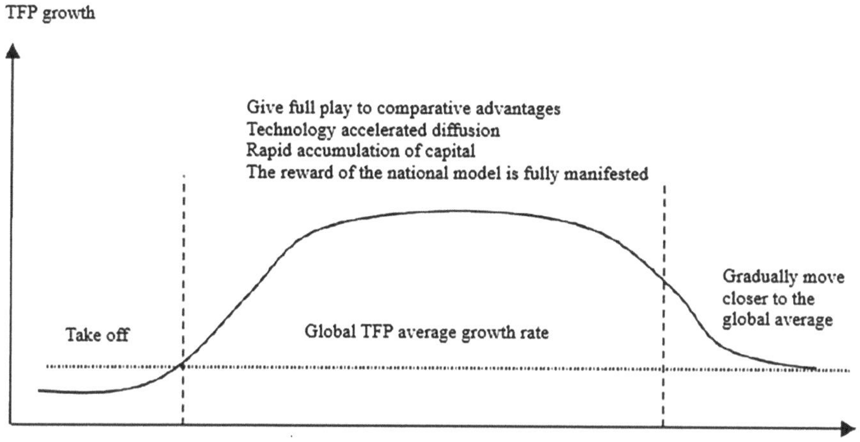

Fig. 3.2 Dynamic evolution of TFP with increased economic accessibility and political cohesion

sustained. When this dividend is released, the comparative advantage will no longer be evident, returns to scale will begin to decline, the factor drive will no longer be effective, learning costs will no longer be cheap, the level of technology will be closer to the world's frontiers, and so on. By this time, the rate of growth of TFP will have declined significantly. Provided that there is no significant slippage in economic accessibility and political cohesion, a country's TFP will gradually converge to the global average. This dynamic process is shown in Fig. 3.2.

3.2 Total Factor Productivity and Evolution of Key Indicators of A-C Theory

Since 1960, 101 economies globally have reached the level of middle-income countries. However, over the past 50 years or so, only 13 of these economies succeeded in entering high-income societies, while most countries remain at the middle-income level for a long period of time after a period of high growth, with some experiencing prolonged stagnation of economic growth or even a decline in absolute levels (Joint Research Team of the World Bank and the Development Research Center of the State Council 2013). The World Bank and the Asian Development Bank refer to this phenomenon as "the middle-income trap". There are many reasons for this phenomenon, but our research found that a common reason behind it is the continuing decline in TFP in economies that fall into the middle-income trap.[5] In this section, we shed light on the common factors behind the volatility of

[5] The paper devoted a case study around the comparative economic growth of Japan vs. Mexico and South Korea vs. the Philippines, examining the divergence in productivity and economic performance of these two groups of economies.

economic growth in different countries based on TFP, which is an indicator of efficiency, combined with the dynamic evolution of economic accessibility and political cohesion.

3.2.1 Evolution of Total Factor Productivity in Chinese Economy Since Reform and Opening Up Under A-C Theory

Over the past 40 years of reform and opening up, China's economic accessibility and political cohesion have been greatly improved, and the TFP of the Chinese economy has nearly doubled, significantly narrowing the gap in TFP with the world's major developed economies. From 1978 to 2016, the average annual growth in TFP in China was about 3.5%, and its contribution to our economic growth averaged 36%. According to Cai and Fu (2017), the TFP growth rate of the Chinese economy since the reform and opening up decomposes into two major parts—technological effect and structural effect—which are broken down into 17 industries. Among them, the structural effect further decomposes into the capital-factor structural transformation effect and labor-factor structural transformation effect. On the basis of this decomposition, we calculated the contribution of the technological effect and structural effect to the growth of TFP and decomposed them into three industries, which are the primary, secondary, and tertiary industries, as shown in Table 3.1.

Based on the contribution of technical and structural effects shown in Table 3.1, we can make the following preliminary judgment.

First, since the reform and opening up, in general, the technological progress prevailing in various industries has been the main source of TFP growth. Between 1978 and 2016, the average contribution of the technology effect to TFP growth was as high as 83.7%, while the average contribution of the structural effect was only 16.3%. Of course, there have been large fluctuations in the magnitude of the contribution of the two effects over time. In terms of the three industries, the contribution of the technology effect was significantly positive for all three industries in most of the time periods, with the tertiary industry contributing significantly positively in every time period. As for the structural effect, the primary industry showed a more significant negative contribution from the mid-1980s onwards, while the tertiary industry showed a more significant and stable positive contribution and the secondary industry showed a positive contribution in most of the periods.

Second, the contribution of the structural effect to TFP growth was generally more prominent in the early years of reform and opening up. The contribution of the structural effect in the period of 1978–1980 was as high as 42.8%, in which the contribution of the labor-factor structure effect of the primary industry was particularly prominent. The contribution of the technology effect in the same period came mainly from the secondary and tertiary industries. The reason behind this may lie in

Table 3.1 Contribution (%) of effects and industries to macro-level TFP growth (1978–2016)

	1978–1980	1980–1985	1985–1990	1990–1995	1995–2000	2000–2005	2005–2010	2010–2016	1978–2016
Technological effect	***57.2***	***89.9***	***117.0***	***86.8***	***117.7***	***82.1***	***72.1***	***40.7***	***83.7***
Primary industry	–57.6	8.8	–47.2	23.3	3.3	23.7	21.8	47.5	14.2
Secondary industry	76.7	21.2	73.6	45.2	82.3	28.9	18.5	–29.4	34.5
Tertiary industry	38.1	59.8	90.6	18.4	32.1	29.5	31.7	22.6	35.0
Structural effect	***42.8***	***10.1***	***–17.0***	***13.2***	***–17.7***	***17.9***	***27.9***	***59.3***	***16.3***
Primary industry	40.9	13.5	–16.0	–22.1	–21.4	–23.7	–28.7	–52.5	–15.5
Secondary industry	2.3	1.3	–11.3	16.7	–21.8	22.5	37.1	88.2	17.4
Tertiary industry	–0.4	–4.7	10.4	18.5	25.5	19.0	19.5	23.5	14.5
Capital-factor structural effect	***5.1***	***1.9***	***28.3***	***5.8***	***– 9.1***	***9.1***	***20.8***	***22.6***	***8.8***
Primary industry	–34.6	–15.9	–72.6	–11.3	–30.5	–11.8	–18.5	–26.7	–18.9
Secondary industry	24.9	10.9	59.4	9.9	17.7	15.1	29.2	32.6	18.4
Tertiary industry	14.8	6.9	41.5	7.1	3.7	5.8	10.2	16.7	9.3
Labor-factor structural effect	***38.5***	***8.3***	***–40.6***	***7.4***	***–7.8***	***9.1***	***7.9***	***37.6***	***7.0***
Primary industry	75.1	29.5	56.6	–10.8	9.1	–11.8	–10.2	–25.8	3.4
Secondary industry	–21.8	–9.6	–66.0	6.8	–38.7	7.4	8.4	56.1	–1.0
Tertiary industry	–14.8	–11.6	–31.1	11.4	21.8	13.6	9.6	7.2	4.7

Note: (1) The data are based on the macro-level GDP growth (percentage points) driven by each factor measured and decomposed, and is calculated based on the ratio of the macro-level GDP growth (percentage points) driven by each factor to the GDP growth (percentage points) driven by macro-level TFP growth. (2) Due to the rounding of decimal points in different sectors, there are slight errors between the sum of the contribution of capital factors and labor factors and the contribution of structural effects the fact that the pioneering and full implementation of rural reforms greatly increased farmers' labor incentives, which directly manifested in a significant increase in individual labor hours per farmer, ultimately translating into a positive labor factor structure effect.[6] The opening up to the outside world introduced advanced technology and equipment from abroad and lessons from management experience, which gave a strong impetus to the development of the industrial and service sectors.

Third, after 1985, the contribution of the technology effect to TFP growth became absolutely dominant. This trend continued after China's entry into the World Trade Organization (WTO) in 2001. Among them, the average contribution rates of the technological effect in the periods of 1985–1990 and 1995–2000 were as high as 117.0% and 117.7%, respectively, and the contribution rates in the periods of 1990–1995 and 2000–2005 were as high as 86.8% and 82.1%, respectively. After the mid-1980s, China's opening up to the outside world continued to expand, and the focus of reform shifted from rural to urban, from agriculture to industry, and so the late-comer's advantage brought about by the huge technological gap between China and Europe and the United States was brought into fuller play. In terms of the sub-industry, the three industries basically show a more obvious technology effect. In terms of the structural effect, the contribution of the structural effect of the primary industry was always negative, that of the secondary industry was basically positive, and that of the tertiary industry was all significantly positive, indicating that factor resources were more allocated to secondary and tertiary industries. The above results are in line with the basic facts of the rapid development of the secondary and tertiary industries in the process of China's comprehensive industrialization.

Fourth, after 2000, the contribution of the technology effect to TFP growth showed a more pronounced downward trend, while the contribution of the structural effect showed a significant increase. In terms of the sub-industry, both the decline in the contribution of the technical effect and the increase in the contribution of the structural effect were largely caused by the secondary industry. The tertiary industry maintained a relatively significant and stable contribution in terms of both the technical and structural effects. One possible explanation is that after nearly two decades of opening up to the outside world, the technological gap between China and the developed economies of the United States and Europe narrowed significantly, making it more difficult for China to achieve overall technological progress through introduction and diffusion. However, due to the continuous advancement of

[6] According to the relevant theory capital factor structure effect and labor factor structure effect can be simplified as respectively: $\varphi_2 \approx (1-\beta)\sum_i \frac{f_i^K}{f^K} \cdot \dot{S}_l^K, \varphi_3 \approx \beta \sum_i \frac{f_i^L}{f^L} \cdot \dot{S}_l^L$. At the beginning of the reform and opening-up period, the lengthening of individual farmer's labor hours brought about a relative increase in the factor share of labor inputs in the primary sector, i.e., $\dot{S}_l^L > 0$, which implies that φ_3 must be positive. In the case of capital factor inputs, the agricultural share is clearly declining, i.e., $\dot{S}_l^K < 0$. The capital factor structure effect should be negative, and our measurements confirmed this.

industrialization and urbanization, more factor resources were allocated to the more efficient secondary and tertiary industries, ultimately maintaining a relatively high growth rate of TFP.

Fifth, after the outbreak of the international financial crisis in 2008, the contribution of the technology effect to TFP growth declined sharply, and the contribution of the structural effect to TFP growth gradually took over the dominant position, highlighted by the significant negative contribution of the technology effect in the secondary industry and the substantial positive contribution of the structural effect. From 2010 to 2016, the average contribution of the structural effect to the growth of TFP was 59.3%, while the average contributions of the technological effect and structural effect from the secondary industry were –29.4% and 88.2%, respectively. In detail, the contributions of the structural effect in 2011, 2012, and 2013 exceeded 100%, namely 138.2%, 108.6%, and 134.4%, respectively. This suggested a distortion in the allocation of factors of production across society, which ultimately manifested itself in a decline in the contribution of the technological effect and an increase in the contribution of the structural effect; however, this trend has improved since 2014.

3.2.2 *Insights from Comparative Economic Growth of Japan-Mexico and South Korea-the Philippines*

In a comparative study of countries around the world based on the A-C theory, we found two very interesting and illustrative groups of comparative countries, which were between Japan and Mexico and between South Korea and the Philippines. The economic growth levels of Mexico and the Philippines in the mid-twentieth century were similar, but they both experienced a slowdown in growth and a decline in TFP in the mid-to-late twentieth century. There is a very obvious differentiation in productivity indicators and economic performance between Japan and Mexico and between South Korea and the Philippines. Behind these differentiations are actually the differentiations among different countries in economic accessibility and political cohesion.

Taking the comparison between Japan and Mexico as an example, as shown in Fig. 3.3, we can see that from 1950 to 1972, Japan's TFP maintained rapid growth for 20 years. In addition, its capital productivity also remained at a high level for those 20 years. Mexico's TFP growth rate was significantly slower, and its capital productivity remained almost unchanged for 60 years. Along with the divergence in TFP and capital productivity, Japan's labor productivity also surpassed Mexico's around 1980.

Japan's ability to achieve sustained TFP growth and maintain the capital output rate at a high level over a long period was due to, on the one hand, the upgrading of the industrial structure and technological level during the period of high growth, especially in the latter part of the high growth period and, on the other hand, the

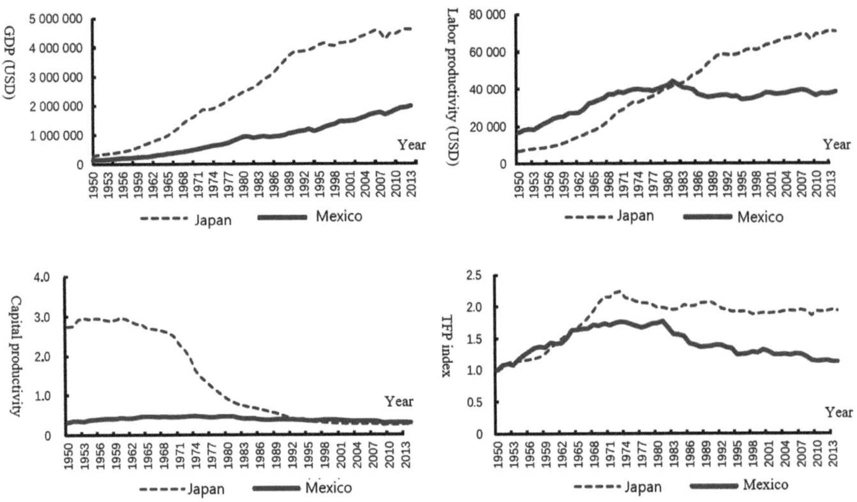

Fig. 3.3 Comparison of economic performance between Japan and Mexico (1950–2014). Source: Penn World Table version 9.0 and authors' own calculations, with the TFP index adjusted to 1 for 1950 for both countries

prominent contradiction of the slowdown in labor productivity during the transition period, for which it took a number of relatively effective countermeasures.

The first was promoting the structural upgrading of Japan's manufacturing industry and accelerating the succession of industrial competitive advantages. In the process of Japan's rapid growth, the proportion of resource-based and raw-material-based heavy industries gradually declined, while the proportion of more technology-intensive heavy industries, such as the equipment industry, continued to rise rapidly, gradually becoming the mainstay of Japan's manufacturing industry and taking a leading position in the world: "The U.S. manufacturing production index grew 99% from 1960 to 1973, the heyday of industrial growth after World War II. Japanese manufacturing, on the other hand, grew by 362% during the same time, with the machinery industry growing by 612%, which is higher than the average for manufacturing as a whole" (Yoshikawa 1998). The rapid development of the manufacturing industry was accompanied by a rapid upgrading of the internal structure of the manufacturing industry, and the proportion of the machinery and metal industry continued to increase: "The industrial composition of Japan's manufacturing industry was characterized by a rapid shift towards a structure centered on the machine-metal industry. In 1971 the machinery and metal industry accounted for 38% of the number of people employed in manufacturing, and by 1990 it had reached 45%" (Yoshikawa 1998). In particular, it is worth pointing out that Japan, in the long-term accumulation of equipment industry technology base, was vigorously developing electronic technology, and the implementation of mechatronics achieved remarkable results. The quality and competitiveness of CNC machinery products quickly ranked among the world's first-class level.

The second countermeasure was encouraging the upgrading of technology and management levels. After the start of the transition from high to medium growth and the outbreak of the oil crisis, Japan continued to implement a series of policies aimed at upgrading technology, including several major aspects. For instance, accelerated depreciation was granted for investments in equipment for the prevention of public hazards. When the Ministry of International Trade and Industry revised the tax system in 1972–1973, it stipulated that facilities for preventing public hazards (such as sewage treatment equipment, soot treatment equipment, etc.) were entitled to special depreciation equal to half of the income gained in the first year, in addition to general depreciation. In 1972, a public hazard prevention reserve system was established for the metal mining, ironmaking, steelmaking, and petroleum refining industries, and enterprises in these industries were allowed to set aside 0.3–0.6% of their revenues as a public hazard prevention reserve. Also, demand-side subsidies were provided to encourage the development of new industries. For example, in order to encourage the development of the electronic computer industry, it was stipulated that the depreciation rate for high-performance computers purchased by enterprises was increased from 20 to 25%. In addition, Japan encouraged investment in energy conservation and alternative energy sources. In 1978, a special depreciation of 25% of the purchase price was provided for energy-saving equipment (Chen and Song 2007). Furthermore, enterprises were encouraged to implement "reduction management" (Hamano et al. 2010), which centered on cost-cutting measures, such as saving energy consumption, reducing debt, and saving labor.

The third countermeasure was providing assistance for the exit of so-called "structurally depressed" industries. The impact of the oil crisis and the appreciation of the yen caused many high-growth energy-intensive heavy industries, such as steel, shipbuilding, and petrochemicals, which required large amounts of imported raw materials, to become so-called structurally depressed industries. It was difficult to improve the operating conditions of these enterprises through general economic revitalization plans and short-term production and price adjustments. Even if the situation temporarily improved, in the medium and long term, the obvious overcapacity would lead to an imbalance between supply and demand. In 1977, the Japanese government began to plan and implement comprehensive economic measures, an important aspect of which was to take more systematic measures to deal with structurally declining industries. The basic aim was to effectively reduce production capacity, while minimizing the impact on employment and social stability. In 1978, the Japanese Diet passed the *Act on Temporary Measures for the Stabilization of Specific Depressed Industries*. Under the Act, by March 1979, a total of 10 industries became subject to the Act. The Act stipulated that the procedure for the disposal of specific depressed industries is that the competent minister first stipulates the establishment of a basic plan for stabilization for the relevant industry, which specifies the criteria for the actions to be taken by the enterprises for the disposal of surplus equipment; when the companies alone are unable to implement the basic plan for stabilization, the competent minister may initiate procedures for joint action by various parties; the Credit Fund for Specific Depressed Industries was established to provide loan guarantees for the elimination of surplus equipment by companies implementing the basic plan for stabilization (The Editorial Committee for the History of Trade of Industry Policy of the Ministry of International Trade and Industry of Japan 1997). The Ministry of International Trade and Industry continued to play a role at this point, forming cartels in these industries to allocate the market share that needed to be cut and to determine the number of employees that needed to be retrained or receive pensions (Johnson 2010).

In the case of South Korea and the Philippines, as shown in Fig. 3.4, both had comparable GDP sizes in 1950–1975, but there was a significant divergence in their economic development from the mid-1970s onward. Especially from around 1975, while South Korea's capital output rate also declined significantly, the performance differences in economic growth between the two were mainly in terms of TFP and labor productivity. The divergence in TFP between the two countries gradually became apparent around 1970, resulting in South Korea's TFP index more than doubling by 2010 but the Philippines seeing a more pronounced decline in TFP rather than a rise during this nearly 40-year period. Comparing the labor productivity of the two countries, before 1975, there was not much difference; after 1975, South Korea's labor productivity grew rapidly, and as of today, South Korea's labor productivity has reached about six times that of the Philippines.

South Korea was able to achieve sustained TFP growth thanks to a variety of reforms and policy measures. The first was the deregulation and accelerated privatization of state-owned enterprises. In order to deregulate administration and promote the development of a market economy, the government conducted a meticulous

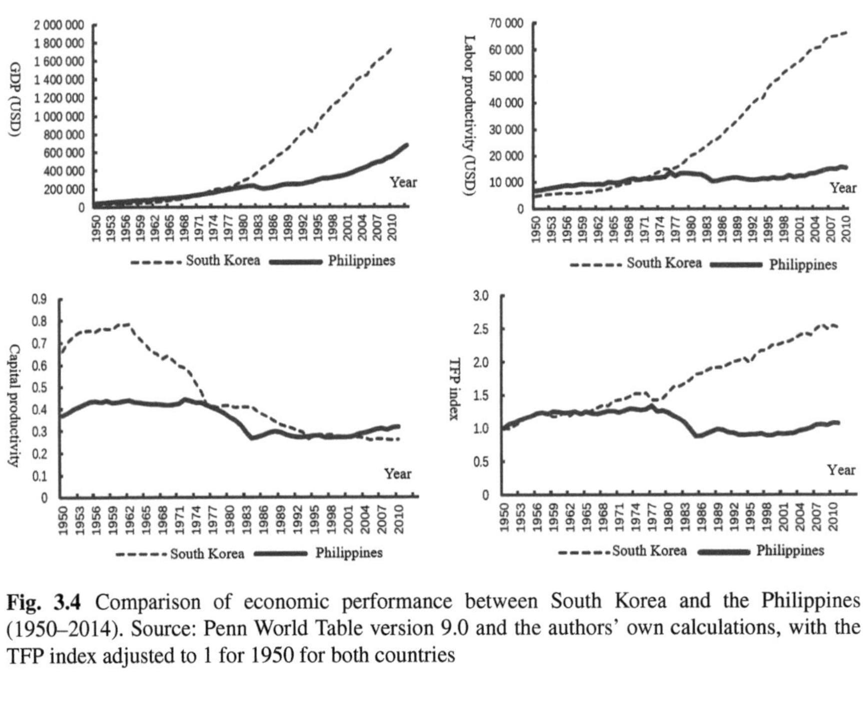

Fig. 3.4 Comparison of economic performance between South Korea and the Philippines (1950–2014). Source: Penn World Table version 9.0 and the authors' own calculations, with the TFP index adjusted to 1 for 1950 for both countries

review of existing regulations, and of the 1125 regulations in the central government departments at the end of 1998, 5430 (48.8%) were repealed and 2411 (21.7%) were improved. Another centralized review in 1999 resulted in the abolition of 503 regulations and the improvement of 570 regulations. In July–August 1998, the government decided to privatize 11 out of 26 public institutions. During the Kim Dae-jung administration, eight state enterprises were privatized. In parallel with privatization, the government retired surplus labor from state-owned enterprises at a rate of 24.8%. The government has also reformed the operating mechanisms of state-owned enterprises and government-funded organizations, establishing an operating mechanism based on responsibility and efficiency and implementing new management measures, such as the open system of management, the annual salary system, and the managerial operating contract system.

The second was establishing a more flexible labor market, while improving the social safety net. South Korea's health insurance, which used to be operated separately by region, work unit, etc., was gradually consolidated from October 1998 to July 2000, promoting the separation of medicine. In April 1999, the national pension insurance was expanded to cover all residents of urban areas, and in 2000, the government introduced a minimum subsistence guarantee system that covers all people. In addition, prior to the Asian financial crisis, the South Korean labor market was too rigid, with a similar phenomenon of lifetime employment in most firms. Trade unions were strong, and wage increases often exceeded labor productivity. In the aftermath of the financial crisis, in order to complement financial, corporate, and public sector reforms, it was necessary to reform the labor-employment system and improve labor market flexibility. In January 1998, a Labor-Management Political Council was established, and a social agreement on structural reforms and hardship sharing was drawn up. The pre-1997 labor law, while allowing for the dismissal of employees, was very restrictive. In February 1998, under the supervision of the International Monetary Fund (IMF), the government amended the labor law, relaxed the conditions for dismissal, enhanced the mobility of the labor market, and promoted the restructuring and adjustment of enterprises and financial institutions. In July 1998, the labor dispatch system was legalized.

The third measure was increasing efforts to build South Korea's capacity in information technology and scientific and technological innovation. The Kim Dae-jung administration considered high-speed broadband networks as an infrastructure for building an information society, and in 1999 the government began to make large-scale investments. As of the end of 2001, South Korea's internet penetration rate was as high as 17.16%, ranking first among OECD member countries and surpassing that of the United States. At the end of 2000, the South Korean government took the opening of the information superhighway as an opportunity to start promoting the construction of e-government, and it formulated the *Basic Law for the Promotion of Informatization*, the *Electronic Signatures Act*, and the *E-Government Act*. South Korea's R&D investment also increased significantly, from 2.34% of GDP in 1998 to 2.63% in 2003. Since the twenty-first century, a large number of new industries, such as cell phones, automobiles, semiconductors, digital home appliances, film and television creativity, special ships, etc., have been growing rapidly, and the industrial structure of South Korea has been optimized and upgraded.

3.3 Statistical Correlation Between Economic Accessibility, Political Cohesion, and Total Factor Productivity

Of course, the above two groups of countries are only relatively representative cases. Next, we tested the statistical relevance of economic accessibility, political cohesion, and total factor productivity based on the database used in this book and the latest version of Penn World Table version 9.0.[7]

We used a simple model setup, where the explanatory variable is the growth rate of TFP and the only core explanatory variables are the indicators: economic accessibility and political cohesion. Considering the autocorrelation of the TFP growth rate, as well as the close correlation between the TFP growth rate and the development stage of an economy, we put the lagged terms of the development stage and TFP growth rate together as control variables in the model. We estimated the mixed cross-section model, the random effects panel model, and the fixed effects panel model separately. From the results of the Hausman test, there was no significant systematic difference between the coefficients of the random effects model and the fixed effects model. As shown in Table 3.2, the coefficient of political cohesion, on the other hand, is significantly positive, indicating that an increase in political cohesion has a significant positive effect on TFP growth, while the coefficient of economic accessibility, although not significant, is positive in most cases. One possible reason for this result is that the data on TFP growth are missing for nearly half of the countries in the sample, which are generally less-developed countries with lower TFP growth and economic accessibility. In addition, the autocorrelation of the TFP growth rate is highly significant and the negative correlation between the TFP growth rate and the stage of development is also highly significant.

3.4 Reasons for Slowdown and Divergence of Total Factor Productivity Growth in China in Recent Years[8]

Since the international financial crisis in 2008, there has been a marked decline in the growth rate of TFP in China. From 2002 to 2007, China's TFP grew at an average annual rate of 5%, while after 2008 it grew at an average annual rate of only

[7] See Appendix A for a detailed description of the database.

[8] This section and part of Sect. 3.5 were first incorporated into the book *Innovative China: Cultivating New Drivers of China's Economic Growth*, jointly published by the Development Research Center of the State Council, the Ministry of Finance, and the World Bank Group in 2019.

Table 3.2 Estimation result of different model settings

	TFP growth rate (y_{it})					
Variable	Pool (1)	Pool (2)	RE (1)	FE (1)	RE (2)	FE (2)
Economic accessibility	0.026 (0.27)	0.076 (0.83)	–0.026 (0.18)	–0.101 (0.53)	0.076 (0.83)	0.002 (0.01)
Political cohesion	0.528*** (4.98)	0.372*** (3.67)	0.649*** (3.82)	0.612** (2.22)	0.372*** (3.67)	0.449 (1.62)
Economic development stage	–0.455*** (8.59)	–0.32*** (6.28)	–0.541*** (5.98)	–0.806*** (4.94)	–0.32*** (6.28)	–0.725*** (4.39)
TFP growth lag y_{it-1}		0.328*** (17.53)			0.328*** (17.53)	0.19*** (9.66)
Constant term	0.373* (1.82)	0.028 (0.14)	0.432 (1.16)	1.492* (1.71)	0.028 (0.14)	1.264 (1.44)
Sample size	2636	2471	2636	2636	2471	2471
Number of countries	118	118	118	118	118	118
Hausman test	–		No significant systematic differences		Significant systematic differences	

Note: (1) Considering that outliers in the TFP growth rate may have greater interference with the regression results, we only retained samples with TFP growth rates between –10 and 10% in the regression analysis. (2) The numbers in parentheses are standard deviations of the estimates. (3) * stands for $p < 0.1$, ** stands for $p < 0.05$, and *** stands for $p < 0.01$. (4) Pool corresponds to a mixed cross-section, RE corresponds to a random effect, and FE corresponds to a fixed effect

about 1.5%, a drop in growth of about 3.5 percentage points. Preliminary calculations show that the growth phase transition factor can explain about 2.0–2.5 percentage points mainly because, as China's development stage improves, the gap between the overall technological level and the frontier narrows, the space for technological catch-up shrinks, and the difficulty of catching up also increases. Cyclical factors can explain about 0.3–0.5 percentage points, as major developed economies also experienced a similar decline in TFP growth during the same period. The remaining approximately 0.7–1.2 percentage points are mainly due to resource mismatches between industries, within industries, and between regions, as well as hindered technology diffusion. Based on international experiences, bridging this part of the growth rate gap will be the main battlefield for China to improve its TFP.

It was later published in the China Economic Times on September 18, 2019, under the title *Cultivating New Drivers of China's Economic Growth with a Focus on Improving Total Factor Productivity.*

3.4.1 Stages

Historical experience shows that as the level of economic development increases, there will be a regular slowdown in TFP growth. As shown in Fig. 3.5, once GDP per capita reaches 10,000 international dollars, the TFP growth rate gradually declines, which is roughly 2% compatible with moderate growth. The more successful catching-up economies, such as Japan and South Korea, have both seen a significant step down in TFP growth at a similar stage of development, and their growth rates decline further as GDP per capita rises. Comparing the experiences and lessons learned from labor productivity catch-up in different economies, the key to achieving a smooth transition from high to medium-high growth lies in the ability to raise TFP in a sustained manner. If an economy's TFP growth stalls, it will eventually face high debt, declining investment returns, asset bubbles, exchange rate depreciation, and other shocks, and the economy will find it difficult to stabilize at a medium- to high-speed growth level.

3.4.2 Cyclical Causes

Accounting for TFP, which is sensitive to changes in the capital stock, is clearly pro-cyclical. Typically, TFP grows faster during periods of economic prosperity. From the international point of view, the TFP growth rate of all countries is characterized by obvious fluctuations in the cycle. The study of TFP can not only look at short-term quantitative changes, where the focus is to analyze the stage of change and to grasp its growth trend.

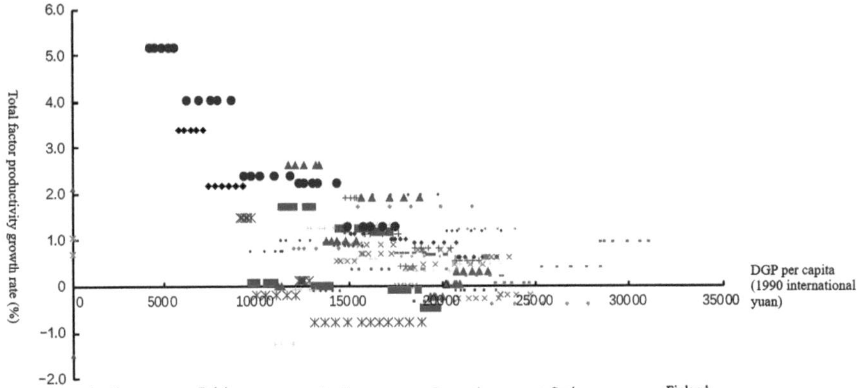

Fig. 3.5 TFP growth rate of some countries. Source: Calculated based on the Penn World Table version 9.0 database

Since 1978, China has broadly experienced three relatively large cycles, the most recent of which was broadly synchronized with the cyclical fluctuations of the major economies in the wake of the international financial crisis. Growth in the major economies slowed down after 2008, during which the TFP growth of the major economies of the United States, Japan, and the euro area slowed down to varying degrees, with an average slowdown of 0.5 percentage points. As China has been deeply integrated into globalization, coupled with a broadly synchronized economic cycle, it is roughly estimated that cyclical factors have contributed 0.3–0.5 percentage points to the decline in China's TFP growth since 2008.

3.4.3 Structural Causes

From the micro level, the slowdown and divergence of China's TFP growth rate are also related to the following structural factors.

First, the TFP growth is generally lower in industries that lack competition. As shown in Fig. 3.6, from 1980 to 2013, the industry with the lowest TFP growth rate was oil extraction and processing, which is a monopoly industry, with an average growth rate of less than –5%. This is followed by the production and supply of water, gas, and electricity, which is an industry with administrative-access restrictions, with an average growth rate of less than 2%. The manufacturing of consumer goods, such as food, clothing, and furniture, and the manufacturing of primary products, such as metal processing, agricultural and sideline products, and plastic products, have an average TFP growth rate of 2–5%. The TFP of high-tech industries, such as computer communication equipment, instrumentation manufacturing, special equipment manufacturing, and pharmaceutical manufacturing, grew rapidly, with an average growth rate of 5–10%. It can be seen that in sectors where natural monopolies and access restrictions are relatively tight, there is a lack of effective competition mechanisms, there are barriers to the entry of high-productivity firms, there is a lack of exit mechanisms for low-productivity firms, and it is difficult to effectively integrate resources within the industry, and hence TFP growth is significantly constrained.

Second, the net TFP-enhancing effect of factor mobility and reallocation within some industries has significantly weakened or even disappeared. For a given industry, the entry of high-productivity firms, the exit of low-productivity firms, and inter-firm mobility are important sources of productivity gains, but in recent years the contribution of intra-industry mobility and the reallocation to TFP in some industries have significantly weakened or even disappeared. Taking the manufacturing industry as an example, we decomposed the TFP growth rate into four contributions: inter-enterprise flow, new enterprise entry, old enterprise exit, and existing enterprise efficiency improvement. The result showed that the increase in TFP in China's manufacturing industry from 1998 to 2007 was mainly brought about by the entry of new enterprises and the improvement of the efficiency of existing enterprises, while in 2007–2013, the contribution of new enterprises almost disappeared.

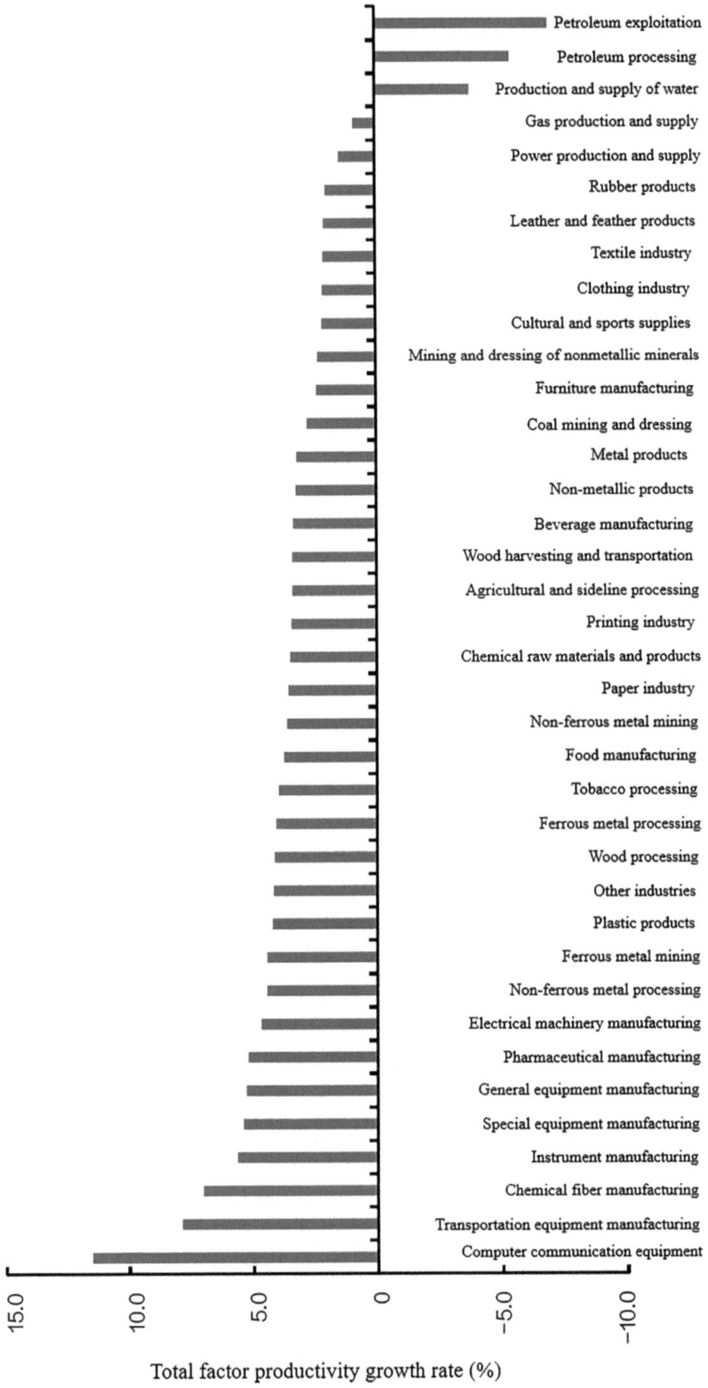

Fig. 3.6 Growth of TFP in the secondary industry (1980–2013). Source: Calculated by the authors

The reason was that the number of new entrants decreased or the productivity of most new entrants was below the industry average. In particular, the existence of a large number of inefficient and ineffective zombie enterprises, which occupy a large amount of economic resources without generating benefits, seriously slowed down the pace of efficiency improvement.

Third, the proliferation of advanced technologies and management styles has slowed down. In recent years, the global TFP growth has slowed down, while the gap between industries and between different enterprises within an industry has widened significantly. A research study by the OECD (2015) shows that the TFP of frontier firms globally continues to grow relatively fast, but the TFP growth of a large number of other firms has slowed down significantly. This suggests that, in addition to the slowdown in technological progress, the diffusion of technology from frontier firms to other firms has also slowed down. Unlike traditional industries, the dissemination of modern technologies and management styles is more servitization in nature, and non-codifiable knowledge tends to be exchanged within a smaller scope, making external imitation and replication more difficult, which to some extent can explain the obvious gap that still exists between the domestic frontier and the global frontier in some industries, especially those with an insufficient degree of openness. In addition, due to the lack of enforcement of intellectual property protection, the uncertainty of enterprise transformation and upgrading has risen, and the pace of technology expansion has slowed down accordingly.

Fourth, a large number of inefficient investments are pulling down China's TFP growth. The country's per capita capital stock generally falls short of that of frontier economies, and there is still a need to maintain a certain rate of capital accumulation. However, in the context of widespread budgetary soft constraints and moral hazards at the local level and in state-owned enterprises, the phenomenon of overinvestment in some areas, resulting in overcapacity, has been prominent in the aftermath of the international financial crisis. Studies have shown that most of the investments made by local governments, either directly or indirectly through state-owned enterprises, have been directed to industries with low productivity, pulling down the efficiency of investment and exacerbating overcapacity and debt risks. More importantly, local governments and state-owned enterprises take up a large amount of resources and, to a certain extent, also crowd out the space for efficient sectors, leading to a serious mismatch of capital, land, and other resources and pulling down the overall TFP.

3.5 Paths to Total Factor Productivity Enhancement Under A-C Theory

From historical experience, a short-term decline in TFP is not terrible. The key is to identify the factors that restrict the improvement of China's TFP, accelerate the pace of reform and innovation, increase the degree of opening up, take targeted reform measures, continuously improve the accessibility of China's economy, maintain the impartiality of political governance, continuously improve the cohesion of political governance, strive to improve the efficiency of resource reallocation, accelerate the process of technological research and development and diffusion, regain the track of TFP growth, strive to maintain China's economy on a medium-to-high-speed growth platform, and continuously promote high-quality development.

In response to the decline in the TFP growth rate that accompanies an increase in the stage of development, emphasis should be placed on rebuilding incentive mechanisms, increasing R&D investment in various industries, and upgrading the technological level of industries themselves in order to solve the problems of insufficient incentives for innovation, lack of rapid technological progress, insufficient human capital, and insufficient added value of products, as well as to promote the integration and development of new technologies and new modes of industry with traditional industries. In response to the decline in TFP growth that accompanies economic cycle fluctuations, emphasis should be placed on upgrading the quality of macroeconomic policies, such as monetary policy, fiscal policy, and expectation management, and on strengthening policy coordination in order to reduce the frequency and magnitude of economic fluctuations, strengthen the countercyclicality of macroeconomic policies, and avoid major ups and downs in the economy. In response to the decline in TFP growth caused by structural factors, China must focus on correcting resource mismatch and resource allocation inefficiency, continue to deepen supply-side structural reforms, improve the institutional environment, and strive to solve the common problems in the country's economic operation, such as entry barriers, poor exit, restrictions on factor mobility, and obstructed price signal transmission. China must promote both entry and effective exit, achieve both frontier expansion and technology diffusion, and narrow the productivity gap within industries, between ownership structures, between industries, between regions, and between international and domestic markets.

Firstly, emphasis should be placed on improving the incentive mechanism for innovation, strengthening the protection of intellectual property rights, and promoting the expansion of technological frontiers. This will reshape the incentive mechanism for knowledge-based labor, stimulate the creativity of researchers, and accelerate the transformation and application of scientific research results. The collaborative development of industry, academia, research, and utilization, and the adaptability of traditional sectors to the digital economy, should be increased. The protection of intellectual property rights should be strengthened, penalties for infringement and enforcement should be increased, and legitimate and remunerative intellectual property transactions and use should be encouraged. In line with the laws of urbanization, China should accelerate the implementation of all policies related to the settlement of the non-domiciled resident population, give play to the aggregation effect of talents, enhance knowledge density, and promote the collision of ideas and the overflow of knowledge. The diversified development of universities should be encouraged to enrich the structure of talents and enhance the quality of human capital. Vocational training should be increased, lifelong learning mechanisms should be encouraged, and the skills of the labor force should be promoted to keep up with the times.

Secondly, China should enhance the quality of macroeconomic policies, strengthen policy coordination, enhance countercyclicality, reduce the magnitude of economic fluctuations, and maintain stable economic growth. It is necessary to change fiscal policy thinking in a timely manner, from "giving equal importance to tax cuts and increased spending" to "cutting taxes while taking into account the adjustment of fiscal expenditure structure", from "high tax rate and low collection rate" to "low tax rate and high collection rate". The government should strengthen and increase the evaluation of fiscal subsidy policies, reduce inefficient fiscal subsidies in some areas, and improve the quality of fiscal policies. The independence of the central bank and the transparency of monetary policy should be improved, with a focus on solving the problem of a poor monetary policy transmission mechanism, dealing with the relationship between monetary policy adjustments and "deleveraging" efforts, and grasping the relationship between macro-prudential and micro-regulation. The communication costs between the central bank and the market and between the central bank and other central banks should be reduced, thus reducing the cost of coordination. China should accelerate the construction of an institutionalized expectation management system, fully develop and utilize various expectation management tools, track changes in market expectations, make clear the main body of expectation management and the main channel of market communication, do a good job of policy adjustment and market communication in a timely manner, improve the quality of expectation management work, and reduce the cost of policy implementation. In addition, domestic and international coordination of macro-policies should be strengthened, the optimal window period for different policies should be grasped, and different policies should be rationally matched in order to achieve optimal macro-control objectives.

Thirdly, the fundamental position of competition policy should be further strengthened, market entry and exit thresholds should be lowered, the internal accessibility of the economy should be improved, price reform should be deepened, factor mobility should be promoted, the price mechanism should be rationalized, and the efficiency of resource allocation should be enhanced. China should fully implement the negative list system for market access, relax restrictions on industry access, and gradually liberalize access restrictions in industries, such as the military, electric power, civil aviation, telecommunications, petroleum, supply and marketing, agricultural reclamation, and railroads, hence removing all types of hidden barriers to entry, lowering the threshold of access for industries or some parts of the industry, permitting the entry of private and offshore capital, and encouraging all types of enterprises to participate in competition. Focusing on price reforms for resource and energy products, public utilities, and public services will further deepen price reforms in monopolized industries, especially electricity, oil and gas, railroads, and highways, and further rationalize the price mechanism. Prices in competitive areas and segments that can be liberalized should be steadily liberalized and regulated by the market; where government pricing is retained, sound cost-monitoring rules and pricing mechanisms should be established to promote scientific pricing. There should be timely initiation of anti-monopoly investigations into suspected price monopolization, as well as punishment in accordance with the law of the conclusion and implementation of price monopoly agreements and abuse of dominant market position, and there should be rectification of provisions and practices of abuse of administrative power that exclude and restrict competition. The government should start revising the Company Law, Bankruptcy Law, Measures for the Administration of Major Asset Restructuring of Listed Companies, Labor Law, Unemployment Insurance Regulations, and other laws and regulations on asset disposal, debt repayment, etc., as soon as possible. It should also lower the threshold for enterprise exit, especially reduce the exit barriers for inefficient production capacity and zombie enterprises, and create more convenient institutional conditions for enterprise bankruptcy liquidation, restructuring, mergers and acquisitions, cancellation and exit, labor reemployment, and reconfiguration of other production factors.

Fourth, China should further break down market segmentation and reduce efficiency differences between industries and regions. Taking the improvement of the legal system for labor and employment as a starting point, the government should also further break down the urban-rural, regional, and industrial divisions and discrimination on the basis of identity and gender, and guarantee equal access to employment in accordance with the law; make efforts to break down the constraints of the dual structure of urban and rural areas to improve the system of property rights in the countryside and push forward equal exchanges of factors between urban and rural areas and a balanced allocation of public resources so as to allow the vast majority of peasants to participate on equal footing in the process of modernization and to share the fruits thereof. China should promote the two-way flow of factor resources between urban and rural areas, increase the scale of agricultural production, and enhance the comprehensive efficiency of agricultural production. The country should also improve industry regulation, increase tolerance for the integration of new technologies and models with traditional sectors, promote the flow of advanced technologies and management experience across industries, and stimulate new vitality in traditional industries. The construction of a unified market should be further strengthened, the interregional division of labor and cooperation should be promoted, duplicative construction and vicious competition should be reduced, and the space for the existence of inefficient enterprises should be compressed.

Fifth, China should deepen its openness to the outside world, increase the external accessibility of the economy, accelerate international technology diffusion, and narrow the productivity gap with frontier countries. Through the implementation of the Foreign Investment Law, the government should further relax foreign investment access; flexibly handle the establishment and management of grassroots party organizations in foreign-invested enterprises; further expand opening up, especially the opening up of information, finance, culture, education, sports, medical, and other service industries; improve the level of trade and investment facilitation; and promote the orderly and free flow of international and domestic factors, efficient allocation of resources, and deep integration of markets. Competition will be achieved through opening up, and China should continuously improve the overall efficiency of its economic operations. On the premise of adhering to the principles of truthfulness and prudence, domestic enterprises should be encouraged to go out, participate in the division of labor in the global value chain as much as possible, and strive to upgrade their position in the global value chain so as to promote China's products and technologies to the middle and high end of global markets.

References

Cai YZ, Fu YF (2017) The technical and structural effects of TFP growth: measurement and decomposition based on China's macro and sector data. Econ Res J 52(1):72–88

Chen GH, Song XY (2007) Japan's fiscal policy. China Financial & Economic Publishing House, Beijing

Coelli TJ, Rao DSP, Donnell CJO et al (2005) The calculation and decomposition of productivity change using frontier methods. In: An introduction to efficiency and productivity analysis. Springer U.S, New York

Hamano K et al (2010) Japanese economic history: 1600-2000 (trans: Peng X). Nanjing University Press, Nanjing

Hulten CR (2000) Total factor productivity: a short biography. NBER working paper no. W7471. https://papers.ssrn.com/sol3/papers.cfm?abstract_%20id=213430

Johnson C (2010) MITI and the Japanese miracle: the growth of industrial policy, 1925-1975 (trans: Jin Y). Jilin Publishing Group Co Ltd, Jilin

Joint Research Team of the World Bank and the Development Research Center of the State Council (2013) China in 2030: building a modern, harmonious and creative society. China Financial & Economic Publishing House, Beijing

Massell BF (1961) A disaggregated view of technical change. J Polit Econ 69(6):547–557

OECD (2001) Measuring productivity-OECD manual measurement of aggregate and industry-level productivity growth 2001. https://www.oecd-ilibrary.org/%20industry-and-services/measuring-productivity-oecd-manual_9789264194519-en

OECD (2009) Measuring capital—OECD manual 2009 second edition. https://www.oecd-ilibrary.org/economics/measuring-capital-oecd-manual-%202009_9789264068476-en

OECD (2015) The future of productivity. https://www.oecd.org/economy/%20growth/OECD-2015-The-future-of-productivity-book.pdf

Solow RM (1957) Technical change and the aggregate production function. Rev Econ Stat 39(3):312–320

Syverson C (2011) What determines productivity? J Econ Lit 49(2):326–365

The Editorial Committee for The History of Trade and Industry Policy of the Ministry of International Trade and Industry of Japan (1997) History of Japan's trade and industrial policy, volume 1 (trans: China's "History of Japanese Trade and Industrial Policy" Compilation Committee). China Youth Publishing Group, Beijing

Yoshikawa H (ed) (1998) Made in Japan: a guide to transforming Japan's manufacturing industry (trans: Wang HJ et al). Shanghai Far East Publisher, Shanghai

Chapter 4
Local Government Competition and Coherent Action

Over the past 40 years of reform and opening up, China's economic development has achieved world-renowned results, in which local governments have played a huge role. For the local governments, their main incentives come from both administrative and economic sources. Among other things, promoting economic growth is the main way of accomplishing performance appraisals and expanding financial resources, so governments at all levels are committed to accelerating economic development. Although incentive mechanisms vary in different periods, competition among the local governments has never stopped, and there was even excessive competition at one point. Especially with the advancement of reform and opening up, the local governments have gained more autonomy in economic construction, and the reform of the fiscal and taxation system further stimulated the vitality of the local governments. The local governments have played an important role in promoting the formation and improvement of a unified national market and continuously improving economic accessibility. Although artificially created market barriers still occur from time to time, overall, the behavior of the local governments in China remains consistent with the decisions of the central government. They are able to take joint actions and form a policy synergy to promote the implementation of policies and the resolution of a series of problems. This is reflected in the continuous improvement of the cohesion of China's political governance, thereby promoting the long-term, sustained, high-speed growth of China's economy.

C. Chen et al., *From Poverty to Prosperity*, Understanding China,
https://doi.org/10.1007/978-981-95-7171-0_4

4.1 Formation and Evolution of Interrelations of Local Governments

Since the founding of China, local intergovernmental relations can be divided into three broad phases—the planned economy period, the early period of reform and opening up, and the market economy period—each with distinctive features closely related to its economic and financial systems.

4.1.1 Interrelations of Local Government in Planned Economy

At the beginning of the founding of New China, China set up regional governments to manage the economic, political, and cultural work of the provinces; the regional governments had a certain degree of autonomy and could guide the work of the provinces in accordance with the actual situation in the region, which played a certain positive role at that time. However, because of problems that arose later, in June 1954, the central government abolished the regional system and replaced it with direct leadership of the provinces. However, the high degree of centralization of power by the central government greatly weakened the independence of the localities, affecting the enthusiasm for local economic construction, and the role of the local governments was not brought into good play. As Chairman Mao said in his report, *On the Ten Great Relationships*, at the enlarged meeting of the Politburo on April 25, 1956, "On the premise of consolidating the unified leadership of the central government, we should expand the power of the localities a little bit, give them more independence, and allow them to do more things. This will be more favorable for us to build a strong socialist country." Therefore, the country's regions were redivided in 1958 and 1960. However, the central government's "lines" had already penetrated the local governments. Under the system of central leadership and local government "dictatorship", the main responsibility of the local governments was to implement central decisions. One result was that the local governments lacked the will and space to independently develop the economy.

In addition, the national system of unified revenue and expenditure discouraged the local governments. The local governments acted only as agents of the central government, carrying out revenue and expenditure tasks without financial autonomy. According to the 1950 Decision on the Unification of the State's Fiscal and Economic Work, all revenues from customs duties, salt taxes, excise taxes, and industrial and commercial taxes, except for authorized local taxes, were to be uniformly dispatched and used by the Ministry of Finance of the Central People's Government. State-owned enterprises at all levels basically contributed all their profits, which constituted the bulk of fiscal revenue. On the expenditure side, the distribution of financial resources was egalitarian, with all of them uniformly deployed by the central government. At this stage, the local governments and all types of state-owned enterprises acted under a centralized plan and lacked incentives to develop and expand the local economy.

Under the centralized administrative system and the unified fiscal system of revenue and expenditure, the local governments had little room to develop the economy independently and lacked corresponding incentive mechanisms. Direct competition among local governments at the economic level was relatively weak and more reflected in the competition for central resources. The local governments strove to get material allocations and fiscal expenditures to be tilted towards the local areas.

4.1.2 *Interrelation of Local Governments in Early Years of Reform and Opening Up*

At the beginning of the reform and opening up, the central government gradually made positive policy and institutional adjustments. At the political level, the highly centralized political system was gradually thawed, with the granting or decentralization of powers, including administrative autonomy and decision-making, that should have belonged to the local governments but were controlled by the central authorities under rules and regulations. The Third Plenary Session of the 11th Central Committee of the Communist Party of China pointed out that measures should be taken to give full play to the initiative, enthusiasm, and creativity of the four aspects of central departments, local governments, enterprises, and individual workers. Since 1978, the central government has gradually "delegated power and profits" to the local governments and state-owned enterprises, giving the local governments a certain degree of administrative autonomy and decision-making power, and the independence and autonomy of the local governments in participating in economic construction have been continuously improved.

In addition, the financial field has gradually changed the original unified revenue and expenditure system. After the implementation of "profit to tax" and "grant to loan" policies, the contract management responsibility system was fully implemented in all fields in 1987. The local governments contracted to the central government, enterprises contracted to the state, and families contracted to collectives. The contracting entities only need to pay the full contract amount, and the remaining part can be retained and distributed independently. In terms of the financial system, the change from centralized management to "separate kitchen" financing has clarified the financial relationship between the central government and the local governments, and the local governments gained a certain degree of autonomy, which greatly stimulated the enthusiasm of the local governments and state-owned enterprises for development.

With the deepening of "decentralization", the sense of independent economic interests of the local governments has gradually increased, and competition among the local governments has begun to intensify, with inter-regional competition for resources and markets intensifying. At this time, the local governments are not only directly involved in microeconomic activities but also compete to adopt local protectionist practices, creating artificial barriers to entry and exit across regions and markets. Not only between provinces but even within the province and within the city of different regions, different departments exist between a territory in a "compete for the boss, grab resources" situation. This kind of beggar-thy-neighbor local protection is what academics usually refer to as the "vassal economy".

During this period, in order to curb vicious inter-regional competition and coordinate inter-regional cooperation and development, the state introduced a series of relevant policies. In 1980, the State Council issued the *Provisional Provisions on the Promotion of Economic Unions*, aimed at promoting the development of various forms of unions; in 1984, the *Decision of the Central Committee of the Communist Party of China on the Reform of the Economic System* explicitly pointed out that "it is necessary to open up to the outside world, and even more so to open up to each other among the various regions within the country". In March 1986, the State Council's *Provisions on Several Issues Concerning Further Promoting Horizontal Economic Integration* proposed that "horizontal economic integration is an important part of economic system reform and a requirement for developing social productivity. It promotes resource development and the rational use of funds, promotes commodity circulation and the formation of a socialist unified market, promotes technological progress and the rational exchange of talents, and promotes the rationalization of economic structure and regional layout." In 1990, the State Council also issued the *Circular on Breaking the Interregional Market Blockade and Further Revitalizing the Circulation of Commodities*, which explicitly required "all regions and departments to consciously stop and correct the erroneous practice of regional blockades."

4.1.3 Interrelation of Local Governments in Market Economy

In 1992, the 14th CPC National Congress formally proposed to establish a socialist market economic system. In 1994, a macroeconomic system reform was officially launched, aiming to establish a macroeconomic control system framework that is compatible with the socialist market economy. Among other things, the reform of the tax-sharing system further smoothed out the financial relationship between the central government and the local governments, providing incentives for the local governments to expand their own disposable financial resources. In addition, China established a cadre appraisal mechanism that is compatible with the development of a socialist market economy. Although the entire appraisal system is based on "moral ability, diligence, performance, and integrity" as the benchmark, in practice, economic indicators are used to assess cadres, especially the assessment of local officials, hence forming a "GDP only"-oriented appraisal system. Under the orientation of "GDP only" assessment, attracting investment became a key task for the local governments at all levels. In order to attract foreign investment, the local governments made bold attempts and actively explored many aspects. Although various problems, such as duplicated construction, arbitrary tax reductions and exemptions, and local protection, have arisen in the process, on the whole, the practice greatly stimulated the autonomy and mobility of the local governments in developing their economies and strongly promoted local economic development.

During this period, there were some new changes in the competition among the local governments. Most notably, in order to attract funds and projects, the local governments stepped up efforts to improve the local infrastructure and business environment, enhance local connectivity with transportation arteries and hubs, accelerate the spillover and dissemination of local management experience, and objectively accelerate the formation of a unified national market. However, unhealthy competition among the local governments has also become more prevalent. For example, in order to attract foreign investment, the local governments, in addition to the central government's "three reductions and two exemptions" policy for foreign-invested enterprises, further expanded the policy scope and extended the policy period, which undermined the country's unified tax system, sacrificed national fiscal revenue, and even led to some irregular practices that did not follow economic laws, which to a certain extent caused waste of resources and inefficiency. In recent years, there have also been some new changes in the fierce competition among the local governments, with homogenization and low-end industry competition evident, the pursuit of the construction of a complete industrial system in various places, and a rise in the degree of convergence of industrial structures. In a southwestern province, for example, 18 of the 20 cities and states have their own new energy vehicle brands and use a lot of financial resources to support them.

In order to promote cooperation and competition among regions and accelerate the formation of a unified market nationwide, the central government further introduced a series of relevant policies. In 1993, the Central Committee of the Communist Party of China issued the *Decision on Several Issues Concerning the Establishment of a Socialist Market Economic System*, which further standardized regional economic cooperation. In April 2001, the State Council issued the *Regulations on the Prohibition of Regional Embargoes in Market Economic Activities*. In October 2003, the *Decision on Several Issues Concerning the Improvement of the Socialist Market Economic System*, adopted at the Third Plenary Session of the Sixteenth Central Committee of the Communist Party of China, emphasized the need for "coordinated regional development" and "the formation of a mechanism to promote coordinated development of the regional economy." The *Outline of the 14th Five-Year Plan for National Economic and Social Development of the People's Republic of China and the Long-Term Goals for 2035*, adopted at the 2021 National People's Congress and the Chinese People's Political Consultative Conference, further emphasized the need to "accelerate the construction of a unified domestic market; optimize the market environment in line with international advanced rules and best practices; promote the coordination and unification of standards, rules, and policies among different regions and industries; and effectively eliminate local protectionism, industry monopoly, and market segmentation." These practices of the central government undoubtedly played a positive role in promoting the formation of an orderly, competitive, and cooperative relationship among the local governments.

From the evolution of the relationship between the local governments in the above three periods, it can be seen that with the advancement of reform and opening up and the establishment and improvement of the socialist market economic system, the enthusiasm of the local governments in developing the economy has continuously increased. Although some local protectionism and vicious competition occur and still exist in this process, on the whole, the competition between the local governments has been controlled to a reasonable degree and has played a positive role in improving the efficiency of resource allocation. The formation of a unified market has been accelerated, and the flow of population, capital, and goods has become freer and more convenient. The overall accessibility of China's economy has continued to improve. In addition, the local governments' actions at all levels have always been consistent with the central government's decisions, which has ensured a continuous improvement in political cohesion since China's reform and opening up.

4.2 Gradual Development of National Infrastructure

The importance of a country's infrastructure to its economic accessibility cannot be overstated. With the gradual completion of national infrastructure, the movement of people becomes more convenient, the diffusion of technology becomes more efficient, and inter-regional economic exchanges become more convenient; with the pace of the formation of a unified national market accelerating, enterprises are able to continuously expand the scope and scale of their operations and the advantages of the economy in terms of scale will continue to emerge. The result of this study's econometric analysis based on inter-provincial panel data has shown that the increasing mileage of railroads and highways has provided strong support for the sustained growth of the local economy. In the process of the gradual formation of China's national infrastructure, governments at all levels have played a very important role, especially in the construction of national railways and highways, which cannot be separated from the support of the central government. The central government established an effective infrastructure of central-local cooperation and financing mechanisms through medium- and long-term planning and financial power control so that infrastructure construction can be financially supported. In particular, this made up for the problem of insufficient national infrastructure supply against the backdrop of fierce competition among the local governments and promoted the formation of a unified market in China.

4.2.1 How Infrastructure Is Perceived

Infrastructure should be commensurate with the level of economic development. The stage of economic development is a continuous spectrum from a low-income agricultural economy all the way to a high-income post-industrialized economy

(Lin 2012), and at any stage, there are different industrial structures, which are continuously upgraded along with economic development, and there will be a corresponding demand for improvement of infrastructure. An agricultural economy is largely self-sufficient, with little large-scale trade and low infrastructure requirements. An industrialized economy emphasizes the scale effect and professional division of labor, and different regions will have to engage in large-scale trade exchanges, which puts higher and higher demands on infrastructure, such as roads. Only when the infrastructure meets the basic requirements can it further promote the industrial division of labor. Hence, the construction of infrastructure is a necessary condition for economic development, and unadapted infrastructure will constrain the long-term development of the economy. In addition, economic development provides the necessary material basis for infrastructure improvements, and so the two are mutually reinforcing. As the level of economic development continues to rise, the scale of the industry grows larger and larger, more products move from the local to the national and even global level, and higher demands are placed on the national and even global infrastructure.

China's governments at all levels, especially the central government, need to play an active role in infrastructure development. According to the theory of public economics, it is difficult to realize the optimal supply of products with externalities through the spontaneous regulation of the market, and it is necessary for a government to play a certain role in increasing the supply of products with positive externalities and reducing the supply of products with negative externalities. It is clear that infrastructure is a public good with strong positive externalities, that adequate infrastructure cannot be built by private or corporate provision alone, and that more infrastructure needs to be provided by the government through taxation and other means. By the same token, the increased emphasis by the local governments in China on infrastructure within their jurisdictions and the apparent lack of willingness to provide regional or national infrastructure require a greater role for the central government. The most significant impact on the financial power of the central government and the local governments is the fiscal and taxation system, and the reform of the fiscal and taxation system had a direct impact on the financial and operational capacity of the central government and the local governments, which in turn affects the level of construction of local and national infrastructures. Therefore, as economic development puts higher demands on national infrastructure, the central government in particular should have some financial power and use it to build regional or national infrastructures in regions where the local government's willingness or ability to invest is insufficient.

Infrastructure includes both physical and non-physical infrastructure. Tangible infrastructure includes railroads, highways, airports, telecommunications, power grids, water conservancy, etc., while intangible infrastructure includes property rights systems, credit systems, business environments, and competition policies. Both physical and non-physical infrastructure should be commensurate with the level of economic development. As the economy develops, while the requirements for infrastructure become higher and higher, the economic development provides basic conditions for infrastructure construction, and hence the two promote each other to continuously advance the process of industrialization; otherwise, lagging infrastructure construction will hinder the process of economic development. In this chapter, the focus is on physical infrastructure, i.e., railroads and highways, the construction of which is a necessary means for the movement of people and goods, and good infrastructure is conducive to accelerating the flow of factors and improving the efficiency of resource allocation and is a necessary condition for the formation of a unified national market. However, the local governments have focused only on building infrastructure within their jurisdictions, resulting in the lack of investments in cross-regional infrastructure, while what the central government wants is infrastructure connectivity, and hence the central government plays an important role in aligning the local governments' behavior with the goals of central policymaking.

4.2.2 Reform of Fiscal and Taxation System and Infrastructure Financing Mechanisms

The absence of China's local governments in the development of national infrastructure requires the central government to fill the gap, i.e., by investing large amounts of central financial resources. The reform of the fiscal and taxation system in 1994 provided financial security for the central government and the local governments; the central investment local matching funding system and the land transfer system established effective financing mechanisms and financial security for infrastructure investment, followed by a rapid increase in the mileage of China's railroads and highways and the realization of inter-regional interconnections, which provided the material basis for the formation of a unified market across the country.

The 1994 reform of the fiscal and taxation system expanded the financial power of all levels of government. Since the reform and opening up, the financial field has undergone a series of reforms. After changing the original unified revenue and expenditure system, the "profit to tax" and "grant to loan" policies were implemented. In particular, a contracting system was implemented in 1987. The central government, the local governments contracted, and enterprises all used the contracting system. After paying the contract amount, they retained all the money. This greatly stimulated the development enthusiasm of the local governments and enterprises. However, this led to a rapid decline in the share of fiscal revenues in GDP and in the share of central government revenues in total fiscal revenues. As can be seen in Fig. 4.1, the state revenue as a share of GDP declined from 30.8% in 1978 to 10.7% in 1994, with the central government accounting for 22.0% of all fiscal revenue in 1993. The reform of the fiscal and taxation system in 1994 stopped the continuous decline by recovering two proportions of revenue. The proportion of the national fiscal revenue gradually recovered, rising to 22.1% in 2015, and then declined to 18.0% in 2020; after 1994, the proportion of central fiscal revenue in total fiscal revenue has always remained above 45%. It can be seen that the reform

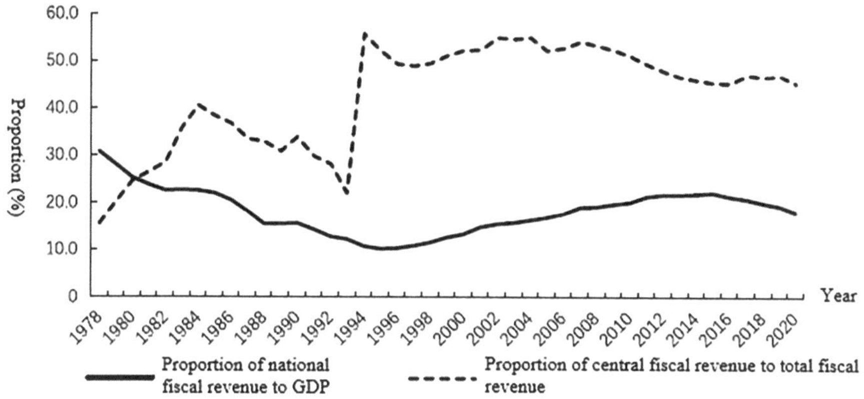

Fig. 4.1 Structure of state revenues. Source: WIND

of the fiscal and taxation system in 1994 led to the gradual restoration of financial power at all levels of government, and the central government in particular was given more financial power. The reform provided a solid guarantee of sources of funding for the construction of infrastructure at the local and national levels.

Road and railroad construction is heavily financed by the government and relevant state-owned enterprises. Regarding the *National Highway Network Plan (2013–2030)*, the Vice Minister of the Ministry of Transport pointed out in an interview with the media: "Taking into account the differences in the service attributes of ordinary national highways and national expressways, if 70% of the construction funds for ordinary national highways are subsidized by central funds, and the remaining part is arranged by provincial finances and other funds, with 30% of the construction funds for national expressways subsidized by central vehicle purchase tax funds and the rest are subsidized by social funds, then the national investment in the construction of the national highway network will be approximately 2.3 trillion yuan." (Feng 2013) This scale accounts for about 49% of the total funds. The construction of railroads is similar in that the central government and the relevant local governments jointly finance the project and partially utilize other financing methods, which are repaid through future earnings. Thus, infrastructure cannot be built and maintained without an active role by the governments of all levels.

The land premium system provides a large source of funding for the local governments. China has a socialist public ownership system of land, with the land in urban areas owned by the state. The land in rural and suburban areas is owned collectively by peasants, except where state ownership is provided for by law. This establishes the basis and the most basic conditions for the state to carry out macroeconomic management through its ownership of land. Because the state owns the land and has a legal basis for expropriation and demolition, it is relatively less difficult to expropriate land, and the cost of expropriation is relatively lower than if the land were privately owned. In addition, land management comes with long-term development, e.g., the planned supply of the land to the market, and production and living facilities in the surrounding area. The commercial value of the land is high, and in addition to the cost of land, attachment compensation, resettlement subsidies, and other costs, the local governments can still deposit a higher income from land grants. Therefore, the local governments have the incentive and ability to carry out land acquisition and transfer, which can not only promote regional economic development but also obtain substantial land transfer fee income. In June 1990, the *Interim Regulations on the Transfer and Assignment of Urban State-Owned Land Use Rights* were promulgated, and the land transfer fee system was formally established. The comprehensive reform of the land grant system and the focus on cultivating the real estate market promoted the expansion of the urban land market and the scope of land transactions, with revenues from land grants becoming a high proportion of local government revenues and the largest source of income in addition to tax revenues. A large amount of these funds are used by the local governments for infrastructure construction and other government functions, as land premiums have become an important source of local financial expenditures, generally referred to as "land finance".

The state issues long-term construction bonds for the purpose of supplementing funds for infrastructure development. The issuance of state bonds is one of the sources of financing for infrastructure development, not only at the central level but also at the local level. For example, in August 1998, the Ministry of Finance issued 10-year Treasury bonds to four major state-owned banks. The banks provided loans specifically for infrastructure construction and enterprise technological transformation, where the investment income of the projects was used to repay the loans, mainly for the construction of agriculture, forestry, water conservancy, transportation and communications, urban infrastructure, urban and rural power grid transformation, state-owned grain reserves, and affordable housing. As another example, in 2009, in order to solve the problem of insufficient supporting funds from the local governments for the central government's investment projects for expanding domestic demand, the central government adopted the method of issuing local government bonds on behalf of the local governments, with clearly defined purposes.

Requiring local matching funds is an effective mechanism for increasing local investment in infrastructure. Local matching funds refer to the requirement that when central or provincial finance allocates funds to lower-level finance for project establishment, the lower-level finance must provide matching funds in a corresponding proportion. The matching proportion requirements vary depending on local, regional, and national projects and on local financial conditions, thereby more effectively achieving the central government's goal of strengthening national infrastructure construction. The channels for the local governments to mobilize matching funds include the general budget funds of the local governments at all levels, various types of governmental funds, such as proceeds from the land concessions of the local governments at all levels, funds from local government bonds issued by the central financial agency, and funds raised through the market mechanism by using governmental financing platforms, and so on. Of course, there are also some problems in the implementation of local matching funds, such as insufficient local matching funds.

Railroad and road construction has accelerated significantly after 1994. As can be seen from Fig. 4.2, the construction of railroads and highways in China is gradually accelerating since 1994, which is attributable to the increased financial capacity of governments at all levels following the reform of the fiscal and taxation system, as well as to the fact that the central government attaches importance to infrastructure construction and has established various effective financing mechanisms. Both road and railroad construction have been given high priority by all levels of government, and the mileage numbers of highways and railroads constructed are almost neck and neck. From 1978 to 1993, the highway mileage increased from 890,200 to 1,083,500 km, with an average annual increase of 12,900 km. From 1994 to 2020, the highway mileage increased from 1,117,800 to 2,715,700 km, with an average annual increase of 61,500 km. The average annual increase was about five times that of the previous period. From 1978 to 1993, the operating mileage of railways increased from 51,700 to 58,600 km, with an average annual increase of 4600 km. From 1994 to 2020, the mileage of highways increased from 59,000 to 146,000 km, with an average annual increase of 33,500 km. The average annual increase was about 7 times that of the previous period. As can be seen, railroad and road construction has accelerated significantly after 1994.

An empirical analysis was conducted to investigate if infrastructure development is closely related to the reform of the fiscal and taxation system. In order to analyze the impact of the reform and the country's economic strength on railway and highway investment, the dependent variable was the annual increase in railway or highway mileage, that is, the annual new mileage kilometers of each province, while the independent variable was the actual GDP value of each province, excluding the price factor. A dummy variable was designed to represent the reform of the fiscal

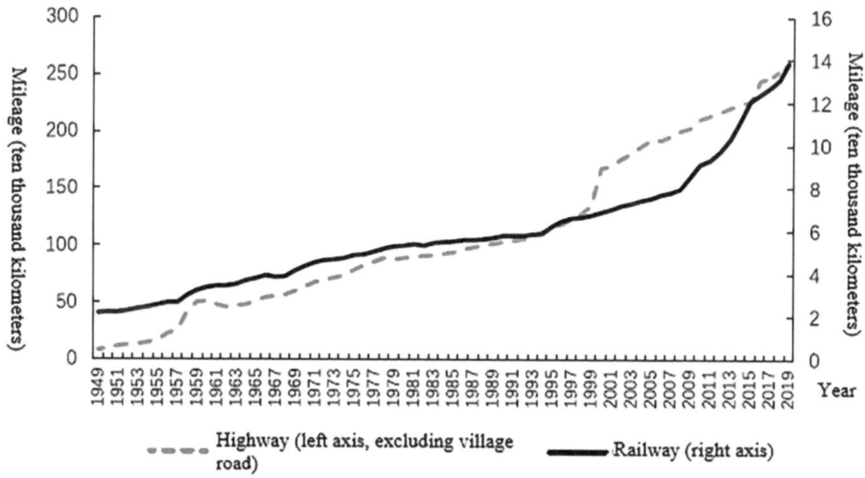

Fig. 4.2 Road and railroad mileages. Source: WIND (data before 2004), Statistical Bulletin on the Development of Road and Waterway Transportation Industry (2005–2012 data), and Statistical Bulletin on the Development of Transportation Industry (data after 2013)

and taxation system, that is, 0 before 1993 and 1 after 1994. The regression analysis of the real value of GDP of each province, autonomous region, and city in the calendar year and the dummy variable of the reform of the fiscal and tax system using the number of increases in the mileage of railroads or highways, respectively, and the regression results are shown as follows, and the coefficients of the dummy variables are very significant, which indicates that the construction of the infrastructure indeed accelerated after the reform of the fiscal and taxation system in 1994. Also, infrastructure development was found to be highly correlated with the economic strength of a region; the larger the economy, the greater the mileage of the new infrastructure.

4.2.3 Importance of Infrastructure Development for Economic Growth

The impact of infrastructure on economic growth is divided into two main channels: one is the pull of infrastructure investment itself on economic growth, and the other is the contribution of stock infrastructure to economic growth. The two effects are intertwined, and we constructed econometric models to assess the two effects separately.

The first is the role of infrastructure investment in driving economic growth. Over the past 40 years, China's economic growth has been investment-driven, where infrastructure investments are an important part. Among infrastructure investments, highway and railroad investments account for a larger proportion. For example, in 2003–2014, fixed-asset investment in road transportation grew at an average annual rate of 19.0% and fixed-asset investment in rail transportation grew at an average annual rate of 24.4%. It is estimated that the construction of 1000 km of highways requires about 1 million tons of steel, 9 million tons of cement, and 800,000 tons of asphalt, as well as a large number of workers and large-scale machinery and equipment. Infrastructure construction is also one of the most important means for the local governments to boost their economy. Large-scale infrastructure investment directly contributes to economic growth, while driving the development of related industries and providing a large number of jobs. In examining the contribution of infrastructure development to economic efficiency, the direct contribution of infrastructure development itself to economic growth needs to be deducted.

The other channel lies in the economic efficiency gains of infrastructure, which can manifest in three ways. The first is transportation efficiency. Shortening the time and lowering the cost of transporting goods between cities further extends the reach of a region's residents, speeds up the flow of goods, increases the variety and convenience of consumption, and releases some of the consumption potential. The second is the scale effect. The wider the scope of goods transportation, such that enterprises can expand the scale of production and further give full play to the comparative advantages of a province and even the country, the more products will be sold to the province and even the country to obtain a greater scale effect. Between different regions, the advantage will be comparative, with industries that implement large-scale production greatly improving production efficiency. The third is factor mobility. Transportation facilitation promotes the cross-regional mobility of capital and people, leading to the reallocation of resources across the country and enhancing allocation efficiency, while also leading to the diffusion of technology and increasing total factor productivity.

An empirical analysis was conducted, and the result shows that both effects are significant. To analyze the impact of railway and highway construction on economic growth, the actual annual GDP value of each province was selected as the dependent variable, and the increase in railway or highway mileage in each province over the years was selected as the independent variable in order to examine the direct driving effect of railway or highway investment on the total economic volume. A lag term of railway or highway mileage was added in order to examine the impact of existing infrastructure on economic benefits. The regression result shows that the coefficients of the lagged terms for railroad or highway mileage are highly significant, indicating that infrastructure plays a significant role in improving economic efficiency and promoting economic growth. In addition, the correlation between incremental infrastructure and total economic volume is also high, indicating that infrastructure investment has a direct contribution to economic growth.

4.3 Freer Movement of People

Unlike other factors, the local governments have relatively little initiative in population management and are more likely to follow a unified, centralized policy that regulates population movement through permits for people to move out and settlement policies for people to move in. Successive population management policies of the central government have had a greater impact on population mobility, which has gradually increased since the reform and opening up of China, especially since the introduction of a series of policies and measures to accelerate the construction of a unified urban and rural labor market after 2005, which has resulted in freer national population mobility and a marked expansion of the scale of population mobility. Following freer population movements, the population gradually gathered in cities, especially in eastern coastal cities, providing a large number of low-cost laborers for the development of important industries, promoting the industrial division of labor among regions, and effectively breaking down local barriers. Judging from the result of the econometric regression of provincial panel data, several important changes in population management policies have effectively lifted the administrative restrictions on population mobility, conformed to the development trend of the market economy, and accelerated the formation of a unified national labor market, and the large-scale population mobility has also provided a continuous impetus for economic development.

4.3.1 How Population Movements Are Perceived

Population mobility should be in line with the level of economic development. The agricultural economy initially accounted for the highest proportion of China's economy when the development of light industry and heavy industry made these sectors the leading industry, and then the service industry gradually grew to become the first major industry. The industrial structure, along with the economic development of the continuous upgrading of the demand for the labor force, is also constantly changing. The agricultural economy is largely self-sufficient, with farmers farming on their own; there is little need for large-scale labor hiring and fewer requirements for population mobility. The industrial economy, especially the early light industry, put forward a large demand for labor. With the employment income in the industrial sector also much higher than that of the agricultural sector and the desire of the surplus labor in agricultural production to migrate, this put forward strong demands for the relaxation of the national population management policy. It was only when the policy finally allowed for the free flow of the population and provided the necessary living security for the floating population that such population movement was carried out legally, compliantly, and on a large scale. In addition, large population flows provide low-cost labor for industrial development, and secondary schools training a large number of industrial workers provide the reserve labor force for further industrial upgrading. Especially with the popularization of compulsory education, higher education, and vocational education, the human capital of China's labor force has been greatly enhanced, which promotes the development of the economy. It can be seen that population mobility is an important driving force and a necessary condition for sustained economic development.

The central government plays an important role in China's population mobility. Since the founding of New China, China's household registration management system can be roughly divided into three phases: before 1958, it was basically a phase of free movement; from 1958 to 1978, population movement was strictly controlled; and after 1978, population movement was gradually liberalized. In 1950, China began to implement the household registration system. In 1951, the Ministry of Public Security officially promulgated the *Provisional Regulations on Urban Household Registration Management*, which was the earliest household registration law after the founding of New China. It basically unified the household registration system in cities across the country. In 1953, based on the first national census, most rural areas established a household registration system. With regard to population movement, the 1954 Constitution of the People's Republic of China clearly stipulates that citizens have "freedom of movement and residence". However, as a large number of rural populations flowed into cities, the state managed and restricted population mobility, especially the *Household Registration Regulations of the People's Republic of China*, promulgated in 1958, which strictly restricted the free flow of population and distinguished between "agricultural household registration" and "non-agricultural household registration". The 1975 Constitution even abolished the provisions on freedom of migration.,[12] As reform and opening up continued to advance and the socialist market economy was gradually established, policies on population migration and residence were gradually relaxed, including allowing farmers to provide their own food and settle in towns,[3] converting agricultural household registration to non-agricultural household registration,[4] and processing permanent urban household registration for employment and home buyers. Later, the processing of permanent household registration in small towns was relaxed.[5] At present, some large cities still implement a strict management system for household registration, but they also implement other policies, such as the work permit system for the migrant population. This shows that government policies have played a key and positive role in population migration and residence in order to promote the formation of a unified labor market and economic development.

A mobile population is mainly defined as the difference between the resident population and the household population. A mobile population may be defined in various ways, for example, as a population that stays in a certain area only for a period of not more than 6 months, as opposed to the permanent resident population. A floating population is referred to in this paper as the remaining portion of the resident population in a given area after deducting the household registration population, which mainly includes the foreign population, those who live permanently in the locality but have not obtained household registration, and those who live temporarily in the locality. For a region, the mobile population flow can be either negative or positive, and if the resident population is greater than the household population, there is a net inflow of people to the region. For the whole country, the sum of all resident population should equal the sum of all household population. At present, first-tier cities and some second-tier cities, for example, Beijing, Shanghai, Shenzhen, and some provincial capitals, have large net inflows of population. Net outflows of population are mainly from some populous provinces and some central and western provinces with relatively lagging economic development.

[1] Refer to Baidu Encyclopedia.

[2] In November 1977, the State Council approved the Ministry of Public Security's *Regulations on the Handling of Household Movements*.

[3] In October 1984, the State Council issued a circular on the issue of farmers settling in market towns.

[4] In June 1997, the State Council approved the Ministry of Public Security's *Pilot Program for Reform of the Household Registration System in Small Towns and Opinions on Improving the Household Registration System in Rural Areas*.

[5] In July 1998, the State Council approved the Ministry of Public Security's *Opinions on Solving Several Outstanding Problems in the Current Administration of Household Registration*.

4.3.2 Migration and Economic Participation

The household registration system has an important impact on population mobility, especially since many public services are related to household registration, such as education, medical care, social security, and other important social resources. Therefore, all previous household registration system reforms have had a far-reaching impact on population migration, especially since 2005, when the policy of urban settlement was greatly relaxed, where population mobility significantly accelerated and the scale of the floating population greatly expanded. There is a significant correlation between the household registration system and population mobility.

The resumption of the college entrance examination in 1977 expanded the channels for population mobility into cities. In 1977, the national examination for admission to institutions of higher learning, which had been suspended for 10 years, was resumed, and talents were selected for admission to universities on the basis of a unified examination and on the basis of merit, with target groups including workers, peasants, young people who had gone up to the mountains to work in the countryside, demobilized soldiers, cadres, and recent high school graduates. More than 5.7 million people took the first exam in 1977, and more than 6 million people enrolled in the 1978 college entrance examination, with the two cohorts of students enrolling in the spring and fall of 1978 just half a year apart.

The restoration of the college entrance examination system has put China's talent training back on a healthy track. More and more graduates of institutions of higher learning and colleges and universities are staying and working in the cities, which has not only changed the destiny of several generations but also accelerated the flow of talents, laying a good foundation of talents for urban construction and national economic development.

The rapid development of the non-public economy is driving rural-urban labor mobility. In 1992, former Chairman Deng's Southern Dialogue set off another climax of China's economic reform, further increasing reform and opening up and ushering in a period of rapid development of the non-public economy, which created a huge demand for labor. There was also a large amount of idle labor in the countryside, and with the abolition of the urban food supply system, the rural labor force accelerated its movement to the cities, solving the problem of cheap labor in the cities, and rural migrant workers grew up with secondary schooling to become industrial workers, which pushed for the realization of urbanization and industrialization. During this period, the central government emphasized the need to reasonably guide rural laborers to work in cities in accordance with the needs of urban development, but the local governments tended to restrict rural laborers from going to the cities and discriminatory policies existed for migrant workers.

Policies to accelerate the construction of a unified urban and rural labor market have been introduced since 2005. On April 4, 2005, the State Council issued *Opinions on Deepening Economic System Reform in 2005 (Guo Fa (2005) No. 9)*, which explicitly called for the acceleration of the construction of a unified urban and rural labor market for further reforming the labor and employment management system, clearing up unreasonable restrictive policies and arbitrary fees for farmers working in cities, and eliminating all kinds of discriminatory regulations on the employment of rural laborers. The state further reformed the household registration management system, promoted the rational and orderly transfer of surplus rural labor, and selected some cities with the necessary conditions to carry out pilot work on integrated urban and rural labor markets. As a policy to implement the above-mentioned opinions, on January 31, 2006, the State Council issued *Several Opinions of the State Council on Solving the Problem of Migrant Workers (Guo Fa (2006) No. 5)*, which called for further improvement of services for the transfer of farmers for employment. Governments at all levels are urged to take the promotion of the transfer of surplus rural labor to employment as an important task. A sound network of public employment services in counties and townships should be established to provide services for the transfer of employment for farmers. The State Council also requires that a high priority is given to the social security of migrant workers, that migrant workers are included in the scope of work-related injury insurance, that the issue of medical protection for migrant workers against serious illnesses is urgently resolved, and that a pension insurance scheme suited to the characteristics of migrant workers is explored. Moreover, it is deemed necessary to effectively provide relevant public services for migrant workers, integrate migrant workers into the urban public service system, guarantee equal access to compulsory education for the children of migrant workers, strengthen the prevention and control of diseases among migrant workers and the immunization of school-age children, and improve the living conditions of migrant workers through a variety of channels. This round of reform of the household registration system significantly relaxed the conditions for people to migrate and settle down and gave great support to various kinds of complementary measures, which, from the point of view of practical effects, effectively promoted population mobility.

The size of the mobile population increased significantly after 2005. The overall mobile population size for the country can be obtained by subtracting the number of permanent residents from the number of householders in each province to obtain the number of mobile people and by summing the number of mobile people in provinces with net population inflow. Adding up the number of net inflows in the provinces with net population inflows gives Fig. 4.3, from which it can be seen that the size of the mobile population has been increasing rapidly since 2008, and as of the end of 2019, the size of the mobile population in provinces with net population inflows exceeded 60 million people. From 1987 to 2005, the size of the mobile population increased from 3,956,800 to 33,512,600, with an average annual increase of 1,642,200 people. The growth rate of the mobile population size slowed down before and after 2005, but the mobile population began to increase rapidly again in 2009, with the size of the mobile population increasing to 62,245,300 people. In fact, the census data show that the size of the country's mobile population is much larger than that calculated by the methodology described above. The Seventh National Population Census in 2020 showed that the national cross-municipal floating population amounted to 375.82 million people, an increase of 69.73% compared with 2010, of which the cross-provincial floating population amounted to 124.84

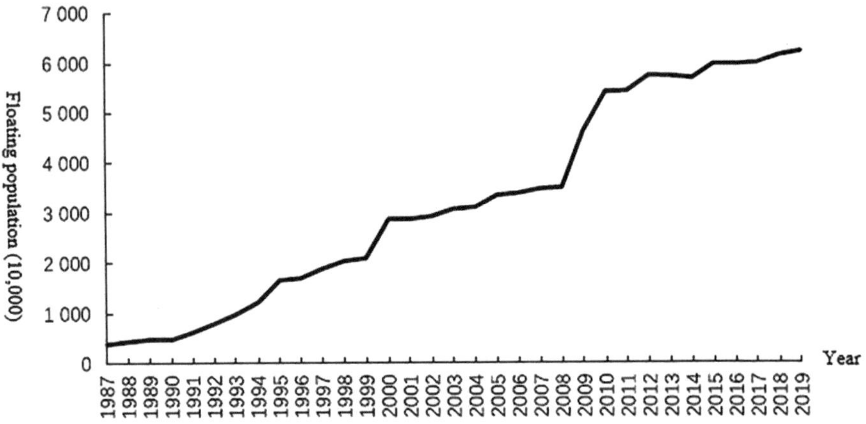

Fig. 4.3 Total mobile population in provinces with net population inflow. Source: WIND; calculated by the authors

million people, and that the scale of China's floating population is rapidly expanding. The gradual liberalization of the household registration system and population mobility policy after 2005 has resulted in a large influx of people into economically developed provinces, such as Guangdong, Shanghai, Beijing, and Zhejiang. In contrast, the net outflow of population is mainly concentrated in Henan, Guizhou, Sichuan, Anhui, and Guangxi.

An empirical analysis was conducted, and the result shows that the reform of the household registration system has a significant impact on population mobility. The dependent variable was the annual number of floating population in each province, i.e., the difference between the number of permanent residents and the number of household population in each province each year, while the independent variable was the GDP per capita of each province, autonomous region, and city in a calendar year. A dummy variable was designed to represent the reform of the household registration system, i.e., it is 0 prior to 2004, and 1 from 2005 onwards, and a cross-term of the dummy variable with GDP per capita was added. Using migrant population, a regression analysis was conducted to analyze the GDP per capita of each province, region, and city in a calendar year, the dummy variable of the reform of the household registration system, and the cross-term of the two. The regression result shows that the coefficients of both the dummy variable and the cross-term of the dummy variable with GDP per capita are highly significant, indicating that the reform of the household registration system in 2005 had a large impact on population mobility. Under the combined impact of the reform of the household registration system, the level of GDP per capita at which population inflow and outflow are balanced is about 48,000 yuan, above which the GDP per capita is more likely to attract a net inflow of population and below which the GDP per capita is more likely to result in a net outflow of population.

4.3.3 Population Mobility and Economic Growth

The impact of population mobility on economic growth is divided into two main channels: one is the driving effect of the stock of mobile population itself on economic growth, and the other is the promotion effect of new mobile population on economic growth. The two effects are intertwined, and we constructed econometric models to assess the two effects separately.

The first is the contribution of the mobile population to economic growth. Over the past 40 years, China's industrial development had been mainly labor-intensive, with the transfer of surplus rural labor from the countryside to urban industries constituting an important driving force for economic growth and with the foreign population making an important contribution to the development of the eastern seaboard. In recent years, various cities have even launched a "war" for talents, especially high-quality talents with certain skills, which has become the focus of competition. As China's economy moves towards high-quality development, talents have become the core resource for future local economic development, which speaks volumes about the importance of mobile populations for economic development.

More important is the second effect, which is the continued contribution of the stock of mobile people to economic growth. When a large number of migrants enter the cities and become permanent residents, they form an integral part of the population of these cities. These migrant populations are distributed across a wide range of industries and have accumulated significant human capital over time, consistently contributing to local economic development. Moreover, these populations have a certain degree of mobility, and if the economic development potential of certain regions declines, they are more likely to opt for inter-regional mobility into regions or sectors with higher production efficiency, which is of great significance in improving the efficiency of resource allocation.

The result of the empirical analysis shows that both effects are more significant. To analyze the impact of population mobility on economic growth, the dependent variable was the annual GDP per capita of each province; the independent variable was the increase in the mobile population in each province, region, and city in order to examine the impact of the mobile population on the total economy; and a lagged term of the mobile population was added in order to examine the impact of the stock of the mobile population on economic efficiency. The regression result shows that the coefficient of the lagged term for the mobile population is highly significant, indicating that the stock of the mobile population contributes to economic growth. In addition, the correlation between the mobile population and the total economy is also very high, and the larger the increase in the mobile population, the higher the level of economic development of the region. It should be noted that the coefficient of the incremental mobile population mainly reflects the direct contribution of population inflow to economic growth, while the coefficient of the mobile population stock mainly reflects the important role played by the original mobile population in economic development.

4.4 Breaking Down Regional Trade Barriers

Among the central government's successive initiatives to break down local trade barriers, the *2001 State Council Provisions on the Prohibition of Regional Embargoes in the Market Economy (State Council Decree No. 303)* were the most stringent, which, together with a number of complementary policies that followed, effectively played a role in breaking down the regional embargo. Since then, local embargoes have been moderated, interregional commodity flows have increased, interregional product competition has intensified, and the market share of competitive commodities has gradually expanded. From the result of the econometric regression of the inter-provincial panel data, the 2001 ban on regional embargoes has indeed restrained regional embargoes, effectively lifted the various restrictions on the flow of commodities imposed by local administrative interventions, responded to the trend of the development of the market economy, accelerated the formation of a unified market for commodities throughout the country, and made the division of labor between regions more common, with the comparative advantages of regions providing an important impetus for economic development.

4.4.1 Regional Embargoes

The creation of regional embargoes is related to the economic system. Local embargoes refer to the abuse of administrative power by local governments to discriminate between local and foreign enterprises or to turn a blind eye to the unfair competition of local enterprises, thereby preventing foreign products and even capital from entering the local market in order to protect the development of local enterprises. The first reason is the fiscal system. The tax system makes the local governments strive to expand the size of the local economy, especially when the value-added tax (VAT) is levied at the factory level. Even if an enterprise has poor profits and cannot pay income tax, it can still pay a sizable amount of VAT, which leads to the incentive for local governments to protect the production and development of local enterprises and to exclude foreign commodities from crowding the market. The second reason is the cadre appraisal system, the "only GDP on heroes" type of performance appraisal system. While the system can expand local employment, improve the level of local economic development, and improve the standard of living of the residents, it can also incentivize local cadres to safeguard the interests of local enterprises after the hard work of expanding the scale of the local economy. The third reason is the administrative management system. For a long period of time, local administrations have been managed by the local governments, and their behaviors are influenced by the local governments, which turns local administrations into administrative means of regional embargoes rather than the maintainers of market unity, and so the vertical management of all kinds of administrations at the sub-provincial level has been implemented one after another later on. The fourth reason is the judicial system. The setting up of the judiciary, as well as its staffing, is territorial, which creates conditions for the local governments to intervene in the judiciary and law enforcement and to judicially protect the division of the market, since even if the vertically managed administrative authorities impose administrative penalties on local enterprises for acts of unfair competition, there may be a judgment upholding the interests of the local enterprises in the event of a review by the judicial authorities.

In the past, regional embargoes were more prevalent. For example, the beer industry was characterized by a serious regional embargo. In 1997, the total national beer production reached 18.665 million tons; basically, all local governments had beer brands that they supported. The country had more than 500 beer enterprises, but the annual output did not exceed one million tons of enterprises. Even some well-known brands had a relatively low share in the national market. An important reason for the market segmentation of the beer industry was local protection, as taxes on beer enterprises were always a big source of profits for the local governments. In order to safeguard their own interests, the local governments increased the sales cost of foreign beer enterprises by setting various tangible or intangible barriers to entry, such as quality inspection standards and various taxes and fees, and even restricted foreign brands from entering local sales by explicitly prohibiting local sales of foreign beer (Li and Sun 2004).

Regional embargoes limit the efficiency of resource allocation. As the early localities had relatively complete categories of industries, such as woolen mills, sugar mills, milk powder factories, breweries, etc., the regional blockade restricted inter-regional product competition, resulting in a wider variety of products in each locality, but on a more limited scale of production. Thus, regional embargoes affected the efficiency of resource allocation in several ways. Firstly, it was difficult to achieve economies of scale. Enterprises in various regions produced only for the consumption of local residents, but the population was limited in size and hence the scale of production could not be expanded. While an industrial enterprise has a strong scale effect, where the cost per unit of production will decline with the expansion of the scale of production, regional embargoes inhibited the reduction of costs through the expansion of the scale. Secondly, it was difficult to utilize comparative advantages. Due to the different resource endowments of different regions, different industrial accumulations, and differences in workers' skills, different regions had their own advantageous industries, and regional embargoes led to a region not focusing on its advantageous industries by expanding production but rather spreading its resources flatly among industries, making it difficult to give full play to its comparative advantages. Thirdly, there was a lack of effective competition. The existence of local protection caused the lack of enterprise awareness and competition and the lack of improvement of technology, which resulted in product quality that was difficult to improve and production costs that were high. Fourthly, it was difficult to meet the needs of the masses. For local residents, the poor availability or the high access cost of goods from outside the country left them with a choice of only local products, and so regional embargoes led to a decline in people's well-being.

4.4.2 *Breaking Regional Embargoes and Facilitating Movement of Commodities*

Local protectionism has always existed, and regional barriers and blockades are hard to break. Despite repeated orders from the central government, the "vassal economy" was still prevalent. The central government has taken many measures, such as adopting vertical management below the provincial level to avoid administrative intervention by the local governments. With the implementation of various measures, regional blockades have eased, and a unified national market has been accelerated. Although there are still many barriers to a unified national market, local protection has been significantly curbed.

Policies to break the regional embargo have been effective since 2001. On April 21, 2001, the State Council issued the *Provisions on the Prohibition of Regional Embargoes in Market Economic Activities (State Council Decree No. 303)*, which explicitly requires that the local governments and their subordinate departments shall not, in contravention of the laws, administrative regulations, and the State Council's stipulations, implement the following acts of regional embargo: (1) restricting, in any way or in disguise, units or individuals to operate, purchase, or use only locally produced products or to receive only services provided by local enterprises, designated enterprises, other economic organizations, or individuals; (2) setting up barriers on roads, stations, ports, airports, or at the borders of the administrative region to hinder the entry of foreign products or the transportation of local products; (3) setting discriminatory charges, prescribing discriminatory prices, or applying discriminatory tariffs for products or services from abroad; (4) adopting technical requirements and testing standards for foreign products or services that are different from those for similar local products or services, or adopting discriminatory technical measures, such as duplicate testing and duplicate certification, for foreign products or services, thereby restricting the entry of foreign products or services into the local market; (5) adopting such means as monopolies, exclusive sales, approvals, licenses, etc., specifically targeting foreign products or services, applying discriminatory treatment, and restricting the entry of foreign products or services into the local market; (6) restricting or excluding foreign enterprises, other economic organizations or individuals from participating in local bidding and tendering activities by setting discriminatory qualification requirements and evaluation criteria or by failing to publish information in accordance with the law; (7) restricting or excluding foreign enterprises, other economic organizations, or individuals from investing in or setting up local branches by adopting unequal treatment for local enterprises, other economic organizations, or individuals or by infringing on lawful rights and interests by applying discriminatory treatment favoring local investments or branches set up by foreign enterprises, other economic organizations, or individuals; and (8) other acts of regional blockade.

The flow of goods accelerated markedly since the curbing of regional embargoes. Still taking the beer industry as an example, the production of beer by well-known brands increased significantly in 2001. After long-term competition, the beer

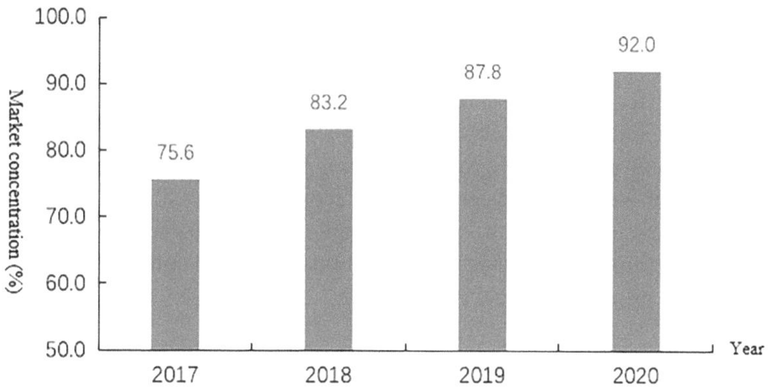

Fig. 4.4 Market concentration in beer industry. Source: China Alcoholic Beverage Association, Prospective Industry Research Institute

industry formed some well-known national or regional brands, such as Tsingtao Beer, Yanjing Beer, Snowflake Beer, Harbin Beer, Zhujiang Beer, Jinwei Beer, Xuejin Beer, Chongqing Beer, Baihui Beer, etc. The headquarters of these beer enterprises are mainly concentrated in Shandong, Beijing, Heilongjiang, Guangdong, Henan, Chongqing, Fujian, Hunan, and other places, and some national well-known brands also set up factories closer to their consumers. In recent years, the market concentration of China's beer industry has further increased; as shown in Fig. 4.4, the market share accounted for by the top five brands rose from 75.6% in 2017 to 92% in 2020. Beer has become less difficult to move between regions, and there has been a marked increase in the production of well-known brands after 2001, especially after 2007, due closely to the regional or national promotion of these brands, reflecting the weakening of regional blockades.

An empirical analysis was conducted and the result shows that the policy of breaking the regional blockade had a significant impact on beer sales. The dependent variable was the annual beer production of each province, and the independent variables were the calendar year GDP and population of each province, region, and city. A category variable was added, with 1 for the location of well-known beer companies and 0 for other regions; a dummy variable was designed to represent the policy of breaking the regional embargo, i.e., 0 for the period prior to 2001 and 1 for the period after 2001; and cross-terms were added for the dummy variable with the GDP, population, and category variables. The regression result shows that the coefficient of the dummy variable is very significant, and the coefficient of the cross-term of the dummy variable and the category variable is also very significant. For provinces where famous beer brands are located, the combined coefficient is positive, while for other provinces, the combined coefficient is negative, which shows that the output of provinces where these famous brands are located increased significantly after 2001, while that of other provinces decreased relatively, indicating increased mobility of beer products in different provinces and improved brand concentration.

4.5 Intergovernmental Relations and Economic Growth

Through the perfect mechanism design, China has formed an effective competitive and cooperative relationship between governments of all levels, realized the consistency of decision-making between the central government and the local governments, and improved political cohesion and economic accessibility, which enables China's economy to maintain a long-term high growth rate. The role of local government competition in achieving the promotion of political cohesion and economic accessibility is summarized below.

4.5.1 Improvement of Central Government's Capacity for Coordination and Coherence in Behavior of All Levels of Government

The local governments are faced with two main incentives: administrative and economic. Administratively, the central government decides the position change and promotion of local government officials through the performance appraisal of the local governments; economically, the central government decides the financial resources of the local governments through tax rebates, transfer payments, and subsidized funds. By improving and optimizing the incentive mechanism of the local governments, the central government's voice can be improved and its macro-control ability can be enhanced. Administrative incentives have been improved through the strengthening of cadre management and the optimization of the cadre appointment and dismissal mechanism, and the regulatory capacity of the government, especially the central government, has been strengthened through the reform of the tax system, which has enhanced the implementation of the central government's decisions by the local governments and the consistency of decision-making at all levels of the government, thereby strengthening political cohesion.

4.5.2 Breaking Regional Embargoes and Building Unified National Market

Initially, there was a serious phenomenon of regional embargoes in local competition, with the establishment of small and all-encompassing industrial systems and a low level of inter-regional economic and trade exchanges, which had a serious impact on the efficiency of economic production. The state has established a vertical management system in the administrative system, and the leadership of central governments over the local governments has been strengthened in various areas, such as quality inspection, industry and commerce, pricing, taxation, and the judiciary, which greatly reduced the administrative intervention of the local governments.

National connectivity has been achieved through large-scale national and regional infrastructure development. Free movement of the population has been realized through the restoration of the college entrance examination and the improvement of the mechanism for seeking education, the transfer of rural migrant workers to urban industries, and the improvement of the household registration management system. The free movement of goods has been realized through the liberalization of market access, the encouragement of market economy development, and free trade. By restructuring the institutional mechanism of economic and social management, effective competition among the local governments within the framework of rules has been promoted, conflicts and vicious competition among the local governments have been curbed, and the cohesiveness of governance has been improved, while the inward openness of the economy has been greatly increased.

4.5.3 Encouragement of Local Pilots and Rapid Replication and Scaling Up of Experiences

In the process of local competition, the central government encourages and accommodates the economic construction of the local governments, and the local governments exert their initiative to carry out batch after batch of pilot works for assessing new proposals, from which a large number of successful cases have been produced and valuable experience accumulated, with the pilot works rapidly popularized to the whole country through local exchanges of learning and other ways. Government officials who performed outstandingly in local economic construction are usually reappointed and entrusted with important duties and transferred to higher levels of government or other places to carry out their work, and they will bring their management experience to more places. Through the implementation of targeted assistance and counterpart support, the developed regions give strong support to the less-developed regions in terms of personnel, capital, and technology to realize a rapid increase in productivity. As a result of effective experience replication and scaling up, regions have a higher degree of acceptance of the economic development model and economic performance, and it is easier to reach a consensus at the national level, which improves political cohesion and accelerates the pace of economic construction in the process.

4.5.4 Full and Free Movement of Factors and Formation of National Industrial Division of Labor

With the breaking of regional embargoes, people, capital, and technology can flow freely. Various factors began to gather in areas with high factor returns, and the comparative advantages of these areas are reflected. Different industrial clusters are formed in various regions, and economies of scale gradually manifest. The pattern of industrial division of labor and cooperation is formed throughout the country, and the national unified market is gradually formed. With the continuous emergence of new products, technologies, and modes, the division of labor between enterprises and regions has become more refined, and the production and operation of enterprises have become more specialized and scaled up, further enhancing their competitiveness in global markets and more conducive to their in-depth integration into the global industrial chain and value chain, to the formation of benign interactions between the external market and the internal market, and to the sustained increase in the degree of opening up of the economy to the outside world and to the inside world.

4.5.5 Formation of a Positive Competition, and Continuous Optimization of the Local Business Environment

At present, China's economy is in an important period of high-quality development. The development, transformation, and upgrading of the local economy should attract more professional and technical talents. All local governments attach great importance to improving the business environment of enterprises, continue to promote the "streamline administration, delegate power, strengthen regulation, and improve services" reform, vigorously promote tax reduction and fee reduction, and continuously optimize the relationship between the government and enterprises. The central government attaches great importance to improving the well-being of the people, and the level of public services, such as education, medical care, and elderly care, has been steadily rising. These have further enhanced political cohesion, while local competition has promoted the optimal allocation of resources, improved the efficiency of resource allocation, facilitated technological progress and technology diffusion, and increased total factor productivity and economic growth.

References

Feng QY (2013) Three questions about the huge investment in highway construction. Economic Daily

Li J, Sun QY (2004) The impact of WTO on eliminating local protection from the perspective of beer market integration. J World Econ 6:37–45+80

Lin YF (2012) New structural economics (trans: Su I). Peking University Press, Beijing

Chapter 5
Manufacturing Powerhouse Supported by Industrial Parks

Over the past 40 years of reform and opening up, industrial parks have played an important role in policy pilots, institutional innovation, industrial growth and upgrading, creation of jobs and tax revenue, creation of economic growth points, and the drive for regional economic development.

Industrial parks break through existing institutional and policy frameworks and take the lead in attracting foreign investment, developing markets, and innovating management systems. They serve as open windows to the outside world and they gather production factors, such as capital, labor, and technology, internally. And they have significantly improved the accessibility of China's economy both internally and externally.

In addition, the promotion of industrial park development experience has driven the development of more regions and industries, supporting the growth and upgrading of important industries. And it has built a consensus on reform, opened up on a larger scale, and improved economic accessibility. It also makes the formulation and implementation of various policies and political governance more coherent, making an important contribution to China's economic growth.

5.1 Emergence and Development of Industrial Parks in China

The industrial park economy is a relatively distinctive model in China's economic development process. Its main feature is to efficiently concentrate production factors and related policies in a certain area and within a certain period of time, cultivate specific economic functions and pillar industries in the region, and drive and lead the development of more fields in a larger scope. As early as the beginning of reform and opening up, the Chinese government proposed a framework for the development of industrial park economies based on economic development zones,

C. Chen et al., *From Poverty to Prosperity*, Understanding China,
https://doi.org/10.1007/978-981-95-7171-0_5

which has since opened the precedent for China's modern industrial park economies. Through the phased development of fixed-point experiments, partial promotion, and nationwide popularization, the industrial park economy has played a very important role in China's economic growth with its advantages of high efficiency, positive externalities, and strong targeting. After more than 40 years of development, a paradigm of industrial park construction and management with Chinese characteristics has been formed. As of October 2020, 475 national-level industrial parks have been established in China, including 219 economic and technological development zones, 169 high-tech industrial development zones, 57 export processing zones, 17 border economic cooperation zones, and 13 bonded zones.[1] These parks have become an important support and new growth point for the development of the national economy and have become innovation highlands, industrial highlands, and talent highlands in the country's development. Taking high-tech zones as an example, in 2019, China's 169 national high-tech zones achieved a gross domestic product of 12.2 trillion yuan, accounting for 12.3% of the country's GDP, and paid 1.9 trillion yuan in taxes and fees, accounting for 11.8% of the country's tax revenue; the R&D expenditure of enterprises in national high-tech zones was 825.9 billion yuan, accounting for half of the total investment of enterprises in the country, while the number of invention patents authorized in national high-tech zones accounted for 37.5% of the country, the number of PCT international patent applications accounted for 44.7% of the country, and every 10,000 employees had 388 valid invention patents, which is 11.3 times the national average.[2]

5.1.1 Historical Background of China's Introduction of Industrial Park Economy

The development of the industrial park economy in China has a special historical background, and it has gone through a rather tortuous process from taking root to flourishing everywhere. In a sense, the development of the industrial park economy in China is the product of a specific historical environment.

In the 1950s, the global economy was showing a new trend. From the perspective of economic trends, the post-war technological revolution was flourishing. On the southwest coast of the United States, a large number of semiconductor-related industries were emerging. Famous universities, such as Stanford, used campus power to build relevant entrepreneurial platforms and infrastructure for young entrepreneurs, forming many industrial parks. High-tech industries began to gather in large numbers, and the microelectronics industry started to develop rapidly.

[1] Data source: List of National Industrial Parks (October 2020 edition), website of the Ministry of Commerce of the People's Republic of China, http://www.mofcom.gov.cn/xglj/kaifaqu.shtml.

[2] Data source: Regular policy briefing of the State Council on July 23, 2020, from the website of the Central People's Government of the People's Republic of China (http://www.gov.cn/xinwen/2020-07/23/content_5529625.htm).

Under the basic concepts of openness, innovation, and fault tolerance, industrial parks gradually grew into world-leading technology centers. Industrial parks were an important growth pole of the post-war US economy and helped the growth of large companies, such as HP, Intel, Cisco, Oracle, Apple, and Nvidia. Various industrial parks, such as Boston's 128 Highway High-Tech Belt and North Carolina's Triangle Research Park in the United States, the Cambridge Science Park in the United Kingdom, and the High-Tech Zone in Scotland, sprang up like mushrooms after rain. The combination of high-tech industries and industrial parks became an important economic development model in the new era, providing an important inspiration for China, which had just entered the reform and opening-up period. In addition, important industrial parks, represented by Japan's Tsukuba Science Park, South Korea's Daejeon Institute of Technology, Singapore's Jurong Industrial Park, and Taiwan's Hsinchu Science Park, emerged one after another and developed rapidly in the 1970s. Driven by the new round of industrial parks, Japan grew into the world's second-largest economy, the economics of the "Four Little Dragons" in Asia took off rapidly, and the surrounding economies achieved rapid economic development through the promotion of industrial parks. The continuous emergence of successful cases provided China with good experience (Wang 2014).

In the early 1980s, the global information wave was surging, and relevant information and theoretical works about high-tech industrial parks around the world were constantly introduced into China. A number of foreign works, such as *The Third Wave*, *Megatrends: Ten New Directions to Change Our Lives*, and *The Coming of Post-Industrial Society*, were introduced into China, providing new perspectives for China's ideological circles and triggering extensive discussions. Since 1983, China's ideological circles launched a great discussion on whether high-tech industries are technological revolutions or industrial revolutions. One view is that high-tech industries are actually a reflection of changes in industrial and social structures rather than a simple revolution in production technology. Another view is that this so-called industrial revolution does not actually exist but is just the self-glorification of capitalism. On October 9, 1983, Zhao Ziyang, then Premier of the State Council, held a symposium in Zhongnanhai and delivered a speech titled *We Should Pay Attention to Studying the New Technological Revolution in the World and Our Countermeasures*, in which the book *Megatrends*[3] by John Naisbitt was mentioned. From 1983 to 1985, relevant departments organized several expert discussions to discuss how to respond to the challenges of the new technological revolution. More than 2000 experts participated in the discussions and determined the idea of seizing the opportunity of the high-tech revolution. In 1984, the State Science and Technology Commission submitted a report titled *Countermeasures to Meet the Challenges and Opportunities of the New Technological Revolution* to the State Council, which clearly proposed to formulate policies for new technology parks and business incubators and to boldly implement them. This opened the door for the birth of industrial park policies. In 1986, China's *High-Tech Research and*

[3] For more details, see Liu Hong (2010).

Development Plan was officially implemented and, in conjunction, the pilot high-tech basic industrial development zone was established.

5.1.2 Development History of Industrial Parks in China

Since the establishment of China's first industrial park in 1979, the Shekou Industrial Zone, China's industrial parks have gone through more than 40 years of history. According to the number of newly established industrial parks, the evolution of industrial park management mechanisms, and the role played by industrial parks, the development of China's industrial parks can be roughly divided into five stages, namely the initial exploration stage (1979–1983), the gradual cultivation stage (1984–1991), the rapid growth stage (1992–2002), the stable development stage (2002–2008), and the innovation and upgrading stage (2009 to present).

Initial Exploration Stage (1979–1983)
In 1979, the establishment of the Shekou Industrial Zone kicked off the construction of industrial parks in China. The development of industrial parks at this stage was in the exploratory stage. The development process was mainly guided by central policies, and local pilot projects and rapid exploration were encouraged. In terms of the management model, industrial parks took policy preferences and simplified procedures as the two main lines. Through relevant policies in the fields of enterprise access and tariff preferences, export-oriented economic development zones were established to attract foreign investment and encourage entrepreneurship. Taking the Shekou Industrial Zone as an example, its positioning was to drive the development of China's export-oriented economy by developing labor-intensive industries, which was consistent with China's national conditions at the time and its comparative advantages in international markets. In addition, the Shekou Industrial Zone boldly tried the employee reward system and proposed "time is money, efficiency is life", becoming a pioneer in breaking the "iron rice bowl" of enterprises and truly taking the lead in policy innovation and institutional mechanism innovation. Also, the Shekou Industrial Zone innovatively allowed the development of private enterprises, allowing many large private enterprises to take root and sprout. For example, Huawei, Vanke, and Ping An all developed in the Shekou Industrial Zone. In 1981, the State Council held a working conference in Guangdong and Fujian provinces and put forward 10 important opinions, which further clarified the direction of industrial parks and became a reference model for future mechanism reforms.

Gradual Cultivation Stage (1984–1991)
This stage was marked by the establishment of 14 economic development zones and 27 high-tech industrial development zones in coastal areas.[4] Industrial parks in

[4]The first batch of 14 economic and technological development zones were approved and established from 1984 to 1988, namely the Qinhuangdao Economic and Technological Development Zone, Ningbo Economic and Technological Development Zone, Qingdao Economic and

eastern coastal provinces and municipalities started one after another, with each province and city establishing 2–4 industrial parks. Even central and western provinces began to establish their first industrial park, and the second echelon of national industrial park development was gradually formed. At this stage, industrial parks were still dominated by labor-intensive industries. The industrial structure was relatively simple, but the state provided a lot of support in terms of local legislation, land allocation, and preferential policies. For example, the *Provisional Regulations of Guangzhou Economic and Technological Development Zone*, issued in 1985 by the State Council, gave foreign-invested enterprises more preferential treatment on the basis of relevant regulations. Various parks actively learned and boldly tried new systems and vigorously carried out the construction of software and hardware facilities to attract investment. The park management system also saw certain breakthroughs. Take Zhongguancun Science Park as an example. In May 1988, the State Council approved the establishment of China's first high-tech zone, the Beijing New Technology Industry Development Experimental Zone, which was the predecessor of the Zhongguancun Science Park. The Zhongguancun Science Park Management Committee, as an agency dispatched by the Beijing Municipal Government, exercises unified leadership and management over the park. In addition, in terms of land use, Shanghai Hongqiao took the lead in implementing the land lease system, and the Guangzhou Development Zone transferred the first piece of industrial land. In terms of decentralization, the Dalian Development Zone adjusted a series of mechanisms in 1986 to expand the autonomy of enterprises in hiring and simplify procedures. By 1991, the 14 national-level economic

Technological Development Zone, Yantai Economic and Technological Development Zone, Dalian Economic and Technological Development Zone, Zhanjiang Economic and Technological Development Zone, Tianjin Economic and Technological Development Zone, Nantong Economic and Technological Development Zone, Lianyungang Economic and Technological Development Zone, Guangzhou Economic and Technological Development Zone, Fuzhou Economic and Technological Development Zone, Hongqiao Economic and Technological Development Zone, Minhang Economic and Technological Development Zone, and Caohejing Emerging Technology Development Zone. The first batch of 27 high-tech industrial development zones were approved and established in March 1991 were Zhongguancun Science and Technology Park, Wuhan East Lake New Technology Development Zone (Optical Valley), Nanjing High-Tech Industrial Development Zone, Shenyang High-Tech Industrial Development Zone, Tianjin New Technology Industrial Park, Xi'an High-Tech Industrial Development Zone, Chengdu High-Tech Industrial Development Zone, Weihai Torch High-Tech Industrial Development Zone, Zhongshan Torch High-Tech Industrial Development Zone, Changchun High-Tech Industrial Development Zone, Harbin High-Tech Industrial Development Zone, Changsha High-Tech Industrial Development Zone, Fuzhou High-Tech Industrial Development Zone, Guangzhou High-Tech Industrial Development Zone, Hefei High-Tech Industrial Development Zone, Chongqing High-Tech Industrial Development Zone, Hangzhou High-Tech Industrial Development Zone, Guilin High-Tech Industrial Development Zone, Zhengzhou High-Tech Technology Industrial Development Zone, Lanzhou High-Tech Industrial Development Zone, Shijiazhuang High-Tech Industrial Development Zone, Jinan High-Tech Industrial Development Zone, Shanghai High-Tech Industrial Development Zone, Dalian High-Tech Industrial Development Zone, Shenzhen High-Tech Industrial Development Zone, Xiamen Torch High School Technology Industrial Development Zone, and Hainan International Science and Technology Industrial Park.

development zones had achieved a total industrial output value of 14.59 billion yuan, tax revenue of 790 million yuan, exports of 6.08 billion yuan, contracted foreign investment of 4.34 billion yuan, and actual foreign investment of 1.93 billion yuan (according to the average exchange rate of the year, the same applies below). By the end of 1991, the cumulative foreign investment was 7.33 billion yuan. Among them, from 1985 to 1991, the average growth rates of GDP, industrial added value, exports, and actual foreign investment of the 14 national-level economic development zones were 133%, 32.4%, 75.5%, and 43.1%, respectively. In 1991, the 27 national-level high-tech zones achieved a total operating income of 8.7 billion yuan, a total industrial output value of 7.1 billion yuan, and export earnings of 960 million yuan (Tongji University Development Institute 2014).

Rapid Growth Stage (1992–2002)

After former CPC Chairman Deng Xiaoping's second Southern Tour, China's reform and opening up entered a new stage. The development of industrial parks accelerated significantly, and the institutional construction and legislative norms related to industrial parks continued to improve. In 1991, the first normative document related to industrial parks was issued at the national level: the *Interim Provisions on Several Policies for National High-Tech Industrial Development Zones*. Local governments accelerated the formulation and issuance of industrial park management regulations in accordance with relevant national laws and regulations, and the positioning, development goals, and reform experiments of industrial parks were clarified. During this period, 16 provinces and cities issued a total number of 22 legal normative documents related to industrial parks, which is a significant improvement compared with that of the previous decade. In addition, the central government also further delegated the management rights of industrial parks to park management agencies, and the parks have more autonomy to carry out market-oriented operations and optimize the mechanisms in terms of foreign investment, land development, and industrial chain aggregation. The industry then gradually shifted from labor-intensive industries to capital-intensive industries. The leading industries of different parks became more diversified and began to extend upstream and downstream of the industrial chain, and various supporting facilities and service industries were established. For example, the Suzhou Industrial Park innovatively implemented small teams and multiple batches of "door-to-door investment promotion", focusing on the use of business-to-business agency investment promotion, industry-themed investment promotion, and other means to establish a flexible and effective investment promotion mechanism. Another example is the Kunshan Economic and Technological Development Zone, which in the early 1990s established the electronic information industry as one of its leading industries, extended its industrial chain, introduced leading large projects, exerted the industrial agglomeration effect, and used flexible mechanisms to support investment promotion, hence making the electronic information industry the first pillar industry of the Kunshan Economic and Technological Development Zone. As the scale becomes larger and more enterprises enter, industrial parks begin to pay attention to providing enterprises with business-supporting services, such as administration and agency, as well as wellbeing-supporting services, such as education, health, business, and leisure, in order to reduce the administrative costs of enterprises and the living costs of workers. The development of the tertiary industry further changed the situation of the single structure and single economic function of industrial parks. As of 2002, the GDP, total industrial output value, industrial added value, tax revenue, actual use of foreign capital, and export earnings of China's 54 national economic and technological development zones were 311 billion yuan, 786.7 billion yuan, 221 billion yuan, 50 billion yuan, 64.06 billion yuan, and 27.5 billion yuan, respectively. Compared with those in 1992, the total industrial output value, tax revenue, actual use of foreign capital, and export earnings increased by 29, 36, 20, and 13 times, respectively. In 2002, the operating income, total industrial output value, industrial added value, net profit, taxes paid, and export earnings of 53 national high-tech zones were 153.26 billion yuan, 129.37 billion yuan, 328.6 billion yuan, 80.1 billion yuan, 76.6 billion yuan, and 32.9 billion yuan, respectively. Compared with those in 1992, the operating income, total industrial output value, net profit, taxes paid, and export earnings increased by 65, 68, 21, 77, and 142 times, respectively (Tongji University Development Institute 2014).

Stable Development Stage (2003–2008)

With the rapid development of industrial parks across the country, some problems began to emerge. Some regions established industrial parks in violation of regulations, and some regions adjusted the development direction and functional scope of industrial parks in violation of regulations. Starting from 2003, in accordance with the State Council's policies, relevant state departments began to clean up and rectify various industrial parks across the country, adjust the preferential policies and management authority of the industrial parks, further improve the construction of industrial park regulations, strictly control land review, strictly adjust the direction and functional scope of industrial parks, and give more emphasis to the structural adjustment, optimization, upgrading, and high-tech industrialization of industrial parks. During this period, new industrial parks were almost no longer built in the southwest, northwest, and northeast regions. Even though new industrial parks were still added in the eastern coastal provinces, most of them were new industrial parks with a high degree of internationalization, such as bonded areas, border economic cooperation zones, and export processing zones. According to the statistics, except for the Ningbo Development Zone, which was promoted to a national economic and technological development zone, the number of the two types of national industrial parks (economic and technological development zones and high-tech zones) has not increased. By mid-2006, the number of development zones in China had dropped from 6866 to 1568, and the planned area was reduced to 9949 km^2 (Tongji University Development Institute 2017). Overall, with the rectification and upgrading, industrial parks have begun to show a trend of scientific and characteristic development, and production quality and efficiency, park services, and enterprise incubation and management have gradually matured. As of 2008, the GDP, total industrial output value, industrial added value, tax revenue, actual foreign investment, and export earnings of China's 54 national economic and technological development zones were 153.13 billion yuan, 459.35 billion yuan, 109.72 billion yuan, 248.1 billion yuan, and US $19.5 billion respectively, up 230%, 255%, 204%, 228%, 89%, and 319% compared with 2003. In 2008, the operating income, total industrial output value, industry-added value, tax revenue, net profit, and export earnings of the 53 national high-tech zones were 659.86 billion yuan, 526.85 billion yuan, 125.07 billion yuan, 319.9 billion yuan, 330.4 billion yuan, and 1334.03 billion yuan, respectively, up 215%, 205%, 188%, 223%, 193%, and 295% compared with 2003 (Tongji University Development Institute 2017).

Innovation and Upgrading Stage (2009 to Present)

After the 2008 financial crisis, in order to cultivate and develop strategic emerging industries, further deepen reform and opening up, and cultivate new momentum for China's economic growth, the country carried out a new round of expansion and reform of industrial parks, and the development of industrial parks ushered in a new climax. In terms of quantity, the number of industrial parks has increased across the country, with most provinces adding more than ten new industrial parks. Jiangsu has 52 new industrial parks, accounting for about 1/6 of the total growth during this period. In terms of park construction, China relies more on new-generation internet technologies, big data technologies, etc., as the focus of industrial development and shifts the focus of park construction from the hard environment of infrastructure to the soft environment, such as development of functional supporting facilities, living supporting facilities, and industrial new towns. In terms of park operations, the central government has further decentralized power, adopted more government-enterprise integration or company-led models, and integrated social resources through the public-private partnership model to give full play to the advantages of multiple parties. In addition, industrial park cooperation has become an important factor in promoting the sustainable development of industrial parks, including cooperation between enterprises within a park, cooperation between a park and its sub-parks, cooperation between parks, industrial integration, international cooperation of parks, and other specific levels, hence encouraging the joint construction of industrial parks in the form of national policies. In addition, the country actively promotes the innovation and upgrading of industrial parks, further explores the innovation potential of industrial parks, accelerates the construction of national independent innovation demonstration zones, creates a policy system of "innovation environment", and promotes the independent innovation capabilities of enterprises in industrial parks. During this stage, the country newly established four national independent innovation demonstration zones, namely Beijing Zhongguancun, Wuhan East Lake, Shanghai Zhangjiang, and Shenzhen Hi-Tech, as well as the Hefei-Wuhu-Bengbu Independent Innovation Comprehensive Experimental Zone, to grant a high degree of freedom for reform and innovation and encourage a new round of innovation.

Looking back on the development history of industrial parks in China over the past 40 years, we can find that the development of industrial parks has gone through five stages: initial exploration, gradual cultivation, rapid growth, stable development, and innovation and upgrading. It has gradually extended from the eastern region to the central and western regions, from policy preferences to system optimization, from hard infrastructure construction to soft environment building, from labor-intensive industries to technology- and knowledge-intensive industries, and from independent development to park cooperation. The role of industrial parks in China's economic development has gradually gained more and more recognition, and some experiences are even being promoted worldwide.

5.2 Examining Role of Industrial Parks in China's Economic Development Based on A-C Theory

Industrial parks are the product of China's economy in a specific period of development and play a very important role in China's reform and opening-up process. From the framework of the A-C theory, industrial parks are institutional "enclaves" opened up under the original institutional framework. Each industrial park is a node for economic opening up. A large number of industrial parks form a channel for interaction between China and the global economy. Global economic factors are injected into China through industrial parks as ports, and Chinese products gradually move from industrial parks to the global markets. This interaction with international markets further mobilizes and releases production factors around industrial parks, forming a cluster of capital, labor, and technology. The platform for other production factors has opened up the opening up of China's economy from point to point and has significantly improved the accessibility of the country's economy both internally and externally. In addition, after more than 40 years of trial and exploration, an industrial park management model with Chinese characteristics has been formed. The promotion of industrial park development experience has driven the development of more regions and more industries, gathered a consensus on reform and opening up on a larger scale, improved the cohesion of political governance, and played an important role in the sustained development of China's economy.

The rapid development of industrial parks is mainly due to China's improved political governance and economic accessibility. From the perspective of political cohesion, the efficient and flat management model of industrial parks has improved decision-making efficiency, reduced administrative intervention, and reduced communication costs between enterprises and the government. In addition, with concentrated financial and policy support, the economic performance of industrial parks has become more outstanding, forming an important position for regional economic development. On the other hand, with industrial parks as the carrier, the mainland economy has gradually integrated with the international community, import and export economic activities have accelerated, and the economy has become more open to the outside world. Also, areas with industrial parks as the core have attracted a large number of capital and labor factors, and the labor force has flowed on a large scale. More factors have been incorporated into the track of economic development, and the economy has also become more open to the inside.

5.2.1 Economic Accessibility: Taking into Account Both External and Internal Accessibility

The development of industrial parks is closely related to the improvement of accessibility. External accessibility defines the trade situation between industrial parks and the external economic environment. Against the backdrop of reform and opening up, China has continuously promoted the opening up of the economy and supported import and export trade from the perspective of policies, laws, and regulations, as well as protecting the legitimate rights and interests of related enterprises. The state successively issued the *Foreign Trade Law* and the *Regulations on the Administration of Import and Export of Goods* and continuously improved the inspection and management of imported and exported goods, the bidding and management of import and export quotas, and revised and implemented relevant laws and regulations. Since the establishment of industrial parks, the total import and export volume of national economic development zones has steadily increased. Especially after China joined the WTO, the import and export of national economic development zones has entered a rapid growth track. It is estimated that the contribution of national economic development zones to the national import and export trade is about 18–20%, and this proportion is still slowly increasing (China Development Zone Association 2017). Overall, the construction of industrial parks has improved the external accessibility of China's economy and accelerated the growth of foreign trade.

Driven by a series of preferential conditions, industrial parks can more efficiently attract labor factors to achieve regional concentration. First, industrial parks improve the accessibility of capital through investment promotion policies. The State Council issued the *Provisional Regulations of the State Council of the People's Republic of China on the Reduction and Exemption of Enterprise Income Tax and Industrial and Commercial Consolidated Tax in Special Economic Zones and Fourteen Coastal Port Cities* in 1984 and the *Regulations on the Implementation of Differential Interest Rates and Subsidies for Development Loans in Special Economic Zones and Economic and Technological Development Zones* in 1987, while the State Science and Technology Commission issued the *Regulations on the Taxation Policy of National High-Tech Industrial Development Zones* in 1991. These relevant policy documents were extremely important in attracting foreign capital. A large amount of foreign capital poured into industrial parks for investment, and industrial parks formed regional capital highlands in a short period of time. From the beginning of the construction of industrial parks to the present, relaxing the capital entry threshold has been a feature of industrial park policies. Today, we can still see that industrial parks across the country are still constantly issuing relevant investment promotion policies, encouraging the use of foreign capital, making the economic activities of the parks full of vitality, and generating stronger economic radiation to the surrounding areas.

In 1986, the Fourth Session of the Sixth National People's Congress passed the *Foreign Investment Enterprise Law of the People's Republic of China*. Since then, China has created favorable policy conditions and support for the introduction and utilization of foreign investment and has continuously improved relevant laws and regulations. In 2000, the Standing Committee of the Ninth National People's Congress once again revised the *Foreign-Invested Enterprises Law* and the *Sino-Foreign Equity Joint Ventures Law* and officially promulgated them for implementation. The core content of the revision was to cancel a number of balancing requirements, further enhance the investment confidence of foreign investors, and create better conditions for attracting foreign investment. The *Regulations on Guiding the Direction of Foreign Investment*, which came into effect on April 1, 2002, further aligned the direction of foreign investment with China's national economic and social development plans. Economic development zones actively responded to the country's policy call to attract foreign investment and have kept pace with the policy. The growth rate of their foreign investment is usually higher than the growth rate of the total foreign investment in the country. As shown in Fig. 5.1, the total amount of foreign investment utilized by national-level economic development zones has been on a steady upward trend, with the growth rate accelerating significantly after 2010. In addition, the proportion of the total amount of foreign investment actually utilized by national-level economic development zones in the total amount of foreign investment actually utilized in the country has also increased rapidly. As shown in Fig. 5.2, in the 5 years from 2009 to 2013 alone, its

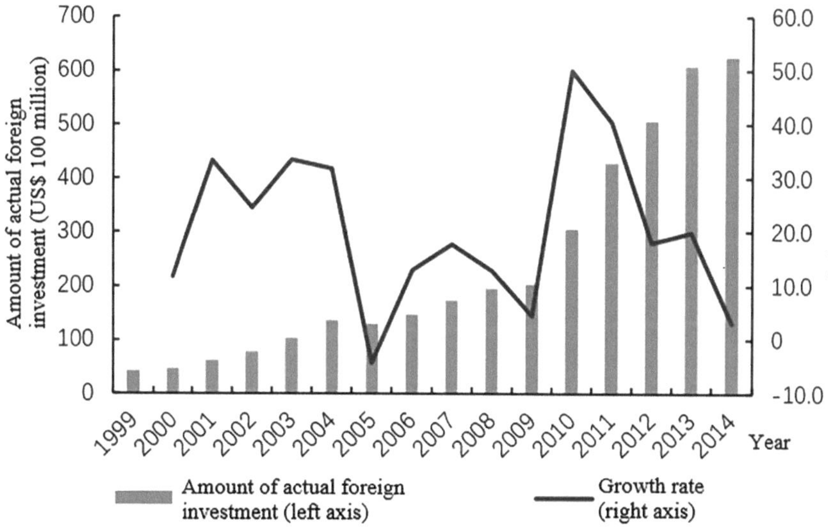

Fig. 5.1 Foreign investment utilization in national economic development zones (1999–2014). Source: China Development Zone Association (2017)

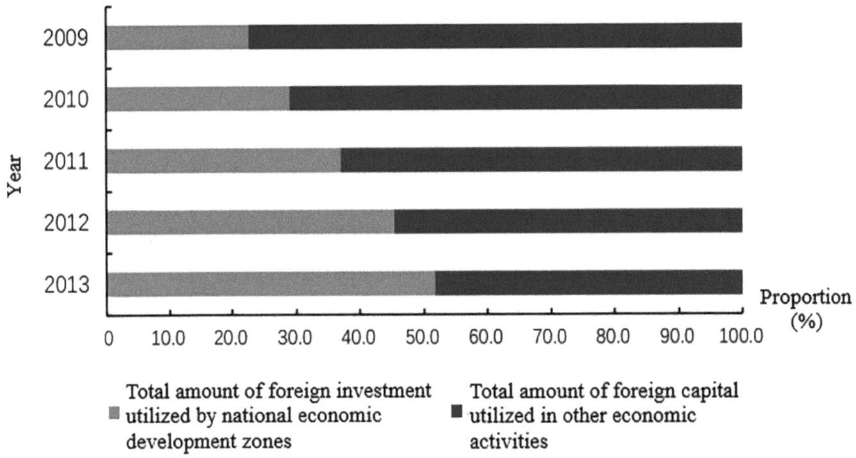

Fig. 5.2 Proportion of foreign investment utilization in national economic development zones to total foreign investment utilization. Source: China Development Zone Association (2017)

proportion of the total amount of foreign investment actually utilized in the country increased from about 20% to more than 50%.

The open recruitment environment and low employment threshold of industrial parks have attracted a large number of laborers to work during the growth period of industrial parks. With the continuous development of economic activities in and around industrial parks, the demand for labor continued to increase, and labor income increased, which led to a large number of agricultural populations pouring into industrial parks and cities, shifting from the primary industry to the secondary and tertiary industries. Since the 1990s, China has seen a wave of migrant workers, with a large number of rural people moving to cities for employment. Although China's household registration system still exists and urban-rural population migration is still restricted by some basic public service systems, objectively speaking, developed and cheap transportation and relatively generous wages have become important driving forces for population transfer. A considerable number of rural laborers who have moved to cities entered various industrial parks. In addition, with the growth of enterprises in industrial parks, especially the growth and increase of high-tech enterprises, the overall skills of the labor force are also constantly improving.

As can be seen in Figs. 5.3 and 5.4, the number of employees of enterprises in national high-tech zones has been growing continuously for a long time, with a growth rate far higher than the growth rate of the national employment population, and the proportion of employees of enterprises in national high-tech zones to the national employment population has also been increasing, from less than 0.5% in 1999 to 2.5% in 2017. These all directly reflect the role of industrial parks in absorbing labor. To some extent, industrial parks are an important driving force for promoting urbanization in China.

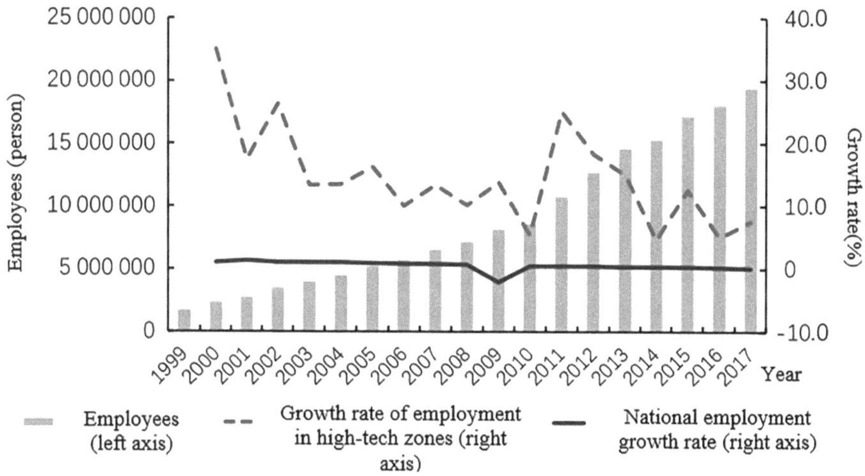

Fig. 5.3 Total number of employees of enterprises in national high-tech zones. Source: China Statistical Yearbook, National Bureau of Statistics

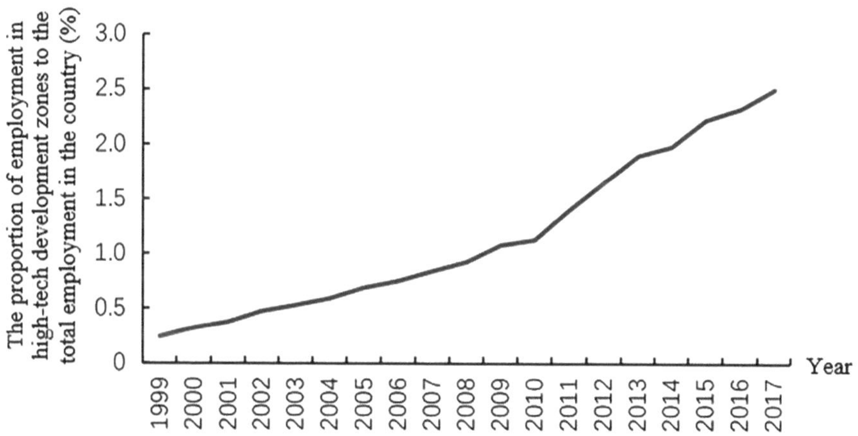

Fig. 5.4 Proportion of employees of enterprises in national high-tech zones to China's total number of employees. Source: China Statistical Yearbook, National Bureau of Statistics

The establishment of industrial parks has also attracted high-tech to flow to industrial parks. If factories and manufacturing enterprises concentrated in industrial parks want to achieve sustainable development, they must continue to innovate technology. In 2005, the Ministry of Commerce, the Ministry of Land and Resources, and the Ministry of Construction jointly issued *Several Opinions on Promoting National Economic and Technological Development Zones to Further Improve Their Development Level*, which proposed that the development of industrial parks should pay more attention to the introduction of high-tech, as well as development and innovation; shift from focusing on technology introduction to focusing on innovation through digestion and absorption; and strive to develop industrial parks into gathering areas for high-tech industries, modern services, and high-quality talents. Issued in 2009, the *Several Opinions on Giving Play to the Role of National High-Tech Industrial Development Zones in Promoting Stable and Rapid Economic Development* further emphasizes the goals of accelerating the agglomeration of high-tech industries, enhancing independent innovation capabilities, and improving public innovation platforms and talent team building. The opinion proposes to strengthen technological innovation and stimulate innovation vitality. These guidelines and related policy support made technological factors more concentrated in industrial parks. Industrial parks have shifted from directly introducing foreign high-tech to combining learning experiences, enhancing their own technology, and introducing and cultivating domestic high-tech talents, patents, equipment, etc. The types of enterprises in industrial parks have also changed from simple, cheap manufacturing to high-tech industries, innovative enterprises, electronic high-tech enterprises, etc., which will inevitably be accompanied by the process of China's industrial upgrading and transformation. These reflect the increasing accessibility of industrial parks' technology.

5.2.2 *Political Cohesion: From Pilot Projects to Experience Promotion*

When the Cultural Revolution ended, CPC Chairman Deng noted: "Among our cadres, especially leading cadres, the problem of emancipating the mind has not been completely solved. Many comrades' minds are still not emancipated, their brains have not been activated, and they are still in a rigid or semi-rigid state."[5] Under such circumstances, there was no consensus on how to promote reform inside and outside the party. Both central ministries and local governments at all levels could not accept local policies that were "not in line with the unified caliber", even if the local policies were based on reality and were correct. Therefore, it was not easy to break through existing rules and regulations and institute reforms, and it was even more difficult to promote large-scale and all-round reforms. The construction of industrial parks in China started in this context.

On January 31, 1979, the CPC Central Committee and the State Council decided to establish the first foreign-oriented industrial zone near Hong Kong in Shekou, Guangdong Province, called the Shekou Industrial Zone, which was also the first experimental zone for China's economic reform. But the foundation was very weak,

[5] See CPC Chairman Deng's speech titled *Emancipate the Mind, Seek Truth from Facts, Unite as One and Look Forward* at the closing meeting of the CPC Central Committee's working conference on December 13, 1978 (Deng 1994). This Central Working Conference made full preparations for the Third Plenary Session of the 11th Central Committee of the Communist Party of China, which was held immediately afterwards. Chairman Deng's speech was actually the theme report of the Third Plenary Session of the 11th CPC Central Committee.

the conditions were very limited, and there was no ability to carry out large-scale infrastructure construction. A report noted: "In December 1979, then Vice Premier of the State Council Comrade Gu Mu led several ministers of the State Council to Shekou for inspection to determine how to support and help the Ministry of Communications' China Merchants Group to develop the Shekou Industrial Zone. In addition, Shekou has a beach and barren mountains, with potholes on the road, and there were no toilets or water for washing faces."[6] Also, because many cadres had been influenced for a long time by the thinking of a planned economic system, no one could grasp how much the management system innovation of the Shekou Industrial Zone could break through under existing rules and regulations. This was also an important reason why the central government chose the China Merchants Group of Hong Kong to be responsible for the construction of the Shekou Industrial Zone. The central government delegated a large amount of power to the China Merchants Group of Hong Kong, allowing the Shekou Industrial Zone to boldly explore and fully combine Guangdong's land and labor with foreign capital, technology, and equipment to break a new path. As a result, the Shekou Industrial Zone was the first to update people's value, time concepts, and talent concepts and was the first to successfully establish a brand-new labor employment system, cadre employment system, salary distribution system, housing system, social insurance system, engineering bidding system, and enterprise shareholding system, as well as the first to try to align the nascent socialist market economic system with international practices and international rules. In the words of Yuan Geng, the CEO of the China Merchants Group of Hong Kong, Shekou is "a test tube for injecting beneficial external economic factors to reform the traditional economic system."[7] By January 1984, when Deng Xiaoping visited the Shekou Industrial Zone, "Shenzhen and Shekou had a very different look, with high-rise buildings everywhere, roads extending in all directions, 10,000-ton docks and helicopter airports in operation, telecommunications, water supply, power supply, flood control, gas supply and sewage treatment taking shape, and a modern industrial new city rising on the frontier of the South China Sea."[8]

By implementing breakthrough reform measures in very small economic units, China not only retained room for policy trial and error, avoided the various resistances that still existed widely in the early stage of reform, and reduced possible risks, but it also concentrated limited advantageous policy resources to build a test field and pilot zone for reform and opening up. Once this reform experiment was successful, it would become a support for further breaking down reform resistance,

---

[6] See the *Report on Accompanying Comrade Deng Xiaoping on His Inspection Tour of Guangdong, Fujian and Shanghai* made to the Central Committee by Comrade Wang Zhen, then a member of the Political Bureau of the CPC Central Committee, on February 27, 1984.

[7] See Yuan Geng's public speech at the Center for Contemporary Asian Studies of the Chinese University of Hong Kong in May 1986.

[8] See the *Report on Accompanying Comrade Deng Xiaoping on His Inspection Tour of Guangdong, Fujian and Shanghai* made to the Central Committee by Comrade Wang Zhen, then a member of the Political Bureau of the CPC Central Committee, on February 27, 1984.

coordinating the interests of multiple parties, and building a consensus on reform. The successful experience gained in the reform experiment also provided a blueprint for expanding the scope of reform. For example, the management committee system,[9] widely implemented in the construction of a large number of industrial parks later, was established in the early exploration. In 1984, the State Council promulgated the *Interim Provisions on Reduction and Exemption of Enterprise Income Tax and Industrial and Commercial Consolidated Tax for Special Economic Zones and Fourteen Coastal Port Cities*, which is both a recognition of previous reform experiments and a promotion of successful reform experiences. In 1987, the People's Bank of China, the State Planning Commission, the Ministry of Finance, and the State Council Special Zone Office jointly issued the *Provisions on the Implementation of Differential Interest Rates and Subsidies for Development Loans in Special Economic Zones and Economic and Technological Development Zones*. In 1988, the General Administration of Customs issued the *Regulations of the Customs of the People's Republic of China on the Administration of Goods Entering and Leaving the Economic and Technological Development Zone*. With the continuous introduction and improvement of national policies, the basic framework for the construction and development of industrial parks gradually took shape to provide a solid foundation.

What is even more commendable is that, with the changes in China's development stage and macro-environment, the central government's policies on industrial parks have kept pace with the times. In 2005, the Ministry of Commerce, the Ministry of Land and Resources, and the Ministry of Construction jointly issued *Several Opinions on Promoting the Further Improvement of the Development Level of National Economic and Technological Development Zones* to ensure economic growth and the quality of industrial park development. In 2009, the Ministry of Commerce and the Ministry of Science and Technology issued *Guiding Opinions*

[9] In most cases, the industrial park management committee is an entity that exercises management functions over industrial parks as a government agency. According to development needs, the management committee has different departments, usually mainly including departments with strong relevance to economic development, such as development and reform, finance, economics and information, commerce, audit, market supervision, and other departments; as well as land, urban construction, environmental protection and other departments with strong relevance to urban construction; and customs, quarantine and other departments with strong relevance to import and export trade. Some industrial parks also added other institutions, such as the Science and Technology Talent Bureau for talent introduction, the Investment Promotion Bureau for foreign investment, and the Enterprise Service Bureau for improving the business environment, according to local actual conditions. The institutional setup of the management committee usually has the characteristics of centralization and flattening. Centralization is mainly reflected in the fact that the management committee usually has only one team, and the decision-making body is more streamlined, and flattening is mainly reflected in the fact that the government is usually only responsible for appointing the director and deputy director of the management committee, while the staff of the departments under the management committee are usually recruited from the society and implement market-oriented management. The two characteristics of centralization and flattening are usually considered to be a successful experience in improving decision-making efficiency and administrative efficiency.

on the Work of National Economic and Technological Development Zones and *Several Opinions on Playing the Role of National High-Tech Industrial Development Zones to Promote Stable and Rapid Economic Development*, respectively, to better the role of industrial parks in resisting the impact of the international financial crisis. In 2014, the General Office of the State Council issued the *Several Opinions on Promoting the Transformation, Upgrading and Innovative Development of National Economic and Technological Development Zones*, which pointed out that institutional and mechanism innovation, the promotion of the development of an open economy, and adherence to green and intensive development are primary tasks for achieving industrial upgrading and breaking through development bottlenecks.

Overall, the growth and development of industrial parks in China did not happen overnight. The development process of industrial parks from pilot zones to expansion and then to full deployment is the process of breaking through resistance, followed by exploring, experimenting, summarizing experience, building a consensus, and finally promoting in full. It is a classic practice of "crossing the river by feeling the stones", a microcosm of the cause of reform and opening up, and a model for continuously improving the cohesion of political governance through economic reform.

5.3 Chapter Summary

Although the growth of industrial parks in China has its own special historical background, and there are even many accidental factors in the development process, it can be seen from the above analysis that the growth and development of industrial parks benefit from the continuous improvement of China's economic accessibility and political cohesion and the benign interaction between the three. In the early stage of reform, the improvement of economic accessibility provided an opportunity for the growth and development of industrial parks, and the promotion of the industrial park model across the country further improved economic accessibility. The success of the pilot provided support for the formation of a reform consensus and the improvement of political cohesion, and the formation of a reform consensus in turn safeguarded the promotion of the industrial park model. Then, the continuous advancement of economic reform continuously improved political cohesion, which in turn further consolidated the consensus on reform. This is a crucial experience for the success of the industrial park model in China, a principle that needs to be adhered to in the process of further reforming and improving the industrial park model and that other developing countries should follow when learning this model.

As reform and opening up continue to deepen and the market economy system continues to improve, the industrial park economy must also adapt to the requirements of high-quality development. China must continue to play a role in gathering and enabling various production factors to participate in high-quality economic activities and in promoting institutional opening up, benchmarking international rules and standards, and building a new pattern of comprehensive opening up. China must also play a leading role in implementing new development concepts, innovating systems and mechanisms, promoting reform experience and low-carbon green development, and achieving substantial progress in common prosperity, and the country must continue to improve the internal and external accessibility of its economy and the cohesion of its political governance.

References

China Development Zone Association (ed) (2017) China development zone yearbook 2016. CUEB Press, Beijing

Deng XP (1994) Selected works of Deng Xiaoping, vol 2. People's Publishing House, Beijing

Liu H (2010) The 1980s and Chinese economists. GXNU Press Group, Guilin

Tongji University Development Institute (2014) Blue book on sustainable development of industrial parks in China. Tongji University Press, Shanghai

Tongji University Development Institute (2017) Blue book on sustainable development of industrial parks in China. Tongji University Press, Shanghai

Wang ZJ (2014) Research on the development of China's high-tech industrial parks. China University of Geoscience Press, Beijing

Chapter 6
Eradicating Absolute Poverty

Poverty is not only the result of insufficient economic accessibility but also a major factor threatening the cohesion of political governance. It is a so-called "silent crisis" faced by all countries in the world, affecting the economic and social development process of all countries. It is also one of the important sources of political turmoil and social instability. Eliminating absolute poverty is not only an effective way to improve the cohesion of political governance but also a thousand-year dream of the Chinese people. After more than 40 years of rapid development and unremitting efforts in reform and opening up, China's poverty alleviation has created a world miracle. Especially since the 18th National Congress of the Communist Party of China, the Chinese government has taken the elimination of poverty as the bottom-line task and landmark indicator for building a well-off society in an all-round way and organized and implemented the unprecedented, most powerful, and most populous poverty alleviation campaign in human history for the arduous task of eliminating absolute poverty. According to the current poverty standard of China's rural residents living below 2300 yuan per person per year (2010 constant price), from 2013 to 2020, 98.99 million rural poor people and 832 poor counties were lifted out of poverty, 128,000 villages were removed from the poverty list, and regional overall poverty was solved. Since the reform and opening up, according to the current poverty standard, 770 million rural poor people in China have escaped poverty. According to the World Bank's international poverty standard, China's poverty reduction population accounts for more than 70% of the global poverty reduction population during the same period (State Council Information Office 2021). China achieved the poverty reduction goals of the United Nations 2030 Agenda for Sustainable Development 10 years ahead of schedule, making significant contributions to the development of global poverty reduction and human development progress.

From the experience of countries around the world, the effectiveness of poverty reduction is not only a reflection of the degree of attention a country pays to poverty reduction and the effectiveness of measures but also an effective test of a country's economic and political system. In this chapter, we introduce the A-C theory into

C. Chen et al., *From Poverty to Prosperity*, Understanding China,
https://doi.org/10.1007/978-981-95-7171-0_6

poverty problem analysis and case studies, which can provide a new perspective for analyzing China's poverty reduction results, and we further summarize China's poverty reduction plans and experiences from the two dimensions of economic system and political governance. We also provide analytical ideas for the next step in solving the long-standing relative poverty problem.

6.1 Historical Process of China's Poverty Alleviation

Since the founding of the People's Republic of China, the party and the government have always been committed to the country's poverty alleviation cause. According to the evolution of the stage of economic development and the basic characteristics of the poor population, as well as the poverty alleviation strategies and policy systems formulated in different historical periods, China's poverty alleviation process can be roughly divided into the following six stages.

The first is the relief-style poverty alleviation stage (1949–1978). At the beginning of the founding of New China, there was a lot of work to be done, the national economic foundation was weak, and the people's living standards were generally low. During this period, poverty alleviation was mainly government-led relief-style poverty alleviation, with the government providing certain social relief to groups that were extremely poor and lacked basic survival capabilities, and poverty alleviation funds were mainly government financial relief funds. After 1959, relief-style poverty alleviation changed from relief for the poor to relief for the poor collective. In the national economic construction expenditure, free investment to support poor communities and teams was added to help poor cooperatives and production teams purchase production equipment and improve production capacity and loan repayment capacity. However, due to the country's limited economic strength and fiscal revenue, the poverty alleviation work at this stage was limited.

The second is the reform-driven poverty alleviation stage (1978–1985). In 1978, the CPC Central Committee made the momentous decision of reforming and opening up, and the reform of the rural economic system kicked off. The implementation of the household contract responsibility system and a series of policies, such as raising the purchase price of agricultural products, effectively promoted the rapid development of the rural economy and drove a large number of rural poor people out of poverty. In addition, for poverty alleviation, some provinces provided agricultural loans to rural poor households, solving production difficulties in the form of interest-free or low-interest loans. In addition, relatively developed regions reformed and innovated horizontal poverty alleviation measures, providing financial, technical, and talent assistance to poverty-stricken areas that received counterpart support and effectively enhancing the development capacity of poverty-stricken areas. However, due to the natural location differences between regions and the different degrees of government economic support policies in the early stage of reform, the income gap between regions widened, such as the gap between coastal areas and inland areas and the gap between urban and rural areas.

The third is the regional-development-oriented poverty alleviation stage (1986–1993). In order to strengthen the guidance of economic development work in poor areas and change the poverty situation in these areas as soon as possible, the State Council established the *Leading Group for Economic Development in Poor Areas* in 1986 to coordinate the national poverty alleviation work. In the same year, the central government issued the *7th Five-Year Plan for the National Economy*, specifically compiling a chapter on the economic development of "old, minority, border, and poor" areas and requiring these areas to develop the economy based on local conditions. In addition, the state implemented a policy of financial support for these areas. Hence, poverty alleviation work entered the stage of regional-development-oriented poverty alleviation. Since then, each 5-year plan for the national economy has taken poverty alleviation as an important content. In this stage, governments at all levels formally established poverty alleviation organizations to achieve the goal of poverty alleviation through large-scale, organized, and planned economic development in poor areas.

The fourth is the *87 Poverty Alleviation Plan* stage (1994–2000). In order to further improve the poverty alleviation work in poor areas, in 1994, the CPC Central Committee formulated the *National 87 Poverty Alleviation Plan*, adjusted and updated the poverty population standard, established corresponding mandatory exit standards, set standards for the classification of poor counties, and made poor counties the main target units for poverty alleviation work. Central fiscal poverty alleviation funds, credit poverty alleviation funds, and work-for-relief and other assistance funds were all tilted towards poor counties, and credit funds were concentrated in poverty alleviation work in poor areas in the western region. In addition, social assistance funds, overseas poverty alleviation assistance funds, etc., provided certain support for poverty reduction in central and western regions.

The fifth is the comprehensive-development poverty alleviation stage (2001–2011). In 2001, the Central Poverty Alleviation and Development Work Conference formulated and adopted the *China Rural Poverty Alleviation and Development Outline (2001–2010)*, which, as the main positioning of poverty alleviation work at this stage, aimed to increase infrastructure construction in poor areas, improve the ecological environment, and narrow the development gap. The poverty alleviation target unit was narrowed from poor counties to poor villages, and comprehensive-development poverty alleviation on a village basis was promoted. Under the guidance of this policy, rural social security construction was continuously improved and labor transfer training was gradually implemented, achieving remarkable results of whole-village poverty alleviation based on local conditions, and poverty alleviation work continues to be carried out in an in-depth direction.

The sixth is the stage of targeted poverty alleviation (2012–2020). Since the 18th CPC National Congress in 2012, China has implemented the strategy of targeted poverty alleviation and poverty reduction via adhering to the core requirements of "six precisions", implementing the "five batches" of poverty alleviation measures, launching new measures for regional development, and continuously increasing central and local fiscal poverty alleviation funds. A series of poverty alleviation measures, such as work-for-relief programs, industrial poverty alleviation, poverty alleviation through relocation, education poverty alleviation, and employment poverty alleviation, have been implemented to widely mobilize the whole society for participating in poverty alleviation, strictly implement poverty alleviation responsibilities, and create new paradigms for poverty alleviation work.

Since 2021, China's poverty reduction focus has shifted to reducing relative poverty, and the focus of rural work has shifted to rural revitalization.

6.2 Typical Cases of China's Poverty Alleviation

From the historical review, we can see that China's poverty alleviation has gone through a process from poverty alleviation in poor areas to poverty alleviation in poor counties, then to poverty alleviation in poor villages, and finally to targeted poverty alleviation. We took two relatively representative poverty alleviation target units—a poor county-level city (City A) and a poor village (Village B)—as cases to summarize the main practices and internal mechanisms of poverty alleviation work and examine the internal consistency behind the practices with the A-C theory.

6.2.1 City A's Poverty Alleviation Process

City A is a county-level city in China's eastern region, with 3 streets, 11 towns, 841 administrative villages, an area of 1793 km^2, and a total population of 525,300. City A is located in a hilly and mountainous area, with mountains accounting for 72.1% of the total area, hills accounting for 21.8%, and plains accounting for only 6.1%. For a long time, the topographic conditions have restricted its economic development, making City A one of the relatively backward areas in the province and even a concentrated area of poverty. At the end of 2016, the number of poor people in City A was 12,862, the poverty incidence rate was higher than 2%, and the annual per capita income of the poor was about 3402 yuan. Under a series of poverty reduction measures, by the end of 2017, the number of poor people in City A decreased by 4028, the poverty incidence rate dropped to 1.5%, and the annual per capita income of the poor was about 3730 yuan. By the end of 2018, the city's poverty incidence rate had dropped to 0%, and the initial task of poverty alleviation was completed. In 2019 and 2020, City A further consolidated and improved the results of poverty alleviation. Although 46 new impoverished households (87 people) emerged during this period, the government promptly included them in the immediate assistance households, achieving the "dynamic elimination" of the impoverished population.

While providing poverty alleviation to households, City A designated villages with a relatively concentrated number of poor people as key poverty-alleviation villages, making the poverty alleviation work more precise and efficient. City A has carried out two rounds of identification of key poverty-alleviation villages. In the first round of identification from 2014 to 2016, six villages and ten villages were identified as provincial-level key poverty-alleviation villages and municipal-level key poverty-alleviation villages, respectively. By the end of 2017, all 16 key villages were lifted out of poverty. In 2018, a new round of municipal-level key poverty-alleviation villages was identified. By the end of 2020, after poverty alleviation, City A basically achieved zero key poverty-alleviation villages.

The infrastructure construction and public service levels in the rural areas of City A also significantly improved. In 2019, City A built 400 rural passenger transport stations, and the notion of "every village is connected to public transportation" was realized for 40 key poverty-alleviation villages. Remarkable results were achieved in improving the rural living environment, with the coverage rate of the beautiful countryside reaching 65.2%. The rural drinking water safety project was completed, benefiting 185,000 people in 417 villages. The income from industrial poverty alleviation projects reached 7.95 million yuan, and financial aid for students from poor families was fully covered.

From 2016 to 2020, City A invested a total of 91.5479 million yuan in special financial poverty-alleviation funds, including 17.9309 million yuan at the provincial level and above, 33.96 million yuan at the municipal level, and 39.657 million yuan at the city level itself.

6.2.2 *Main Experience of City A in Successfully Alleviating Poverty*

Looking back on City A's successful poverty alleviation process, we can summarize three major experiences.

First, paying attention to system construction was an important condition for the significant results of poverty alleviation in City A. In the process of poverty alleviation, City A, with projects as the carrier, gradually established a system consisting of a project management system,[1] a fund-use supervision system,[2] and a

[1] In order to standardize project management and operation, City A successively issued *City A's "Two-Level Carrying and Three-Level Supervision" Poverty Alleviation Project Income Distribution Management Measures (Trial), City A's Poverty Alleviation Key Village Industrial Development Project Management Measures, City A's Implementation Measures for Improving the Construction of the Poverty Alleviation Project Database (Trial), City A's Poverty Alleviation Project Database Management Implementation Rules (Trial)*, and other institutional documents.

[2] In order to strictly supervise the huge scale of special financial poverty-alleviation funds, City A, based on careful research on poverty alleviation project policies at all levels, based on reality and based on the research and demonstration of the Municipal Finance Bureau and Audit Bureau, clarified the relevant issues of village-level financial accounting of poverty alleviation funds and issued *Notice on Poverty Alleviation Asset Management (Trial) in City A, Opinions on the Supervision of the Use of Poverty Alleviation Funds in 2020*, and other relevant institutional documents.

dual-assistance-responsibility system[3] and supplemented it with a dynamic and flexible immediate-assistance mechanism,[4] continuously forming and consolidating the consensus on poverty alleviation in the city, effectively improving the cohesion of local governance, and ensuring that the city would complete poverty alleviation. Under the guarantee of these systems, from 2016 to 2020, City A developed a total of 184 poverty alleviation projects and invested a total of 68.7135 million yuan in special financial poverty-alleviation funds to improve infrastructure construction and support the development of industries in poor villages, achieving good results led by leading enterprises, with investment, photovoltaic, planting and breeding, entrusted operation, infrastructure, and other projects blooming in many places, and the income generated by industrial projects being mainly used to help local registered poor households.

Second, there was a focus on forming a synergy of multiple policies. In order to ensure that poverty alleviation takes root, City A adopts a multi-pronged approach of financial poverty alleviation, education poverty alleviation, preferential insurance poverty alleviation, filial piety and elderly care poverty alleviation, and public welfare special post poverty alleviation, etc., to jointly promote the steady progress of poverty alleviation. For example, City A established a financial poverty-alleviation work mechanism with "the municipal government leading, the municipal people's bank taking the lead, and financial institutions taking the responsibility." All parties jointly formulate poverty-alleviation loan issuance procedures and interest subsidy methods to promote banking institutions to play the role of financing in promoting poverty alleviation. For example, City A implemented the *Yu Lu Plan* in 2016, which provides a subsidy of 3000 yuan per student per school year to children of registered poor families—those who have been lifted out of poverty, who have returned to poverty, or have become newly impoverished—for receiving secondary and higher vocational education. Starting in 2017, City A pays for commercial supplementary medical insurance and accidental injury insurance for poor households who have benefited from the poverty alleviation policy and has strengthened the medical security of the poor through health poverty alleviation, hence reducing the

[3] The so-called "dual assistance-responsibility system" stipulates that each poor household must have two assistance-responsible persons, with county cadres as the first assistance-responsible person and town and village cadres as the second assistance-responsible person. These two assistance-responsible persons jointly fulfill their assistance responsibilities, are responsible for the poor households they assist, and implement effective and precise assistance measures to ensure stable poverty alleviation, prevent relapse into poverty, and achieve full coverage of paired assistance.

[4] The so-called "dynamic and flexible immediate assistance mechanism" is based on the principle of "immediate inclusion, immediate assistance, and dynamic management". For farmers who are outside the National Poverty Alleviation and Development Information System and have temporary problems in "two no-worries and three guarantees" due to sudden reasons, such as illness, disasters, education, and accidents, they will be discovered immediately, identified according to standards and procedures, included in the immediate assistance ledger, and managed in accordance with the population enjoying poverty alleviation policies, and assistance policies and measures will be implemented.

occurrence of returning to poverty due to illness; in 2018, City A began to implement the special public-welfare post-poverty-alleviation policy, with government funding or social fundraising and with towns and villages developing a certain number of non-profit public management or social welfare service posts to support the poor with certain labor capacity and employment desire to achieve employment and increase income, as well as helping the elderly, the weak, the sick, and the disabled and other special groups to get out of poverty. In addition, City A established a poverty-alleviation filial piety fund in 2018. Relevant departments signed maintenance agreements with the children of registered poor elderly people over the age of 60. If the maintenance fee is paid regularly and in full, a certain amount of filial piety pension reward and subsidy funds will be issued to the elderly to guide and encourage the children of the family to fulfill their maintenance obligations. City A also supervises the departments of civil affairs, disabled persons' federation, education, health, medical insurance, housing and construction, water conservancy, and other departments to increase the implementation of poverty alleviation policies, such as rural subsistence allowances, special hardship support, temporary assistance, disability protection, medical care, health, education, and housing, so as to achieve "two no-worries, three guarantees" (the poor not having to worry about food and clothing and given guarantees on their education, basic medical treatment, and housing security), as well as drinking water safety, which effectively lay a solid foundation for the poor to escape poverty.

Third, City A attaches great importance to improving the business environment and using market forces to reduce poverty. The city uses investment promotion as the goal to force the improvement of the business environment. City A fully implemented the strategy of opening up and attracting investment and implemented a series of investment promotion measures, such as the *Golden Shield Huishang Project* and the investment promotion liaison system, so that external capital can enter smoothly. Since 2012, City A has focused on promoting reform through opening up, fully promoting double attraction, and deepening various reforms, such as administrative approval, government services, and budget management systems, as well as continuously optimizing the business environment, actively connecting with developed regions in provinces and cities, and focusing on taking over industrial transfers from Beijing-Tianjin-Hebei, Jiangsu, Zhejiang, and Shanghai. The city also has formulated and improved preferential policies for investment promotion and carried out several projects, such as industrial investment promotion and targeted investment promotion. In 2019, 161 projects were introduced.

The city also improves upon population mobility. City A has continuously increased the construction of urban and rural transportation facilities, actively applied for and implemented the planning and construction of high-speed railways, and promoted the external and internal smoothness of the road network system, with newly rebuilt roads radiating to the surrounding towns and villages of the city. In addition, inter-city bus routes, rural passenger stations, and poverty-alleviation village buses greatly improved the convenience of entering and leaving the city, effectively promoting the mobility of urban and rural populations and freedom of employment. City A has also continuously increased its efforts to attract talent, promoted the recruitment of talent, and cooperated with major universities and scientific research institutions to establish industrial research institutes and workstations, which provide important intellectual support for local economic development.

Furthermore, the city increases the flow of information. Taking the agricultural development of City A as an example, in order to further expand the popularity and influence of local brands, the city held the National Brand Agricultural and Commercial Development Conference to attract well-known brands from all over the country to participate in the exhibition. It has also held the City A Fruit Industry Art Festival for many consecutive years to expand the popularity of the festival. In addition, City A has also continuously developed e-commerce, introduced major e-commerce brands to settle in, and promoted the fruit industry of City A to the world through online sales.

In addition, the city promotes the enhancement of corporate vitality. City A fully supports the development of private enterprises and has issued policy documents, such as the *Implementation Opinions on Supporting the High-Quality Development of the Private Economy*. The city also relied on the provincial financial service platform to finance enterprises and enhance the development potential of enterprises. Moreover, it continuously accelerates the listing process of enterprises, standardizes the corporate system reform of enterprises, and strengthens the cultivation of enterprise echelons to promote the agglomeration of the city's cultural tourism, education and training, and medical and health industries.

6.2.3 Poverty Alleviation Story of Village B

Village B is an administrative village in a poverty-stricken area of the central region of China. It has seven natural villages under its jurisdiction. The total cultivated land area of the village is 2177 acres, with 766 households and 3160 people, divided into 12 villager groups. Village B is located in a plain area with yellow sand soil, a humid and warm climate, sufficient sunlight, abundant rainfall, four distinct seasons, 219 days of frost-free period, and an average annual precipitation of 820 mm. Good soil and climate conditions have promoted the development of local agriculture, especially planting, which has become the dominant industry and the main source of income for villagers. Influenced by traditional planting habits and limited resources, such as technology and talents, most villagers engage in the planting of grain crops, such as wheat, corn, soybeans, and sweet potatoes. In recent years, the planting of cash crops, such as vegetables, has gradually emerged, but it has not yet reached scale in the early stages of development. Due to the continuous increase in agricultural operating costs, the single-family planting method has poor operating efficiency, and the relatively simple planting structure has stretched the farmers' lives for many years. With the development of urbanization, like other rural areas, some farmers in Village B began to leave the land to make a living and find a job in the city, earning a second income besides agricultural planting. At present, the permanent population in the village is only about one-third of the total population. In addition, the transfer of land in Village B has gradually appeared, and the land transfer area of the whole village is about 600 acres.

At the end of 2016, there were 41 registered poor households with 128 people in Village B, 7 low-income poor households with 19 people, and 10 five-guarantee poor households with 11 people, with a poverty incidence rate of about 4%. In the decisive battle against poverty, with the support of party committees and governments at all levels and the leadership of village cadres, the ideological awareness of the poor people was continuously improved, and the poor gradually achieved employment and poverty alleviation through participating in industrial breeding, planting, land transfer, and clothing processing in poverty alleviation workshops. In 2018, Village B achieved poverty alleviation for the entire village. In 2019, 10 new poor households and 25 people were lifted out of poverty. In 2020, the last 6 poor households and 10 people were successfully lifted out of poverty.

In the process of achieving poverty alleviation, the main practices of Village B are as follows. First, it promotes land transfer and develops characteristic industries. In the past, each household in Village B owned scattered land and planted alone, with low management efficiency. Recognizing that only scale can produce higher benefits, the village collective decided to promote land transfer in the village, establish a village-level shareholding economic cooperative, and develop agricultural scale management and characteristic management. However, in the beginning, some people did not understand and believed that growing grain was stable and reliable, and so they were unwilling to rent out their land, which hindered the development of rural industries. The village "two committees" team faced the difficulties and worked tirelessly. They went to the villagers' homes many times to patiently enlighten them. On the premise of promising that the land property rights would not be changed, they also actively helped them to connect and let the villagers work in the cooperative, dispelling the villagers' concerns one by one, and finally promoted the transfer of land in the village, taking the first step in industrial development. In terms of developing characteristic industries, Village B chose to develop strawberry planting. Using the transferred land and integrating the support funds from the higher authorities, the village collective first built greenhouses, dug wells, and coordinated the transformation of the rural power grid. Then, it contacted the agricultural department to collect new varieties, new materials, and new technologies and invited agricultural experts to teach strawberry planting experience. In addition, it actively contacted large commercial companies in the county and even the province to expand sales channels and ensure that strawberries can be grown and sold. As the strawberry planting in the village achieved very good results, more villagers were willing to transfer their land and participate in the work of the cooperative. In this process, villagers not only provide land leasing services for the industrial base through land transfer and obtain land transfer rental income, but they also obtain labor income by providing labor services to the cooperative. At present, strawberry planting in Village B has increased to more than 160 acres, gradually developing into an industry, and Village B was listed as a Provincial Agricultural Science Demonstration Base by the Municipal Science and Technology Association and obtained the next round of financial support.

The second is Village B's poverty alleviation workshops to improve labor productivity. Based on the knowledge level of the villagers, the age of the permanent population, and the labor capacity, Village B ran poverty alleviation workshops and introduced a garment-making enterprise in the county to provide simple jobs for registered poor households and other villagers so that poor households can improve their ability to escape poverty through their own hands. Employees can receive a monthly salary ranging from 1000 to 2500 yuan, which really improves their income level. For instance, a villager used to work outside all year round and after learning that there was a poverty alleviation workshop in the village, he immediately came back to work. Now, he not only has an income of 2000–3000 yuan a month but also can take care of his family. "Left-behind children have company, empty-nest elderly have support, and left-behind women have jobs", as the adage goes. The poverty alleviation workshops in Village B enabled the people of Village B to realize their dream of working at their doorsteps and ignited the hope of local cadres and masses to get rid of poverty.

Third, Village B attaches importance to infrastructure construction and creates conditions for improving life. Under the guidance of national policies and the assistance of governments at all levels, Village B developed "village-to-village" and "household-to-household" projects. Over the past 10 years, village-to-village projects led a highway to the countryside, and rural roads changed from muddy roads to asphalt roads, from narrow to wide, from curved to straight, and from lines to networks, opening up the "last kilometer" of the village's connection with the outside world. Household-to-household projects hardened the "three-meter lane" and achieved seamless connection from the villagers' doorstep to the main road in the village, allowing villagers to bid farewell to the embarrassment of "covered in dirt on sunny days and covered in mud on rainy days" and opening up the "last meter" of improving the quality of life of villagers. In addition, Village B also built a new 650-m rural road in 2019, which greatly facilitated agricultural production and the transportation of agricultural products and extended the "road to wealth" for farmers. In terms of water, gas, and network, Village B has achieved tap water and natural gas access to every household, solving the villagers' long-standing water problem and improving the quality of domestic water. Rural villagers connected to natural gas can also enjoy national subsidies for using natural gas for cooking and heating. The use of firewood piles and black coal balls ended, which is environmentally friendly, hygienic, and also convenient for villagers' lives. At present, Village B has completed the access of radio, television, and broadband to households, and has achieved full coverage of the internet, information, and services. New innovations, such as rural e-commerce and distance education, have taken root in Village B, breaking through the information barriers between villagers and the outside world, broadening villagers' learning opportunities, and enriching villagers' cultural experiences. In terms of living environment, Village B has planted 1200 green trees, painted 3000 m^2 of walls, dispatched large vehicles 30 times, cleaned up more than 100 m^3 of garbage, and spent more than 60,000 yuan. The situation of garbage everywhere has disappeared, and the people's living environment and sense of gain have improved. Village B has also invested funds to build walls and install gates for poor people, effectively improving their living conditions. In addition, Village B is also gradually promoting the renovation of rural household toilets. After the standardized renovation of the original dry toilets, there are no more pungent odors and flying flies, and the living conditions of the villagers further improve.

Fourth, the village attaches importance to the development of education and strives to eliminate ideological poverty. As the saying goes: "It takes ten years to grow a tree but a hundred years to cultivate a person." Poverty alleviation must eventually start with education. At first, some people in Village B did not pay enough attention to education, and many students dropped out of school before graduating from junior high school. After discovering this situation, the village cadres of Village B personally went to the homes of students and their parents to persuade them to explain the importance of going to school and urge the students to return to school. In the past few years, the village cadres of Village B had persuaded more than 10 students to return to the classroom. Furthermore, in order to ensure that the children of the poor can dispel their economic concerns and go to school with peace of mind, the village cadres of Village B contacted relevant functional departments to apply for education subsidies for poor college students and established a long-term student aid plan for the children of poor families to ensure that these children can afford compulsory education and do not drop out of school due to poverty. In addition, Village B also organized the original and new labor force of poor families to participate in skills training so that the qualified poverty-alleviation targets can master one or two vocational skills and rural practical technologies and can make a living independently by technology and labor.

Fifth, the village strengthens medical security and refuses to let the poor fall into poverty due to illness. With the help of the higher-level government, Village B has its own village clinic, and villagers no longer need to go to the town clinic for minor symptoms, such as colds and fevers. In addition, the village cadres of Village B actively cooperate with the health department to implement national and provincial cooperative medical care and major disease assistance policies to ensure that the poor can afford medical treatment and are not burdened by illness.

The sixth is Village B constructing village organizations and giving full play to the power of grassroots organizations. In order to build a poverty alleviation team, the central and provincial governments have targeted and assigned cadres with high political quality, strong working ability, and familiarity with the "three rural" work to serve as the main leaders of the party and government in poor townships. Based on the actual needs of poor villages, secretaries and village work teams are also selected. The village cadres consciously abide by the "five days and four nights" work discipline requirements and they eat in the village, live in the village, and work in the village. They do not become part-time cadres but integrate with the masses and play the leading role of grassroots party organizations. Village B has increased the double promotion of poverty alleviation and grassroots party building, actively guided capable and talented young people to join the Communist Party, cultivated and expanded the team of party members who are leaders in poverty alleviation work, opened up the "last mile" of contact and service to the masses, and built the party branch of Village B into a strong fighting fortress to lead the masses out of poverty.

6.3 Examining China's Experience in Poverty Alleviation Based on A-C Theory

The poverty alleviation process of City A and Village B is a microcosm of China's poverty reduction cause. From a national perspective, the reason why such significant historic achievements can be achieved is mainly based on a complete policy system that promotes the formation of a social consensus on getting rid of poverty and promotes poverty alleviation through industry development, job transfer, relocation, education, and a series of other measures to continuously improve the accessibility of the market economy to poor areas and poor people, to give full play to the decisive role of the market in resource allocation, to better the role of governments at all levels, to promote poverty reduction and eradication in poor areas, and to achieve endogenous and sustainable development. We believe this to be the most important experience in the success of China's poverty reduction practice, and its internal logic and basic mechanism are fully consistent with the core connotation of the A-C theory.

6.3.1 China's Policy System for Poverty Reduction

In general, in the past 70 years of poverty reduction, China has gradually formed a complete policy system, which mainly includes the implicit poverty-reduction policy system under sustained economic growth, the explicit poverty-reduction policy system under special government plans, the poverty-reduction fund investment system, the poverty-alleviation mobilization and assistance system, and the poverty-alleviation responsibility and assessment system. This policy system is the basis for the whole society to form a consensus on the issue of poverty alleviation and prosperity, and it is also the institutional guarantee for China to win the battle against poverty.

Implicit Poverty-Reduction Policy System Under Sustained Economic Growth China has promoted national economic growth by vigorously promoting industrialization, urbanization, and agricultural modernization and has driven poverty reduction through economic growth. However, because the poverty reduction effect is hidden behind economic growth, the policy system that promotes economic growth can also be regarded as an implicit poverty-reduction policy system. Both theoretical and empirical studies have shown that economic growth has a significant poverty reduction effect on China (Dollar and Kraay 2002; Rozelle et al. 2000; Lin 2003; Sen et al. 2006). In addition, in the process of China giving priority to the development of the eastern region and then driving the economic growth of the central and western regions, the eastern region has exerted a trickle-down effect on the central and western regions and has effectively promoted poverty reduction in the poor areas of the central and western regions by absorbing the labor force from the central and western regions, transferring industries to the central and western regions and providing counterpart assistance.

Explicit Poverty-Reduction Policy System Under Special Government Plans
Special poverty-alleviation plans and various poverty-alleviation policies issued by governments at all levels constitute China's explicit poverty-reduction policy system. In order to promote effective progress in poverty alleviation, China has issued special poverty-alleviation plans from top to bottom, forming a vertical and systematic poverty-alleviation policy system. The special plan at the central level is centered on the *13th Five-Year Plan for Poverty Alleviation*, promulgated in November 2016, the first of special 5-year plans for poverty alleviation and prosperity. The *13th Five-Year Plan* clarifies the overall ideas, basic goals, and main tasks and guarantees measures for poverty alleviation during the 5-year period, and it puts forward a timetable and roadmap for winning the battle against poverty. It is an action guide for all regions and departments to promote poverty alleviation and is also an important basis for formulating relevant special poverty-alleviation plans. The *13th Five-Year Plan* proposes to accurately target, adapt, and implement policies in a categorized manner and to give full play to the leading role of the central government, the local governments, and the market. It also closely combines targeted poverty alleviation with overall regional advancement and innovates the system and mechanism of poverty alleviation from aspects of targeted poverty alleviation, poverty-alleviation resource mobilization, poor population participation, project fund management, and assessment incentives so as to build a large pattern of the mechanisms of poverty alleviation and prosperity promoted by the central government, local governments, the market, and the society. The *13th Five-Year Plan* profoundly reflects the people-centered governance concept under China's single-peak unbiased political governance, with strong policy formulation, implementation capabilities, and social mobilization capabilities. Various projects, such as industrial poverty alleviation, transfer employment poverty alleviation, and infrastructure construction projects, strive to stimulate the endogenous driving force of poverty alleviation in poor areas by improving the economic accessibility of poor areas and accelerating the construction of a unified market. Under the guidance of the *13th Five-Year Plan*, local governments also formulate their own poverty alleviation plans according to local conditions and formulate specific implementation plans, such as the *Three-Batch Action Plan for Health Poverty Alleviation Project* and the *Three-Year Action Plan for Agricultural Industry Poverty Alleviation*, to promote the in-depth development of targeted poverty alleviation in various fields and effectively improve the effectiveness of poverty alleviation assistance.

Poverty-Reduction Fund Investment System
China has established a poverty-reduction fund investment system, which includes special central poverty-alleviation funds, local poverty-alleviation funds, and

special financial poverty-alleviation loans. The use of poverty alleviation funds provides financial support for poverty reduction work and is a guarantee for the implementation of poverty reduction policies. According to data from the Ministry of Finance, from 2016 to 2019, the central government allocated a total of 384.38 billion yuan in special poverty-alleviation funds, with an average annual growth of 28.6%. According to the *Report on the State Council's Work on Poverty Alleviation*, from 2013 to 2017, China's provincial and lower-level fiscal poverty alleviation funds also increased significantly, arranging 120 billion yuan in local government debt to improve production and living conditions in poor areas and arranging 99.4 billion yuan in local government debt and 50 billion yuan in special construction funds for poverty alleviation relocation. In addition, China's financial poverty-alleviation efforts increased significantly. During the *13th Five-Year Plan* period, more than 350 billion yuan of special loans for poverty alleviation relocation were issued. The government also introduced a poverty alleviation re-loan policy, and the securities industry, insurance industry, land policies, and other efforts to help poverty alleviation also significantly strengthened.

Poverty-Alleviation Mobilization and Assistance System
Giving full play to the advantages of the socialist system, concentrating efforts on major tasks, and mobilizing all forces to work together to overcome poverty are the starting point and foothold for China to establish a poverty alleviation mobilization and assistance system. China's poverty alleviation mobilization and assistance system includes the following aspects. The first is the poverty alleviation assistance between the eastern and the western regions. This includes achieving full coverage of assistance to 30 ethnic autonomous prefectures across the country through the east-west poverty alleviation cooperation, clarifying the poverty alleviation cooperation tasks between the authorities in Beijing and Tianjin, as well as Zhangjiakou, Chengde and Baoding in Hebei Province, in the coordinated development of Beijing, Tianjin, and Hebei, as well as implementing the concept of working "hand in hand to achieve a well-off society", in which 267 economically developed counties (cities and districts) in the eastern region pair up to help 434 poor counties in the western region. The second is the targeted poverty-alleviation work, which includes 320 central units targeted to help 592 poor counties, and the army and armed police forces targeted to help more than 3500 poor villages. The third is enterprise assistance actions, including central enterprises setting up industrial investment funds in poor areas, carrying out the "100 counties and 10,000 villages" poverty-alleviation action, and private enterprises carrying out the "10,000 enterprises help 10,000 villages" action.

Poverty-Alleviation Accountability Assessment System
China has issued implementation measures of the poverty alleviation responsibility system in accordance with the system and mechanism of "central coordination, provincial overall responsibility, and city and county implementation", and established a responsibility system in which each party bears its own responsibilities and works together to overcome difficulties. The work deployment of this system requires the decomposition and implementation of the 101 important policy measures in the

Decision of the CPC Central Committee and the State Council on Winning the Battle Against Poverty, which clarifies the division of tasks of 76 relevant departments of central state organs. The responsible comrades of the party and government in 22 provinces in central and western regions of China sign a poverty-alleviation responsibility letter of oath to the central government and issue military orders. The leading party and government positions in poor counties remain stable during the poverty alleviation period. In addition, in order to ensure that the poverty alleviation results are real, recognized by the society and the masses, and can stand the test of practice and history, the central government has issued assessment measures for the effectiveness of the work on poverty alleviation and prosperity by provincial party committees and governments and implemented the most stringent assessment and evaluation system. For example, the State Council Leading Group for Poverty Alleviation and Development organized a formal assessment of the effectiveness of the poverty alleviation work of provincial party committees and governments in 2016 based on the trial assessment of the work results in 2015. With the approval of the CPC Central Committee and the State Council, provinces with good comprehensive evaluations were commended, provinces with poor comprehensive evaluations and outstanding problems were summoned for talks by the main responsible party and government officials, provinces with average comprehensive evaluations or outstanding problems in certain areas were summoned for talks by the responsible officials in charge, and the evaluation results were sent to the Central Organization Department as an important basis for the comprehensive evaluation of provincial party committees, government main responsible persons, and leadership teams.

6.3.2 Cohesive Political Governance Is Fundamental Starting Point and Institutional Guarantee for China's Poverty Alleviation Efforts

The Communist Party of China takes the vital interests of all Chinese people as its direction of efforts, which constitutes the basis for all forces in China for reaching a consensus and promoting effective actions. Eliminating poverty, improving people's livelihood, and achieving common prosperity are the essential requirements of socialism. It is in the process of adhering to single-peak unbiased political governance that China gathers the consensus of the whole society and obtains tremendous strength, and the cause of poverty alleviation has been comprehensively coordinated and accurately promoted. The cohesion of political governance in the process of poverty alleviation is fully reflected in three aspects: the concept of unbiased poverty-alleviation policy, strong resource-mobilization ability, and strong execution ability.

First, the poverty alleviation concept of "no one left behind" is consistent with the inherent logic of unbiased political governance, which is an important basis for forming a consensus on poverty alleviation and prosperity in the whole society. In the historical process of poverty reduction, China's poverty reduction concept has been continuously adjusted and optimized according to the actual conditions at different stages of development. At the beginning of the founding of New China, due to the country's limited economic strength, poverty reduction was mainly based on relief-style poverty alleviation. After the reform and opening up, the concept of poverty reduction has undergone a major change. Initially, in response to the situation of numerous poor areas and a huge number of poor people, China promoted poverty reduction by promoting economic development and regional development and achieved remarkable results in the "flooding" method of poverty alleviation for a vast number of poor groups. With the continuous reduction of the number of poor people, the distribution of poor groups gradually showed a sporadic distribution feature, and the flooding method was no longer applicable. The targeted poverty-alleviation strategy, proposed in 2013, marked another major change in China's poverty alleviation concept. Poverty alleviation work gradually moves towards refinement, precision, and accuracy, that is, "implementing refined management of poverty alleviation targets, implementing precise allocation of poverty alleviation resources, implementing precise support for poverty alleviation targets, and ensuring that poverty alleviation resources are truly used on poverty alleviation targets and truly used in poverty-stricken areas."[5] The continuous development and innovation of the concept of poverty reduction reflects the continuous improvement process of cohesive political governance. The policy design concept aims to achieve a well-off society in all respects and common prosperity, where no one is left behind, so that the society is more "unbiased". In addition, the policy design is more scientific, resources are fully utilized in the most effective way, and the policy focus is more "unbiased". Poverty reduction policies are also being continuously optimized, and the quality is constantly improving. From development-oriented poverty alleviation to comprehensive poverty alleviation and then to precise poverty alleviation, poverty alleviation policies have gradually changed from rough to refined, and the precision of poverty alleviation has changed from poor counties to poor villages, and then to poor households and poor people. Policies are more based on the local poverty status and causes of poverty, and policy quality is fully guaranteed. Also, poverty alleviation policies have gradually shifted from single financial relief to diversified poverty alleviation, the policy function has gradually changed from "blood transfusion" to "blood production", and the policy direction has gradually changed from "reducing poverty" to "preventing poverty from occurring". These have led to the continuous improvement of the social recognition of the policies and the corresponding improvement of the policy quality, thereby enhancing the cohesion of political governance.

Second, China's strong resource-mobilization capabilities and effective organizational execution are the driving forces for the collective actions to promote poverty alleviation and prosperity. Poverty alleviation cannot be achieved without a

---

[5] In March 2014, General Secretary Xi Jinping delivered a speech during the deliberation of the Guizhou delegation at the Second Session of the 12th National People's Congress.

large amount of investment in people, funds, and materials. It is impossible to achieve poverty alleviation by relying on the governments, the market, and the society alone. In the process of promoting China's poverty alleviation, the party and the government, with their extraordinary organizational mobilization capabilities, overall coordination capabilities, and implementation capabilities, have led the whole society to participate in poverty alleviation, effectively gathered outstanding talents, effectively integrated idle resources, and gathered a strong force to win the battle against poverty, laying a dynamic foundation for the final victory of poverty alleviation. During this process, the CPC has insisted on putting people at the center, and multiple parties, such as government departments, public institutions, state-owned enterprises, private enterprises, and public welfare organizations, have participated extensively. The enthusiasm of countless units and individuals has been demonstrated, and a series of new practices, such as industrial poverty alleviation, educational poverty alleviation, health poverty alleviation, financial poverty alleviation, ecological poverty alleviation, e-commerce poverty alleviation, and photovoltaic poverty alleviation have emerged. The top-level policy deployment can be smoothly transmitted to grassroots cadres and the masses, and every poor household benefits from it to escape from poverty and move towards a well-off society. The people's sense of gain and identity with the central government's policies has continued to increase, and cohesive political governance has been most fully reflected.

Third, efficient policy execution is an important guarantee for China's success in alleviating poverty. The effective implementation of established rules and policies is an important sign of high cohesion of political governance, which is prominently manifested in the poverty alleviation process as a sound management system, an efficient working mechanism, a strong grassroots work capacity, and strong accountability constraints. Increased improvements in the poverty alleviation management system provide a guarantee for improving the efficiency of poverty alleviation. For example, in the case analysis above, the methods established by City A, including the project management system, fund-use supervision system, rural poor population immediate assistance mechanism, and dual assistance-responsibility system, are relatively representative in the national poverty alleviation work. The system institutionalizes and systematizes various tasks, such as the use of poverty alleviation funds, implementation of poverty alleviation projects, assistance to poor people, and implementation of poverty alleviation responsibilities, effectively improving the implementation of various poverty alleviation policies and providing a basis for the accountability of policy implementation. Also, the clarity of the work responsibility system at all levels guarantees that poverty alleviation policies are passed down from top to bottom. In the process of poverty alleviation, in order to smoothly implement various poverty alleviation policies and ensure the efficiency of poverty alleviation work, comrades from party committees and governments at all levels signed a poverty-alleviation responsibility letter of oath and continuously strengthen organizational construction around the work on poverty alleviation and prosperity, strictly implement the main responsibilities, and establish a responsibility mechanism for poverty alleviation from the five levels of provincial, municipal, county, township, and village secretaries to ensure the implementation of poverty alleviation responsibilities. Under the unified leadership of the central government, all provinces, cities, and counties have established poverty alleviation and development leading group offices, with the party committee secretary as the first group leader to lead poverty alleviation and development work. Poverty alleviation working groups have been established at the town and village levels, with five levels of linkage and efficient operation, promoting the connection of resources, intelligence, and information from the central government to provinces, cities, counties, townships, and even villages. In addition, strong accountability constraints are an important guarantee for execution. In the process of poverty alleviation, the central and local discipline inspection commissions carry out special governance on the issues of corruption and work style in the field of poverty alleviation, aiming to ensure the implementation of poverty alleviation policies and accurate use of poverty alleviation funds. Those who do not attach enough importance to their thoughts, who focus on approval but not supervision, who focus on deployment but not implementation, and who fail to fully play their functions will be held accountable. This forms a strong constraint on the implementation of poverty alleviation work, ensuring that the results of policy implementation meet the requirements of policy design purposes and that poverty alleviation policies are implemented. In addition, in the process of poverty alleviation, the central government attaches great importance to the construction of grassroots organizations, especially the improvement of the working ability of grassroots cadres. To this end, while discovering and cultivating local talents, all poor counties and villages also focus on the introduction of external talents, especially the introduction of highly educated young talents, and successfully explore effective models, such as the "first secretary responsibility system" and "village assistance mechanism", hence reducing the resistance to unifying thoughts, reaching a consensus on understanding and action across the country, effectively solving the "last mile" problem in the process of policy implementation, and significantly improving the efficiency of policy implementation. This is also an important manifestation of the high degree of cohesion in China's political governance.

6.3.3 Improving Economic Accessibility Is Main Means to Achieve Poverty Reduction

Poverty is often caused by people not having the opportunity to participate in various economic activities. To eliminate poverty, society must eliminate the obstacles that prevent people and other factors from participating in economic activities, value creation, and wealth distribution. Improving economic accessibility is like opening a door to wealth for people. Only when this door is opened can the story of economic development happen. From China's experience in poverty reduction, improving economic accessibility, especially accessibility to poor areas and poor people, is the main means to achieve poverty reduction.

The first factor is China creating conditions for the flow and aggregation of capital factors to poor areas and achieving poverty reduction by developing industries in poor areas. An important reason for the underdeveloped economy and society in poor areas is the lack of funds. However, to fundamentally improve the relatively backward social production and living conditions in poor areas and promote a virtuous cycle of economic development, a large amount of funds must be supported. Since the 18th National Congress of the Communist Party of China, the central government and the local governments have continuously increased their financial poverty-alleviation investment, providing guarantees for improving infrastructure and public services in poor areas, developing industries, and creating jobs. The central government and various provinces and cities have also actively guided social capital to go to the countryside in an orderly manner, optimized resource allocation, and formulated a series of policy documents, such as the *Guidelines for Social Capital Investment in Agriculture and Rural Areas*, to call on, guide, and encourage social capital to support the development of poor areas, and hence the sources of funds have been continuously broadened. In addition, various policies, such as leading cadres at all levels and talents to go to the countryside, have provided high-quality human capital for the development of poor areas and become the source of capital inflow and industrial development. Therefore, not only traditional agricultural enterprises, modern real estate, e-commerce enterprises, etc., come to poverty-stricken areas, but science and technology and social services in related fields also participate in the development and construction of poverty-stricken areas. Moreover, many poverty-stricken areas rely on their own characteristics and advantages to develop rural tourism, homestays, and other industries. Vegetables, fruits, tea, cattle and sheep breeding, and other characteristic industries are developing rapidly and even gradually spreading to the whole industrial chain, developing agricultural industrial parks, and industrial towns. As of 2019, 22 provinces and 832 poverty-stricken counties in the country have formulated industrial poverty alleviation plans, developed 14,000 leading enterprises at or above the municipal level, and 126,000 poverty-stricken villages have developed 260,000 farmers' cooperatives. Around 92% of the poor households in the country have participated in industrial development, and more than two-thirds of the poor households have achieved the drive of new business entities.[6]

Second, through transfer employment and relocation, the freedom of labor and the convenience of participating in the economic process are continuously improved. Since there are few employment opportunities in poor areas themselves, transferring the labor force in poor areas to large cities or developed areas with more employment opportunities naturally becomes an important means of poverty alleviation. In this process, the government usually provides a lot of support for transfer employment, such as vigorously carrying out vocational training, strengthening public services for the transferred employed population, and carrying out labor

[6] Ministry of Agriculture and Rural Affairs: Industrial poverty alleviation has covered 92% of poor households, September 2, 2019, https://www.sohu.com/a/338055320_428290.

cooperation between regions. Taking Weinan City in Shaanxi Province as an example, the central government has taken multiple measures and coordinated resources to support leading rural industrialization enterprises through various forms, such as on-the-job employment and flexible employment, providing a large number of jobs, of which migrant workers account for more than 70%. Since 2020, the city's poor labor force has achieved transfer employment for an additional 18,300 people, and newly developed public welfare positions have provided employment for 2890 poor laborers. A total of 10,922 poor laborers have been employed through the development of the "three posts" for employment poverty alleviation.[7] Jishou City in Hunan Province, for example, has successively carried out free training for "two young people" and e-commerce knowledge training, which has effectively improved the labor skills of poor households. It has also signed cooperation agreements with 15 labor cooperation units in and outside the province to smooth employment channels, provide employment information and opportunities for poor households, and consolidate the foundation for the transfer of employment of poor labor. For people in poor living environments, with a lack of basic development conditions, fragile ecological environment, and prohibited or restricted development areas, relocation improves their basic living conditions, such as drinking water safety, travel, and electricity, and the poor are given convenient and accessible basic public services, such as education and medical care, ensuring that poor families with labor capacity have ways to develop in the future and have channels for transfer employment and that their income levels continue to improve, thereby achieving poverty alleviation for the country. During the *13th Five-Year Plan* period, the country invested a total of about 600 billion yuan in various funds, built about 35,000 centralized resettlement areas, and built more than 2.66 million resettlement houses with a total construction area of 210 million square meters, resulting in more than 9.6 million registered poor people moving into new homes. More than 80% of relocated families with labor capacity achieved employment for one or more people. According to the statistics, the per capita net income of registered poor households in the country for poverty alleviation relocation increased from 4221 yuan in 2016 to 9313 yuan in 2019, with an average annual increase of 30.2%.[8]

Third, China has increased efforts in infrastructure construction and continuously shortened the distance between poor areas and the market. Relatively backward transportation conditions restrict the smooth entry of factors and commodities in poor areas into the market. Since the 18th National Congress of the Communist Party of China, the party and the government have attached increasing importance to the construction of transportation infrastructure in poor areas. The investment of fiscal funds in railway and highway construction in poor areas has increased, and

[7] An additional 18,300 poor laborers in the city have found employment through transfer, September 2, 2020, http://dy.163.com/article/FLGO8NR80530KJPT.html.

[8] On December 3, 2020, Zhao Chenxin, the Secretary-General of the National Development and Reform Commission, introduced the data at a press conference on poverty alleviation through relocation, held by the State Council Information Office (http://www.scio.gov.cn/xwfbh/xwbfbh/wqfbh/42311/44410/index.htm).

the central government has encouraged and guided central enterprises, state-owned enterprises, and other types of social capital to invest in transportation facilities in poor areas, actively innovated the cooperation model between the government and social capital, stimulated the enthusiasm of market players to participate in investment, effectively expanded the source of funds, and provided a broader channel for the development of transportation in poor areas. By the end of 2019, the cumulative completion rate of transportation poverty alleviation construction tasks in all provinces across the country reached more than 80%, all qualified towns and villages were connected to hardened roads, the transportation conditions of national and provincial trunk lines and rural roads were greatly improved, and the levels of passenger and freight services were improved. With the improvement of railway and road transportation in poor areas, the increasingly convenient transportation and logistics conditions have provided convenient channels and conditions for the entry of goods, services, and labor in poor areas into the national market, and provided more opportunities for poor areas to participate in the national market and economic development. In addition, governments at all levels have continuously increased the construction of power and internet facilities in poor areas and provided relevant technology and knowledge popularization and training for the development of e-commerce for the poor, hence promoting e-commerce to help poor areas export goods, as well as promoting industrial development and economic growth.

6.3.4 Poverty Reduction Depends on Positive Interaction Between Cohesive Political Governance and Economic Accessibility

Poverty alleviation work needs to pay attention to the organic integration of government and market. The extensive participation of market players and social players in poverty alleviation makes poverty alleviation work no longer shouldered by the government alone, but the forces of government, market, and society can cooperate with each other effectively. In this process, the relationship between the government and the market can also be improved and optimized. The Chinese government gradually abandoned the inertial thinking of "taking on everything", gradually realized the high efficiency of the market in resource allocation, and took the initiative to give competitive areas to the market. This stimulated the enthusiasm of market players and improved market autonomy so that the government could lighten its load, devote its energy to service and regulatory capacity building, and play a guiding role in policies and funds. In this case, the central government and the market are no longer independent of each other. Both strive for a common goal and are organically integrated into a whole. The central government has increased various subsidies for poor areas, strengthened policy incentives, and guided market players to gradually tilt towards poor areas and weak links in terms of resource allocation, thus further improving local market openness. Poor areas can mobilize and combine local labor factors and means of production factors according to broader market demand to ensure that the means of production factors are fully utilized. However, the market focuses on efficiency and sometimes ignores fairness in resource allocation and primary distribution, and hence an effective role of the central government in distribution makes up for this deficiency. The market can then ensure that poor people who participate in economic activities are allocated rewards according to labor factors or means of production factors, thereby helping these poor people escape poverty and become well-off. The government, on the other hand, can mainly target poor people who have no labor ability or lack the means of production and guarantee that these poor people can obtain wealth through fiscal policies, thereby achieving poverty alleviation.

Poverty alleviation also cannot be separated from the mutual promotion of political stability and economic development. Whether compared with the history of poverty alleviation in modern China or with the progress of poverty alleviation in other developing countries in the world, the reason why the miracle of poverty alleviation is realized in China today is that China's political stability is an important guaranteeing factor. Stability is the premise of development. Only a stable regime can concentrate on economic construction and poverty alleviation. As the fruits of economic development benefit more and more ordinary people, people's support for the ruling party and government will deepen and political stability will be further guaranteed. With the continuous development and improvement of China's democratic politics, the demands of poor or low-income people are increasingly included in government decision-making and the barriers that hinder the flow of production factors in the economic development of poor areas are gradually removed, forming more effective competition in the economy and gradually moving towards prosperity. Hence, when the cohesion of political governance increases, economic accessibility further develops. It is precisely because of the efforts to achieve the interaction and balance between the two that the great miracle of China's poverty alleviation was realized and a new chapter in the history of human anti-poverty has been written.

References

Dollar D, Kraay A (2002) Growth is good for the poor. J Econ Growth 7(3):195–225

Lin BQ (2003) China's economic growth, poverty reduction, and policy choices. Econ Res J 12:15–25+90

Rozelle S, Zhang L, Huang J (2000) China's war on poverty. Working Paper No. 60, Center for Economic Research on Economic Development and Policy Reform, Stanford Institute for Economic Policy Research, Stanford University

Sen A et al (2006) India: economic development and social opportunity (trans: Huang FJ). Social Sciences Academic Press, Beijing

State Council Information Office, the People's Republic of China (2021) Building a well off society in an all-round way: a brilliant chapter in the development of China's human rights cause. The State Council Information Office, the People's Republic of China

Chapter 7
Expanding Middle-Income Group

The middle-income group is the backbone of economic development, the cornerstone of social harmony, and the foundation for building the so-called "olive-shaped" social structure. Efforts to expand the proportion of middle-income earners are related to whether people-centered development ideas can be implemented and whether the broad masses of people can share the fruits of reform and development. After more than 40 years of economic reform and opening up, China's GDP and people's living standards have increased rapidly, forming the world's largest middle-income group. Through the continuous struggle of the whole CPC and people of all ethnic groups across the country, China has achieved its first centenary goal, which is to build an all-around well-off society, thereby historically solving the problem of absolute poverty, and is moving towards its second centenary goal of building a modern socialist power. Looking at the process of China's expansion of the middle-income group since the founding of the People's Republic of China, we can find that the expansion of the size of the middle-income group is mainly achieved through the continuous improvement of China's internal and external economic accessibility and the continuous improvement of its single-peak unbiased cohesive governance. In the future, whether the goal is to achieve the level of a moderately developed country by 2035 or to achieve common prosperity, expanding the proportion of middle-income earners will still be the focus of the next economic construction work. To this end, it is also necessary to continue to improve economic accessibility, while ensuring the cohesion of political governance.

C. Chen et al., *From Poverty to Prosperity*, Understanding China,
https://doi.org/10.1007/978-981-95-7171-0_7

7.1 Theoretical Background of Expanding Middle-Income Group

7.1.1 Definition of Middle-Income Group

Middle-income earners are referred to as the group of people in a country who live a relatively comfortable life and have reached a certain level of income. Internationally, the middle class is usually used to describe the middle-income group. This group usually has a good educational background, similar values and lifestyles, and strong consumption capacity and focuses on public participation and the pursuit of self-value realization. They are the main support for economic and social development. There are many ways to measure middle-income earners, and the judgment criteria are not unified. At present, the World Bank's standard of household daily expenditure of US $10–US $100 per capita is more commonly used. The lower limit of this standard is the average poverty line of two developed countries with the lowest poverty lines (Portugal and Italy), and the upper limit is twice the median income of the richest developed country (Luxembourg), thereby excluding the poor in low-income developed countries and the rich in high-income developed countries. Wang Yiming et al. (2017) proposed the standard of household annual income of 32,000–80,000 yuan per capita (calculated based on 2014 data) in light of China's national conditions. The lower limit of this standard is the annual income level per capita of urban households, and the upper limit is 2.5 times the lower limit. These two standards are proposed from the perspectives of expenditure and income, respectively, and the results of the calculation of the size of middle-income earners are roughly similar. On January 15, 2019, the National Bureau of Statistics released the *2018 National Time Use Survey Bulletin*, which gave specific classification standards for different income groups, among which the group with a monthly income of 2000–5000 yuan is the middle-income group.

7.1.2 Western Society's Discussion on Social Functions of Middle-Income Group

Foreign scholars have varying discussions on the social functions of the middle-income group, but most believe that the middle-income group is both a "buffer" between social classes and a "stabilizer" for maintaining social development.

The theory that the middle-income group is a stabilizer can be traced back to Aristotle (Miao 1994). He believed that when the middle class reaches a certain number and power, the gap between the rich and the poor in society will inevitably narrow and social stability will be greatly improved. He advocated narrowing the gap between the rich and the poor and alleviating social conflicts by cultivating the middle class.

Regarding the middle-income group as a buffer, Lipset et al. (1993) believed that as the proportion of the middle class in the social stratification system increases, the role of the middle class in regulating conflicts between upper and lower classes, easing the political attitudes of the lower class, and promoting resource sharing between classes will become increasingly important. Therefore, the larger the size of the middle class, the more stable the society. Wright Mills (2006), in *White Collar: The America's Middle Classes*, stated that the middle class is a buffer class between the monopoly bourgeoisie and the proletariat and plays a stabilizing role in society. De Tocqueville (2009) pointed out in *Democracy in America* that the American middle class attaches importance to material enjoyment, cares about property, and has a devout belief in religion, which makes it tend to be conservative and hence conducive to maintaining social stability.

A small number of scholars have raised the potential "subversiveness" of the middle class. In *The Old Regime and the Revolution*, De Tocqueville (2013) pointed out that the middle class during feudal France was a revolutionary class that despised the path of reform and advocated a thorough transformation of French society. It played a huge role in destroying the old French system and was the "gravedigger" of the French feudal government. Huntington (2008) discussed the impact of the middle class on political stability, emphasizing that the middle class in the growth stage, especially intellectuals, tends to be radical and revolutionary politically, which is an important factor in political instability.

7.1.3 Social Significance of Expanding Middle-Income Group

The growth of the middle-income group gives a continuous arrangement between the opposing poles of the rich and poor. Every member of society can see the hope of climbing up the ladder, which helps to ease the antagonistic emotions accumulated by the gap between the rich and the poor, as well as the series of social problems derived from it. An income distribution system that can achieve prosperity cannot only make a few people rich, hence producing polarization. Marx (1891) mentioned in *Critique of the Gotha Program*: "A person who has no other property except his own labor power, in any social and cultural state, has to be a slave to others who have become the owners of the material conditions of labor." (p. 8) If a small number of people at the top of the pyramid occupy the vast majority of wealth, then such a distribution method will greatly lead to social unrest and damage economic prosperity. A harmonious society is the product of the dynamic balance of various social forces, and such harmony is difficult to achieve in a society with serious polarization. Aristotle pointed out incisively that "social unrest is often caused by "inequality"" and "internal strife always grows from the root of the desire for "equality"." A country with a serious gap between the rich and the poor will inevitably form an unbalanced and unreasonable pyramid-shaped social structure: an oligarchic upper class with a very small number of people but the vast majority of social wealth, and a poor lower class with a large number of people but very little wealth. If a country is in this "inverted pyramid" social structure for a long time, it will not only mean that the country cannot achieve modernization but also that a large number of lower-class people will gradually distrust the government, eventually leading to the opposition between the very small number of the upper rich class and the large number of the lower class and even causing social unrest in serious cases. Such a split will pose a great challenge to the impartiality of governance in a unimodal society and will easily cause multi-modal conflicts in a multi-modal society. The contradictions between the lower class and the upper class, and between the rich class and the poor class, will lead to a decrease in the cohesion of political governance and affect economic prosperity.

Take Latin American countries, the "most unfair region in the world", for example. Starting from the labor force brought by the triangular trade in the sixteenth century, coupled with more than 100 years of industrialization and modernization since the end of the nineteenth century, economic development has achieved some results. However, the exploitation of Blacks, Indians, and lower-class working people has led to an extremely disparate income gap—a development called "a voyage with more victims than navigators" (Galeano 2001). After 400 years of evolution, when entering the new century, wealth has been concentrated in the hands of a very small number of the upper class, social policies are too concerned about the interests of powerful groups, the development of small- and medium-sized enterprises (SMEs) is subject to multiple restrictions, the middle class is difficult to develop, and economic accessibility is very low. In addition, the contradictions and conflicts of multi-peak governance are becoming more and more intensified. The Peruvian presidential election, which began on April 11, 2021, was plagued by riots, assassinations, and other vicious incidents due to people's dissatisfaction with the voting results and disappointment with politics. The homicide rate was as high as 25.1 per 100,000 people, which greatly reduced the cohesion of political governance and seriously affected the country's progress towards prosperity. It can be seen that an unbalanced development caused by low economic accessibility and reduced political cohesion will lead to social unrest. Therefore, in order to achieve prosperity, an income distribution system must avoid polarization, and expanding the proportion of middle-income earners plays an important role in this.

7.2 China's Efforts to Expand Middle-Income Group Since Founding of People's Republic of China

Since the founding of the People's Republic of China, the efforts made to expand the middle-income group have been gradual and in line with the times, and the challenges faced in achieving such a distribution pattern are long-term, arduous, and complex. In the process of economic development, the relationship between productivity and production constantly changes. Therefore, income distribution in correspondence to the relationship between productivity and production also changes.

Since the founding of the People's Republic of China, the country's income distribution pattern has undergone many changes. The reasons behind this are also complex because there are many factors that promote and hinder the change in the size of the middle-income group in a certain period. There are factors that promote the transformation of low-income people into the middle-income group, and there are factors that hinder the transformation of low-income people into the middle-income group. Even the same factor played different roles in different periods. And it is precisely because of the influence of multiple factors and their interactions that the effect on expanding the middle-income group is different. Therefore, it is necessary to analyze the evolution of China's middle-income group after the founding of the People's Republic of China and its relationship with economic accessibility and political cohesion and to find the internal logic and development trend. Based on the reform processes, the income distribution pattern since the founding of the People's Republic of China can be divided into four stages, discussed as follows.

7.2.1 Fair Starting Point Brought About by Land Reform (1949–1956)

The founding of New China provided the ground for the emergence of the middle-income group. Before the founding of New China, the basic characteristics of China's income distribution were "the disparity between the rich and the poor among the residents in a poor country, and the country's poverty was caused by the backwardness of productivity and the destruction of long-term wars. The disparity between the rich and the poor was caused by two exploitation systems—the feudal system and the capitalist system and the corresponding two pairs of opposing classes—the landlord class and the tenant class, the capitalist class and the working class" (Zhao 2007). In the early days of the founding of New China, China was in a period of national economic recovery and development. By confiscating bureaucratic capital and implementing land reform movements, China carried out the Three Major Reforms, which involved the areas of agriculture, private handicrafts, and private capitalist industry and commerce, as well as establishing a socialist collective economic system and implementing a planned economic policy. The Three Major Reforms adopted mild transitional policies, such as agricultural collectivization and asset redemption, relying on in-depth and powerful mobilization capabilities, and the reforms were completely completed in just 3 years. During the process of transformation, the state vigorously developed commerce, expanded urban and rural logistics exchanges, especially the purchase of agricultural products, and supported agricultural cooperatives. This was precisely the embodiment of the improved political cohesion brought about by the implementation of single-peak unbiased governance in New China. Land reform, in accordance with the *Instructions on Establishing Land Reform Committees in People's Governments at All Levels and Organizing Farmers' Associations at All Levels to Directly Lead the Land Reform*

Movement issued by the CPC Central Committee in January 1950, by the spring of 1953, land reform was generally implemented throughout the country, except for ethnic minority areas, such as Xinjiang, Tibet, and Taiwan Province, and the reform completely changed the distribution of social wealth. More than 300 million farmers in the country received about 700 million *mu* of land and a large number of means of production for free, allowing workers from different regions, different nationalities, and different incomes to have an equal starting point for income distribution and share the same opportunities for economic access, which stimulated the enthusiasm of farmers for production. The agricultural output value increased by 48.5% from 32.59 billion yuan in 1949 to 48.29 billion yuan in 1952. Under the combined effect of increased economic accessibility and improved political cohesion, the problem of the rich-poor gap left over from the old China was gradually controlled and narrowed. It provided the possibility for the transformation of the low-income group into the middle-income group. It is worth noting that although the budding of the middle-income group had appeared in rural areas, there was still a long way to go before its real rise. For instance, the *Regulations on Household Registration of the People's Republic of China*, promulgated by the state in 1958, stipulated that farmers cannot transfer their agricultural household registration to non-agricultural household registration without approval and established a household registration separation system between urban and rural areas, which affected economic accessibility and created a gap in the labor return rate between industry and agriculture, hindering the development of the middle-income group in rural areas.

7.2.2 *Arrested Development from Egalitarian Distribution (1957–1978)*

The rise of China's middle-income group was not smooth sailing. Because China's socialist distribution system was pure egalitarianism, the enthusiasm of the vast majority of grassroots workers was severely hit under the influence of egalitarianism, which such adage that "it doesn't matter whether you work more or less, work well or badly, or work or not." During this period, although the income gap between urban and rural residents continued to narrow, where the income ratio between urban and rural residents narrowed from 3.23 in 1957 to 2.57 in 1966, such a narrowing of the income gap did not bring about a large number of middle-income earners. On the contrary, the income of urban and rural residents showed a downward trend to a certain extent, and the budding of the newly emerging middle-income group was quickly suppressed.

The main issues affecting income distribution during this period are as follows. The first is that the Great Leap Forward movement, launched in 1958, ignored the objective laws of production and tried to achieve communism in one step. On May 5, 1958, the Second Session of the Eighth National Congress of the Communist

Party of China was held in Beijing. The Congress formally adopted the general line and basic points of "working hard, striving for excellence, and building socialism faster, better, and more economically" proposed by the Central Committee of the Communist Party of China based on Mao Zedong's initiative. Following this, the country launched the Great Leap Forward movement from agriculture to industry, from "10,000 *catties* of grain per *mu*" in agriculture to "making steel in a big way to catch up with and surpass the United Kingdom and the United States" in industry. The low cohesion of political governance was manifested in the separation between the policymakers and the implementing officials and workers, as well as the pursuit of unrealistic productivity across the country. Under the influence of "high targets" and "exaggeration", the national labor output did not increase but rather decreased, and it was naturally impossible to achieve the transformation of the low-income group into the middle-income group.

The second issue is the people's commune system, which overemphasized the "big pot" distribution system, failed to play the incentive role of distribution and was not conducive to the production enthusiasm of workers. Against the backdrop of the Great Leap Forward movement, the purpose of the people's commune system, which at the beginning was "concentrating forces to do big things" when building water conservancy and farmland, evolved into a general mass movement that ignored objective conditions and competed to promote the transition of agricultural collective production organizations to so-called "higher forms". Under such a system, although the income distribution gap was forcibly eliminated, due to the lack of incentives for workers and scientific researchers, the vast majority of the poor people in the country lacked the means and conditions to transform into middle-income earners.

The third point is that the Cultural Revolution, which lasted for 10 years until 1966, ignored the material basis, the productivity basis, and the political and cultural basis required for a good income distribution pattern. Not only did it fail to make the economy prosperous, but the economy fell into stagnation or even recession, which significantly hindered the growth of the middle-income group. In December 1977, Li Xiannian made an estimate at the National Planning Conference that the national income lost RMB500 billion in the 10 years of the Cultural Revolution. This figure exceeded the total fixed assets of the country in the 30 years since the founding of New China. Furthermore, the conflicts between different groups in society seriously expanded, and China's single-peak unbiased governance encountered twists and turns in the class struggle, which seriously affected the process of prosperity.

7.2.3 Growth Vitality from Reform and Opening Up (1979–2001)

The reform and opening up injected tremendous energy into China. With the advancement of China's social transformation, large-scale social class differentiation emerged. The social class structure changed from simple to diversified, from closed to open. A modern social class structure took shape, and the growth potential of China's contemporary middle-income group was activated.

The rise of the middle-income group began with a series of reforms centered on the rural economy, which led to a substantial increase in farmers' income and a gradual increase in the middle-income group. Starting with the "big contract responsibility system" of dividing land among households in Xiaogang Village, Fengyang, Anhui, rural areas formally piloted and promoted the household contract responsibility system. Although the collective ownership system of land was not changed and the ownership of land was given to farmers, this major reform changed the distribution system, giving farmers the right to use land and to long-term income, allowing farmers to obtain excess economic surplus distribution, which overcame the "free-riding" behavior under the people's commune system, increased economic accessibility, and greatly mobilized farmers' enthusiasm. In addition, the focus of the initial reform from a planned economy to a socialist market economy was to adjust the price structure. In 1979, the state significantly increased the purchase price of 18 major agricultural and sideline products, with an average increase of 24.8%. Among them, the purchase of grain and cotton beyond the plan was also increased by 50% (Zhang 2008). Both the price increases and the big contract responsibility system increased agricultural productivity, stimulated the increase in agricultural production, significantly increased farmers' income, and promoted the large-scale transformation of the low-income group in rural areas into the middle-income group.

The urban middle-income group also continued to grow with the development of the private economy. Before the reform and opening up, the private economy in China almost disappeared. After a long period of political turmoil and economic depression, economic development was very urgent. In order to solve the problem of a large number of young people returning to the city for employment, the development of the self-employed and private economy was gradually relaxed. In 1978, the state supported the restoration and development of some individual economies in towns and cities based on local conditions. Subsequently, according to the suggestions of the 13th National Congress of the Communist Party of China, the State Council promulgated the *Provisional Regulations on Private Enterprises of the People's Republic of China*, which formally confirmed the legal status of China's private economy. The rapid increase in the number of self-employed households formed a special class of small owners, some members of which gradually grew into private enterprise bosses, and a group of private business owners began to appear. The emergence of the group of private business owners during this period was brought about by the reform and opening up that improved economic accessibility and became the reserve force of the middle-income group in the city. Next, in the 1990s, market-oriented reforms, reforms of state-owned enterprises, the "grasping large and letting go of small" of urban state-owned enterprises, and the restructuring of township enterprises led to the rapid expansion of private enterprises and the individual economy. Many government officials and intellectuals went into business, which triggered the large-scale growth of the private enterprise economy and the rapid expansion of the private enterprise class. In addition, the role of human capital was increasingly strengthened. Intellectuals, managers, professionals, and technical personnel from all walks of life also have the opportunity to benefit from reform and opening up and become middle-income earners.

In terms of scale, when China started the reform and opening up in 1978, its economic scale was only RMB364.5 billion, but it crossed the 10 trillion mark in 2001.[1] Since then, with the continuous integration of political governance after the reform and opening up, economic accessibility has continued to increase. A middle-income group with a higher income, higher education, and decent jobs from different industries has taken shape.

7.2.4 *Rapid Growth of Middle-Income Population (2002–Present)*

As early as in his July 1 speech in 2001, Jiang Zemin pointed out that "since the reform and opening up, the composition of China's social classes has undergone new changes, and a group of new social classes have emerged," which "are also builders of the cause of socialism with Chinese characteristics." The report of the 16th National Congress of the Communist Party of China in 2002 included expanding the proportion of middle-income earners in the central documents for the first time, which provided support for the development of China's middle-income group and recognized the political legitimacy of the middle-income group. The fourth part of the *Economic Construction and Economic System Reform* report by the 16th National Congress proposed to "standardize the distribution order, reasonably adjust the excessive income of a few monopolistic industries, and ban illegal income" during the deepening of the reform of the distribution system and the improving of the social security system. With the goal of common prosperity, the state sought to expand the proportion of middle-income earners and improve the income level of low-income earners. Closely linking the development of the middle-income group with the ultimate goal of achieving common prosperity showed that the party regarded expanding the proportion of middle-income earners as a path to achieving the ultimate goal of common prosperity.

This new proposition had great practical significance and far-reaching historical significance. The 17th National Congress of the Communist Party of China further

[1] Data are from *China Statistical Yearbook* by the National Bureau of Statistics.

proposed that "a reasonable and orderly income distribution pattern will be basically formed, middle-income earners will account for the majority, and absolute poverty will be basically eliminated." The 18th National Congress of the Communist Party of China also proposed that "the income distribution gap will be narrowed, the middle-income group will continue to expand, and the number of poverty alleviation targets will be greatly reduced." The *Decision of the CPC Central Committee on Several Major Issues Concerning Comprehensively Deepening Reforms*, adopted at the Third Plenary Session of the 18th Central Committee of the Communist Party of China, pointed out the necessity to "reform the income distribution system and gradually form an olive-shaped distribution pattern." These guiding opinions all show that the party and the state attach great importance to the growth of the middle-income group, recognize the social function of the middle-income group as a "stabilizer", and regard the cultivation of the middle-income group as a major policy goal. The rapidly expanding middle-income group has become a bridge to ease the contradictions between the rich and the poor, and the middle-income group has been given the political significance of improving the cohesion of political governance.

Since the twenty-first century, with the further development of the reform and modernization of China's socialist market economic system, the middle-income group has continued to expand. According to the standard of annual household income per capita, the number of middle-income earners in China exceeded 100 million in 2008 and has increased year by year since then, reaching 400 million in 2019, and the proportion of the total population increased from 8.3% in 2008 to 30.7% in 2019, forming the world's largest middle-income group. Such achievements are inseparable from the continuous efforts made by the party and the central government to improve economic accessibility and political cohesion.

7.3 Examining Importance of Expanding Middle-Income Group in Economic Development Based on A-C Theory

By analyzing the evolution of the middle-income group since the founding of the People's Republic of China, we can find that there is a positive relationship between the expansion of the middle-income group and economic growth. In the early stages of national development, while aiming to achieve wealth accumulation and productivity improvement, a government must pay attention to improving economic accessibility and government cohesion. Only then can the proportion of middle-income earners continue to grow, and the growing middle-income group will play its role as a social stabilizer and further promote economic growth by promoting consumption and improving labor productivity. In this way, China's growing economy and the growing middle-income group, combined with an open economic system and cohesive political governance, realized the path of common prosperity that the Chinese people have pursued for thousands of years.

7.3.1 Expanding Middle-Income Group Is of Great Significance to Economic Development

7.3.1.1 Expanding Middle-Income Group Helps Improve Economic Accessibility

In economics, it is often assumed that the marginal propensity to consume is diminishing. Therefore, the high-income group's marginal propensity to consume is lower than that of the low-income group, while the middle-income group's marginal propensity to consume is somewhere in between. Although the high-income group has a higher income and occupies most of the economic surplus, their demand for consumer goods is close to saturation, their marginal propensity to consume is very low, and they do not have a strong willingness to consume, which objectively reduces the demand for capital and goods. On the other hand, although the low-income group has strong consumption motivation, they own very little social wealth and their current flow income is not much, resulting in the lack of ability to form a long-term stable effective demand in social and economic life. When this group of people reaches a certain scale, society will have the problem of insufficient demand, which will significantly reduce economic accessibility.

In contrast, the middle-income group has a certain income level and relatively stable and diversified economic sources, which makes this group not only have a strong consumption capacity but also more active consumption willingness than the high-income group. Due to the circulation effect of capital, it can continue to participate in production and distribution. As time goes by, the size of the middle-income group gradually expands, the size of the population that can participate in the distribution is also expanding, and economic accessibility will continue to improve. In addition, this will form a long-term and relatively fixed consumer group in social and economic life, which has a positive effect on promoting a sustained and stable growth of the social economy.

In practice, China's economic development has entered a new normal. China's industrial structure is at a low level and mainly relies on low-cost advantages to participate in international competitiveness, advantages that are gradually declining. Expanding the middle-income group is conducive to improving the education level of workers, the quality of workers, and the internal and external accessibility of the economy. It can promote industrial transformation and upgrading internally and improve the country's international competitiveness externally. Compared with the low-income group, the middle-income group has a higher education level, in addition to a higher consumption capacity. Such an education level often brings more scientific and technological knowledge and corporate management capabilities, which makes the middle-income group not only a passive consumer and labor force in the cycle of social and economic growth but also an agent of key tasks, such as factor input, scientific achievement transformation, and technological innovation. Whether it is technology investment, investment of idle funds, or operation in the form of SMEs, the middle-income group is constantly exerting its subjective initiative to spread advanced knowledge and experience in the process of such role transformation, stimulating the business vitality and productivity of SMEs, promoting economic transformation and industrial upgrading within the economy, adjusting and alleviating structural contradictions within the economy, and increasing the scale of new employment, thus enabling more people to join the middle-income group, allowing more people to release potential and huge consumer demand, and finally achieving stable and fast economic growth, all of which forming a virtuous circle. Outside the economy, as the increase in the middle-income group brings about industrial upgrading, China's export enterprises can enhance their productivity level in terms of capital, technology, experience, etc., and can participate and be in a favorable position in increasingly fierce international competition, thus achieving an expansion of the internal and external accessibility of the economy.

7.3.1.2 Expanding Middle-Income Group Helps Improve Cohesion of Political Governance

Cohesive political governance is a political governance form that can maintain social stability and order, promote social compromise and consensus, and effectively promote collective action under a specific political power distribution structure. In order to achieve such a consensus, a cohesive political governance form requires a "glue", and one of the important "glue" is the middle-income group.

As mentioned in the previous article, the middle-income group is a relatively conservative class and a structural factor in maintaining social stability. Rousseau (2003) wrote in *The Social Contract*: "To make the country stable, the two poles should be as close as possible; neither the rich nor the poor are allowed." The size of the middle-income group has an important impact on social functions. The middle-income group is a buffer layer between the upper and lower classes of society. The economic interests and political demands of the middle class are not heterogeneous in form with other classes, but in degree, they are between the two without being extreme and can effectively bond other classes. When the middle class is dominant in a social structure, the contradictions between the upper and lower classes of society will be eased, and the degree of political cohesion will also increase.

From the perspective of the class structure of the middle-income group, firstly, most of the middle class have a good educational background. The influence of higher education enables them to have their own thoughts on problems, and they are more inclined to rational thinking and can analyze problems calmly. Compared with fierce protests, they prefer to express their political wishes rationally in accordance with legal procedures, respect law and order, pursue harmony, and be open-minded. It is easier to form a consensus in society and effectively promote collective action. Secondly, the middle class has stable and comfortable working and living conditions, which makes their interests closely related to the current social order. Therefore, they will have a higher sense of identity with the current social order, have a relatively mild attitude towards society, and tend to be conservative in ideological and political consciousness. From their own interests, they generally do not approve of using drastic methods to resolve social contradictions and conflicts. Therefore, as long as the proportion of the middle class continues to rise, the possibility of major political conflicts or unrest will be smaller, and social stability and order can be maintained. These two points—the self-cultivation of the middle class and their recognition of the mainstream ideology—make the middle class the main force in maintaining the cohesion of political governance.

7.3.2 *Economic Development Provides Guarantee for Expanding Middle-Income Group*

7.3.2.1 Expanding Middle-Income Group Requires Continuous Improvement in Economic Accessibility

The expansion of the middle-income group is achieved by firstly improving economic accessibility, promoting the free flow of factors, breaking monopolies to optimize factor allocation, and then improving labor productivity. When "local blockades" are broken, personnel, capital, and technology start to flow freely. Various production factors begin to converge in regions with higher factor returns. The comparative advantages of these regions are reflected, and different industrial clusters are formed in various regions. The economies of scale are also gradually reflected. A country forms an industrial division of labor and cooperation pattern of "you have me, I have you", and a unified national market is gradually formed. With the continuous emergence of new products, new technologies, and new models, the division of labor between enterprises and regions becomes more refined, and the production and operation of enterprises become more specialized and large-scale. The competitiveness in global markets is further improved, which is more conducive to deep integration into the global industrial chain value chain, and the external market and the internal market form a benign interaction. The degree of internal and external economic openness continues to increase, and the social income distribution pattern tends to be "olive-shaped". In contrast, in an economic structure with low economic accessibility, the situation is just the opposite. The circulation of factor resources is restricted, which can easily lead to monopolies or barriers. The entry of human capital into the industry is also restricted, which will lead to a gap in profit margins between industries, and the social income distribution pattern will present a "dumbbell-shaped" distribution.

Secondly, the expansion of the middle-income group is achieved by improving economic accessibility and increasing social class mobility. An economy is affected by multiple factors, such as historical path dependency. Any society may face problems, such as excessively high incomes in monopoly industries, rent-seeking, and special interest groups controlling the distribution pattern. In response to these situations, a government needs to introduce targeted measures to correct existing problems in the distribution order and form a benign social mobility mechanism, while promoting the expansion of the proportion of middle-income earners. For example, Japan and South Korea both gave priority to education. On the basis of universal compulsory education, they strictly implemented large-scale regular rotation of teachers and nearby enrollment of students and evenly allocated educational resources, achieving a balanced and universal improvement of human capital in the whole society and laying a solid foundation for the expansion of the middle-income group. In the 1980s, South Korea established the National Fair Trade Commission, which focused on eliminating the economic monopoly and political corruption of the old *chaebols* and effectively blocking the channels for special interest groups to seek monopoly and special interests.

Thirdly, any society and region has some economically backward areas or vulnerable groups due to innate conditions and industry characteristics. Only by properly solving the poverty problem in backward areas can measures to expand the middle-income group be implemented smoothly. In order to achieve the goal of poverty alleviation, improving economic accessibility and allowing more backward areas and poor people to participate in economic activities is the most direct and efficient solution. Whether to support backward areas or vulnerable groups, policy measures need to cover many areas, including increasing public investment, giving tax incentives, developing new industries, and strengthening transfer payments.

Finally, improving economic accessibility can promote the expansion of the middle-income group by narrowing the wage gap between industries and adjusting income distribution. In modern society, wages are the main source of income for the vast majority of residents and are also the main focus of countries in improving the income distribution pattern and expanding the proportion of middle-income earners. Through the minimum wage system or wage negotiation mechanism, policymakers not only ensure a reasonable increase in the wage level of the low-income group but also drive the overall improvement of wage income levels through the spillover effect and narrow the factor income gap between labor and capital. As the wage gap between industries decreases, more people can enter economic life to participate in production and distribution, and the proportion of middle-income earners will continue to rise.

7.3.2.2 Expanding Middle-Income Group Requires Increasingly Cohesive Political Governance

When measuring the cohesiveness of political governance, there is a very important sub-indicator: a government's social mobilization ability and execution ability as measured by the government's taxation capacity.[2] With cohesive political governance, a government can effectively formulate and implement fiscal policies uniformly throughout the country. In order to deal with income inequality and increase the proportion of middle-income earners, giving full play to the regulatory role of

[2] For specific indicators of political cohesion, please see Chap. 9 of this book.

taxation is the most basic and important means. On the income side, China's tax policies can adjust personal income and property through a progressive tax system, reduce or exempt personal income and property taxes for the low-income group, and ensure the path of the transformation of low-income earners into the middle-income group. On the expenditure side, the reform of China's fiscal and taxation system provides financial support for local governments with weak financial resources, improves the investment capacity of local governments, and cooperates with local governments via the land transfer system to establish an effective financing mechanism and financial guarantee for infrastructure investment, which rapidly increased China's railway and highway construction mileage, achieved regional interconnection, accelerated the formation of a unified national market, and enabled the transformation of more low-income earners into the middle-income group.

Secondly, the improved cohesion of China's political governance has promoted the consistent actions of local governments and the central government, accelerated the reform of the household registration system, promoted social mobility, and expanded the proportion of middle-income earners. For megacities with a high proportion of floating population, China has established a "point-based settlement" system to promote the orderly settlement of the floating population with stable employment and residence. The state also has improved the mobility of the labor force, promoted the transfer of agricultural population to non-agricultural sectors, improved labor productivity, enhanced the flexibility of the labor market, and promoted the free flow of labor between regions, industries, and enterprises. In addition, the state has lowered the invisible threshold for employment, improved the transparency and fairness of personnel selection and employment, encouraged social members to achieve their life goals through hard work, encouraged mass entrepreneurship and innovation, stimulated social vitality, and provided a broader development space and smoother flow channels for ambitious and capable young people in society. As the subjective initiative of the rural poor is mobilized and their income increases, this group will become the source of the expansion of the proportion of middle-income earners.

Thirdly, with the improvement of political cohesion, China's strong resource-allocation capabilities have been realized. The central government, local governments, the market, and the whole society have reached a consensus on income distribution to actively participate in the cause of expanding the middle-income group under the leadership of the party, gathering outstanding talents, and integrating idle resources. Against the backdrop of the continuous improvement of a single-peak unbiased governance model, the institutional and mechanism barriers in the factor market, urban-rural system, property rights system, public services, etc., have been gradually removed and various sources of creating social wealth, such as labor, knowledge, technology, management, and capital, have been flowing fully, such that social wealth can be reasonably distributed among various factors, breaking down the barriers and obstacles that hinder the reasonable distribution of factor benefits. In addition, a good incentive mechanism can be formed throughout the country to establish a good social atmosphere of respecting labor, knowledge, talents, and creativity; encourage people to realize their value through creative labor; let entrepreneurs, workers, farmers, intellectuals, and cadres at all levels do their best and get what they deserve; and form a vivid situation where everyone participates, fulfills their responsibilities, strives to become stronger, and enjoys the opportunity to make a difference in life and make their dreams come true. Under the joint effect of the incentive mechanism and the supporting system, the low-income group can smoothly transform into the middle-income group.

Finally, cohesive political governance has promoted the advanced experience of China's developed regions to provide support to poor areas with more low-income people via competition and cooperation among local governments, and so more poor people can be transformed into the middle-income group. Under the encouragement of the central government, the developed regions have carried out batches of pilot projects, among which a large number of successful cases have emerged and valuable experience has been accumulated. These practices and experiences are quickly popularized throughout the country through local exchanges and learning. In addition, government officials who perform outstandingly in local economic construction are generally reenlisted, entrusted with important tasks, or transferred to higher-level governments or other places, bringing their management experience to more places. Through targeted assistance and counterpart support, developed regions have given strong support to underdeveloped regions in terms of personnel, funds, technology, etc., such that the size of the middle-income group in underdeveloped regions has increased rapidly.

7.4 Conclusion and Outlook

After the difficult journey in the early days of the founding of the People's Republic of China and the great exploration of reform and opening up over the past 40 years, although the proportion of the country's middle-income earners is still not as high as that of Western developed countries, China has formed the world's largest middle-income group. In China's transition from poverty to prosperity, the middle-income group plays an important role. Looking back at history, we can find that there is a relationship between the expansion of the middle-income group and economic growth. With the expansion of the middle-income group, the economic system can be better transformed from a restricted to an open economy, and the cohesion of political governance can also be improved through the function of the middle-income class as a "buffer". In addition, based on the great exploration of reform and opening up over the past 40 years, the expansion of the proportion of middle-income earners is also inseparable from the continuous increase in internal and external economic accessibility and the cohesion of political governance, creating a social environment for the continuous transformation of the low-income group into the middle-income group.

Although New China has made remarkable achievements in expanding the middle-income group, there is still a lot of room for progress. Whether the goal is to achieve the level of a moderately developed country by 2035 or to achieve common prosperity, the proportion of middle-income earners needs to be further expanded. To this end, China must continue to improve economic accessibility, while ensuring the impartiality of political governance. China must unite everyone politically, lower market access thresholds economically, consolidate the foundation of the national economy, and establish and improve the security system. The income distribution system also needs to be further improved. China needs to encourage the rich to have the motivation and willingness to create opportunities for the poor to participate in economic development and distribution and truly enjoy the fruits of China's transformation from poverty to prosperity. In order to achieve such a goal, China's overall policy orientation should have the following points.

First, the main battle is to promote low-income people into the ranks of middle-income people. The most realistic and main source of expanding the middle-income group is to promote low-income people, especially those who are close to the middle-income threshold, into the middle-income group. Against the backdrop of the gradual weakening of China's labor force advantage, stabilizing employment and improving employment quality are the keys to promoting steady income growth for this group. Targeted reforms should be carried out in the labor market, in addition to skills training, salary system, public services, and social security, in order to enhance economic accessibility and create conditions for more low-income people to transform into middle-income earners.

The second is raising human capital and labor productivity. This is not only in line with China's fundamental system of distribution according to work but also an inherent requirement for promoting China's industries to move towards medium- and high-end levels. The accumulation and quality of human capital are the basis for raising wages. Only by focusing on raising labor productivity and human capital can China realize a virtuous cycle in which economic growth, the growth of the middle-income group, and the improvement of the pattern of income distribution are mutually reinforcing.

Third, the establishment of a new incentive mechanism is the main impetus. The most fundamental impetus for raising income and growing the middle-income group is to rationalize the incentive mechanism and strengthen the bond of political governance. For everyone can enjoy the opportunity to excel in life and make his or her dreams come true, China has to establish a favorable social atmosphere of respect for labor, knowledge, talents, and creativity; motivate people to realize their value through creative labor; enable entrepreneurs, workers, farmers, intellectuals, and cadres at all levels to make the best use of their abilities; and create a lively situation in which everyone participates in the work of the community, does his or her best, and strives to be strong and vigorous.

Fourth, the breakthrough is the removal of institutional barriers. At present, the removal of China's institutional and institutional barriers in factor markets, urban and rural systems, property rights systems, and public services should be used as a breakthrough in order to enhance the cohesiveness of political governance and to allow the full flow of labor, knowledge, technology, management, capital, and other sources of social wealth creation. Social wealth should be rationally distributed among various factors, and barriers and obstacles to the rational distribution of factor returns should be broken down; in particular, support for the participation of labor, knowledge, and other factors in distribution should be strengthened.

References

De Tocqueville A (2009) Democracy in America (trans: Dong GL). The Commercial Press, Beijing
De Tocqueville A (2013) The old regime and the revolution (trans: Xing XY). National Academy of Governance Press, Beijing
Galeano E (2001) Open veins of Latin America (trans: Wang M et al). People's Literature Publishing House, Beijing
Huntington SP (2008) Political order in changing societies (trans: Wang GH). Shanghai People's Publishing House, Shanghai
Lipset et al (1993) A comparative analysis of the social requisites of democracy. Int Soc Sci J 45(2):155–175
Marx (1891) Critique of the Gotha program (trans: the Central Compilation and Translation Bureau of the Communist Party of China for Marx's Works). People's Publishing House, Beijing
Miao LT (ed) (1994) Complete works of Aristotle (trans: Miao LT), vol 9. China Renmin University Press, Beijing
Mills CM (2006) White collar: the American middle classes (trans: Zhou XH). Nanjing University Press, Nanjing
Rousseau JJ (2003) The social contract (trans: He ZW). The Commercial Press, Beijing
Wang YM et al (2017) Research on the issue of increasing the proportion of middle-income earners
Zhang ZY (2008) Thirty years of price reform in China: achievements, history and prospects. Econ Rev J 12:3–10
Zhao DX (2007) 1949-2002: Two approaches to common prosperity and their practical experience. Contemp China Hist Stud 2:29–38+125

Chapter 8
Attitude Towards New Ideas

In the course of human social development, with the emergence of new technologies and new forms of business, the dynamics of economic growth, the composition of social strata, and the demand for resource allocation all continue to change, and new interests and even new interest groups are constantly created. At this point, the original political governance system and economic system may not be able to adapt to economic and social development and may even be at risk of ossification or degradation. For example, the degree of political cohesion may decline—single-peak unbiased governance may degenerate into single-peak biased governance, while multi-peak reconciliatory governance may degenerate into multi-peak conflictual governance—and an advanced economic system that promotes internal and external openness may ossify into a backward economic system that hinders the flow of factors and distorts the allocation of resources, and thus the degradation in political cohesion and economic accessibility fails to adapt to, or even hinders, the further development of the economy and society. Therefore, only through timely adjustments to its political governance and economic system, in close coordination with the needs of economic and social development, can a country ensure a high level of economic accessibility and political cohesion and thus provide fundamental institutional safeguards for high-quality and sustainable economic and social development. In this chapter, we take financial technology, or "fintech", as an example, and we review the development history of this new phenomenon in China, explore the reasons for its rapid development at the institutional level, and further discuss the role of the rapid development of fintech in improving China's economic accessibility and political cohesion. On this basis, we will also discuss how a government can deal with emerging issues in order to maintain a high level of economic accessibility and political cohesion. We believe this will be instructive for China and many other countries in the future.

C. Chen et al., *From Poverty to Prosperity*, Understanding China,
https://doi.org/10.1007/978-981-95-7171-0_8

8.1 Evolution of Fintech in China

Science and technology have always had a wide impact on the development of the financial industry, where especially the rapid development of information technology (IT) has deepened the impact on the financial industry. Not only have financial institutions set up internal IT departments and used IT and hardware and software equipment in financial business to reduce operating costs and improve service efficiency, some technology enterprises also are utilizing software and technology to provide innovative financial services to the market, with new business forms constantly appearing, the service scope of the financial industry constantly extending, and the financial attributes of some traditional technology enterprises becoming stronger and stronger. In this context, fintech[1] has experienced rapid development, its scope and extension have continuously expanded,[2] the integration of technology and finance has deepened, and even the entire financial industry is facing reshaping. According to the definition by the Financial Stability Board (2016), fintech refers to "the promotion of financial innovation through technological means to form business models, technological applications, and processes and products that have a significant impact on financial markets, institutions, and financial services." We can get a small glimpse of the depth of the integration of finance and technology today. As a developing country, China has already made remarkable achievements in emerging financial technologies, such as mobile payments, and is even ahead of some developed countries to a certain extent. In the next subchapters, the development of fintech in China in the context of the development of mobile payment, internet crowdfunding, internet insurance, and other fields, are briefly reviewed.

8.1.1 Evolution of Mobile Payments

Although mobile payment technology was not born in China, the development of mobile payment in China is remarkable. With the maturity of the e-commerce market and the popularization of smartphones and 4G/5G mobile internet, mobile payment based on smartphones and mobile networks has developed rapidly by virtue of its advantage of breaking the constraints of time and space and has been deeply

[1] The term "fintech" originated from a development project called the Financial Services Technology Alliance, initiated by Citibank in the 1990s, which was later shortened to Financial Technology, or FinTech (Xie and Zhou 2017).

[2] For example, in the FinTech 1.0 era, the bank clearing system and the credit system are represented in the bank office system, and ATMs and POS machines are represented in the external service windows, while the Fintech 2.0 era saw the emergence of mobile payment business and internet finance, such as third-party payment, P2P lending, internet crowdfunding, etc., and the rapid growth of some technology enterprises with financial attributes; in the Fintech 3.0 era, there is the in-depth fusion of latest technologies in the financial industry, such as big data, artificial intelligence, and blockchain.

integrated into every aspect of consumers' clothing, food, housing, and transportation, becoming one of the essential lifestyles of the common people.

Mobile payment first appeared in 1999, when China Mobile cooperated with the Bank of China, the Industrial and Commercial Bank of China, and the China Merchants Bank to launch mobile payment services in 17 provinces and cities, including Beijing. In the following 10 years, the domestic mobile payment field has been a race to the bottom, with China UnionPay, mobile operators, cell phone manufacturers, and third-party payment platforms attempting to launch mobile payment services in their own niche areas. Other than launching mobile payment products to compete for business, all parties also fiercely competed for payment standards. For example, China UnionPay conducted a lot of exploration at the early stage of the development of mobile payment in China, launching various products, such as SD cards and "Apple Skin" (a customized case for Apple cell phones) in cooperation with banks and NFC-SIM solutions in cooperation with mobile operators, and even taking the lead in testing 2D code payment services in some areas.

Since 2013, the rise of third-party mobile payment platforms, such as Alipay and WeChat Pay, has ushered in new opportunities for mobile payment in China. Because online shopping is low-priced and convenient, it is easy to satisfy consumers, especially those in rural areas where shopping facilities are not well developed, and the subject of a transaction only needs a smartphone to satisfy daily payment needs. Hence, mobile payment, which is an important part of online shopping, has also seen a spurt of growth. According to the statistics by the People's Bank of China, the number of annual transactions of mobile payment increased from 1.674 billion in 2013 to 123.22 billion in 2020, which is a 73.6-fold increase in 6 years, and the transaction amount of mobile payment increased from 9.64 trillion yuan in 2013 to 432.16 trillion yuan in 2020, which is a 44.8-fold increase. The percentages of transaction and turnover of mobile payments increased from 6% and 0.9%, respectively, of all electronic payments in 2013 to 52.4% and 15.9%, respectively, in 2020. The number of transactions and turnover of mobile payments have increased from 6% and 0.9% of all electronic payments in 2013 to 52.4% and 15.9% of all electronic payments in 2020.[3]

At present, mobile payment remains a hotspot for innovation, and service innovations around cell phones, applications, QR codes, and other payment methods continue to emerge, leading to continued growth in the scale of mobile payment transactions, such as cell phone flash payment and QR codes. China UnionPay, commercial banks, and non-bank payment institutions have continued to strengthen the operation of user-side applications, actively build an open ecosystem for mobile phones, and iterate application versions so as to provide users with richer functions and services.

[3] Source: *Payment System Operation Overall Situation* published by the People's Bank of China annually (2013–2020).

8.1.2 Evolution of Internet Crowdfunding

Compared with other forms of internet finance, internet crowdfunding started relatively late in China. It was only in July 2011 that the first crowdfunding website was launched in China, and in the whole year of 2011, there were three crowdfunding platforms online; in 2012 and 2013, there were 11 and 20, respectively.[4] However, due to the high-speed development of internet finance, the internet crowdfunding industry has been developing very fast in China. In 2014, domestic crowdfunding platforms saw explosive growth, with a total of 166 platforms online in the whole year,[5] while the types of crowdfunding platforms accelerated and diversified, with equity-type, equity-type, property-type, public welfare-type, and comprehensive crowdfunding platforms appearing one after another.[6] In 2015, the number of crowdfunding platforms continued to increase, with a total of 288 platforms going online in the whole year,[7] and the market segments covered a wide range of fields, such as used cars, technology, physical venues, tourism, agriculture, film and television, music, publishing, and games.

However, with more and more industry giants entering the crowdfunding industry,[8] the competitive pressure in this field has been increasing day by day, and many platforms themselves face problems to a greater or lesser extent, such as the uneven quality of projects and insufficient professionalism of platforms, etc., coupled with the lack of regulatory rules in the early stage of the industry's development Some risks and problems that accumulated in the process of the industry's high-speed development began to be exposed, and the industry's reputation and investors' confidence suffered a serious setback. With large organizations exiting the industry out of branding and risk concerns, large startup organizations withdrawing from the industry due to brand and risk concerns, and startup

[4] Data source: Human Creation Consulting (2017).

[5] Data source: ibid.

[6] Equity-based crowdfunding refers to non-public equity financing over the internet, that is, the financier participates in equity financing through equity crowdfunding by way of non-public offering on an internet platform. Equity-based crowdfunding refers to the provision of products or services by an individual or company initiating a project in return for investment. Property crowdfunding refers to raising funds from the public through the internet for the acquisition of physical assets and obtaining profits through the appreciation and realization of assets. Public interest crowdfunding means that the individual or company initiating a project receives donations from supporters without compensation. Integrated platforms are platforms that include two or more crowdfunding models.

[7] Data source: Human Creation Consulting (2017).

[8] In 2015, JD.com, Alibaba, 360, and other platforms successively laid out crowdfunding businesses. In 2016, Suning, Xiaomi, and other platforms launched equity crowdfunding platforms "Suning Private Equity Financing Platform" and "Mi Chou Jinfu", an addition to their existing equity crowdfunding businesses. Baidu and NetEase also began to lay out crowdfunding businesses in 2016. In April, Baidu launched the "Baidu Baizhong" private equity financing platform, and NetEase launched the "Sanshi Crowdfunding" platform focusing on equity crowdfunding at the end of October, deepening its presence in the pan-entertainment field.

companies encountering a cold spell of capital and finding it difficult to expand their development, the development of the industry gradually entered a bottleneck. According to statistics, the number of newly launched crowdfunding platforms in 2016 was 264, which was lower than that in 2015, while more platforms went offline or were transformed. At the end of 2016, the cumulative number of online internet crowdfunding platforms totaled 752, but only 532 platforms were in operation, while 220 platforms were taken offline or transformed. Out of the 288 platforms that went online in 2015 alone, 108 platforms were taken offline or transformed.[9]

As part of the national special rectification work on internet financial risks,[10] relevant government departments began to issue policies and regulations to strengthen the supervision of internet crowdfunding platforms and create a better order environment for the healthy and sustainable development of the industry by rectifying and clearing up the chaos in the industry. On April 12, 2016, the Shenzhen Internet Finance Association issued the *Notice of the Shenzhen Internet Finance Association on Stopping Real Estate Crowdfunding Business*, which requires all internet financial companies in the city to stop conducting real estate crowdfunding business and to conduct self-examination, self-correction, and business cleanup. The next day, the Guangzhou Financial Bureau convened a meeting with the Guangzhou Internet Finance Association and the Guangzhou Financial Industry Association and required real estate crowdfunding companies to suspend business and do a good job in risk investigation. On August 24, the China Banking Regulatory Commission and other departments jointly issued the *Interim Measures for the Management of Business Activities of Online Lending Information Intermediaries*, clarifying 13 activities that online lending information intermediaries are not allowed to engage in or accept commissions to engage in, including asset-like securitization business, equity crowdfunding, and other businesses. On October 13, the China Securities Regulatory Commission and 15 other departments issued the *Implementation Plan for the Special Rectification of Equity Crowdfunding Risks*, which included eight behaviors as the focus of rectification, such as internet equity financing platforms engaging in equity financing business under the name of equity crowdfunding. In addition, relevant departments and policies have fully recognized platforms or models with better development. For example, in August 2016, the Ministry of Civil Affairs announced the first batch of 13 internet fundraising information platforms,[11] which was actually an official recognition of the donation

[9] Data source: Human Creation Consulting (2017).

[10] In order to regulate the development of internet finance, in July 2015, the People's Bank of China and 10 other departments jointly issued the *Guiding Opinions on Promoting the Healthy Development of Internet Finance*. In April 2016, the General Office of the State Council issued the *Implementation Plan for Special Rectification of Internet Financial Risks*.

[11] The first batch of 13 internet fundraising information platforms announced by the Ministry of Civil Affairs were Tencent Charity, Taobao, Ant Financial Charity Platform, Sina Weibo (Weibo Charity), Qingsongchou, China Charity Information Platform, JD Charity, Foundation Center Network, Baidu Charity Donation Platform, Gongyibao, Xinhua Charity Service Platform, Lianquan.com, and Guangzhou Charity Association Charity Information Platform.

crowdfunding model. In December 2016, the State Council issued the *13th Five--Year Plan for the Development of National Strategic Emerging Industries*, which mentioned "crowdfunding" three times and clearly included "building a crowdfunding platform" as one of the 69 key tasks of the national strategic emerging industries during the *13th Five-Year Plan*, indicating that crowdfunding has been elevated to the height of national strategic priorities.

After a deep reshuffle in 2016–2017, the internet crowdfunding industry began to shift from blind expansion to refined development. First, despite the decline in the number of new platforms and the number of normally operating platforms, the number of financing projects and the total amount of financing in the internet crowdfunding industry still maintained a growing trend. The number of successful projects in 2016 was as high as 48,437, more than three times the 15,218 in 2015, and the total amount of financing was 21.74 billion yuan, about twice the total amount of financing of all successful projects in 2015.[12] The number of successful projects and the total amount of financing in 2017 were 69,637 and 26 billion yuan, respectively, up 43.8% and 19.6% from 2016.[13] In the first half of 2018, the national crowdfunding platforms saw a total of 48,935 projects, 40,274 of which were successfully financed, with a financing amount of 13.711 billion yuan, far exceeding that of the same period in 2017.[14] Second, platforms with poor management withdrew from the market, and platforms that did well found their own development paths and expanded vigorously, with a rapid increase in market share, and the concentration of the entire industry increased accordingly. Third, China's localized internet crowdfunding model has begun to emerge. The most representative one is physical venue crowdfunding, whose down-to-earth crowdfunding model has cultivated a group of loyal users and leading platforms in the industry. In 2017, initiated by Zhongchoujia, 11 units, which were Zhongchoujia, Kaishiba, Kaoputou, Duocaitou, Renrentou, Renrenchuang, Diwuchuang, Dianchou.com, Tongchengzhongtou, Qingsongchou, and Zhengongfu, jointly established the New Entity Financial Service Alliance, which is committed to better realizing the value of crowdfunding services for the real economy.

8.1.3 Development History of Internet Insurance

In recent years, as part of financial technology, the development of internet insurance has also accelerated significantly. In particular, the new round of information technology revolution represented by various technologies, such as big data, cloud computing, artificial intelligence, and blockchain, has driven internet insurance into the fast lane. The number of insurance companies operating an internet insurance

[12] Data source: Human Creation Consulting (2017).

[13] Data source: Human Creation Consulting (2018).

[14] Data sources: Crowdfunding, Forward-Looking Industry Research Institute, etc.

business has increased from 34 in 2012 to 134 in 2020, and the premium income of internet insurance increased from 3.2 billion yuan in 2011 to 290.9 billion yuan in 2020, with an annualized growth rate of 65.1%, in comparison with an annualized growth rate of premiums of only 13.6% in the entire insurance industry during the same period.[15]

Similar to internet crowdfunding, the development of the internet insurance industry also experienced a transition from wild expansion in the early stages of development to standardized operations under stricter supervision. As early as before 2015, the number of insurance companies newly added to operate internet insurance business was no less than 25 each year, and the internet penetration rate increased by about 10 percentage points each year. In 2015, the total income of internet insurance premiums nationwide increased by as much as 160%. However, some problems and chaos also emerged in the internet insurance industry. For example, some insurance companies violated regulations in operating high-cash-value internet insurance businesses, selling insurance products through the internet, and making misleading descriptions, such as false descriptions and one-sided or exaggerated publicity of past performance, as well as making false declarations of income or losses. There were also some insurance institutions that conducted online cross-border business, cooperated with third-party network platforms that did not have the qualifications to operate to carry out internet insurance business, and cooperated with internet credit platforms that provide credit enhancement services, set up fund pools, and illegally raise funds. Imperfect risk control measures and inadequate internal control management were apparent, and there were even signs of risk transmission to the insurance field. There were unlicensed institutions illegally carrying out internet insurance business, companies with no business qualifications carrying out internet insurance business in disguised forms, such as mutual assistance, as well as illegal institutions using the name of insurance companies or the credit of insurance companies to illegally raise funds online. Faced with these situations and potential risk points, the China Insurance Regulatory Commission, together with 14 departments, including the People's Bank of China, issued the *Implementation Plan for Special Rectification of Internet Insurance Risks* in April 2016[16] and carried out a 1-year special rectification work through cracking down on various illegal and irregular activities and widely investigating the internet business model and insurance products of the insurance industry in order to standardize the internet insurance business model, improve the regulatory system rules, and optimize the market development environment.

With the launch of the special rectification work on internet insurance in 2016, the enthusiasm of institutions for internet insurance faded to a certain extent, the business of internet insurance began to decline significantly, and the growth rate of premium income slowed down sharply and even shrunk to a certain extent. In 2016,

---

[15] Data source: Data submitted by member companies of the China Insurance Association.

[16] The special rectification work targeting the internet insurance industry was also part of the national special rectification work on internet financial risks in 2016.

the total premium income of internet insurance nationwide reached 229.9 billion yuan, an increase of 6.5 billion yuan from the previous year's premium income of 223.4 billion yuan, a year-on-year increase of only 2.9%, far lower than the growth rate of 160% in 2015. In 2017, internet insurance only achieved premium income of 187.7 billion yuan, a sharp decline of 18.4% from 2016, and only increased by 0.6% in 2018.[17] In the long run, this kind of industry growth fluctuation brought about by the standardization of market order is not necessarily bad news. When the industry rushes to the front, it often leads to chasing hot spots and creating gimmicks, which causes real innovation to be ignored. Under strict supervision, the industry's standardized operation will be able to separate the true from the false, thereby stimulating more effective and beneficial innovations. As the industry reshuffle was coming to an end, coupled with the driving effect of the hot sales of short-term health insurance, such as the Million Medical insurance, internet insurance premium income resumed its upward trend in 2019. In that year, internet insurance premium income reached 269.6 billion yuan, a record high, with a year-on-year increase of 42.8%.[18]

At present, the most obvious benefit of technology empowerment is the insurance sales link. Technologically advanced institutions have begun using big data analysis and other means to achieve differentiated premiums and even differentiated insurance products, use intelligent robots to replace manual customer service, and realize automatic online claims through image recognition to optimize product services. With the further innovation and development of technology, in the future, insurance technology will penetrate into all links of the insurance industry chain, including product design, pricing, marketing, underwriting, insurance, risk control, claims, operations, etc., to enhance companies' operational capabilities and risk control level and provide more space for the development of the internet insurance industry. With the penetration and empowerment of artificial intelligence, big data, the Internet of Things, blockchain, and other technologies, some problems and pain points that have long plagued China's insurance market are expected to be solved, and we look forward to the insurance industry ushering in a new breakthrough.

8.2 Market Accessibility Is Always Prerequisite for Development of Financial Technology

8.2.1 Telecommunications Network Infrastructure Supply Makes Development of Financial Technology Possible

Compared with traditional finance, today's financial technology has two unique features. First, technology has shifted the focus of financial activities from a physical space to a virtual space of information, further expanding the coverage of long-tail

[17] Data source: China Insurance Association, China Insurance Research Institute.

[18] Ibid.

customers (a large group of customers with low individual contribution and dispersed demand); second, the online transaction data, social data, and behavioral data of customers have greatly enriched the data foundation of financial institutions, making customer portraits more accurate, greatly reducing business costs, and improving risk control capabilities. Both of these characteristics are inseparable from the information-based, networked, and mobile electronic communication infrastructure. Only by establishing an electronic communication network with wide coverage, fast speed, and low fees can the financial entry threshold for customers be lowered and the coverage of more financial service demand entities be achieved, and only by achieving extensive coverage of demand entities can the advantages and scale effects of big data be brought into play and the development of financial technology be further promoted.

With the development of financial technology, the Chinese government has promoted the expansion of internet infrastructure coverage and the reduction of internet usage costs in the construction of telecommunications network infrastructure and service provision so as to enable the supply side to obtain basic qualifications for internet access and transform the potential demand on the demand side into actual demand.

China has actively expanded the coverage of broadband and mobile internet and built a physical infrastructure foundation to improve the accessibility of the fintech market. At present, China has built the world's largest fiber-optic broadband network and 4G network. As of the end of March 2020, the proportion of fiber-optic users in the country exceeded 93% of broadband users, and the proportion of 4G users reached 80%. The coverage rate of fiber-optic broadband networks and 4G networks in administrative villages across the country exceeded 98%; 198,000 5G base stations have been built, resulting in more than 50 million 5G package users and more than 20 million 5G terminals connected to the 5G network.[19] The wide-area coverage of telecommunications infrastructure has created the possibility for more than one billion people and tens of thousands of corporate entities to enter the fintech market.

In addition, the Chinese government has created high-quality and low-cost network services by increasing network speed and reducing fees, which has truly lowered the threshold for low- and middle-income people to obtain financial services through financial technology. Since 2015, China has continued to increase network speed and reduce fees, vigorously promoted the construction of high-speed fiber-optic broadband networks and 4G networks, persuaded telecommunications companies to cancel domestic long-distance roaming fees and data roaming fees for mobile phones, and significantly reduced international long-distance charges. According to the statistics from the Ministry of Industry and Information Technology, in 2020, the penetration rate of mobile phone users in China reached 113.9 households/100 people, far higher than the global average of 102.94 households/100 people.

---

[19] Press conference on the development of the industrial communications industry in the first quarter of 2020 held by the State Council Information Office on April 23, 2020 (http://www.scio.gov.cn/xwfbh/xwbfbh/qfbh/42311/42928/wz42930/Document/1677785/1677785.htm).

Presently, there are 27 provinces, autonomous regions, and municipalities in the country with a mobile phone penetration rate of more than 100 households/100 people, and the price of mobile internet traffic has dropped to 4.4 yuan/gigabyte. The increase in telecommunications network speed and the reduction in fees have enabled many low- and middle-income people to have access to financial technology at a lower cost.

The increase in the supply of mobile internet infrastructure has further lowered the threshold for financial services, and the market scale effect has also reduced service costs and risk control costs. China's large market of more than one billion people is one of the few in the world. The huge market size has created two extremely important favorable conditions for promoting the explosive development of the fintech industry. First, the huge market size can support a sufficient number of fintech companies, which can conduct independent and diverse explorations in terms of technology routes, business models, and operating methods. Second, the increasing returns to scale brought about by the huge market size can enable fintech companies to quickly reduce the marginal cost of providing financial services, thereby allowing the companies to quickly accumulate a large amount of profits for the necessary funding of the company's technology R&D and rapid product iteration and optimization, thereby promoting the rapid development of the entire fintech industry.

8.2.2 Inclusive Regulation and Ex Post Facto Recognition Provide Space for Development of Financial Technology

In the early stages of development and rapid growth, China's fintech industry was centered on internet finance. At that time, China's internet companies and internet financial businesses faced many market access restrictions set by laws and policies. Some of the measures taken by internet companies to circumvent restrictions faced certain legal and policy risks to a certain extent. However, the Chinese government has maintained a considerable degree of tolerance and patience on the subject. Following the valuable experience of "crossing the river by feeling the stones" accumulated during the process of reform and opening up, the Chinese government has adopted an inclusive regulatory and ex post facto approach to the development of internet finance, ensuring the accessibility of this emerging field.

In the early days, internet financial services were mostly carried out by internet companies, and the development of internet companies itself faced restrictions on foreign investment. In the early days of China's internet era, internet companies had difficulty obtaining loans from the banking system due to the lack of collateral in their asset-light operation model. China also lacked venture capital due to the scarcity of local capital and the imperfect capital market. Internet companies had to seek venture capital and listing financing from abroad. However, China's early foreign investment regulations prohibited foreign investment in the telecommunications industry. The relevant competent authorities stipulated that only domestic companies could apply for value-added telecommunications business licenses. To circumvent regulatory restrictions, most internet companies that provide value-added telecommunications services adopted the variable interest entity (VIE) structure, pioneered by the Sina Corporation, by using VIEs established overseas to control nominally fully domestic companies through agreements rather than equity to operate internet businesses in order to raise funds from foreign investors. This model has enabled foreign-funded enterprises to enter industries that are only open to domestic enterprises by Chinese laws.

In the process of carrying out internet financial business, internet companies also face the problem of access restrictions in the financial industry. In practice, the Chinese government respects the financial innovation formed spontaneously by the market and adopts relatively loose supervision and supportive ex post facto recognition for internet financial businesses. Internet financial businesses originated from non-financial institutions' online transactions of payment services. Traditional payment services are generally undertaken by the banking sector, but non-financial internet institutions intervene in the payment service system by providing payment services to market traders using information and communications technology (ICT). ICT payment services provided by non-financial internet institutions have proven to play a positive role in enriching payment service methods, expanding the coverage of payment services, promoting the development of e-commerce, and even promoting competition and efficiency improvement in the financial industry, especially the banking industry. An important example of ex post facto recognition of financial technology and internet financial business is the issuance and management of the payment business license of non-financial institutions by financial regulatory authorities. In June 2010, the People's Bank of China promulgated the *Administrative Measures for Payment Services of Non-Financial Institutions*, which required that "non-financial institutions providing payment services shall obtain the payment business license in accordance with the provisions of these measures." Regarding qualifications, the policy stipulated that companies applying for the payment business license must be a "limited liability company or joint stock limited company established in accordance with the law within the territory of the People's Republic of China" and that "the business scope of foreign-invested payment institutions, the qualifications of overseas investors, the proportion of investment, etc., shall be separately stipulated by the People's Bank of China and reported to the State Council for approval." At that time, many domestic non-financial internet institutions themselves, or their parent companies, were controlled by foreign capital through VIEs registered outside China. For example, Alipay (China) Network Technology Co., Ltd., which had the largest share of domestic third-party payment services at the time, was wholly owned by overseas-registered Alipay E-commerce, which in turn was wholly owned by the Alibaba Group, and nearly 70% of Alibaba Group's shares were held by foreign capital (Wei 2019). This equity structure and governance structure arrangement caused concerns among Alipay companies, which believed that the existing payment service business faced huge policy risks, and finally chose to dismantle the agreement control to become a completely domestic company. However, in the first batch of non-financial institutions that obtained the payment business license announced by the central bank in May 2011, in addition to Alipay, some companies, such as Tenpay, which were affiliated with internet companies and maintained an agreement holding structure, were also listed. In March 2018, the central bank issued the *People's Bank of China Announcement [2018] No. 7*, which officially lifted access restrictions for foreign-invested payment institutions to conduct business in China, greatly improving the accessibility of financial technology and internet finance industries to external markets and, in fact, further strengthening the ex post facto recognition of existing internet finance businesses with large foreign investment participation.

8.2.3 Adjusting and Regulating Industry Order Will Lay Solid Foundation for Sustainable and Healthy Development of Financial Technology

In the early days of internet finance, the problems caused by industry irregularities were not obvious. However, with the rapid expansion of the industry, a series of risks and problems that accumulated in the early stage began to be exposed. For example, a large number of peer-to-peer (P2P) businesses became Ponzi schemes because the platforms promised investors too high of a return, which eventually led to the closure of a large number of platforms and the frequent occurrence of controllers running away with the money. Another example is some financing entities taking advantage of the rise of blockchain-encrypted digital currencies and raising so-called "virtual currencies", such as Bitcoin and Ethereum, from investors through the illegal issuance and circulation of tokens. For a period of time, more than 80% of the world's virtual currency transactions and initial coin offering financing took place in China (Zhang and Pan 2018). This was essentially an illegal public financing behavior via illegal issuance of token tickets, illegal issuance of securities, illegal fundraising, financial fraud, pyramid schemes, and other illegal and criminal activities. Some financial technology companies were also hiding disorderly expansion of capital, unlimited leverage, and accumulation of potential financial risks. The Ant Group's prospectus for listing on the Science and Technology Innovation Board showed that, as of June 30, 2020, the company's platform facilitated a credit balance of 2.1 trillion yuan, of which about 98% were lent or securitized by the company's financial institution partners (Ant Group 2020). The Ant Group has tied up a large number of financial institutions through large-scale and high-frequency asset securitization operations. Once its liquidity problems arise, it may evolve into systemic financial risks through inter-institutional contagion in the asset securitization market, endangering the stability of the entire financial system.

In order to prevent systemic financial risks and maintain national financial stability and the long-term development of financial technology, the Chinese government has begun to gradually standardize the supervision of the fintech industry. In September 2017, the People's Bank of China and seven other departments issued the *Announcement on Preventing the Risks of Token Issuance and Financing*, which clarified that all types of token issuance and financing activities are illegal and should be stopped immediately. In 2020, the number of P2P platforms, which exceeded 5000 at its peak, was completely cleared.[20] At the end of 2020, the Central Political Bureau meeting and the Central Economic Work Conference proposed for the first time "strengthening anti-monopoly and preventing disorderly expansion of capital" and that "financial innovation must be carried out under the premise of prudent supervision." In April 2021, financial management departments of multiple countries jointly interviewed the Ant Group and put forward rectification requirements for the Ant Group in five key business areas. All its financial activities were included in the scope of financial supervision. The People's Bank of China and other financial regulatory authorities have made it clear that future supervision of financial technology platform companies will adhere to the principle of "finance-based, technology-enabled", serve the real economy and prevent financial risks, severely investigate and punish illegal business operations in accordance with the law, insist on incorporating all financial activities into financial supervision and on financial business operating with a license, adhere to the balance of development and regulation, strengthen supervision in accordance with the law, regulate market order, prevent market monopoly, protect data property rights and personal privacy, grasp the development laws of the platform economy, improve the financial service experience, and consolidate and enhance the international competitiveness of platform companies.

We sorted out and analyzed the main policy documents and major events of domestic fintech industry supervision since the Third Plenary Session of the 18th Central Committee of the Communist Party of China in 2013 proposed to develop inclusive finance, encourage financial innovation, and enrich the levels and products of the financial market. It can be seen that in the early stage of fintech development, the Chinese government was willing to take an inclusive attitude towards the trial-and-error development of financial technology. This inclusive supervision has continuously improved the accessibility of the financial market and promoted the large-scale integration of various technology companies into the financial market. With the development of the industry, the regulatory policies on financial technology have gradually become standardized, from loose to strict, with the regulatory thinking and context becoming clearer and clearer and attention being paid to achieving a balance between promoting the development of financial technology and preventing financial risks. Moderate, reasonable, and standardized supervision can eliminate the drawbacks of industry development, ensure that financial technology companies operate legally and in compliance with regulations, ensure that risks are controllable, maintain the accessibility of the market, and create an open, inclusive, and safe ecological environment for financial technology. Standardized

[20] On the afternoon of January 15, 2021, the State Council Information Office held a press conference. At the press conference, Chen Yulu, Deputy Governor of the People's Bank of China, said that the battle to prevent and resolve financial risks in 2020 had achieved important phased results and all P2P platforms had been cleared.

supervision can also promote fair and orderly competition, encourage technological innovation and efficiency improvement, and achieve the goals of promoting the healthy development of financial technology and improving the level of development of the financial industry.

8.3 Positive Interaction Between Development of Financial Technology and Unilateral and Unbiased Political Governance

8.3.1 Fintech Makes Inclusive Finance a Reality and Improves Cohesion of Political Governance

Compared with developed countries, the development of China's financial industry was relatively backward. For example, the financial system had long been dominated by traditional large state-owned commercial banks, lacking sufficient openness and competition both internally and externally. The state's control over interest rates had not yet been completely relaxed. The backwardness of the credit reporting system led to a heavy reliance on asset mortgages for credit creation. In addition, traditional large state-owned commercial banks naturally preferred asset-heavy and large-scale customers and had a strong rejection towards small and microenterprises and emerging retail businesses, the credit risks of which were difficult to identify due to the lack of collateral. The problem of financing difficulties and high financing costs for SMEs were not solved for a long time. Traditional financial institutions either could not cover, or were unwilling to serve, those in remote areas, the low-income group, and many small and micro enterprises, and hence it was difficult for these groups to obtain basic financial services. These problems were unacceptable from both the perspectives of financial ethics and common prosperity. In 2005, the construction of an inclusive financial system was officially put on the international agenda,[21] requiring each country to "provide appropriate and effective financial services at affordable costs to all social classes and groups with financial service needs based on the requirements of equal opportunities and the principle of commercial sustainability."[22]

From the above definition, inclusive finance includes at least the following four aspects. The first is availability from the demand side. From the perspective of financial ethics, everyone has the right to obtain financial services. The words "based on requirements equal opportunities" and "all social classes and groups"

[21] In 2005, the United Nations mobilized many experts to draft a blue paper on inclusive financial systems through online surveys, expert interviews, conference discussions, etc, and held a global launch conference on building an inclusive financial system in Geneva in May of that year.

[22] This is the official definition of inclusive finance given by the United Nations in its 2006 publication, "Building an Inclusive Financial System for Development".

reflect the requirements of inclusive financial availability. The second aspect is sustainability from the supply side. Inclusive finance is essentially finance, not financial poverty alleviation. Only when the supply side gets a certain return can the availability of financial services be sustainable. From this perspective, sustainability and availability complement each other, and the words "principle of commercial sustainability" in the definition reflect this. The third is appropriate financial services. This requirement means that in addition to providing credit financial services, it is also necessary to provide various types and multi-level financial services, such as insurance services, remittance settlement services, etc. Finally, the fourth aspect is that on the basis of satisfying all the above contents, financial efficiency is further considered, which is expressed as "effective financial services" in the definition.

Judging from the above requirements, it is not easy to build an inclusive financial system in a country like China, with its vast territory and great regional differences. For a long time after the United Nations officially proposed this concept, China made little progress in building an inclusive financial system, even though the *Decision of the Central Committee of the Communist Party of China on Several Major Issues Concerning Comprehensively Deepening Reforms* adopted at the Third Plenary Session of the 18th Central Committee of the Communist Party of China in 2013 clearly proposed for the first time to the goal to "develop inclusive finance". What really made China's inclusive finance develop rapidly was the rapid development of financial technology in recent years, especially the development of mobile payments and the emergence of online loan platforms.

Fintech has some unique advantages that traditional finance does not have. It can enable financial service demand entities to enjoy multi-level financial services in a more convenient, efficient, and low-cost mode. These unique advantages are mainly reflected in the following three aspects. First, fintech promotes financial services that can cover long-tail customers and reduce the average cost of financial services. Since it is based on internet technology, fintech makes financial services more information-based, networked, and mobile, which greatly improves the availability of financial services, especially to those in remote areas or the low-income group. As the customer scale expands, the average cost of providing financial services is also greatly reduced. For example, the popularity of smart terminals has made mobile payments ubiquitous, greatly enhancing the accessibility of payment services, and the emergence of online loan platforms has greatly expanded the regional scope of traditional credit. Not only that, smart terminals have also changed the traditional model of account opening, making remote account opening possible. The second aspect is that fintech reconstructs data processing methods and improves the risk control capabilities of financial institutions. Internet-based transaction data, social data, and behavioral data can greatly enrich the data foundation of financial institutions and make customer portraits more accurate. Credit investigation based on behavioral data also provides financial institutions with new risk management methods. The third aspect is that financial technology can greatly enhance customer "stickiness" by optimizing user experience. For example, the popularity of mobile terminals allows users to enjoy online financial services without leaving their homes. The improvement of massive information and computing power provides financial institutions with the possibility of conducting precision marketing, further improving customer loyalty.

In general, the rapid development of financial technology has made inclusive finance a reality, enabling "everyone to enjoy timely, dignified, convenient, high-quality financial services of all types at an appropriate price when they need it",[23] especially for meeting the financial service needs of low-income people, residents in remote areas, farmers, and many small and microenterprises, which are groups that traditional financial institutions cannot cover or are unwilling to serve. In addition, financial technology has enriched the types of financial services, reduced the cost of obtaining financial services, and significantly improved these groups' sense of identity and gain in the party's policies, effectively improving the cohesion of political governance.

8.3.2 Emphasis on Financial Technology in Political Decision-Making Fully Reflects Tolerance of New Technologies

Since financial technology is an emerging technology with an important strategic position, the party and the government have paid full attention to financial technology since its early development. In the process of formulating development strategies, the state has conducted long-term and continuous research on financial technology to fully grasp its development trends, opportunities, and challenges and to gradually form a comprehensive and scientific understanding of financial technology. In this process, the state has established a close communication and contact mechanism with financial technology companies. For example, research think tanks, colleges, universities, and government research institutes at all levels have established research cooperation mechanisms with some leading financial technology companies to timely and fully understand the development trends and policy demands in the field of financial technology, as well as submitting research reports to governments at all levels and the relevant departments to provide decision-making references for the formulation of national and local development strategies and related policies. For example, at the press conference on Financial Reform and Development held by the central bank on March 10, 2017, Zhou Xiaochuan, the governor of the People's Bank of China, said that "the People's Bank of China highly encourages and also cooperates with various industries to promote the development of financial technology." In May 2017, the People's Bank of China formally established the Financial Technology Committee to strengthen the research planning and overall coordination of financial technology work. In August 2019, the People's Bank of China issued the *Financial Technology (FinTech) Development*

[23] This was a reference made to the definition of inclusive finance given by Zhou Xiaochuan when he talked about deepening financial system reform on November 25, 2015.

Plan (2019–2021) to give full play to the enabling role of financial technology; promote the high-quality development of China's financial industry; establish and improve the "four beams and eight pillars" of China's financial technology development by 2021; further enhance the financial industry's technology application capabilities; achieve deep integration and coordinated development of finance and technology; significantly enhance the people's satisfaction with digital, networked, and intelligent financial products and services; and promote China's fintech development to be at the international leading level so as to achieve advanced and controllable financial technology applications, steadily enhance financial service capabilities, significantly improve financial risk control levels, continuously improve financial regulatory efficiency, continuously improve financial technology support, and prosper the fintech industry. In this sense, the national economic decision-making process is actively open to emerging economic technologies, such as financial technology.

In addition to being open to fintech during the research and preparation of the political decision-making process, the party and the government also maintain an open and welcoming attitude towards the direct political participation of corporate representatives from the field of fintech. For example, fintech entrepreneurs have been nominated as deputies to the National People's Congress or recommended as members of the Chinese People's Political Consultative Conference, the Communist Party of China, democratic parties, the Youth League, the Federation of Industry and Commerce, etc., due to their outstanding social contributions, and they have even been recommended to hold positions in various mass organizations with a close relationship with the governments at all levels. Some entrepreneurs have been awarded honorary titles or political commendations, such as "Outstanding Entrepreneur" and "Reform Pioneer", by the central government or the local governments. These social positions, political honors, and political treatments enable the entrepreneurs to exercise political rights, such as the right to vote and the right to make suggestions on behalf of the entire industry in the country's political journey and to express their own interests legally, smoothly, and efficiently within the existing political governance framework. Objectively, the process of representative entrepreneurs exercising their political rights can enable emerging industries, such as fintech, to obtain appropriate policy support and inclination in the allocation of national strategic resources, which is conducive to uniting and absorbing new interest groups that have grown up in emerging technologies and industries into the existing political governance framework, reducing the possibility of conflicts of interest, maintaining political stability, and improving the cohesion of governance.

In general, China's political decision-making process is pragmatic and inclusive to emerging economic issues, which fundamentally ensures that the CPC can always represent the fundamental interests of the vast majority of the people, consolidates the ruling foundation of the CPC, promotes effective information exchange and benign interaction among various interest groups in society, improves the efficiency of political decision-making and execution, and truly realizes multi-party participation and democratic decision-making in the political decision-making process. This is an important guarantee for China's political governance to be able to adhere to and accommodate emerging new interest groups during drastic economic structural changes and maintain single-peak unbiased political governance under the leadership of the CPC.

8.3.3 State Keeps Pace with the Times and Explores Use of Financial Technology

In the rapid development of financial technology supported by new technologies, such as the internet, big data, cloud computing, artificial intelligence, biometrics, and blockchain, in addition to enterprises exploring innovation in full swing, Chinese government agencies have also begun to take more and more actions. For example, in recent years, China's monetary management department has made very active explorations in the application of blockchain technology to issue digital currencies.

As early as 2014, the People's Bank of China proposed the idea of building a digital currency and set up a special team to conduct special research on digital currency, including the issuance framework, key technologies, issuance and circulation environment, and related international experiences. In 2017, the People's Bank of China officially established the Digital Currency Research Institute of the Central Bank, the world's earliest official institution dedicated to the research and development of the digital RMB system, with the aim to create a new type of RMB in digital form to meet the public's cash needs in a digital economy and to create a reliable, stable, fast, and efficient system with continuous innovation and open competition in the retail payment field. Financial infrastructure was built to support the development of China's digital economy, improve the level of inclusive financial development, and improve the efficiency of the currency and payment system. At the end of 2019, the digital RMB system started pilot testing in Shenzhen, Suzhou, Xiongan New Area, Chengdu, and the future Winter Olympics scene. In October 2020, six more pilot test areas were added: Shanghai, Hainan, Changsha, Xi'an, Qingdao, and Dalian.

Blockchain technology, in addition to its application in the issuance and use of digital currency, can be applied to many typical scenarios and fields in the financial field, such as payment, digital assets, bills, clearing and settlement, securities, credit, supply chain finance, etc. These financial transaction processes generally face frequent and large amounts of information transmission and value transfer. With the help of blockchain technology, through a decentralized and trusted transaction network, the processes can be simplified and shortened. In addition, data immutability and traceability of blockchain technology can provide an important technical foundation for regulatory authorities to build appropriate regulatory tools, which is helpful for protecting the rights and interests of financial consumers and preventing the accumulation and outbreak of risks. Especially in areas where finance is relatively lacking, this promotes the development of protection work. In 2018, the

China Electronics Standardization Institute, under the guidance of the Ministry of Industry and Information Technology, compiled the *China Blockchain Technology and Application Development White Paper*, a result of a special joint study with a number of financial technology companies on the development trend of blockchain technology and applications. The white paper points out that blockchain technology has the potential to reconstruct the financial industry's infrastructure due to its high reliability, simplified processes, traceable transactions, cost savings, reduced errors, and improved data quality.

The exploration of China's monetary management department and financial regulatory department in applying blockchain technology fully reflects the state's recognition and embrace of emerging technologies and fully demonstrates the cohesion, tolerance, and open absorption of emerging technologies by China's political governance system. This will not only help consolidate the market's recognition of emerging technologies but also be conducive to the further development of emerging technologies.

8.4 Chapter Summary

Over the past 40 years of reform and opening up, China's rapid and sustained development has benefited greatly from the consistent maintenance of cohesive single-peak unbiased political governance and the continuous improvement of economic accessibility, which is what the country should continue to adhere to in the future. However, it must be admitted that new technologies and interest groups will continue to emerge in the process of economic and social development. If the economy cannot be open to them and politics cannot be inclusive of them, China's political governance system and economic system will be at risk of rigidification or degeneration. From the review and analysis of the attitude and practices of the Chinese government towards the emergence of financial technology, it can be seen that improving China's open and accessible economic system is not a one-time solution. This chapter takes the development of the fintech industry as an example to analyze the Chinese government's methods of maintaining cohesive political governance and economic accessibility.

In terms of improving the accessibility of an economy when it comes to emerging technologies, at least the following three tasks can be started. First, a government should build on a large scale the infrastructure necessary for the development of emerging technologies (for example, the telecommunications network for financial technology), which not only can provide the basic environment for production and operation on the supply side of emerging technologies but also, on the demand side, meet the actual demand from emerging technologies. The improvement of market accessibility can also bring about economies of scale and further promote the development of emerging technologies. Second, a government can adopt inclusive supervision and ex post facto recognition for emerging technologies. In the early stages of development, emerging technologies often face multiple paths and multiple models. During this time, supervision that is too strict will compress the "trial-and-error space" of emerging technologies and be detrimental to their development. The Chinese government has always maintained a highly open and inclusive attitude towards emerging technologies, giving them a relaxed regulatory environment. Under the premise of no major risks, it allows new technologies, new models, and new formats to enter the market freely. In addition, it keeps close track of problems that arise in the development of emerging technologies and ex post facto recognizes successfully tried technologies and models and their development results. Third, as emerging technologies grow, a government should take reasonable policy measures in a timely manner, formulate appropriate rules, regulate market order, and maintain high market accessibility. For example, first-mover companies in the development of emerging technologies will use their market advantages to exclude peers and seek industry monopoly. This monopoly behavior will greatly reduce the openness and competitiveness of the market and thus harm the long-term development of emerging technologies. The government needs to take appropriate regulatory measures at this time, including anti-monopoly and anti-unfair competition, to maintain market accessibility.

In terms of maintaining the cohesion of political governance, the following three tasks can be started. First, a government should attach great importance to emerging technologies and industries that represent the development direction of advanced productive forces; it should support the development of emerging technologies and improve the recognition and sense of gain of its target groups on state policies, thereby improving the cohesion of political governance. Second, the political decision-making process should focus on openness to emerging technologies, including conducting research, listening to opinions and interests from all sides, and forming a scientific and comprehensive understanding of emerging technologies, as well as actively absorbing representative entrepreneurs and relevant interest groups to create opportunities for them to participate in politics and even directly participate in the national political decision-making process. Third, while encouraging and supporting the exploration and development of emerging technologies based on market principles, a government can also actively carry out the applications of new technologies and new innovations in public affairs and public services, which will not only help consolidate the market's recognition of emerging technologies but also help the political governance system to be cohesive, inclusive, and open to emerging technologies.

References

Ant Group (2020) Ant technology group Co, Ltd. initial public offering and listing on the science and technology innovation board prospectus (application draft). Shanghai Stock Exchange

Financial Stability Board (2016) Fintech: describing the landscape and a framework for analysis. Unpublished Working Paper

Human Creation Consulting (2017) https://mp.weixin.qq.com/s/8pLUDicXGiNyx_sNRC8VA

Human Creation Consulting (2018) https://mp.weixin.qq.com/s/xZ6okC2RuOqm7TpJyYkqWg

Wei X (2019) Alipay split. https://www.sohu.com/a/304675235_100023184
Xie P, Zhou CW (eds) (2017) Fintech: decoding the fusion of finance and technology. China Financial Publishing House, Beijing
Zhang QS, Pan GS (2018) Internet finance or financial technology should be subject to stricter supervision. Shanghai Securities News

Chapter 9
Economic Development and Performance of Countries Under A-C Theory

As mentioned, the main purpose of our A-C theory is to explain the course of China's economic development and to try to find the deeper common factors behind the different development models of China, developed Western countries, and developing countries. In this chapter, we used the A-C theory to provide a new perspective on the development type and performance of the global economy. First, we constructed a series of indicators for the A-C theory and grouped countries based on their political cohesion and economic accessibility in order to have an overall understanding of the position of each country under the framework of the theory. Then, we used the historical data of the countries and adopted some econometric methods to empirically test the core conclusions of the A-C theory.

9.1 Portraits of Countries Around the World Under Framework of A-C Theory

Taking into account the availability and completeness of data, we selected basic data from 209 countries and regions from 1996 to 2018 and constructed the political cohesion index and economic accessibility index of each country by year (see Appendix A for details on the construction method). On this basis, we examined the distribution of the countries under the framework of the A-C theory, as well as the evolution of the distribution over time.

Based on the logic of Fig. 1.1 in Chap. 1, we established a two-dimensional space consisting of two indicators, which are political cohesion and economic accessibility, namely the A-C space. Since the indicators are standardized when constructed, the A-C space is a finite two-dimensional 5×5 space. In addition,

C. Chen et al., *From Poverty to Prosperity*, Understanding China,
https://doi.org/10.1007/978-981-95-7171-0_9

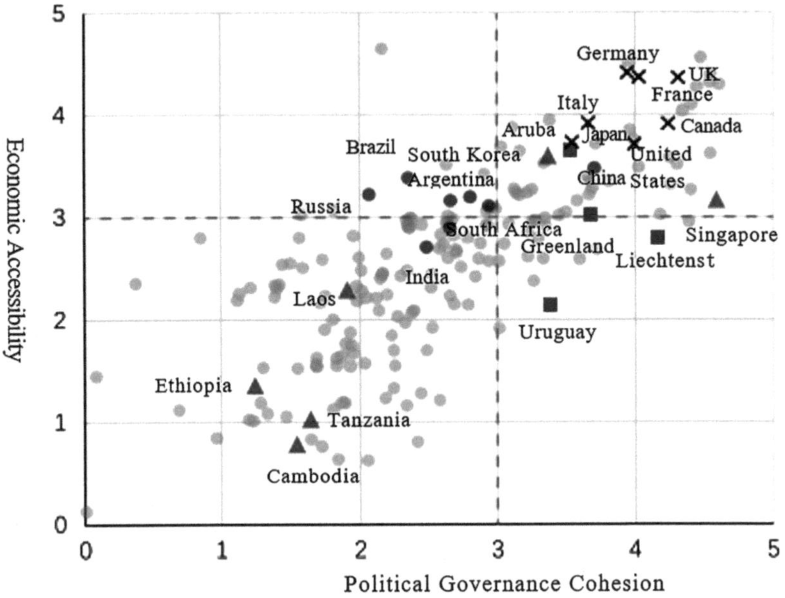

Fig. 9.1 Distribution of countries and regions in A-C space in 1996

based on the "passing value"[1] of the horizontal and vertical axes, the space is divided into four quadrants, as corresponding to Fig. 1.1. Based on the specific indicator's value of a country in a certain year, we determined the country's position in the A-C space. Figures 9.1, 9.2, and 9.3 show the distribution of the selected countries and regions in this two-dimensional space in three representative years, which are 1996, 2006, and 2018, respectively.

Generally speaking, developed countries, represented by G7 countries or OECD countries, have always been in the quadrant of high political cohesion and high economic accessibility, and both their GDP per capita and GDP growth rate are significantly higher than those of other quadrant; while least-developed economies, represented by most countries, have been in the quadrant of low political cohesion and low economic accessibility for a long time.

From the development process of the past two decades, although the number of countries in the quadrant of high political cohesion and high economic accessibility

[1] From the perspective of the development stage (GDP per capita level) of each economy and the dynamic evolution of the three indicators of economic accessibility and political cohesion, when economic accessibility and political cohesion reach the value of 3, their contribution to economic growth changes significantly. For details, please refer to the regression analysis results. From the characteristics of the distribution in 2018, the third quintile (i.e., 60%) of economic accessibility and political cohesion are both around 3. From a direct perspective, we might as well regard the value of 3 as the "passing value" of the two dimensions. Therefore, when dividing the A-C space, we use the "passing value" of the two dimensions of economic accessibility and political cohesion as the benchmark, i.e., the value of 3 on the horizontal and vertical axes.

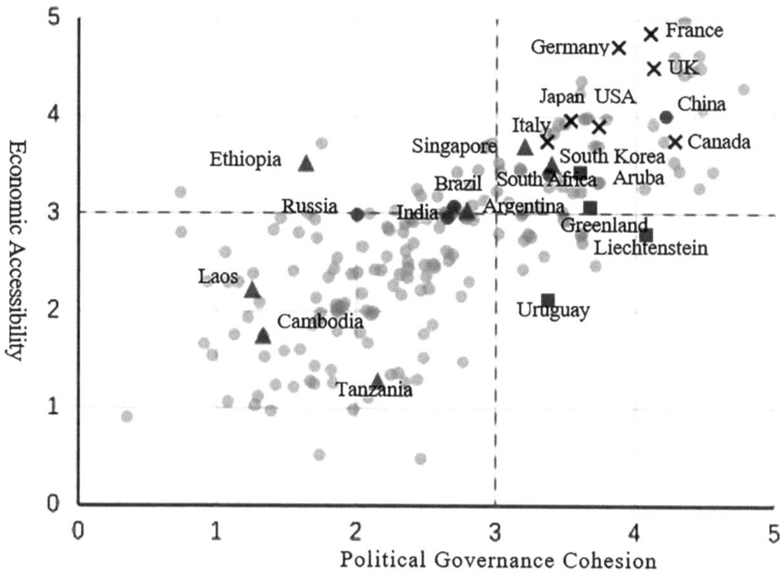

Fig. 9.2 Distribution of countries and regions in A-C space in 2006

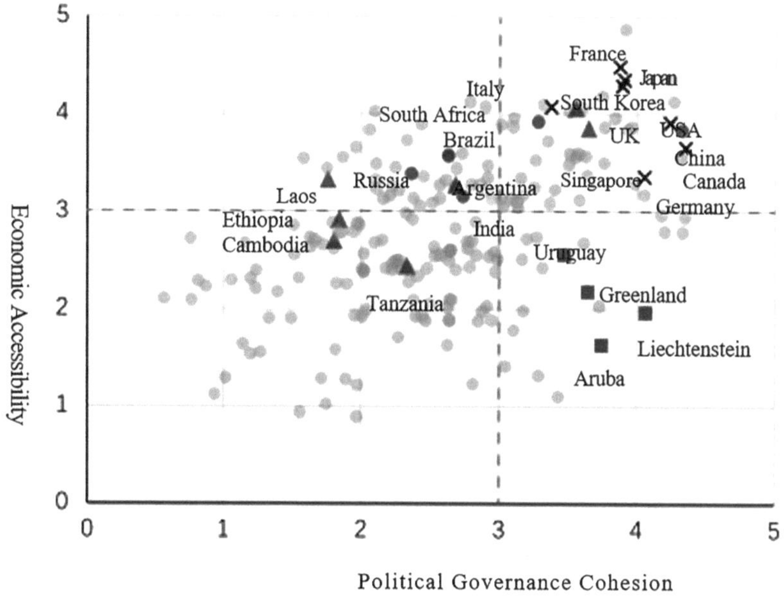

Fig. 9.3 Distribution of countries and regions in A-C space in 2018

is relatively stable, many countries have experienced changes in one or even both dimensions. For example, China's economic accessibility index improved significantly from 1996 to 2006, and the improvement in China's political cohesion index from 2006 to 2018 is even more obvious. On the contrary, the political cohesion index of developed countries, such as the United Kingdom and France, declined significantly from 2006 to 2018. Russia's political cohesion index also declined significantly from 1996 to 2006, even degenerating from the quadrant of high political cohesion and high economic accessibility to the quadrant of low political cohesion and high economic accessibility. In addition, many countries in the quadrant of low political cohesion and low economic accessibility also achieved improvements in one or even both dimensions. For example, the economic accessibility index of least-developed countries, such as Ethiopia, Tanzania, Laos, and Cambodia, experienced a significant increase in the past two decades. It can be seen that a country also has the possibility of not advancing, or even regressing, in terms of political cohesion or economic accessibility. The possibility of such degeneration is greater in countries with low political cohesion or low economic accessibility.

By introducing economic growth, we further examined the relationship between political cohesion, economic accessibility, and economic growth. As shown in Table 9.1, the economic growth rates of countries and regions in the quadrant of high political cohesion and high economic accessibility are generally higher than those in other quadrants, while the economic growth rates of countries and regions in the quadrant of low political cohesion and low economic accessibility are generally lower than those in other quadrants.

In addition, there is also a clear correlation between a country's political cohesion and economic accessibility. We set countries with below-average and above-average political cohesion index scores as control groups for difference-in-difference regression, and we found that the improvement of political cohesion improved economic accessibility. The result is shown in Table 9.2. We adopted the same strategy to test the potential causal effect of accessibility on political cohesion, but as shown in Table 9.3, the difference-in-difference regression result did not support this causal relationship.

We also studied the causal relationship between economic accessibility and political cohesion by controlling the development stage, the result of which is shown in Table 9.4. It is worth noting that for GDP per capita less than US $4000 or exceeding US $12,000, there is no significant causal relationship between the two indicators. However, for GDP per capita in the US $4000–12,000 range, the causal relationship between the two indicators is significant. For GDP per capita within US $8000–12,000, both directions of causality are very significant.

Table 9.1 Overall distribution of countries and regions in A-C space in three representative years

Distribution	Variables	1996	2006	2018
High political cohesion, high economic accessibility (Quadrant 1)	Mean of economic accessibility index	3.38	3.39	3.42
	Mean of political cohesion index	3.39	3.59	3.48
	Median GDP per capita (US$)	28,787	32,352	30,036
	Median GDP per capita growth rate	3.06%	4.23%	2.77%
	Number of countries	74	65	71
High political cohesion, low economic accessibility (Quadrant 2)	Mean of economic accessibility index	1.58	1.55	1.70
	Mean of political cohesion index	3.27	3.28	3.26
	Median GDP per capita (US$)	4303	8177	12715
	Median GDP per capita growth rate	4.27%	5.04%	2.26%
	Number of countries	59	62	63
Low political cohesion, low economic accessibility (Quadrant 3)	Mean of economic accessibility index	1.34	1.31	1.51
	Mean of political cohesion index	1.73	1.83	1.65
	Median GDP per capita (US$)	3532	3084	3463
	Median GDP per capita growth rate	1.55%	3.24%	1.27%
	Number of countries	49	62	45
Low political cohesion, high economic accessibility (Quadrant 4)	Mean of economic accessibility index	3.10	3.13	3.08
	Mean of political cohesion index	1.82	2.03	1.89
	Median GDP per capita (US$)	12,592	17,810	18,087
	Median GDP per capita growth rate	4.21%	3.64%	2.03%
	Number of countries	27	20	30

Note: (1) The currency unit of GDP per capita is the constant price of 2017 US dollars. The median of GDP per capita and the median of GDP per capita growth rate are the medians of a country in each quadrant. (2) Due to the lack of data of individual countries and regions in earlier years, the numbers of the countries in the three representative years are not the same

Table 9.2 Impact of political cohesion on economic accessibility

Variables		Economic accessibility	Standard deviation	t	$P > t$
(1)	Control (C)	−35.052			
	Test (T)	−33.658			
	(T–C)	1.394	9.538	0.15	0.884
(2)	Control (C)	−35.033			
	Test (T)	−33.640			
	(T–C)	−1.393	9.533	0.15	0.884
Difference in difference		−0.000	0.005	−0.10	0.921

Note: Means and standard deviations were estimated based on linear regression

Table 9.3 Impact of economic accessibility on political cohesion

Variables		Political cohesion	Standard deviation	t	$P > t$
(1)	Control (C)	−4.498			
	Test (T)	8.241			
	(T–C)	12.739	7.736	1.65	0.100*
(2)	Control (C)	−4.494			
	Test (T)	−29.956			
	(T–C)	−8.239	7.732	1.65	0.100*
Difference in difference		12.733	0.004	−1.61	0.107

Note: (1) Means and standard deviations were estimated based on linear regression. (2) * represents $p < 0.1$

Table 9.4 Causal relationship between economic accessibility and political cohesion

GDP per capita by development stage	Economic accessibility as a factor	Political cohesion as a factor
Stage 1: US $0–4000	0.131	0.779
Stage 2: US $4000–8000	0.018*	0.1*
Stage 3: US $8000–12,000	0.007**	0.008***
Stage 4: US $12,000–16,000	0.438	0.821

Note: (1) Means and standard deviations were estimated based on linear regression. (2) * represents $p < 0.1$, ** represents $p < 0.05$, and *** represents $p < 0.01$

9.2 Empirical Test of Core Conclusions of A-C Theory

Combining the above observations and the summary of the core ideas of the A-C theory in Chap. 1, we put forward the core conclusions of the A-C theory in the form of three theoretical conjectures in order to conduct empirical tests using data from countries around the world:

Hypothesis 1 Improving the cohesion of political governance can promote economic growth.

Hypothesis 2 Improving economic accessibility can promote economic growth.

Hypothesis 3 Single-peak governance and multi-peak governance are neutral for a country's economic growth.

9.2.1 *Setting of Econometric Model*

Based on the above discussion on indicator construction and data, we used a dynamic panel model to test these three theoretical conjectures. The specific settings of the model are as follows:

$$y_{it} = \alpha + \beta X_{it} + \gamma Z_{it} + u_{it} \tag{9.1}$$

where, for i-th country in year t:

y_{it} is the growth rate of GDP per capita (constant price, local currency)
X_{it} is the vector of explanatory variables (x_{1it}, x_{2it}, x_{3it}, x_{4it})
x_{1it} is the economic accessibility index
x_{2it} is the political governance index
x_{3it} is the political concentration index
x_{4it} is the development stage
Z_{it} is control variables, including lag terms, population, area, etc.
β is the coefficient vector of X_{it} (β_1, β_2, β_3, β_4)
γ is the coefficient vector before Z_{it}
u_{it} is the error term of the model

Since our data were standardized, the coefficient estimates did not say anything about the relative importance of the explanatory variables; we were more concerned with the sign (positive or negative) of these coefficients. If the conjecture proposed above is true, then model parameters β_1 and β_2 should both be positive, while model parameter β_3 is not significantly different from 0. Furthermore, based on the relevant literature in development economics, we expected β_4 to be negative; that is, economies at higher stages of development will have lower economic growth rates.

9.2.2 Estimation Result of Econometric Model Based on Panel Data

Taking into account the panel characteristics of the data structure and the autoregressive characteristics of economic growth, we estimated random-effect and fixed-effect models with different lag terms of y_{it} and conducted a Hausman test on the two models. The result shows that there are significant systematic differences between the coefficients, as shown in Table 9.5, and the systematic differences are robust to model specifications with different numbers of lag terms and control variables. Therefore, we mainly used the fixed-effect model to test the core conclusions of the A-C theory.

From the three fixed-effect model settings in Table 9.5, which are FE (1), FE (2), and FE (3), we can see that the coefficients of the economic accessibility and political cohesion indexes are significantly positive, indicating that Conjecture 1 and Conjecture 2 are statistically supported; in addition, the insignificant coefficient before the political concentration index means that we cannot reject Conjecture 3. Furthermore, the coefficient of the development stage is significantly negative, which confirms that economies at higher stages of development grow at lower rates.

Table 9.5 Estimation result of random-effect model and fixed-effect model

Variable	GDP per capita growth rate (y_{it})					
	FE (1)	RE(1)	FE (2)	RE (2)	FE (3)	RE (3)
Economic accessibility	0.952*** (3.28)	0.25*** (2.23)	0.85*** (2.86)	0.208* (1.76)	0.928*** (3.08)	0.213* (1.79)
Political cohesion	1.444*** (3.46)	−0.075 −0.61	1.584*** (3.57)	−0.021 −0.17	1.617*** (3.44)	0.002 −0.02
Political concentration	−0.165 −1.31	−0.076 −1.04	−0.156 −1.18	−0.061 −0.82	0.008 −0.06	−0.041 −0.55
Economic development stage	−1.123*** (5.26)	−0.219*** (3.82)	−1.079*** (4.72)	−0.242*** (4.12)	−0.989*** (4.06)	−0.247*** (4.15)
y_{it-1}	0.238*** (14.80)	0.389*** (26.44)	0.225*** (13.18)	0.339*** (20.60)	0.221*** (12.74)	0.336*** (20.01)
y_{it-2}			−0.02 −1.19	0.083*** (5.14)	−0.04*** (2.32)	0.038** (2.18)
y_{it-3}					0.006 −0.37	0.1*** (6.22)
Constant term	−1.238 −0.95	1.731*** (6.64)	−1.422 −1.03	1.621*** (6.05)	−2.287 −1.58	1.405*** (5.16)
Sample size	3772	3772	3555	3555	3341	3341
Hausman test	Significant systematic differences		Significant systematic differences		Significant systematic differences	

Note: (1) Considering that outliers in the GDP per capita growth rate may have a significant impact on the regression results, we only retained countries with a GDP per capita growth rate of between −20 and 50% for regression analysis. (2) The number in the bracket is the standard deviation of the estimate. (3) * represents $p < 0.1$, ** represents $p < 0.05$, and *** represents $p < 0.01$. (4) RE corresponds to random effects, and FE corresponds to fixed effects

9.2.3 Robustness Test

Next, we conducted a test to verify the robustness of the baseline model's results. First, we tested the robustness of the model by adding control variables, which were population (which represents a country's basic resources), area (which can approximately represent a country's or region's natural resources), and GDP per capita (which represents the size of the economy). Numerically, there is no significant change in the regression result, especially the sign of the correlation coefficient. Furthermore, when we replaced either the variable of area or population with the variable of area per capita, we also found no significant changes. Due to space limitations, relevant result details are not reported here.

Secondly, we studied the interaction between the core variables and the stage of economic development, focusing on the interaction between unimodal and multimodal governance models, political cohesion, and economic accessibility at different stages of economic development. As shown in Table 9.6, the relationship between the impact of economic accessibility on economic growth and the stage of economic development is not significant; in other words, regardless of the development stage of an economy, the impact of economic accessibility on economic growth is not significant, i.e., the importance is the same. In contrast, as the stage of economic development increases, political cohesion seems to play an increasingly important role. However, there is no significant interaction between indicators of political concentration and the stage of economic development; the effect of political concentration on economic growth appears to be neutral in countries at any stage of economic development.

Third, since the sample covered a period of more than 20 years during exactly the period of rapid economic growth in China, China's influence on the entire sample could inevitably be questioned. Therefore, we specifically removed China's data from the sample and repeated the robustness test. As shown in Table 9.6, the regression result is almost unchanged after China's data were removed.

9.3 Chapter Summary

Based on the theoretical model, we put forward three theoretical conjectures: (1) the improvement of political cohesion can promote economic growth; (2) the improvement of economic accessibility can promote economic growth; and (3) unimodal governance and multimodal governance are neutral to a country's economic growth. Based on the panel data of 209 economies from 1996 to 2018, we conducted an empirical test on these three conjectures. The regression result shows that the coefficient of economic accessibility is significantly positive, which supports Conjecture 1, that is, the improvement of economic accessibility helps to promote economic growth; in addition, the coefficient of political cohesion is also significantly positive, which supports Conjecture 2, that is, political governance that is more cohesive

Table 9.6 Result of robustness test

Variable	GDP per capita growth (y_{it})								
	Interaction between core variables and stage of economic development					Sample with China's data removed			
	FE (1)	FE (2)	FE (3)	FE (4)	FE (5)	FE (6)	FE (7)	FE (8	FE (9)
Economic accessibility	0.952*** (3.28)	0.728 −1.57	0.952*** (3.29)	0.952*** (3.28)	1.153** (2.43)	0.715 −1.53	0.945*** (3.26)	0.947*** (3.25)	1.144** (2.40)
Political cohesion	1.444*** (3.46)	1.451*** (3.48)	−0.212 −0.37	1.445*** (3.46)	−0.363 −0.61	1.458*** (3.49)	−0.207 −0.36	1.452*** (3.47)	−0.355 −0.6
Political concentration	−0.165 −1.31	−0.162 −1.28	−0.131 −1.04	−0.146 −0.72	0.044 −0.21	−0.162 −1.28	−0.132 −1.04	−0.144 −0.71	0.043 −0.2
Economic development stage	−1.123*** (5.26)	−1.38*** (2.91)	−2.71*** (6.26)	−1.097*** (3.55)	−2.373*** (4.20)	−1.393*** (2.92)	−2.714*** (6.23)	−1.092*** (3.49)	−2.38*** (4.20)
y_{it-1}	0.238*** (14.80)	0.238*** (14.81)	0.233*** (14.49)	0.238*** (14.80)	0.232*** (14.41)	0.238*** (14.75)	0.233*** (14.43)	0.238*** (14.73)	0.232*** (14.35)
Economic accessibility × economic development stage		0.091 −0.62			−0.084 −0.55	0.095 −0.64			−0.083 −0.53
Political cohesion × economic development stage			0.684*** (4.21)		0.749*** (4.34)		0.685*** (4.20)		0.749*** (4.32)
Political concentration × economic development stage				−0.012 −0.12	−0.107 −1.07			−0.013 −0.13	−0.106 −1.06
Constant term	−1.238 −0.95	−0.708 −0.45	1.83 −1.23	−1.28 −0.94	1.239 −0.75	−0.717 −0.46	1.824 −1.21	−1.312 −0.96	1.236 −0.74
Sample size	3772	3772	3772	3772	3772	3753	3753	3753	3753

Note: (1) The number in bracket is the standard deviation of the estimate. (2) * represents $p < 0.1$, ** represents $p < 0.05$, and *** represents $p < 0.01$. (3) FE corresponds to fixed effects is more conducive to sustainable economic growth. However, the coefficient of the political concentration index is not significant, which indicates that Conjecture 3 cannot be rejected, that is, a unimodal or multimodal political governance model is neutral to a country's economic growth. Our empirical result also supplements the literature on the relationship between economic growth and the stage of economic development; it can be found from the empirical result that economies at a higher stage of development showed lower economic growth rates.

For robustness testing, by introducing additional control variables to test the interaction between the core variables and the stage of economic development and replacing the original variables with sub-indicators, we obtained more accurate results. Judging from the result of the robustness test, although there are differences in the regression coefficients of the main variables, the significance of the core variables is still robust, which provides statistical support for our theoretical results.

Chapter 10
Singapore: Model of Openness and Cohesion in Asia

Singapore's economic success and political stability are regarded as a model by many developing countries. Compared with other economically developed countries, Singapore's success has attracted the world's attention because, apart from its strategic location and the port facilities built during the British colonial period to promote regional transportation and logistics, Singapore has almost no natural resources. It is a small island city-state with a small area and unsustainable industrial and domestic water. However, as shown in Fig. 10.1, the country achieved tremendous economic development achievements in a few decades and completed its economic takeoff and industrialization process in only half a century to become one of the high-income countries,[1] which established its status as one of the "Four Asian Tigers" and has maintained its sustained rapid economic growth and social stability.

Studying Singapore's development history, we can find that the two key factors for Singapore's success are completely consistent with the A–C theory. Firstly, since the independence of the Republic of Singapore, under the leadership of prime ministers from Lee Kuan Yew and Goh Chok Tong to Lee Hsien Loong, the People's Action Party (PAP) has always been in power. As the ruling party, the PAP has adopted and adhered to a set of effective policies at the political level to promote and maintain the integration and unity of multi-ethnic and multi-cultural groups and to build a single-peak, unbiased, and cohesive political governance structure, which not only ensures the long-term stability of Singaporean society but also provides the necessary political cohesion for Singapore's sustainable development. Secondly, on the basis of political stability and people's unity, the Singaporean government is highly involved in the development of the market economy. The government has built a highly open economic structure and formulated economic development strategies and plans. Under its guidance, through powerful industrial policies and development models, the internal accessibility and external accessibility of the economic

[1]According to the World Bank's WDI database, Singapore's GDP per capita was US$65,600 in 2019, ranked tenth in the world behind those of Monaco, Bermuda, Luxembourg, the Cayman Islands, Macau, China, Switzerland, Ireland, Norway, and Iceland.

C. Chen et al., *From Poverty to Prosperity*, Understanding China,
https://doi.org/10.1007/978-981-95-7171-0_10

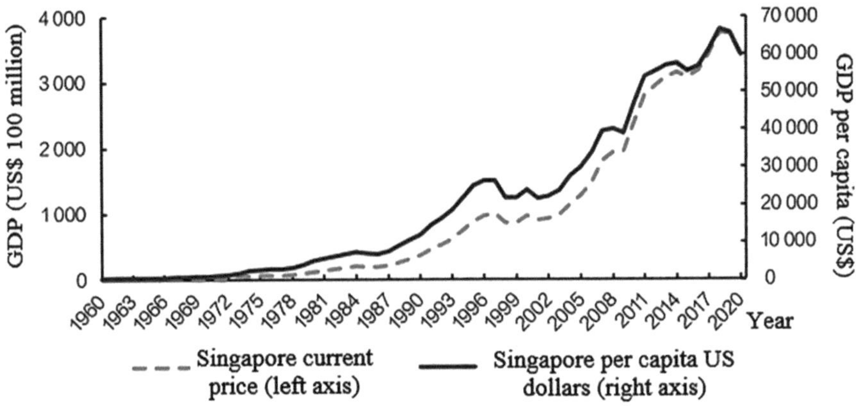

Fig. 10.1 Singapore's GDP and GDP per capita over past 60 years. *Source*: World Bank WDI database

system have been greatly expanded so that all individuals involved in economic participation can obtain economic development opportunities to the greatest extent, thereby continuously and effectively promoting the continuous development of the economy.

10.1 Phase I: Opening Up to Outside World and Integrating with Inside World

10.1.1 Government-Led Economic Development Model of Continuous Opening up to Outside World

Singapore's remarkable journey from relative poverty to remarkable prosperity began with its unplanned independence in August 1965. During this period, Singapore was abruptly forced to withdraw from the Federation of Malaysia, faced the loss of its traditional hinterland, and faced a military standoff with Indonesia due to the Malaysia-Indonesia conflict. Malaysia even tried to bypass Singapore's ports by setting up tariff barriers on Singapore's industrial products to protect the economic development projects on the peninsular mainland. This seriously threatened Singapore's traditional role as the fiscal, financial, and shipping center of the Malay Peninsula, and its economic prospects were bleak. In 1965, Singapore was a port with a stagnant economy, large slums, and an unemployment rate of more than 10%. To survive, the government had to create jobs as quickly as possible and provide people with housing, education, and other infrastructure projects. Therefore, the state needed to play an important role in creating the prerequisites for economic growth, hence prompting the adoption of effective policies to solve economic and social problems.

In the context of the time, most least-developed countries adopted import substitution policies, developing their own production capacity by establishing protective tariff barriers, implementing import restrictions, and keeping a distance from large multinational corporations. However, as a city-state, Singapore faced the most basic limitation: the lack of economic space, including natural resources and a huge domestic market. Singapore's policymakers had to solve key problems of overcoming scale limitations, expanding economic space, and achieving sustained GDP growth.

As a node in the Commonwealth's transportation, capital, and communication networks during the British colonial period, Singapore had close ties with many Commonwealth countries. As a result, the government decided to adopt a government-led export-oriented development strategy with foreign direct investment as the main body, making full use of its strategic resource advantages and its relationship with Commonwealth countries and adopting a completely open economic model: not only trading in goods and services but also the flow of capital and labor. Singapore opened its doors to foreign direct investment in the 1960s and allowed the free inflow of foreign talents in the early twenty-first century. The *Economic Growth Incentives Act of 1967* gave Singapore's Economic Development Board a "pioneer" status, with the responsibility of introducing multinational corporations to Singapore and providing foreign companies with a five-year tax reduction (extended continuously in the late 1970s), as well as sparing no effort in recruiting large foreign companies and attracting them to settle in Singapore with incentives. In this way, Singapore could obtain foreign capital, technology, and management expertise and integrate into the global production network and supply chain of multinational corporations.

In July 1968, the Economic Development Board was reorganized, and the function of providing financial support for development was transferred to the Development Bank of Singapore, which provided long-term financing services to manufacturing enterprises and invested in a large number of emerging industry enterprises that were invested and built by private capital. Then, the International Trade Company was established, which was jointly owned by the government, the Development Bank of Singapore, and private capital. In 1968, Singapore became the headquarters of the Asian dollar market. In 1969, Singapore became a gold market and quickly surpassed Hong Kong and Beirut in size. Singapore quickly grew into a financial center and capital market.

Singapore achieved great success in attracting foreign direct investment by developing an open-door model and an export-oriented development strategy, which was consistent with the practice of many countries in the 1970s to reduce production costs through cheap labor and raw materials. In these developed countries, union activities, production costs, high taxes, and competition were rising, and the business sector found that it could reap more benefits by moving production to low-cost countries. Many multinational corporations from the United States, Europe, and Japan wanted to move to countries that could provide efficient and low-cost operating environments due to rising domestic costs or the need to find new markets. Singapore thus became a regional production and distribution location favored by multinational corporations. By the end of the 1980s, Singapore received 4.6% of the world's foreign direct investment and 14.6% of the total foreign direct investment from developing countries.

In addition, the development and changes in the international situation also provided favorable conditions for Singapore's economic development. In June 1966, the Malaysia-Indonesia conflict ended, and the trade volume between Singapore and Indonesia increased. The United States gradually increased its investment in the Vietnam War, which also benefited Singapore as a major supply center. In 1967, the "Seven Days War" broke out in the Middle East and the Suez Canal was closed, which led to the prosperity of Singapore's ship repair business.

Hence, the government planned to make Singapore the second largest shipping, ship repair, and shipbuilding center in Asia after Japan. In 1968, Singapore established a local ship registry. Two years later, the government offered duty-free registration to foreign ships, established the first "Flag of Convenience" system in Asia, and established the state-owned Orient Neptune Lines. From 1966 to 1968, the volume of shipbuilding and ship repair business increased sharply. In 1969, Singapore became the busiest port in the Commonwealth.

Because Singapore had a high demand for Malaysian oil and its geographical location and facilities were well suited to the establishment of related supporting industries, capital, equipment, and professional talents poured into Singapore. By 1970, oil became Singapore's main export industry, accounting for 40% of total industrial manufactured goods. In 1973, Singapore became the world's third-largest refining center (after Houston in the United States and Rotterdam in Holland).

As a result, under the leadership of the government, Singapore entered a new stage of accelerated economic development through a series of domestic and foreign economic openings to improve economic accessibility.

10.1.2 Unimodal and Unbiased Cohesive Political Governance

The continued rule of the PAP has created a high degree of continuity in Singapore's unimodal, unbiased, cohesive political governance. Singapore has been ruled by the PAP since 1959, and for most of this period, the PAP has won all seats in regular parliamentary elections. Lee Kuan Yew led Singapore's government from the 1960s until his retirement in 1990, becoming the world's longest-serving prime minister.

The PAP government has done a good job of meeting the basic needs and aspirations of its citizens. The government under its leadership adhered to an open economic strategy, creating a large number of jobs with fairly strong economic growth, such that almost full employment was achieved in the early 1970s. In addition, a large-scale public housing construction program brought high-quality housing to the vast majority of people, and by the mid-1990s, more than 90% of Singaporeans owned their own homes. Great efforts have also been made to provide educational opportunities at the primary, secondary, vocational, and higher education levels, providing people with opportunities to move to higher social classes and thus gaining the support of the people despite the government's tough policies. The party's long-term rule has also brought stability and predictability to national policies, and its governance has long-term planning and continuity, which also helped to attract foreign investment and achieve its strategy of economic growth driven by foreign direct investment.

In addition, one of the important prerequisites for sustained economic development is social stability. In order to achieve this goal, the PAP government reached a "social contract" between the government and the people in the early days of Singapore's independence. In this contract, some civil rights are transferred to the state power. When the government conducted social governance, it followed the principle of the social contract and redistributed the transferred civil rights, thereby ensuring social stability and sustained economic development. The rapid growth of GDP laid the foundation for the PAP to provide various public services and consolidate its ruling position. The PAP government maintains an almost absolute dominant position on the political stage, and so it can continue to implement such a social contract for more than 30 years after the founding of the country, focusing on developing the domestic economy without being disturbed by other political issues.

In addition, the government relies on a strong civil service system, statutory commissions, and other state institutions to implement its policies. In general, these state institutions are based on meritocracy and fighting corruption. To minimize corruption in the public service, the government has adopted a "carrot and stick" approach. In cracking down on corruption, raising civil servants' salaries to a level comparable to private sector salaries has enabled the government to attract and retain talents and reduce the incentives for corruption.

In addition, Singapore has successively promulgated various laws and regulations, such as corporate law, foreign investment law, foreign trade law, financial law, accounting law, tax law, etc., and gradually formed a systematic legal system. By establishing and continuously improving the legal system, a harmonious environment has been created for Singapore's economic development.

10.1.3 Government Intervention in Economy and Industry

The Singaporean government intervenes in industries that it deems important but that the private sector does not have the capacity or resources to develop. For example, the government and state-owned enterprises have played an important role in developing emerging and strategic sectors of the domestic economy—banking, telecommunications, industrial estates, ports, airports, air and maritime transport, shipbuilding and repair, and defense technology.

In order to make Singapore an efficient production and distribution center for multinational corporations, the government has invested heavily in a range of infrastructures, including transportation, logistics, telecommunication systems, etc. These infrastructures are essential to maintaining Singapore's main natural competitive advantages, such as its strategic location and strong regional and global connections, improving the efficiency of the business environment, and reducing the operating costs of multinational corporations. For example, Singapore's ports and airports are consistently ranked as one of the most efficient ports in the world.

The establishment of state-owned enterprises, such as Singapore Airlines and Neptune Lines, promoted Singapore's international connectivity and trade links. The government also established the Development Bank of Singapore (now DBS Bank) and the Post Office Savings Bank of Singapore to mobilize large amounts of savings through deposit activities to provide financing for Singapore's early development, especially the construction of productive projects.

10.1.4 Gradual Opening Up of Standardized Labor Policies

At the beginning of Singapore's independence, labor was its only "natural resource", but for a long time, the labor market was often turbulent, which also affected political stability. Since the early 1960s, the PAP government has taken various legislative and administrative measures to curb hostile trade union forces and promote the stable development of industry.

Prime Minister Lee Kuan Yew cracked down on left-wing unions, effectively breaking up the independent labor movement. After the National Trades Union Congress was formed, it eventually institutionalized unions as the only official union federation in Singapore. In 1968, the government passed two labor bills to control labor costs and improve the investment climate. The *Employment Act 1968* regulated employment terms and conditions and placed limits on negotiable fringe benefits. The *Industrial Relations (Amendment) Act* set out procedures for labor-management negotiations and conflict resolution. These laws successfully depoliticized the labor movement, established *de facto* government control over unions, gave employers considerable bargaining power, and greatly facilitated the growth of labor-intensive factory jobs, especially for young women, while also bringing about major social and demographic changes. In less than a decade, export manufacturing by multinational corporations reduced the backlog of unemployment. Since then, Singapore has maintained full employment, save for a few brief recessions in 1973–1974, 1985–1986, 1997–1998, and 2008–2009.

In the 1970s, the government made two major interventions in the labor market. First, it relaxed immigration rules to allow employers with labor shortages to bring in foreign workers. In the 1970s, the influx of unskilled foreign workers was a small part of the workforce, employed mainly in manufacturing and from Singapore's traditional heartland of Malaysia. However, as labor shortages became more common, the government began to allow employers to bring in workers from non-traditional sources into non-manufacturing industries and introduced programs to make it easier for foreign entrepreneurs and investors to obtain Singapore permanent residency. Normally, the requirement for obtaining Singapore citizenship is 10 years of permanent residency. Qualified professionals, entrepreneurs, and investors can apply for Singapore citizenship two years after obtaining permanent residency, while other permanent residents with special skills and qualifications can apply for citizenship after five years of residence.

Second, the government set up the National Wages Council, consisting of the government, employer groups, and labor representatives, to establish the framework of the "triplet labor relations" system (employers, employees, and the government) to help determine wage standards. This system has played a great role in reducing tripartite friction and helped to maintain a stable investment environment, which is important to foreign investors, and maintain the competitive position of Singapore's labor-intensive manufacturing industry.

In addition, the government began to focus on public investment in human resources. To enhance the global competitiveness of the workforce, it advocated English as the main office language and invested in vocational and skills training. The government actively utilized the training capacity of multinational companies and their own governments to ensure that the workforce had the appropriate skills to engage in export-oriented manufacturing by setting up joint training institutions and providing training via the Ministry of Education's Human Resources Development Department to offer vocational training courses. The government responded to the changing needs of multinational companies and the economy and invested in training for different skills. For example, the National Computer Board, established in 1981, promoted companies to learn and apply information technology-related skills.

10.1.5 Homeownership Policies That Promote Cohesive Governance

When Singapore gained independence, the government faced a number of housing-related problems, such as a large number of immigrants, a growing population, a chronic housing shortage, and insufficient resources and capacity in the private sector.

In the 1960s, Singapore laid the foundations of its real estate and housing policy, which comprised three important components: the establishment of the Housing Development Board (HDB) in 1960,[2] the enactment of the *Land Acquisition Act* in 1966, and the expansion of the role of the Central Provident Fund (CPF) as a housing finance agency in 1968.

The HDB began operations on 1 February 1960. It was established as a statutory board with the objective of "providing decent housing with modern facilities to all who need it" and a target of constructing 110,000 residential units by 1970. From 1964, the HDB began selling homes on a 99-year lease under its Home Ownership Scheme, hence providing affordable housing for families with a monthly income of

[2] The HDB is a statutory body under the Ministry of National Development in charge of public housing. For more information, please visit its official website at http://www.hdb.gov.sg.

no more than S$800 by offering loans where owners would pay less in mortgage payments each month than they would pay in rent.

The political and economic motivations behind the homeownership policy are perhaps best understood in the words of Prime Minister Lee Kuan Yew: "My first priority is to enable every citizen to participate in the country and its future. I want to build a society where every family owns a home. I saw the contrast between the badly abused and poorly maintained low-cost rental flats and the proud owners of their homes, and I was convinced that the country would be more stable if every family owned their own home. … I saw that voters in the capital always tended to vote against the government of the day, and I was determined to make our citizens homeowners, otherwise we would not have political stability. Another important motivation for me was to convince all parents that if their sons had to serve the country, then their sons were defending their own interests. If a soldier's family does not own his own home, he will soon conclude that he will be protecting the property of the rich. I believe this sense of ownership is essential for our new society, which has no common historical experience" (Lee 2013).

In the 30 years since Singapore's independence, the improvement of Singapore's urban environment and housing standards has greatly promoted political cohesion and stability, providing a very solid foundation for the success of the economic development and housing strategies adopted by the government. In short, the social development benefits brought about by the Home Ownership Scheme launched by the government during this period can be summarized as follows.

10.1.5.1 Increasing Savings Rate

When the CPF homeownership program was launched in 1968, total national savings were less than 20% of GDP, which was insufficient to meet the country's investment needs (32% of GDP). By 1990, the CPF had significantly increased the savings rate to 44% of GDP, one of the highest savings rates in the world and sufficient to meet the country's investment needs.

10.1.5.2 Increase Quantity and Quality of Housing Stock

The Home Ownership Scheme enabled Singapore to mobilize long-term demand-side resources to support the public sector in rapidly providing housing with minimal government spending. This resource mobilization significantly improved the living standards for all people, improved Singapore's built environment, and created a real estate boom.

10.1.5.3 Promote Racial Integration

The implementation of the Home Ownership Scheme has played an extremely important role in shaping Singaporean society. Singapore is a multi-ethnic and multi-religious country. In 2014, Chinese residents accounted for 74.3% of the total population, Malays accounted for 13.3%, Indians accounted for 9.1%, and other races accounted for 3.3%. The actual planning of the Home Ownership Scheme is to include different income and ethnic groups in the public housing program, which avoids the development of low-income or ethnic enclaves. In Singapore's early town planning, the colonial government pursued a policy of racial segregation. Starting in the 1970s, the Housing and Development Board allocated new towns to different new towns in a "racially well-distributed" manner. However, by 1988, the trend of residents of the same ethnic group re-aggregating through the resale market became prominent, which was a problem caused by the Home Ownership Scheme. In 1989, the HDB implemented a racial integration policy that set racial limits for HDB neighborhoods and blocks: when a neighborhood/block reaches the set racial limit, those who wish to sell their HDB flat in that neighborhood/block must sell it to another family from the same ethnic group. The government stresses that the multiracial policy must continue if Singapore is to develop a more cohesive and integrated society. Singapore's racial harmony, long-term stability, and even viability as a nation depend on it.

10.2 Phase II: High-Tech Manufacturing and Regional Service Industry Centers

10.2.1 Transformation of Manufacturing Industry

10.2.1.1 1980–Early Twenty-First Century: Manufacturing Dominated, with Service Industry Developed Rapidly

In the late 1970s, with the emergence of labor shortages, Singapore's industrial strategy gradually shifted to high-tech, high-value-added manufacturing and service industries to adapt to changes in economic structural adjustment. This strategy was driven by the government's industrial promotion policy. In the early days of the founding of the country, Singapore's leading industries were oriented towards the domestic market and were dominated by the printing, publishing, and food and beverage manufacturing industries; in the 1980s, the leading industries gradually shifted to export-oriented, namely refined petroleum product manufacturing, other transportation equipment manufacturing (mainly ships), and computer, electronic and optical manufacturing; since the beginning of the twenty-first century, as shown in Table 10.1, computer, electronic, and optical manufacturing, as well as pharmaceuticals and biological products, other transportation equipment manufacturing

Table 10.1 Singapore's manufacturing output and value added by industry (2007–2019)

Industry	Manufacturing output value (million US dollars)		Manufacturing value added (million US dollars)		Manufacturing output value Proportion (%)		Proportion of manufacturing industry value added (%)	
	2007	2019	2007	2019	2007	2019	2007	2019
Manufacturing industry overall	244,733	322875.4	57179.5	97174.8	100	100	100	100
Food, beverage, and tobacco industry	5862.3	10482.3	1446.7	4128.6	2.40	3.25	2.53	4.25
Textile and clothing industry	135.7	52	36.3	24.6	0.06	0.02	0.06	0.03
Clothing Industry	626.6	386	219	117.7	0.26	0.12	0.38	0.12
Leather, fur, feathers and products thereof, and footwear	242.5	133	59.7	48.7	0.10	0.04	0.10	0.05
Wood processing and products industry	238.3	246.7	69.7	112.2	0.10	0.08	0.12	0.12
Paper and paper products industry	1016.9	1051.9	249.1	219.6	0.42	0.33	0.44	0.23
Printing and recorded media reproduction industry	2953.1	1502.4	1389.4	746.7	1.21	0.47	2.43	0.77
Refined petroleum products manufacturing	47,869	38261.5	1769.6	801.7	19.56	11.85	3.09	0.83
Chemical raw materials and chemical products manufacturing	33962.8	43961.9	5089.2	9510.4	13.88	13.62	8.90	9.79
Pharmaceutical and biological manufacturing	20,315	19966.3	12819.6	13065.4	8.30	6.18	22.42	13.45
Rubber and plastics products industry	2541.5	1776.1	827	740.8	1.04	0.55	1.45	0.76
Non-metallic mineral products	1883.6	1510.7	506.4	231.3	0.77	0.47	0.89	0.24

(continued)

Table 10.1 (continued)

Industry	Manufacturing output value (million US dollars)		Manufacturing value added (million US dollars)		Manufacturing output value Proportion (%)		Proportion of manufacturing industry value added (%)	
	2007	2019	2007	2019	2007	2019	2007	2019
Metal smelting and rolling processing industry	1355.7	1021	318.8	76.1	0.55	0.32	0.56	0.08
Metal products industry	8871.1	7549.8	2448.5	2442.7	3.62	2.34	4.28	2.51
Computer, electronics, and optics manufacturing	77443.6	131548.7	17669.9	42095.5	31.64	40.74	30.90	43.32
Electrical machinery and equipment manufacturing	2999.8	3681.8	703.8	1039.5	1.23	1.14	1.23	1.07
Mechanical equipment manufacturing	18477.9	26170.5	4708.5	7712.5	7.55	8.11	8.23	7.94
Automotive manufacturing	743	1360.2	199.1	408.9	0.30	0.42	0.35	0.42
Other transportation equipment manufacturing	13502.8	16897.6	5135.1	6843	5.52	5.23	8.98	7.04
Furniture manufacturing	482.1	742.5	188.6	281.3	0.20	0.23	0.33	0.29
Other manufacturing industries	3209.5	14572.5	1325.7	6527.4	1.31	4.51	2.32	6.72

Source: Singapore Ministry of Trade and Industry, *Yearbook of Statistics Singapore*

(mainly ships), and mechanical equipment manufacturing, have been the leading industries.

In addition, Singapore also developed into a regional service center, connecting the Southeast Asian hinterland with the rest of the world through financial, shipping, and air transport activities. Its competitive advantages included the following: strategic geographical location; well-developed mobile connectivity network and telecommunications infrastructure; business practitioners trained in business, finance, and infrastructure management; mostly well-educated people with the ability to speak English; strict and fair legal environment; minimal restrictions on business rights; relatively friendly tax system; no controls on capital flows and foreign exchange transactions; and political, social, and economic stability. With these advantages, Singapore became the regional headquarters of many American, European, and Japanese multinational companies during this period.

10.2.1.2 Twenty-First Century to Present

In 2003, the Economic Review Committee (ERC),[3] a government committee set up to formulate a medium-term economic growth strategy, identified the industries of biosciences, global banking and finance, wealth management, lifestyle industries, arts and culture, media and design, education and health as examples of industries to be prioritized for development. Although manufacturing will continue to be one of the main pillars of the economy, accounting for 20% to 25% of GDP, the focus will be on encouraging manufacturing with a higher level of innovation and placing greater emphasis on the development of the service sector, especially tradable services, which has the ability to take advantage of the size of its global market.

At this stage, the government observed that to attract and build innovation-driven industries, while efficiency was still important, more important was a sufficient number of innovative talents. If there was not enough supply of creative talents domestically to meet the needs of many clusters, Singapore should once again take advantage of globalization and look abroad for the talents it needed. In response to this challenge, the reports by the Economic Review Committee (2003) and the Economic Strategies Committee (2010) both emphasized the importance of making Singapore a "leading global city—a hub for talent, enterprise, and innovation" and "the most open and international city in Asia, and one of the best places to live and work."[4] This decision marked a fundamental shift in Singapore's development strategy—from attracting multinational companies to attracting foreign talents. In order to successfully attract foreign creative talents, Singapore has to position itself as a global city. The new focus is not only on investing in efficiency-enhancing infra-

[3] The ERC, established in 2001, is composed of 20 representatives from the government, trade unions, and private enterprises and is chaired by the Minister of Finance. Responsible for restructuring Singapore's economy, the ERC aims to overcome current economic problems and formulate plans for future economic development. The first chairman of the committee was Lee Hsien Loong, then Deputy Prime Minister and Minister of Finance of Singapore. In 2009, the Singapore government established the Economic Strategies Committee to study the country's long-term economic development strategy. The committee is chaired by Tharman Shanmugaratnam, then Minister of Finance of Singapore, and its members were experts from the government and the private sector. In 2015, the Singapore government established the "Future Economy Committee", which consists of 30 members including five cabinet ministers, as well as old, middle-aged, and young business leaders, entrepreneurs, and investors, and was chaired by Heng Swee Keat, then Minister of Finance of Singapore. The committee is committed to transforming Singapore into an innovative and value-creating economy around the Five Futures, namely future jobs, enterprises, resources, technology, and markets, in order to develop a future-oriented economic strategy that will enable Singapore to become an economy that grows sustainably, creates value and opportunities, and is vibrant and resilient.

[4] See *Report of the Committee on Foreign Relations* (2003), pp. 51–60, and *Report of the Economic and Social Commission for Asia and the Pacific* (2010), pp. 7–10.

structure but also on improving Singapore's international talent appeal so that creative talents from all over the world would choose to live and work in Singapore. The government's economic policy objectives, which are high GDP growth and surplus accumulation, still have not changed. What has changed is that economic growth will now be driven by foreign talents rather than foreign investment.

The government acted quickly and pragmatically, making a series of major policy adjustments. First, it significantly relaxed immigration and foreign labor policies, greatly relaxing the approval standards and procedures for work visas, permanent residency, and citizenship. This relaxation was particularly targeted at creative talents, entrepreneurs, professionals, high-net-worth individuals, and international students. Second, a new employment pass called the S-Pass was introduced to accelerate the introduction of potential entrepreneurial and creative workers, and the number of foreign workers and new residents rose sharply.

10.2.2 Transformation of Service Industry

Since independence, Singapore has always adhered to a state-led, export-oriented development model. For more than 40 years, it has achieved high GDP growth through factor accumulation, mainly foreign manufacturing investment, high domestic savings, and a large number of skilled and unskilled foreign labor. Faced with the inherent deficiencies of a small land area, dense population, and scarce resources, Singapore has completed a huge leap from a single re-export trade to the comprehensive development of modern service industries in just a few decades. Its successful experience provides a good reference for economies that are in the stage of economic transformation and upgrading.

First, the Singaporean government has guided and created an internal environment conducive to the development of the modern service industry. The government realized early that the modern service industry would become the main driving force of Singapore's future economic development, so it quickly adjusted its economic development strategy to give priority to the development of industries related to the modern service industry. For this purpose, the government established a special agency responsible for guiding the development of the modern service industry, timely discovering and solving existing and emerging problems in the development process of industries related to the modern service industry, and guiding the healthy development of the modern service industry through a series of industrial support policies. In addition, the government also pays great attention to the upgrading of "software", and vigorously promotes the bilingual advantage and high level of informatization as Singapore's core competitiveness to provide a good environment for the development of the modern service industry.

Secondly, the government has improved the legal system and provided the foundation for the healthy development of the modern service industry. Over the years, the government has continuously improved the relevant legislation to protect and regulate the modern service industry, strengthened the legal supervision of the modern service industry, and unified rules and standards. Additionally, in accordance with changes and new problems arising in the development process of the modern service industry, the government has been regularly reviewing and promptly revising relevant laws and regulations that are incompatible with the development of the industry or even are a hindrance to it. In addition, the government has gradually relaxed the entry control of the modern service industry, hence greatly increasing the participation of private and external capital in related industries and injecting new vitality into market competition.

The third is that the government has introduced support policies to inject vitality into the development of the enterprises of the modern service industry. In order to support the operation and development of domestic enterprises, the government has introduced a variety of economic support programs, such as the Capacity Development Subsidy Program, the Credit Comprehensive Funding Assistance Program, and the Market Readiness Assistance Program. The government has also introduced a series of funding support programs to help domestic enterprises grow and develop locally, while also actively expanding into overseas markets. In March 2020, the Economic Development Board expanded the scope of the Market Readiness Assistance Program to help SMEs increase their brand awareness in overseas markets by providing up to 70% of funding assistance. The assistance can be used by Singaporean companies for promotion and publicity activities in overseas markets, developing e-commerce marketing strategies, and promoting online and digital media marketing, as well as participating in large-scale trade fairs.

Finally, Singapore's talent-oriented policies have ensured the sustainability of talent supply. In response to the development needs of the modern service industry, the government has targeted and strengthened the training program for professional talents. It has also increased specialized on-the-job training and continuing education in various related industries in the modern service industry. Although the government has tightened its foreign labor policy in recent years, the talent introduction program continues to be implemented and strengthened as a national policy of Singapore. In response to the rapid development of the modern service industry and the urgent need for high-quality talents, the government continues to recruit top talents from around the world to work in Singapore. In addition, the government has sought to attract outstanding talents to stay in the country through the introduction of a series of preferential measures, such as continuously improving salary levels, solving housing and identity problems, and improving the entrepreneurial employment environment, hence providing a solid talent guarantee for the sustained and rapid development of Singapore's modern service industry. Singapore has made a large investment in one of its few resources—human resources. Because the investment in talent education and training is targeted at economic needs, Singapore can minimize the mismatch between the skills provided by the labor force and the skills required by the industry. In Singapore, as the economy evolves and shifts more towards knowledge-based activities, the proportion of people with university degrees in the workforce has also increased. As shown in Fig. 10.2, this proportion started to increase rapidly in the early 1990s. In the early 1970s, less than 2.4% of the working population had a university degree, and this increased to 6.3% in 1990.

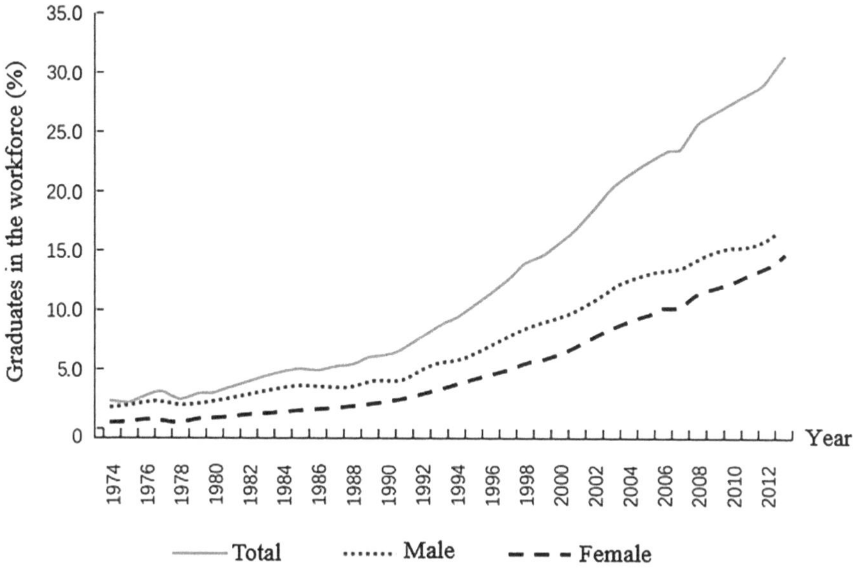

Fig. 10.2 Proportion of Singapore's resident labor force with university degree. *Source*: Department of Statistics STS database and Singapore Statistical Yearbook

However, over the next 20 years, this proportion increased rapidly to 31% in 2013. Table 10.2 shows the distribution of university enrollment by course and gender. The vast majority of university enrollments are in engineering sciences, although there is a gender gap in enrollment in this field and a recent downward trend. University enrollments in business and social sciences have been increasing as the service sector expands.

10.2.3 Development of Home Ownership Scheme

In this subchapter, the main housing issues faced by Singaporean administrations from a historical perspective, and their respective responses, are explained.

10.2.3.1 Deregulating Markets and Increasing Assets

When Goh Chok Tong succeeded Lee Kuan Yew as prime minister in 1990, the housing shortage had been resolved. About 88% of households own their own homes and 87% own HDB flats. In the 1990s, the HDB shifted its focus to providing larger and better-quality homes for middle- and upper-income families,

Table 10.2 Enrollment rates for first-degree programs at universities in Singapore

Course	Gender	1995	2000	2005	2010	2013
Engineering Science	M	50.0	60.7	56.7	43.4	40.7
	F	10.3	23.0	23.9	17.3	17.3
Accounting, Business, and Administration	M	14.7	9.6	11.8	14.1	15.5
	F	29.5	23.0	21.8	19.6	19.4
Natural, Physical, and Mathematical Sciences	M	8.1	6.4	8.5	11.1	10.4
	F	13.1	13.4	15.4	15.6	15.3
Humanities and Social Sciences	M	9.6	8.2	8.4	11.0	11.8
	F	30.6	24.6	21.7	22.9	23.4
Information Technology	M	7.2	6.3	5.5	7.7	8.7
	F	5.0	3.8	3.3	3.6	4.2
Medicine, Dentistry, Health Sciences	M	4.5	3.9	3.6	3.7	4.0
	F	3.1	3.4	4.1	5.3	6.2
Architecture and Buildings	M	3.2	3.0	2.6	2.4	2.5
	F	4.1	4.7	3.9	3.9	3.7
Law	M	2.3	1.3	1.5	2.3	2.5
	F	2.8	1.9	2.3	2.7	2.4
Education, Applied Arts, Mass Communication, Services	M	0.5	0.8	1.3	4.3	3.8
	F	1.7	2.1	3.6	9.3	8.0

Note: Calculation based on data of each year from Singapore Statistical Yearbook

redeveloping old estates, and retrofitting existing homes. The development of an active secondary market and a system that allows eligible households to apply for a second (usually larger) subsidized home after the minimum occupation period has facilitated households' upgrading to larger HDB flats.

In the early 1990s, the emphasis of land planning shifted accordingly in a more forward-looking direction, which was providing a larger market space for private developers to meet the demand for exclusive housing for growing population groups. During this period, the government sold land to private developers, which led to a significant increase in the supply of private housing. Revenue from the sale of state-owned land leases accounted for a prominent proportion of government revenues, especially during the "boom" period of the 1990s.

The administration's housing policy was characterized by market deregulation, "asset enhancement", and "home upgrading" policies. The government viewed housing in Singapore as an asset and a potential source of old-age security. Policies implemented included deregulating the HDB resale market, increasing housing loan support for HDB flat resales to promote liquidity, physical upgrading of HDB flats and neighborhoods, and introducing demand-side subsidies in the form of CPF housing grants. These policies contributed in part to the rapid rise in housing prices in the early 1990s.

The liquidity or trading ease of an asset largely determines how easily people can access it and, more importantly, the efficiency of the market. Therefore, while promoting the ownership of new subsidized HDB flats, the government also formulated policies on the secondary housing market, clarifying the liquidity conditions and trading rules of HDB flats. From a public policy perspective, people were concerned early on that HDB flats should not be a tool for speculation, given the widespread housing shortage at the time. Therefore, in the early days of the housing program, the regulations on house resale were extremely strict. As the housing shortage eased, the HDB gradually relaxed relevant regulations.

Before 1971, there was no resale market for the flats. The HDB required owners who wished to sell their flats to resell them to the HDB at the original purchase price plus depreciated renovation costs. In 1971, the HDB established a resale market by allowing owners who had lived in their flats for at least three years to sell their flats at market price to buyers who met HDB's eligibility requirements. However, the families who resold their flats were prohibited from applying for public housing for one year. In 1975, the prohibition period was increased to two and a half years. In 1973, the minimum period of residence before reselling was increased to five years and has remained so ever since.

The lock-up period was a huge disincentive for any household considering selling its home. In 1979, the government abolished the lock-up period, thereby greatly facilitating exchange within the public housing sector. It was replaced by a 5% tax on the transaction price of a home to "reduce windfalls for households". In 1982, a tiered resale tax depending on the type of home was introduced, and the rules regarding the circumstances under which the tax could be exempted were fine-tuned in the 1980s. The resale tax system ensured that households received less subsidy for their second new home from HDB than that for their first HDB flat.

Prior to 1989, only citizens, non-owners of any other residential property, and families of at least two people whose household income was below the income ceiling set by the HDB were eligible to purchase new or resale HDB flats. In 1989, the income ceiling for resale HDB flats was removed, which increased housing mobility, and the resale market was also opened to permanent residents and private owners, as long as they planned to live in the flats. HDB flat owners, who previously could not own any other residential property, were also able to invest in privately built homes. From 1991, single aged 35 and above are allowed to purchase resale HDB flats for their own residence.

The HDB also provides loans to buyers of resale HDB flats. In terms of price, loans before 1993 were based on 80% of the price of a new HDB flat in 1984. As new and resale prices rose, a growing proportion of households buying resale properties paid in cash, as shown in Fig. 10.3. In 1993, the HDB brought its mortgage loan terms closer to market practice, granting loans of up to 80% of the current valuation or the declared resale price of the property, whichever is lower. In 1993, the CPF Board also began to allow CPF savings to be withdrawn to pay mortgage interest on resale HDB flats and private homes.

The deregulation of the HDB resale market was accompanied by an increase in HDB resale transactions. The volume of HDB resale transactions increased from less than 800 units in 1979 to 13,000 units in 1987, 60,000 units in 1999, and 31,000 units in 2004. Resale transactions accounted for 3%, 37%, 64%, and 68% of total owner-occupied public housing transactions (new and resale) in 1979, 1987,

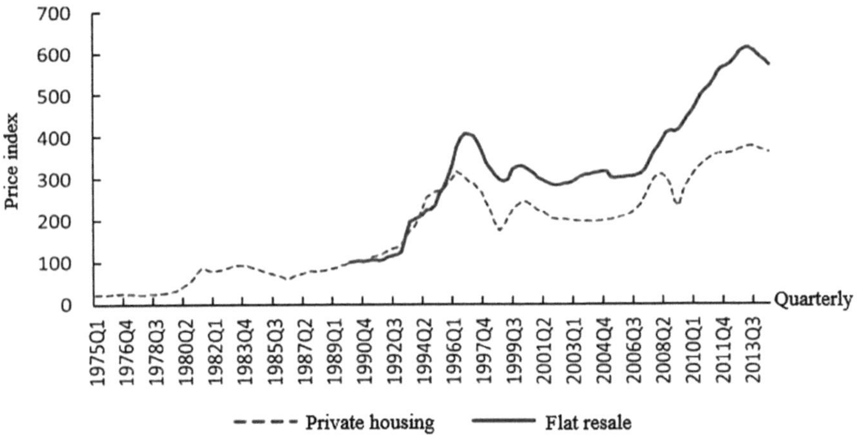

Fig. 10.3 Singapore's house price inde. *Note*: Private housing price index, 1975–2014 (Q1 1990 = 100); HDB resale price index, 1990–2014 (Q1 1990 = 100). *Sources*: Singaporean government agencies, Urban Redevelopment Authority, Real Estate Information System (REALIS); Housing and Development Board website

1999, and 2004, respectively. The increase in demand for resale housing in the second half of the 1990s was partly due to the introduction of demand-side housing subsidies.

The introduction in 1994 of demand-side subsidies in the form of CPF Housing Grants for the purchase of resale flats marked a shift from a system that relied entirely on subsidies linked to new flats to a hybrid system that relied partly on subsidies linked to resale flats. The grant was deposited into the CPF account of eligible households when they applied to resell or sell their flats. Under the scheme, the government provided a grant of S$30,000 to first-time applicants for the purchase of a resale flat close to the residence of their parents or married children. In 1995, the grant was increased to S$50,000. The government also provided a more general grant of S$40,000 to eligible households purchasing resale flats without having to meet the criterion of being close to the residence of their parents or married children.

By the late 1980s, a spatial age gradient in HDB flats was already evident. The older flats were located closer to central business districts, while new towns were built further away from the districts. There was also a clear trend of young families moving out of older HDB towns, as they were allocated new flats in the outer new towns. In 1989, the government announced an ambitious long-term HDB upgrading program to upgrade existing flats. The nature and scale of the upgrading programs varied, with the government subsidizing between 53% and 93% of the upgrades, depending on the type of flat. The government also introduced the Selective Group Redevelopment Scheme in 1995. Under the program, old low-density HDB flats were demolished and the occupants moved to brand-new high-density developments within the same estate.

10.2.3.2 Managing Housing Demand and Extracting Assets to Fund Retirement

Lee Hsien Loong had been a Member of Parliament since 1984 and a member of the Cabinet since 1987 when he became Singapore's third prime minister in August 2004. At the start of his tenure, the housing market had stabilized, the Housing and Building Authority had begun to downsize, and the Singapore economy was still recovering from the shock of the 2003 SARS crisis. The 1997 Asian financial crisis and the subsequent property price decline demonstrated the risks of housing bubbles, job losses, and reliance on housing as a retirement asset. Over the years, the rapidly aging population and declining total fertility rates have posed significant demographic challenges. Policy attention has shifted to how older households can monetize their housing assets, as well as to the better targeting of housing policies to benefit lower-income households and the regulation of the housing market and housing loans.

In 2005, the government decided to develop two integrated resorts based on casinos. This decision can be said to mark the beginning of another stage in Singapore's economic development as an international city. In terms of population, the country's immigration and foreign labor policies have led to a rapid growth in the number of foreigners in Singapore.

10.2.3.3 Analysis of Home Ownership Scheme

Singapore has been able to effectively implement its plans and regulations because of a network of qualified and reliable organizations that together provide the public sector's wide-ranging capacity. The high quality of Singapore's public administration is due to merit-based recruitment, competitive remuneration benchmarked against private sector wages, extensive digitalization, and a civil service culture with zero tolerance for corruption. If the government and the public sector leadership are weak and/or corrupt, extensive intervention and government control over resource allocation can be abused, and the cost can be higher than inaction.

In the analysis of the Home Ownership Scheme, first, although the government's heavy hand in the market is very obvious and the market is very important, creating an environment that enables the market to operate more effectively is a very worthy area of attention for Singapore's housing policy. Second, the government's involvement has been very helpful in providing timely real estate market information, establishing a sustainable housing supply system and mortgage institutions, and improving the liquidity of housing assets. A full understanding is necessary of the short-term and long-term impacts of housing subsidies throughout the system, whether explicit or implicit, and whether the subsidies are on the supply side or the demand side. Third, retirement savings can be used to pay for housing mortgages. However, the CPF itself does not provide loans to its members—it is not a good practice for the CPF to become a direct lender of housing, as this may cause confusion over its objectives. Fourth, the government's extensive regulation of the housing market and introduction of a series of measures have curbed speculative demand and mitigated the development of asset bubbles. Finally, strong legislation and appropriate fund governance structures have ensured that the interests of provident fund members are fully protected.

10.3 Singapore's Political Cohesion and Economic Accessibility Indexes

In the previous two subchapters, the history of Singapore's political and economic development was studied. In this subchapter, an analysis of Singapore's performance in terms of the quantitative indicators of political cohesion and economic accessibility under the framework of the A–C theory is presented. Due to data availability, the period for the relevant indicators is 1996–2018.

10.3.1 Political Cohesion Index

As shown in Fig. 10.4, Singapore's political cohesion index (standardized with the score of 5 as the upper limit) has been maintained for a long time at an extremely high level, much higher than the averages for the world and G7 countries. The extremely high political cohesion index means that in Singapore, various interest groups of citizens have a strong social consensus and that government policies have a high execution efficiency, which can provide a stable social operation order for economic development, as seen in the correlation between Singapore's political cohesion index and economic growth shown in Fig. 10.5.

10.3.2 Economic Accessibility Index

Economic accessibility is another important explanatory factor in explaining economic growth in the A–C theory. Higher economic accessibility means that an economy has created a unified, effective, open, and competitive market environment internally and externally. As shown in Fig. 10.6, Singapore's economic accessibility index score is around 4.5 and its economic accessibility is extremely high, not only far higher than the world's average but also higher than the average index of G7 countries, indicating that Singapore has a highly open economy.

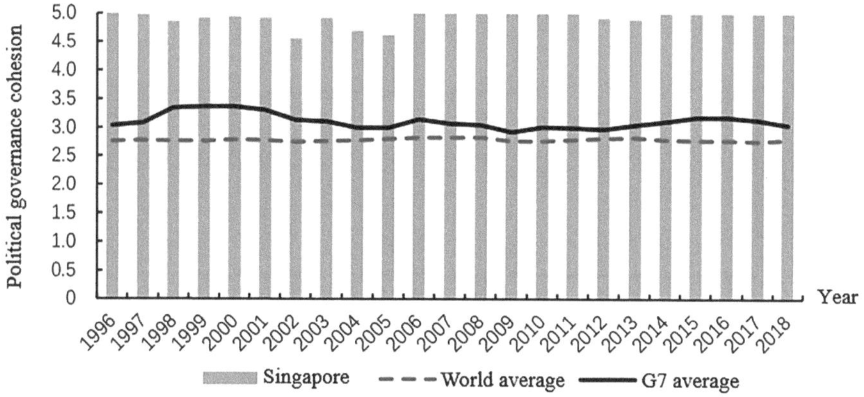

Fig. 10.4 Singapore's political cohesion. *Data source*: Calculation by the authors' research team based on data from the Maddison Project Database

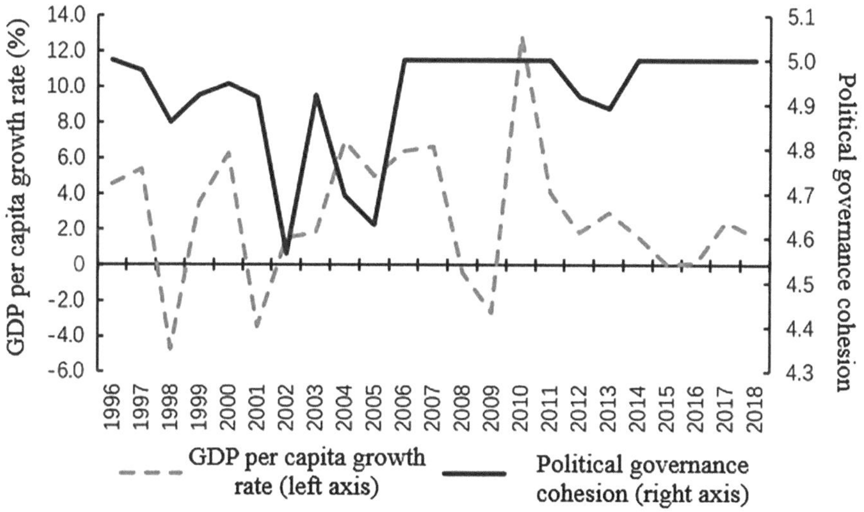

Fig. 10.5 Singapore's GDP per capita growth rate and political cohesion index. *Data source*: Calculation by authors' research team based on data from the Maddison Project Database

10.3.2.1 Internal Economic Accessibility Index

As shown in Fig. 10.7, Singapore's internal economic accessibility index performs well, with a score of 4.5 or above, which is higher than the averages of the world and G7 countries. This means that Singapore's internal market is unified, open, competitive, and orderly and that the efficiency of product circulation and factor flow is very high.

There are four main reasons. First, the average cost of starting a business in Singapore is very low, lower than those of the world and G7 countries, indicating

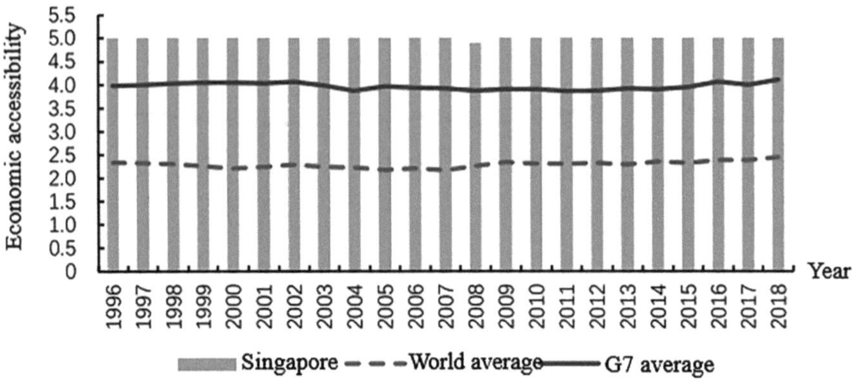

Fig. 10.6 Singapore's economic accessibility. *Data source*: Calculation by authors' research team

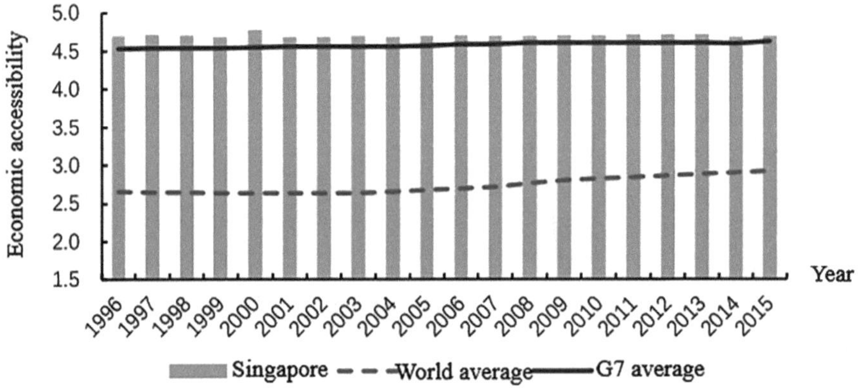

Fig. 10.7 Internal accessibility index of Singapore's economy. *Source*: Calculation by authors' research team

that Singapore has high capital accessibility. Second, Singapore has a high level of infrastructure construction, roughly equivalent to the level of G7 countries. Third, Singapore has good logistics conditions and hence its commodity market accessibility is higher than those of the world and G7 countries. Finally, fourth, the proportion of Singapore's workforce with formal jobs protected by labor contracts is high, and hence the accessibility of Singapore's labor market is higher than the world's average and is roughly equivalent to the G7's average.

10.3.2.2 External Economic Accessibility Index

Singapore is a highly export-oriented economy, with an external economic accessibility score of about 4.5, much higher than the averages of the world and G7 countries, as shown in Fig. 10.8. This reflects that Singapore has always been at the

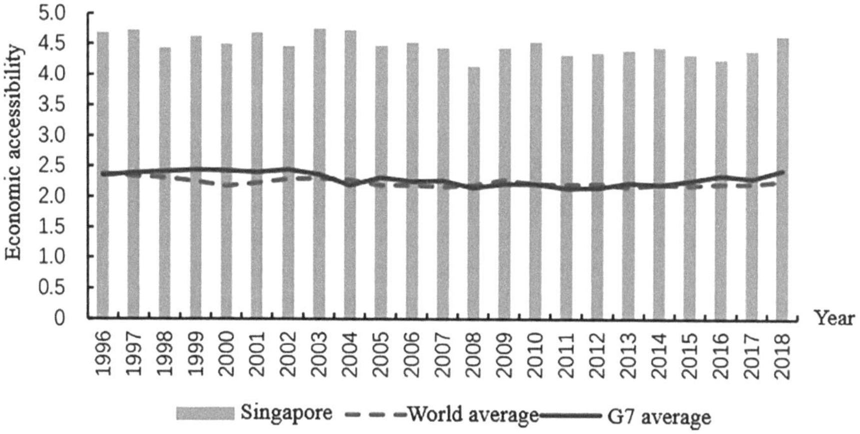

Fig. 10.8 External accessibility index of Singapore's economy. *Source*: Calculation by authors' research team

forefront of the world in opening up to the outside world, and through a high degree of openness, it has participated in global economic activities, broken through its own resource endowment and market capacity limitations, and fully utilized its comparative advantages to gain the international market share, providing exogenous impetus for economic development.

10.4 Chapter Summary

From the framework of the A–C theory, there is no doubt that political cohesion—as manifested in Singapore's political stability—played a key role in the country's economic success. The Singapore model of state intervention in the economy during the initial stages of Singapore's development from the 1960s to the 1980s was successful in achieving high economic growth and transforming a developing economy into a fairly developed economy, with policies oriented towards innovation and foundation. In addition to the normal macroeconomic control exercised by the government through monetary, financial scale, and exchange rate policies, Singapore gradually expanded its control over domestic capital (e.g., "forced savings" through the CPF, persistent budget surpluses, large foreign exchange reserves, and a world-scale sovereign wealth fund), land and real estate (e.g., housing for more than 80% of the population through the HDB, and the development of commercial and residential private properties through state-linked entities), and the labor market. In addition, the role of foreign investment or multinational corporations is itself heavily influenced by the government's industrial policies, especially investment promotion activities led by the Economic Development Board, which not only affects labor market policies and outcomes but also the broader resource allocation. The basic policies of tax incentives, infrastructure subsidies, and labor policies to attract foreign investors have not changed for decades. Singapore's single-peak unbiased governance that is stable and cohesive, as well as its gradual economic opening process and balanced growth strategy with dynamic adjustments in line with the economic development trends, have been the guarantee for the continuous deepening of the country's industrialization process, creating conditions for its industrial upgrading, its climb in the global industrial chain niche, and ultimately its successful economic catch-up. This is consistent with the assumption that a development model based on the combination of cohesive political governance and open-access economy proposed in the A–C theory can promote national development to the greatest extent and in the best way.

In addition to Singapore's experience, the experience of other East Asian and Southeast Asian economies can also fully illustrate the importance of political stability for sustainable economic growth. Political stability is an independent variable: leadership is crucial to achieving political stability. Singapore's government is composed of highly skilled professionals from different professions, and the high remuneration makes politics attractive to these professionals. All of this ensures peace and stability and creates a good environment for rapid economic development. However, political stability cannot guarantee the quality of national governance. Autocratic regimes can also bring political stability, but we do not see the prosperity of their national economies. Therefore, cohesive political governance must be combined with access to internal and external markets for economic resources. The research conducted in this study around the case of Singapore shows that although the external environment has prompted Singapore to adopt an open economic policy and although the quality of governance of the leadership is also worthy of full recognition, what is more important is that Singapore's People's Action Party has always been in control of the country's political power, which ensures the country's political cohesion and the continuity of its economic development policies. In short, combining political cohesion and openness to economic resources can maximize the development and progress of a country, and Singapore's successful experience is clear proof of this.

References

Economic Review Committee (2003) Report of the committee on foreign relations. Economic Review Committee, pp 51–60

Economic Review Committee (2010) Report of the economic and social commission for Asia and the Pacific. Economic Strategies Committee, pp 7–10

Lee KY (2013) The Singapore story: memoirs of Lee Kuan Yew. Yilin Press, Nanjing

Chapter 11
South Korea: "Han River Miracle" of Successful Catch-Up

During its founding, South Korea was one of the poorest countries in the world. According to the Maddison Project Database, South Korea's GDP per capita in 1950 in terms of purchasing power parity was only 1178 international yuan, ranked 105th among 140 countries, which was only 7.7% of the GDP per capita of the US, 14.4% that of Western Europe, 27.9% that of Latin America, 117.2% that of East Asia, and 32.1% that of the world's average. However, the South Korean economy began to take off after the 1960s, and the country became a member of the OECD in 1996 and a high-income country, as defined by the United Nations, in 2001, hence achieving a rapid catch-up by a late-developing economy. As shown in Fig. 11.1, in 2016, South Korea's GDP per capita reached 36,103 international dollars, an increase of 29.6 times compared with that in 1950, reaching 68.1% that of the United States, 93.4% that of Western Europe, 260.7% that of Latin America, 343.5% that of East Asia, and 245.7% that of the world's average.

South Korea's economic development history is a typical example of the East Asian economic model, comprising a formerly authoritarian political model, a government-planned economy, policies of industrial development and subsidy, and an "official financial system" of financial suppression policies. In addition, South Korea's economy has its own uniqueness, such as the *chaebol* group economy inherited from the colonial period. South Korea's successful experience is another classic example of the dual-pillar development of cohesive governance and the opening up of internal and external economic accessibility, which can provide a valuable experience for late-developing economies in political governance, economic opening up, market cultivation, and other aspects. Moreover, the problems that emerged in South Korea during its economic development, such as *chaebol* monopoly, lack of market vitality, and serious polarization between the rich and the poor, can also provide important lessons for developing economies in terms of social equity and market system.

C. Chen et al., *From Poverty to Prosperity*, Understanding China,
https://doi.org/10.1007/978-981-95-7171-0_11

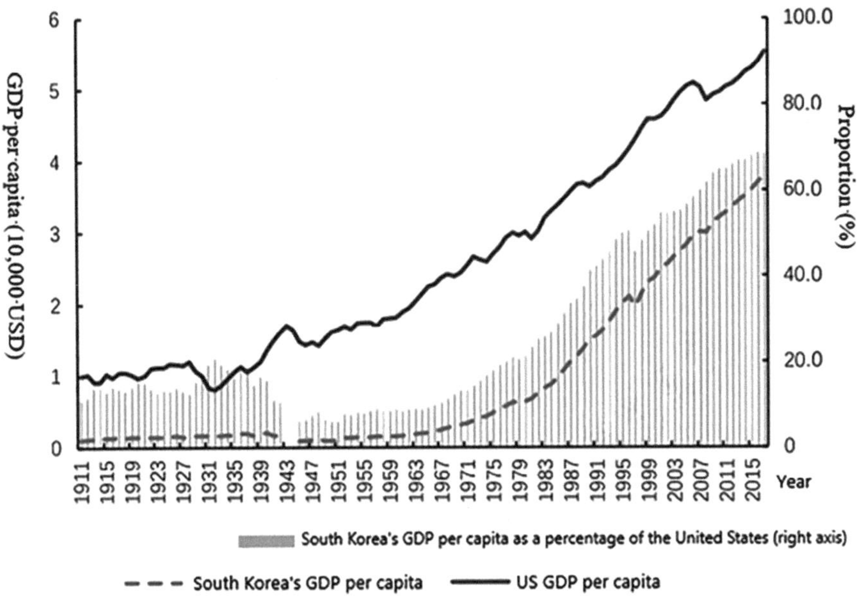

Fig. 11.1 GDP per capita: South Korea vs. the United States. *Source*: The Maddison Project Database; data from 1941 to 1949 were supplemented by linear interpolation

11.1 Brief History of South Korea's Political Economy

Since the founding of South Korea after World War II, its political and economic history has gone through three stages: the period of dictatorship, the period of military authoritarian rule, and the period of modern democratic politics. South Korea's political form changed from multi-peak conflictual governance to single-peak unbiased governance and then to multi-peak reconciliatory governance after the failure of the country's exploration of single-peak unbiased governance. South Korea's economic policy has changed from an import substitution strategy to a planned economy for national development and then to a free market economy. The establishment of national integration and political order has provided a stable institutional environment for economic development, enabling South Korea to achieve the so-called "Han River Miracle" of a transformation from an extremely poor country to an emerging industrialized country.

11.1.1 Intensification of Multi-peak Conflictual Governance: Period of Dictatorship

In 1948, the southern region of Korea held parliamentary elections with the support of the United States. The Constitution of the Republic of Korea, passed by the Constitutional Assembly, established the Republic of Korea and stipulated that the government should implement a presidential central system. Syngman Rhee, former President of the Korean Provisional Government during the Japanese rule in Korea, was indirectly elected as the first president of the South Korean government, and South Korea entered the first republic period. Subsequently, the government of the Republic of Korea received the formal transfer of power from the U.S. occupation government and was recognized by the United Nations as the legitimate government on the Korean Peninsula. The three cornerstones of the Syngman Rhee government were a National Assembly controlled by right-wing conservative forces, violent organizations centered on the police force, and the support of the U.S. government. Based on this, Syngman Rhee's pro-American conservative forces established a dictatorship. However, because Syngman Rhee had long been trying to build a country through diplomatic activities overseas, he lacked direct forces and popular support on the Korean Peninsula, and there were differences between his political programs and those of other political forces. Therefore, his dictatorship was multi-peak conflictual governance, which suppressed the original pro-Japanese conservative forces and left-wing progressive forces by winning over the peasant class and balancing military forces.

Of the 200 seats in the first National Assembly, the National Independence Promotion Association, led by Syngman Rhee, held 55 seats, while the Korea Democratic Party held 29 seats, the Taedong Youth League held 12 seats, the National Youth League held 6 seats, and other small parties, such as the Korea Independence Party, held 13 seats. The remaining 85 seats were held by non-partisans (Kim 2014). Although Syngman Rhee's forces were the largest party in the National Assembly, they were far from having an absolute majority and were always challenged by other factions of conservative forces and left-wing democratic forces. Among them was the conservative anti-communist coalition established by pro-Japanese forces in southern Korea in 1945 (Zhao 1995). Another was the Democratic Party of Korea (abbreviated as the Korea Democratic Party), an important right-wing conservative party, which was reorganized into the Democratic Kuomintang (abbreviated as the Democratic Party) in early 1949. The Republic of Korea Party, although often conflicted with Syngman Rhee's conservative forces due to its advocacy of a responsible cabinet system and its pro-Japanese stance, generally united with the conservative forces in the face of the demands from the young progressive forces to punish pro-Japanese forces. After the "South Workers' Party Spy Incident", which was fabricated to defeat young progressive forces, the Korean Nationalist Party, formed by Syngman Rhee at the end of 1949, became the ruling party with a majority of seats. Syngman Rhee's forces, which controlled the National Assembly, successively passed laws restricting citizens' rights, such as the

National Security Law, the Anti-National Behavior Punishment Law, and the Press Law. Following the second National Assembly election in 1950, the right-wing and left-wing opposition forces expanded and jointly prevented Syngman Rhee from being re-elected and fought fiercely with forces from the Republic of Korea Party. However, the outbreak of the Korean War allowed Syngman Rhee to invoke the Wartime Presidential Powers Act with the support of the United States to defeat the opposition. In order to ensure his reelection, Syngman Rhee reorganized the Korean Nationalist Party into the Liberal Party in 1951 and forced the National Assembly to pass the Third Constitutional Amendment (known as the Best Constitutional Amendment) in mid-1952, which was centered on direct presidential elections and a bicameral system, thereby achieving re-election that year. In 1954, Syngman Rhee further manipulated the National Assembly to pass the constitutional amendment for a lifelong presidency and continued to be re-elected president by cheating. In 1958, amendments to the National Security Law to strengthen the anti-communist system and amendments to the Local Autonomy Law to strengthen intervention in local administration were passed, further strengthening Syngman Rhee's dictatorial rule. Although the Syngman Rhee government's interference and control over the National Assembly was constantly increasing, it also caused the political struggle to gradually develop to an irreconcilable level.

After the founding of the country, the police force and the military police were the main organizations that the Syngman Rhee government relied on to oppose the Soviet Union and the Communist Party. In addition, semi-fascist organizations, such as the Korean Youth League, served as important thugs for Syngman Rhee's forces. Syngman Rhee used these organizations to interfere with the operation of the National Assembly, such as forcing the National Assembly to pass bills by surrounding the National Assembly, arresting or detaining National Assembly members, and fabricating various incidents to attack opposition parties. In 1948, the National Assembly established a special investigation committee on anti-national behavior, in accordance with the Special Punishment Law for Anti-National Behavior, to purge pro-Japanese elements, which affected the interests of many conservative forces. The police launched the "June Offensive" and "Progressive Party Incident", etc., and used kidnapping, assassination, arrest, and other methods to attack left-wing progressive forces. In addition, the police clamped down on public opinion, resulting in the "Literary College Pen Disaster Incident" and the "Ham Seok-hun Pen Disaster Incident", and suppressed public demonstrations. Although the dictatorial measures helped the Syngman Rhee government to rule in the short term, they intensified the contradictions between various interest groups in society and isolated the government.

After independence, the Republic of Korea faced an extremely depressed domestic economy, with agriculture dominating the industrial structure and a serious lack of industrial production capacity. In 1953, after the armistice of the Korean War, the added value of the secondary industry in South Korea accounted for only 12.1% of GDP (Groningen Growth and Development Centre 2014). In order to consolidate the regime and develop the economy, the Syngman Rhee government mainly adopted the following three major economic measures.

The first was to deal with the problem of excessive land concentration and to appease farmers with no or little land. The government's Agricultural Land Reform Law adopted the principle of "compensated confiscation and paid distribution." The government purchased land that did not belong to farmers or was not self-cultivated, as well as land of more than 3 *chobu* (about 2.94 hectares), and distributed the land to farmers with no or little land at an equal value. The land reform reduced the proportion of hired farmers in South Korea from 48.9% in 1945 to 5.2% in 1964. During the same period, the proportion of self-cultivating farmers increased from 13.8% to 71.6%. By the end of 1951, all landlords who owned more than 5 *chobu* had disappeared (Ju 1991); the proportion of self-cultivated land in cultivated land increased from 35% to 96% (Zhang 2005). The establishment of a small peasant economy system with self-cultivating farmers as the main body helped the Syngman Rhee government stabilize its regime.

The second measure was relying on the "scissors gap" between industrial and agricultural product prices and the US economic aid to implement an economic development strategy based on import substitution. From 1948 to 1961, the purchase prices stipulated in the Grain Purchase Act were much lower than the production cost and market price of agricultural products. In addition, from 1956 to 1960, the annual food provided by the United States to South Korea accounted for about 15% of South Korea's domestic food production (Ministry of Agriculture and Forestry of South Korea 1964). Low food prices reduced costs for the government to develop the urban industrial economy. From 1954 to 1960, 10% of South Korea's GDP, more than 50% of total investment, and 38% of government revenue came from foreign aid, mainly from the United States. The Nathan Plan and the Tasca Plan, which were aimed at helping South Korea's economic revival and development, built 51 industrial projects for South Korea from 1954 to 1957, mainly focusing on certain industries, such as cement, textiles, and flat glass. The Syngman Rhee government also tried its best to promote the development of heavy industry due to war needs. In order to achieve the goal of import substitution, the Syngman Rhee government adopted the policies of raising trade barriers, overvaluing the currency exchange rate, and implementing foreign exchange controls to reduce the import of consumer manufactured goods and expand the import of intermediate capital goods. However, the import substitution strategy suppressed the external accessibility of the South Korean economy, causing its light industry, represented by the "three white industries" (flour, sugar, and cotton yarn), which originally had comparative advantages, to have overcapacity due to insufficient demand (Mason 1981).

The third is the *chaebol* economic system based on political and economic privileges.[1] According to the 1948 Agreement on the Transfer of Finance and Property between South Korea and the United States, major natural resources, such as

[1] The term "chaebol", which originated in Japan before World War II, refers to a centralized business group whose ownership and management rights are concentrated in the head family and have a significant impact on the national economy. South Koreans are accustomed to referring as *chaebol* the top 30 companies in terms of assets and business groups that meet the above characteristics.

mountains, forests, wilderness, and land, buildings, and cultural relics of historical value, property with permanent preservation value or needed by the government and public groups, as well as enterprises, important mines, steel, and machinery industries that are urgently needed for national defense and national life, were all owned by the state and the public, and the rest were all handled by individuals and legal persons. In addition to those that were nationalized and publicly owned, the remaining enterprises and movable and immovable properties handled by the private sector were preferentially handled to trusted employees, "national meritorious persons", and their surviving families according to the shares, and the remaining parts were auctioned within the designated scope (Kim 2014). In 1953, South Korea decided to "transform from a semi-free, semi-controlled management economic system to a free economic system" and further privatized government-owned enterprises other than public utilities such as communications and transportation (Kim 2014). Those with political privileges and large landowners who had obtained capital through government land redemption often obtained ownership of assets at a price far below the actual value of the assets during the disposal and privatization of "owned" assets. Some family groups that controlled a series of enterprises, such as Samsung and Dongyang, gradually grew into *chaebols* with a significant impact on the economy. *Chaebol* enterprises enjoyed the advantage of priority access to production materials and credit funds allocated by the government, which suppressed the internal accessibility of the South Korean economy, causing the share of SMEs with less than 200 employees in South Korea's GDP to drop from 66.3% in 1958 to 43.7% (Kim 2014).

Due to excessive reliance on US economic aid and the failure of the import substitution strategy, South Korea's economic growth was very unstable during this period. Calculated at constant prices, South Korea's GDP grew at a compound annual rate of 4.0% from 1953 to 1960. It reached 6.7% in 1957, when US grants reached their peak. After the US aid was converted from grants to interest-bearing loans, and then gradually shrank, South Korea's GDP growth rate fell all the way to 1.2% in 1960. In addition, South Korea's inflation rate remained at around 40% from 1954 to 1960 (Mason 1981). In early 1958, the number of unemployed people in South Korea reached 4.2 million (Kim 2014). The March 15, 1960, presidential election fraud case became the fuse for the public to express their dissatisfaction. A series of demonstrations and bloodshed across the country, especially the "April 19" movement and the "Current Situation Declaration" of the university professors' group, caused the Syngman Rhee government to lose its popular support. The military forces, which had never been completely controlled by the government, chose to remain neutral. Under the persuasion of the United States, Syngman Rhee finally stepped down at the end of April of that year.

Under the auspices of the Heo Jeong transitional government, the National Assembly, controlled by the Democratic Party, passed a constitutional amendment centered on the cabinet responsibility system and won an absolute majority of seats in the elections of both houses after the constitutional amendment. In the end, Yun Bo-sun, a member of the old Democratic Party (later formed the New Democratic Party), was elected president, and Chang Myon, a member of the new Democratic

Party (still using the name of the Democratic Party), was elected prime minister, and the Second Republic of Korea was established. The Chang Myon government adopted an ambiguous and negative attitude in being held accountable for election fraud, bloodshed, and collusion between officials and businessmen. It turned from supporting to suppressing the expanding mass movement and was unable to restore the severely impacted economy in a short period of time, making it a new target of struggle for the mass movement. The Chang Myon government of the Second Republic was overthrown by the military after only 10 months.

11.1.2 Exploration of Single-Peak Governance: Period of Military Authoritarian Rule

In 1961, military forces led by General Park Chung-hee launched the May 16 coup and gained control of the country, quickly stabilized the domestic situation, and obtained recognition from the United States, thus opening a 30-year period of military authoritarian rule in South Korea. From the "Revolutionary Pact" of the coup to "The Road of the Nation" and "I, the Nation, and the Revolution", Park Chung-hee's military government's adherence to developmentalism regarding economic development was the most important source of legitimacy of the regime. Politically, the regime relied on the authoritarian system, technical bureaucrats, and the *chaebol* group to achieve cohesive governance and made important explorations towards single-peak governance; in terms of the economy, the regime implemented "guided capitalism" that was in line with national conditions (Korea Economic Development Plan Evaluation Professor Group 1967) and built a highly open economic development pattern at home and abroad. The economic development plan created the "Han River Miracle" of economic growth, but it also activated more interest groups expressing their own interests, which led to increasingly intensifying conflicts with the authoritarian system, a system that was deepening in order to maintain growth, and ultimately led to the decline of South Korea's single-peak governance, with major interest groups closely encircling the military government.

In parliamentary politics, the ruling group has always maintained the unity of the state's administrative and legislative powers, and the opposition or opposition parties do not have the ability to truly challenge the ruling party. During the military regime from 1961 to 1963, the parliament and political parties were all dissolved, and the Military Revolutionary Committee/National Supreme Reconstruction Conference held state power. In 1963, in a civilian transfer of power, Park Chung-hee was elected president with 46.6% of the votes; in the National Assembly election, Park Chung-hee's Republican Party won 110 seats of the 175 seats, while the Democratic Party won 41 seats, the Democratic Party won 13 seats, and other parties won 11 seats. With the 1963 election, South Korea entered the Third Republic period. In 1967, Park Chung-hee was re-elected president with 51.4% of the votes; in the National Assembly election, the Republican Party won 129 seats of the 175 seats, the New Democratic Party won 45 seats, and a minor party won 1 seat. In 1969, the Constitutional Amendment aimed at achieving the re-election of an incumbent president for three consecutive terms was passed by a two-thirds majority in the National Assembly and 67.5% in the national vote. In the 1971 presidential election, Park Chung-hee was elected with 53.2% of the votes and his party won 204 seats in the National Assembly election. At the end of 1971, Park Chung-hee launched a self-coup and announced a state of emergency; in October 1972, he issued the Reform Declaration and dissolved the National Assembly. In November, the Reform Constitution was approved with 91.5% of the votes in the national referendum. At the end of 1972, Park Chung-hee was elected president for the fourth time, the Reform Constitution was promulgated, and South Korea entered the Fourth Republic. The presidential and congressional elections and the passage of constitutional amendments show that although Park Chung-hee restricted the political rights of citizens, he was still supported by the majority of citizens and interest groups because of the development achievements he made during his administration. He made extremely useful explorations in forming a single-peak unbiased governance, with the Republican Party as the core. The only democratic force that put pressure on the government was the college students in Seoul, but it was not enough to threaten the stability of the entire political situation at that time.

In terms of the administrative system, the Park Chung-hee government vigorously strengthened the power of the central government, which centered on the president, as well as using intelligence agencies and economic and technical bureaucrats and improving the country's mobilization capabilities to implement economic development plans. The Central Intelligence Department, established during the military government period, was a comprehensive intelligence agency for the Park Chung-hee government to maintain power, fight political opponents, and strengthen rule. It is the core agency of the government to ensure national security and promote political progress, which strengthened Park Chung-hee's political authority but not his political legitimacy. Park Chung-hee also built an economic development administration by expanding the team of technical bureaucrats. In 1961, the military government carried out a comprehensive cleanup and rectification of civil servants at all levels based on the principles of giving priority to examinations and performance appraisals, established a National Reconstruction Movement organization from the central to the grassroots level involving every household, strengthened the authority of the presidential secretariat, and established the Economic Planning Board and its subordinate Land Planning Agency, thus building a large, efficient, and professional administrative team to effectively implement the national economic development plan.

In terms of economic policies, the Park Chung-hee government established a national development era under a planned economy by means of state control and the alliance with the *chaebols*. First, the government compiled the *National Economic Five-Year Development Plan* as a blueprint for economic development. The resulting *First Five-Year Economic Development Plan (1962–1966)* was inherited from the unimplemented *Three-Year Economic Development Plan (1960–1962)* of the Syngman Rhee government and the *Five-Year Economic Development Plan* of the Chang Myon government, and hence still followed the strategy of import substitution and heavy industrialization. Following the failure of the currency reform and the Industrial Development Corporation plan as the core content, the Economic Planning Board revised the *First Five-Year Plan*. Due to the backward economic level and serious lack of capital, South Korean economic bureaucrats, such as Zhang Jirong, Jin Helie, Jin Zhenglian, and Wu Yuanzhe, advocated learning from Japan's experience and starting with export-oriented industries to gradually upgrade to heavy industries and high-tech industries. The development strategy relied on lowering the exchange rate to attract external demand to drive economic growth and on export earnings to meet capital investment needs (Jin 1990). The *First Five-Year Plan*, revised in 1964, formally established the export-oriented industrialization strategy, and the subsequent *Second Five-Year Plan* (1967–1971) continued this strategy. In the 1970s, during the *Third Five-Year Plan* (1972–1976), the *Fourth Five-Year Plan* (1977–1981), and the *Declaration on Heavy Chemical Industrialization*, the government's industrial policy began to encourage the development of capital-intensive industries, such as steel and shipbuilding, while adhering to the export-oriented strategy. Although this shift later laid a debt risk for the South Korean economy, it was crucial for further promoting the sustained high-speed growth of the economy.

Second, the government supported *chaebol* enterprises as a means to implement national strategies. In the process of determining the export-oriented strategy, the *chaebol* group played an important role. The Federation of Korean Industries (FKI), established in 1961, includes large companies that are representative of almost all industries in South Korea and is the political spokesperson for the *chaebol* interest group. The "export first" doctrine proposed by the FKI was adopted by the government, and the Export Industry Promotion Committee was established in 1963 to encourage labor-intensive export processing trade. When the government began to develop a heavy chemical industry on a large scale, it needed large *chaebol* enterprises as executors of the development strategy. The government supported *chaebol* enterprises through credit rationing, export preferences, industrial guidance, etc., making the two sides a deeply bound community of interests. A typical policy means establishing a "government-governed" finance system and providing low-cost financing for *chaebol* enterprises through financial suppression policies that significantly lower interest rates. In 1962, South Korea implemented the nationalization of the banking industry and revised the Central Bank Law to achieve direct government control over the central bank.

Third, the government actively took various measures to obtain foreign exchange to support economic development. In 1965, South Korea–Japan relations were normalized, and the *South Korea–Japan Claims and Economic Cooperation Agreement* signed by the two sides stipulated that Japan would provide South Korea with US$500 million in claims funds and more than US$300 million in commercial loans in the next 10 years. In the same year, South Korea participated in the Vietnam War in exchange for US loans, technology, investment, and military aid. From 1965 to 1972, the profits earned by South Korean companies and the wages and compensation received by soldiers and workers totaled about US$750 million (Kim 2014).

In 1975, the government passed the Overseas Construction Promotion Act to support the export of construction labor to the Middle East and obtained a total of US$2.977 billion in foreign exchange from 1975 to 1979 (Shin 2002). Against this background, from 1961 to 1979, the South Korean economy took off, with the annual compound growth rate of GDP, calculated at constant prices, reaching 9.3%.

The reforms, as well as the martial law declaration of the *Presidential Emergency Measures Order No. 9* in 1975, aroused more and more resistance by democratic forces and resulted in conflicts, such as the "Myeongdong Cathedral Incident" and the "Buma Incident", which intensified the division and struggle between the government and the opposition. The contradiction between the working and peasant classes and the *chaebol* group was also intensifying due to the uneven distribution of benefits in the development process and various disputes, such as the "YH Trading Company Incident" and the "Hampyeong Sweet Potato Acquisition Incident", occurred. When the international oil crisis in 1979 hit the South Korean economy, Park Chung-hee's government had to seek help from the IMF and issue a tightening comprehensive economic stabilization measure. Amid the many contradictions, Park Chung-hee's forces were debating about the reforms. Eventually, Park Chung-hee was assassinated by Kim Jae-gyu, the Minister of Central Intelligence, in October of that year.

South Korea's political landscape from 1979 to 1992 saw the decline of the exploration of single-peak unbiased governance and the beginning of a democratic transformation process. After Park Chung-hee was assassinated, South Korea saw a brief resurgence of the democratic movement (known as the "Seoul Spring"), but military forces represented by General Chun Doo-hwan and General Roh Tae-woo gradually seized power through the "December 12th Coup" in 1979 and the "May 17th Coup" in 1980. The military's authoritarian political system continued, marked by the bloody suppression of the "Gwangju Incident" of popular protest. In September 1980, Chun Doo-hwan took office as president, and in October, the Constitution of the Fifth Republic, known as the Second Restoration Constitution, was passed by a national referendum. The new constitution stipulated that the president is elected by the electoral college and has the power to dissolve the National Assembly and political parties. Chun Doo-hwan won 90.23% of the votes of the electoral college and was elected president; of the 276 seats in the National Assembly, the Democratic Justice Party (DJP), a party founded by the military, won 151 seats, while the Min-Korean Party won 81 seats, the Kuomintang won 25 seats, and other parties and non-partisans won only 19 seats (Kim 2014). The National Assembly was nominally a multi-party system, but because the funds for the activities of the opposition parties came from the government, the opposition became "official opposition parties" under the control of the ruling party (Political Department of Korea Daily News 1994). It was not until the establishment of the New Korea Democratic Party in 1985 and the establishment of the first opposition party after the February National Assembly election that the opposition parties truly had the nature of fighting against the ruling party. The democratic movement became stronger during this period. In addition to the active student groups, the middle class also began to move closer towards the opposition parties. The growing working class shifted from demands on economic rights to the path of combining economic and democratic rights. The military authoritarian government, which was originally close to single-peak unbiased political governance, was declining.

In 1987, Chun Doo-hwan issued the *April 13 Constitutional Protection Measures* to postpone constitutional amendments, which triggered the largest opposition movement in South Korea since 1961, with 8.3 million participants, known as the "June Protest" (Kim 2014). At this time, the military split. Roh Tae-woo issued the *June 29 Declaration*, advocating for negotiated constitutional amendments, amending the presidential election law, releasing political prisoners, expanding and protecting human rights, freedom of speech, local autonomy, improving party activities, carrying out dialogue politics, and creating a social community of mutual trust and vitality (Gong 2014). Chun Doo-hwan finally accepted the declaration, and the Fifth Republic entered the Roh Tae-woo period. The subsequent political talks resulted in the ruling and opposition parties reaching an agreement on constitutional amendments. The new constitution, which stipulated the direct election of the president, was passed by the National Assembly with 93.1% of the votes, and South Korea entered the Sixth Republic. In the presidential election at the end of 1987, due to the breakdown of negotiations between the two camps of Kim Young-sam and Kim Dae-jung within the democratic forces, both announced their candidacy for the presidency. In the end, Roh Tae-woo was elected president with a relative majority of only 36.6%. In the 1988 National Assembly election, Roh Tae-woo's Democratic Justice Party only won 125 seats out of 299 seats. The opposition parties, including the Unified Democratic Party led by Kim Young-sam, the Peace Democratic Party led by Kim Dae-jung, and the New Democratic Republic led by Kim Jong-pil, won 174 seats, forming the pattern of a "small ruling party and large opposition party" (Zheng Kuan-yong "Historical Criticism" No. 16). This pattern did not change until 1990 when the Democratic Justice Party merged with the Democratic Party and the Republican Party to form the Democratic Liberal Party. As an extension of the military authoritarian political system, the Roh Tae-woo government nevertheless achieved the first peaceful transfer of power in South Korea since 1960. In addition, the election result also reflected the further decline of the military authoritarian government.

In terms of economic policy, the governments under Chun Doo-hwan and Roh Tae-woo generally continued the development concept of the Park Chung-hee government and successively implemented the *Fifth Five-Year Plan (1982–1986)* and the *Sixth Five-Year Plan (1987–1991)*. The two governments insisted on long-term investment in infrastructure, such as electricity, railways, and ports. The "Plaza Accord" in 1985 caused the Korean won to depreciate against the US dollar and the Japanese yen, stimulating South Korea's exports and expanding its trade surplus, and the regulation of wages, utility charges, and interest rates played a role in promoting the expansion of investment. Along with the political transition to democracy, the two governments also implemented liberalization and democratization reforms in economic policy. Chun Doo-hwan proposed the transition to a private-led economic system in his 1981 policy speech, while the Roh Tae-woo government took economic democratization as the direction of economic reform. The two governments formulated reform measures, such as privatization of state-owned enterprises, price system reform, and financial and import liberalization, but the implementation was not ideal. The privatization of state-owned enterprises transformed large state-owned enterprises, including important industries, such as steel, oil refining, and shipbuilding, into private enterprises. Financial liberalization enhanced the control of *chaebols* over the financial system, which further strengthened the dominant position of the *chaebol* group in the economy. However, the setting of wages, prices, interest rates, and the exchange rate was still under government control. Even bathing fees, coffee prices, and *jjajangmyeon* prices were still determined by the government. Therefore, "the market liberalization policy implemented in the 1980s was not to replace the role of the state with market functions," but was just a "new form of state intervention. The state has never given up its dominance over monopoly capital, the market, and labor. In other words, the domestic liberalization policy in the 1980s was nothing more than a state-led policy that rationalized monopoly capital (*chaebols*)" (Zhang 2018). Because of the continuation of the overall development economic policy, South Korea still achieved extremely excellent growth results from 1980 to 1992, with a compound annual growth rate of GDP reaching 9.6%, slightly higher than that during the period of Park Chung-hee's government.

11.1.3 Realization of Multimodal Reconciliatory Governance: Modern Democratic Political Period

The political democratization transformation during the Roh Tae-woo administration eventually achieved results. Since then, the military has stopped interfering in politics, and South Korea's political activities have been carried out in the framework of the Constitution of the Sixth Republic through democratic elections and legislative politics. Political parties representing different interest groups obtain national administrative and legislative powers through elections and have continuously reached compromises and reconciliations through political talks in the National Assembly to promote the country's development process. The establishment of multi-peak reconciliatory governance enabled South Korean society to enter a period of stable development.

In the 1992 National Assembly election, there were a total of 299 seats contested. The ruling Democratic Liberal Party, a merger of political parties that include Kim Young-sam's Unified Democratic Party, won 149 seats, while the Democratic Party, a union of opposition democratic parties co-led by Kim Dae-jung, won 79 seats, and the Unified National Party, founded by Chung Ju-yung, won 31 seats. In the subsequent presidential election, Kim Young-sam won 41.4% of the votes and officially took office in 1993 (Kim 2014). The main political measures of the Kim Young-sam government included reforming the political system of military intervention, clearing up the coup and corruption crimes of the Chun Doo-hwan and Roh Tae-woo governments, and strengthening local government elections and autonomy. In 1997, Kim Dae-jung, who was on the left side of the political spectrum, completely turned conservative in order to win the presidential election. He formed a coalition with the right-wing conservative Liberal Democratic Alliance led by Kim Jong-pil and was elected president with 40.3% of the votes (Kim 2014). However, the ruling coalition did not have a majority of seats in the National Assembly for a long time, and the Grand National Party (reorganized from the Democratic Liberal Party—New Korea Party), as the opposition party, was an important constraint on the Kim Dae-jung government. During the Kim Dae-jung administration, the policies of the government mainly focused on responding to the Asian financial crisis, streamlining government agencies, relaxing the political environment, and improving human rights.

The core content of South Korea's national economic policy in the modern democratic political period is economic liberalization reform. The government-led economic system gradually gave way to a market-led economy. The main work of this transformation was basically completed during the two governments of Kim Young-sam and Kim Dae-jung. This change was determined by many factors. First, the government no longer had the ability to fully lead economic development. In the period of economic catch-up, the government has more information advantages than micro-subjects and could compensate for the positive externalities generated by the trial-and-error process of pioneering enterprises, so it could choose industries that conform to the country's comparative advantages for economic development. At this time, the cost of economic distortion caused by the command-based planning system was far less than the benefits, which was the best choice for the government. However, as the economy enters the mature stage, the government no longer has these advantages, the cost and benefit of the command-based planning system have reversed, and so the market economy system becomes a more appropriate choice. Second, the *chaebol* group had developed from being government-dependent to a check and balance of the government. In 1990, Kim Young-sam, a liberal who had long been in the opposition party, joined the ruling party in exchange for the support of conservative right-wing forces. In 1997, Kim Dae-jung, who also belonged to the left, became conservative in his political stance in order to win the presidential election. All these show that any political party in South Korea needs to obtain the support of conservative forces represented by the *chaebol* group if it wants to govern. Third, with the deepening degree of integration into international markets, South Korea has also put forward objective requirements for economic system reform. After three decades of economic opening, South Korea has become an open economy deeply integrated into the global division of labor. As part of the world economy, the South Korean government's industrial policy of intervening in microeconomic entities has been increasingly criticized by the United States and other countries. With South Korea joining the WTO in 1995, it no longer enjoys preferential treatment as a developing country. If the country continues to implement asymmetric trade protection measures, it may be retaliated against or sanctioned by trading partners. Responding to external economic opening requirements with liberalization reform measures has become an inevitable choice for South Korea.

Although the *New Economic Five-Year Plan (1993–1998)* launched by the Kim Young-sam government ended hastily in 1996, its advocacy of the financial real-estate system, financial liberalization, market liberalization, and amendment of the Labor Law made substantial progress. The mandatory implementation of the Real-Name Financial Transaction System in 1993 laid the foundation for the standardized operation of the financial market. In 1994, the Economic Planning Board, a symbol of the planned economy in the economic development era, was abolished and merged with the Ministry of Finance to form the Financial and Economic Agency. In 1995, market liberalization measures, including the privatization of state-owned enterprises, were implemented, and the year was also regarded as the first year of South Korea's formal transformation from a planned economy to a market economy (Zhang 2018). However, the amendment to the Labor Law passed in 1997 expanded the rights of employers to dismiss workers, adjust working hours, and replace striking workers with temporary workers and non-union workers, which exacerbated labor-capital conflicts. In addition, the financial liberalization policies stimulated South Korean companies to invest in debt, resulting in the growth of short-term foreign debt being particularly significant. The increase in debt burden to an unbearable level became the fuse for the outbreak of the financial crisis in South Korea.

Hence, the economic policies of the Kim Dae-jung government were focused on coping with the financial crisis, including rectifying the financial system, adjusting the industrial structure, and softening the labor market. In order to quickly restore the financial system, the government actively sought assistance from the IMF to avoid national bankruptcy and then carried out the bankruptcy reorganization of banks with seriously bad asset conditions, opened the securities market, and guided foreign investment into the South Korean banking system. In order to help the corporate sector reduce its asset-liability ratio and promote industrial exchanges between the *chaebols* to enhance their competitiveness, the upper limit of foreign investment holdings was lifted to reduce corporate leverage. To develop the information technology industry, venture capital and information technology companies were encouraged to start businesses, and the Korean Securities Dealers Automated Quotations (KOSDAQ), the SME trading market division of the Korea Exchange trading board, was established to promote the transformation and upgrading of South Korean industries. State-owned enterprises were further privatized, and 8 of the 11 core state-owned enterprises were privatized (Kim 2014). The layoff system and labor dispatch system were implemented in the labor market in the hope of strengthening the flexibility of the labor market. Under the promotion of a series of policies, South Korea quickly recovered from the recession caused by the financial crisis. South Korea's economic liberalization reforms were basically completed, and the market economy system has been established. South Korea experienced a shift in economic growth during the modern democratic political situation and has entered a stage of medium-speed and stable growth. From 1993 to 2017, South Korea's GDP compound annual growth rate was 4.6%.

11.2 Summary of South Korea's Economic and Social Development Experience Based on A-C Theory

The success of South Korea's economic development, from an extremely backward agricultural country to an industrialized country, is inseparable from the systematic efforts and explorations of the South Korean government in consolidating a development consensus, improving political cohesion, cultivating markets, and expanding openness to improve the internal and external accessibility of the economy.

11.2.1 Construction and Improvement of Political Cohesion

From a historical perspective, the improvement of South Korea's political cohesion has provided a stable social order, common development goals, and strong implementation guarantees for the country's economic development and was the political foundation for the "Han River Miracle" from the 1960s to the 1990s. The South Korean government's construction of political cohesion mainly includes various elements, which are discussed in the following subchapters.

11.2.1.1 Establishment of Centralized Leadership System to Improve Efficiency of National Actions

When Park Chung-hee came to power through a coup in 1961, South Korea experienced a 30-year military authoritarian rule, during which the centralized leadership system was established and strengthened. At the central government level, the Park Chung-hee government restructured the executive power by strengthening the presidential power, improving the status of the presidential secretariat, and establishing the Economic Planning Board and the Korean Central Intelligence Agency. It also controlled the legislative power by establishing the Democratic Republican Party to control the National Assembly. At the level of central-local relations, the central government abolished local government autonomy by promulgating the *Local Government Temporary Measures Act*, which realized the centralization and unification of power and the direct management of local affairs. After taking power, the military group represented by Park Chung-hee implanted the military style of emphasizing discipline, efficiency, and obedience into the administrative system and established a professional, efficient, and executive bureaucratic team from top to bottom, becoming the core force for implementing the central government's policies. The military authoritarian system also tried its best to suppress all kinds of opposition forces, which while to a certain extent undermined political democracy and suppressed economic freedom, it should be admitted that this also reduced the meaningless internal friction of the entire country and played an extremely important role in building a stable overall social order and in the government completing the initial capital accumulation for economic development.

11.2.1.2 Development-Oriented Government System, Building a Consensus on National Development

When the military authoritarian government was established, South Korea was still an extremely poor agricultural country, with a GDP per capita of less than 10% of that of the United States. Obtaining food and clothing was the most urgent desire of the people. After the establishment of the centralized system, the central government chose to position itself as a development-oriented government, taking economic development as the common goal of uniting the people and maintaining its legitimacy of governance by sharing the fruits of development with the people, thereby enhancing the cohesion of political governance. The government formulated and promoted a national economic development plan, and through detailed development plans and industrial policies, it provided a clear path for national development and set a vision for the growth of national income. The main social issues shifted from democracy and freedom to economic development, which achieved cooperation and progress among different social classes. Due to the outstanding economic achievements, the military authoritarian government's legitimacy was recognized by the majority of the people, and the opposition became a minority in the national group. The government thus gained more power granted by the people and strengthened its ability to promote economic development.

11.2.1.3 Establishment of System of Urban and Rural Mobilization to Connect Cities and Villages

When Park Chung-hee came to power in 1961, South Korea was still a country dominated by agricultural employment, and the development of rural areas had not been given much attention by the government. In order to mobilize the people to participate in national construction to the greatest extent, the central government mainly took two measures. First, the Park Chung-hee government launched the Pan-National Movement. Its leadership system was a National Reconstruction Movement Headquarters at the central level, branches in each province and special city, and a promotion association in districts and counties. At least one person from each household was required to participate in related activities. The establishment of a vertical administrative system provided an organizational guarantee for the overall layout, coordinated mobilization, and grassroots implementation of the central government's policies. Second, in the 1970s, the New Village Movement was launched. By training rural leaders on national development and economic development knowledge on a large scale, rural enlightenment and government governance were completed, and the vast rural areas and farmers, who accounted for about 70% of the national population, were gradually integrated into national development. The long-standing *Chaoxiaoyeda* distribution in South Korea's National Assembly, where the ruling party has fewer seats than the opposition party, and the presidential elections at that time was an example of the government winning the support of the majority of farmers.

11.2.2 Construction and Improvement of Economic Accessibility

During the period of rapid growth from the 1960s to the 1990s, South Korea's construction of economic accessibility mainly included the implementation of appropriate industrial guidance policies, large-scale infrastructure construction, and effective human capital investment. Industrial policies were used to build an internationally competitive export sector, and infrastructure construction and human capital investment were used to build effective product markets and labor markets.

11.2.2.1 Implementation of Appropriate Industrial Guidance Policies

South Korea's economic takeoff was driven by the rapid transformation from agriculture to industry. As the private sector lacked capital, talents, and technology to enter the industrial field immediately, the South Korean government adopted the method of promoting economic development plans and industrial policies to improve the capital accessibility of the economy. The government opened up the industrial field by establishing state-owned enterprises and providing industrial demand and facility capital support for the private sector. Furthermore, the government also created an endogenous driving force for economic development by subsidizing private enterprises to enter appropriate target industries.

South Korea's industrial guidance policy was centered on industrialization and followed the path of labor-intensive, capital-intensive, and technology-intensive industrial upgrading. The labor-intensive export industry, which best fit South Korea's early comparative advantage, could rely on the immediate entry of the private sector, but each subsequent step of industrial upgrading was successfully achieved under the intervention of the government. Because cost accounting based on micro-enterprises showed that the initial cost was greater than the benefits for some enterprises undertaking industrial upgrading tasks, capital-intensive or technology-intensive enterprises had no motivation to enter in the early stage and needed to be supported by the government's industrial policy. In order to provide cheap capital goods and raw materials to labor-intensive light industries, reduce corporate production costs, and improve the overall competitiveness of the economy, the South Korean government established a series of large state-owned enterprises in the heavy industry, such as steel and petrochemicals. Among them, Pohang Iron and Steel, which was created in 1973, not only provided cheap raw materials for domestic enterprises and saved a lot of money in terms of foreign exchange but also quickly entered international markets and became the world's second-largest crude steel producer in 1993.

Because the government's direct management capacity was limited, the South Korean government also encouraged private enterprise investment in various ways in terms of subsidies, in addition to establishing state-owned enterprises. The government provided cheap or even free land to enterprises in the form of industrial parks, low-interest loans through financial suppression, tax incentives and financial subsidies through fiscal means, and important raw materials for production through material allocation at below market prices. Key industries of the national economy, such as shipbuilding, automobiles, and petrochemicals, were established with the full support, cooperation, and even orders of the government. Under the guidance of appropriate industrial policies, South Korea's investment level began to rise rapidly. As shown in Fig. 11.2, South Korea's capital formation rate in 1961 was only 12.9%, lower than Argentina's 15.6%; however, it rose rapidly in the more than 30 years after the implementation of the national development plans, and its trend was very similar to that of Japan's rapid economic recovery in the 1950s and 1970s. The peak in 1996 even reached 51.3%, 8.1 percentage points higher than Japan's peak of 43.2%. The rise in the investment rate has provided strong support for South Korea's economic development.

11.2.2.2 Large-Scale Construction of Infrastructure

A country's commodity and labor markets are not necessarily uniformly open. Especially under the economic conditions dominated by agriculture, the domestic market is actually divided into many self-sufficient small markets by transportation capacity and supply system. For South Korea, in order to build a unified domestic

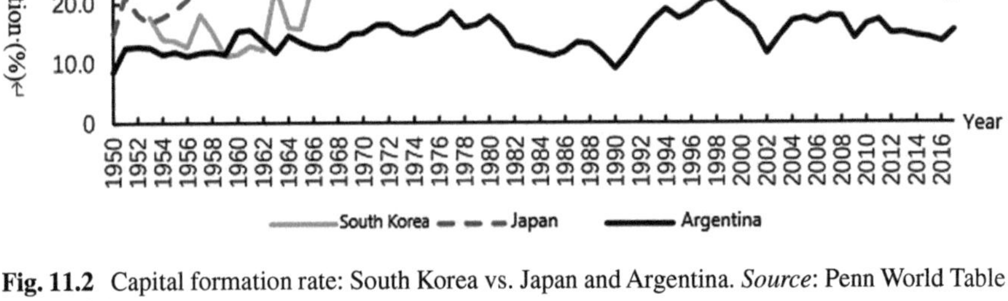

Fig. 11.2 Capital formation rate: South Korea vs. Japan and Argentina. *Source*: Penn World Table version 9.1

market and smooth the allocation channels of economic resources, the government has built a large number of infrastructures through national development plans, which has played an important role in improving the accessibility of the economy.

Infrastructure construction in South Korea is a process from point to surface. In the early days, due to funding constraints, it was impossible to support national infrastructure construction. The South Korean government concentrated resources to build industrial parks, which could exert scale effects within a limited scope, and formed the focus of the national industrial layout on this basis. These parks were built in important locations across the country, each with a focused industry, such as the Seoul Guro Industrial Park (export processing), the Ulsan Park (petrochemicals), the Changwon Park (comprehensive machinery), the Geoje Island Park (shipbuilding), the Gumi Park (electronics), and the Onsan Park (non-ferrous metals). The government provided supporting facilities, such as land, roads, water, electricity, and communications for the industrial parks, while enterprises only needed to invest in plant equipment to start production. The continuous development of industrial parks has further promoted the development of infrastructure networks. As can be seen in Fig. 11.3, the construction of highways in South Korea accelerated significantly since the 1960s, with the highway mileage increased to about 60,000 kilometers by the mid-1990s. With the deepening of the national industrial layout, the construction of national transportation infrastructure was put on the agenda of the South Korean government. In the late 1960s and early 1980s, there were two national highway construction booms, and the expressway mileage increased by more than two-fold. The Gyeongbu Expressway, built from 1967 to 1970, is the first expressway in South Korea; it runs 428 kilometers long from the northwest to the southeast of the country and not only connects the two major economic circles of Seoul and Busan but also drives the development of cities along the route. The Gyeongbu Expressway and the subsequently built Gyeongin Expressway, Honam Expressway, Namhae Expressway, and Yeongdong Expressway constitute South

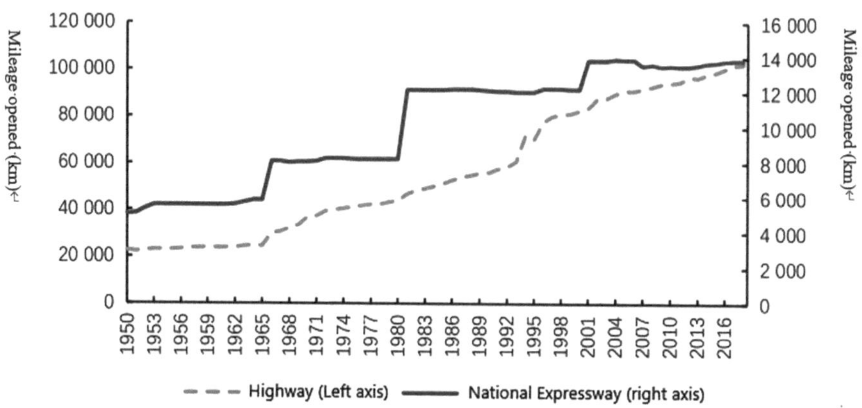

Fig. 11.3 South Korea's transportation infrastructure construction *Source*: Korea Statistical Information Service

Korea's main highway network, greatly enhancing the country's internal regional connectivity and the ability to mobilize national economic resources.

Another important condition for South Korea's successful transformation from agriculture to industry was the improvement of rural infrastructure and agricultural productivity, upon which the agricultural labor force could achieve a rapid transfer into industries. After the large-scale construction of rural infrastructure through the New Village Movement launched in the late 1960s, South Korea's natural village access rate increased from 61% in 1968 to 100% in the late 1970s, the number of farming households with electricity increased from 12% in 1964 to 98.7% in the late 1970s, and the telephone installation rate increased from 36% in 1983 to 89% in 1988. The improvement of rural infrastructure provided preparations for agricultural mechanization and modernization. The number of rural hand tractors increased from 12,000 in 1971 to 290,000 in 1980. The popularization of high-yield rice varieties and modern cultivation bases also greatly improved South Korea's agricultural productivity. From 1972 to 1977, the rice yield per hectare increased from 3.34 tons to 4.94 tons, and domestic demand was basically self-sufficient (Kim 2014). The improvement of agricultural productivity had reduced the number of laborers required for agriculture, and the enhanced connectivity with urban areas further drove the outflow of rural labor. As shown in Fig. 11.4, the proportion of agricultural employment in South Korea in 1963 was 61.9%, but by 1991 it was only 15.6%, a decrease of 46.3 percentage points. On the other hand, the proportion of employment in the manufacturing industry increased from 11.8% to a historical peak of 36.2%, and the proportion of employment in the service industry increased from 26.3% to 48.2%.

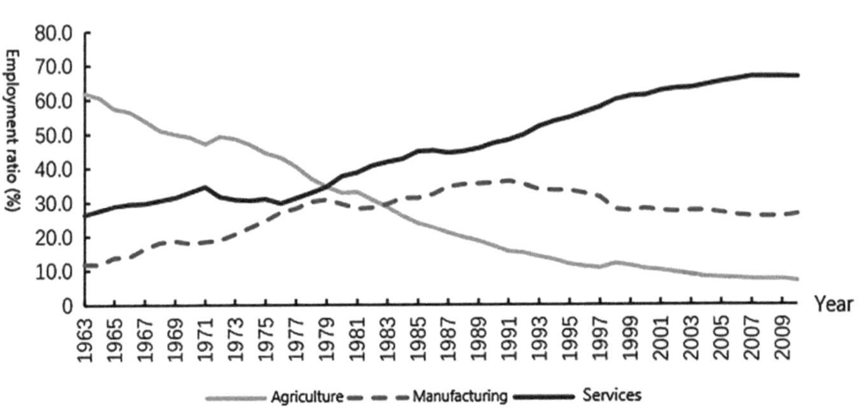

Fig. 11.4 Changes in South Korea's employment structure. *Source*: Groningen Growth and Development Centre (2014), 10-Sector Database

11.2.2.3 Employment and Human Capital Investment

The rapid development of labor-intensive industries under South Korea's industrial guidance policy in the 1960s created a labor market with strong demand, while the improvement of infrastructure construction significantly lowered the entry threshold to the labor market. The improvement of market accessibility enabled domestic labor, especially in rural areas, to participate more in economic development. The labor participation rate of the population over 15 years old increased from 49.3% in 1963 to 59.4% in 1997, of which the male rate increased from 65.0% to 70.7%. As shown in Fig. 11.5, the labor market of women also effectively improved, with its labor participation rate increasing from 33.9% to 48.4%. The smooth entry of labor into production activities made an important contribution to South Korea's economic growth. Relevant growth accounting shows that the contribution of employment growth to GDP growth per capita in South Korea was as high as 57.6% from 1971 to 1979 and 40.6% from 1982 to 1989 (Eichengreen et al. 2015).

Industrial policy support and increased infrastructure have lowered the general market entry threshold for labor, while the improvement of human capital levels helped labor cross specific skill thresholds and become an effective labor supply that could truly meet market demand. South Korea has been attaching great importance to human capital investment. Its secondary school enrollment rate exceeded Argentina's in 1976, and its college enrollment rate was basically the same as Argentina's in 1983. However, as shown in Fig. 11.6, South Korea's GDPs per capita were only 34.3% and 53.2% those of Argentina in 1976 and 1983, respectively. Although traditional growth accounting shows that the contribution of human capital growth to GDP growth per capita in South Korea was not high at only 5.0% in 1971–1979 and 4.6% in 1982–1989 (Eichengreen et al. 2015), which was similar to those of other East Asian economies, we cannot deny that the increase in human capital had brought about efficiency gains in production organization and

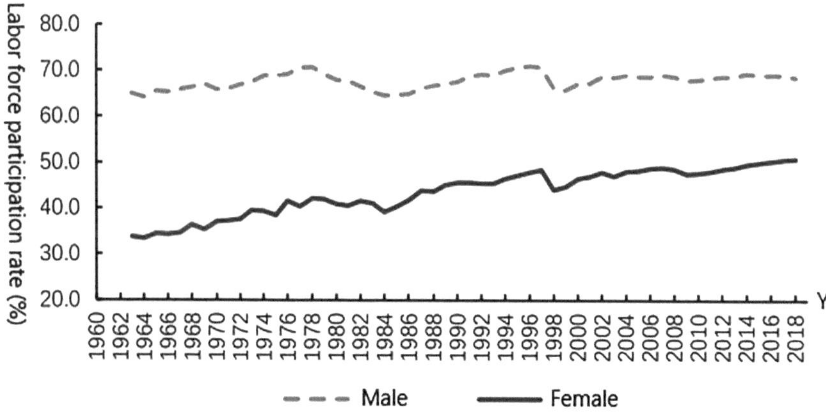

Fig. 11.5 Labor force participation rate in South Korea. *Source*: Korea Statistical Information Service and World Bank (2020)

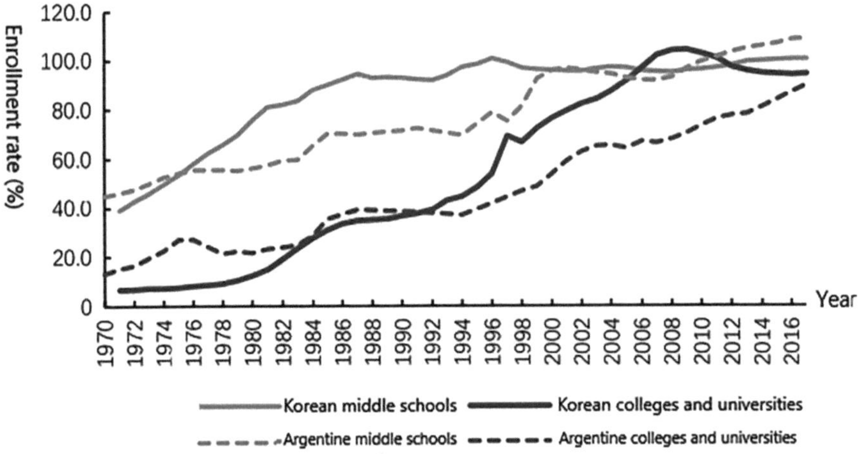

Fig. 11.6 Education enrollment rate: South Korea vs. Argentina. *Source*: World Bank (2020)

management and the use of machinery and equipment through the improvement of labor skills. This efficiency improvement may be reflected in the increase in the quantity and quality of physical capital and in the contribution of physical capital investment to economic growth. The human capital investment provided South Korea with a high-quality and highly skilled workforce and especially played an extremely important role in helping South Korea gradually establish comparative advantages in capital-intensive and technology-intensive industries where it originally did not have the foundation and experience.

11.2.3 Continuous Improvement of Economic Accessibility to Outside World

In order to integrate into the world economic system and rely on exports brought by external demand to drive economic growth, the South Korean government improved its economic accessibility to the outside world by strengthening relations with the United States and Japan, continuously upgrading export-oriented industries, and implementing a competitive exchange rate policy.

11.2.3.1 Connecting with International Markets of the United States and Japan

It is no secret that the South Korean government after World War II was established entirely with the support of the United States, and its political, military, and economic policies were all influenced and controlled by the United States. Because of the history of Japanese colonial aggression before World War II, relations with Japan were also the diplomatic focus of the South Korean government. In order to obtain the demand of international markets centered on the United States and Japan, the Park Chung-hee regime took improving relations with the United States and Japan as a diplomatic breakthrough for its economic development policy.

As the forefront of the Cold War confrontation, South Korea received a large amount of military and economic assistance from the United States in the 1950s. The core of the Park Chung-hee regime when it came to power in 1961 was an anti-communist, pro-US, and pro-development government. Park Chung-hee visited the United States that year and obtained the United States' commitment to support the normalization of South Korea–Japan relations and South Korea's economic development plan. Within a year, South Korea received US$445 million in economic assistance from the United States (Kim 2014). Subsequently, the Economic Planning Board received a lot of support from the United States in formulating South Korea's economic development plan. In 1965, South Korea received a large number of military and economic aid from the United States on the condition of sending troops to participate in the Vietnam War, which played an extremely important role in opening up international markets for South Korean companies and driving South Korea's economic growth.

Normalizing the conflicting diplomatic relations between South Korea and Japan was also an important measure for the Park Chung-hee regime to increase foreign economic ties. As a low-income country, South Korea had a huge gap in capital investment for economic development. In addition to the United States, Japan was another important source of foreign investment for South Korea. In addition, the normalization of diplomatic relations between South Korea and Japan was in the interests of both the United States and Japan. The United States could build a stable anti-communist triangular alliance with Japan and South Korea and reduce the pressure of aid, and Japan could consolidate its own security and open up overseas markets for the "flying geese model" of economic development and industrial transfer. In order to increase Japanese investment, Park Chung-hee actively conducted normalization negotiations with Japan at the beginning of his term. In 1965, the two sides formally signed a series of documents, such as the *Treaty of Basic Relations Between South Korea and Japan* and the *Agreement on Claims and Economic Cooperation Between South Korea and Japan*, which helped South Korea obtain a 10-year economic assistance from Japan in the form of US$500 million in claims funds and more than US$300 million in commercial loans. Due to the treaty, Park Chung-hee and Kim Jong-pil, the top two figures in the South Korean government, were regarded as traitors, but the economic assistance and the deepening of bilateral economic cooperation in exchange were crucial to South Korea's economy.

The management of relations with the United States and Japan brought South Korea valuable development funds and promoted the construction of a series of important projects. For example, the total investment in the construction of Pohang Iron and Steel was US$304 million, of which US$168 million came from Japan (Kim 2014), and the construction fund for the Ulsan Petrochemical Industrial Park came from US loans, etc. From 1966 to 1971, the total amount of loans obtained by

South Korea from abroad even exceeded the total amount of domestic loans (Steinberg and Wang 2018). More importantly, South Korea entered the world's largest single market (the United States) and Asia's largest single market (Japan). The United States and Japan were ranked first and second, respectively, as South Korea's major export destinations for many years. In 1988, South Korea's exports to the United States and Japan accounted for 35.4% and 19.8%, respectively, accounting for half of South Korea's exports, as shown in Table 11.1.

11.2.3.2 Continuous Upgrading of Export-Oriented Industries

The Park Chung-hee regime abandoned the import substitution strategy of the previous era and established an export-oriented economic development strategy. The government established a ministerial export industrial park committee in 1963, promulgated the *Export Industrial Park Development Act* in 1964, and designated 12 large enterprises as comprehensive trading companies in 1975. The interest rate for export loans provided by state-owned banks was only half of that for general loans, and systematic industrial policies were used to support the development of export-oriented industries. Subsequently, these industries quickly opened up to international markets with highly competitive prices, and the average annual growth rate of goods exports at constant prices surged from 9.8% in the 1950s to 29.0% in the 1960s, as shown in Table 11.2. The growing exports of goods rapidly improved South Korea's current account, and a sustained trade surplus was achieved starting from the 1970s, which reached more than 5% of GDP, making an important contribution to South Korea's economic growth, as shown in Fig. 11.7.

It is worth noting that, with the country's economic development in the 1960s, South Korea's export industry cultivation did not stop at labor-intensive industries, such as clothing, but was gradually upgraded to capital-intensive heavy industries and the technology-intensive electronic communication industry. In the early 1970s, South Korea's export-oriented labor-intensive light industries crossed the high-speed growth period, while the growth of domestic demand for heavy industrial products, such as industrial raw materials and machinery and equipment, had caused the country's current account to deteriorate. In addition, the disintegration of the Bretton Woods system and the oil crisis made developed countries, led by the United States, to turn to conservative trade policies: in order to protect domestic employment, they imposed tariffs on imported light industrial products, which hit the South Korean export industry, as the United States was its main sales market. In order to expand exports and maintain economic growth, the South Korean government followed the new trend of world industrial division of labor and actively entered relatively capital-intensive heavy industries, such as steel, petrochemicals, shipbuilding, automobile assembly, and electronic assembly. Unlike some countries in the 1940s and 1950s that faced a lack of comparative advantage and the inability to enter international markets when developing their heavy chemical industry, South Korea's heavy chemical industry had international competitiveness. For example, the production cost of Posco Steel, which was put into production in 1973, was US$251/

Table 11.1 Top five destinations for South Korea's exports

1988		1991		1994		1997		2000		2003		2006	
Country/region	Allotment	Country/region	Allotment	Country/region	Allotment	Country/region	Allotment	Country/region	Allotment	Country/region	Allotment	Country/region	Allotment
United States	35.4	United States	25.7	United States	20.4	United States	15.2	United States	21.9	China	18.1	China	21.3
Japan	19.8	Japan	17.1	Japan	13.3	Japan	10.3	Japan	11.9	United States	17.7	United States	13.3
Hong Kong, China	5.9	Hong Kong, China	6.6	Hong Kong, China	7.9	China	9.4	China	10.7	Japan	8.9	Japan	8.1
Germany	3.9	Germany	4.4	China	6.1	Hong Kong, China	8.1	Hong Kong, China	6.2	Hong Kong, China	7.6	Hong Kong, China	5.9
United Kingdom	3.2	Singapore	3.7	Germany	4.3	Singapore	4.0	Singapore	3.3	Germany	2.9	Germany	3.1

Source: Eichengreen et al. (2015)

Table 11.2 Growth rate of South Korea's exports (constant prices)

Period	Average growth rate of real exports
1950s	9.8
1960s	29.0
1970s	18.7
1980s	10.3
1990s	14.5
2000–2007	10.4

Note: The growth rate in the first 10 years of the twenty-first century represents the growth rate from 2000 to 2007 (Eichengreen et al. 2015)

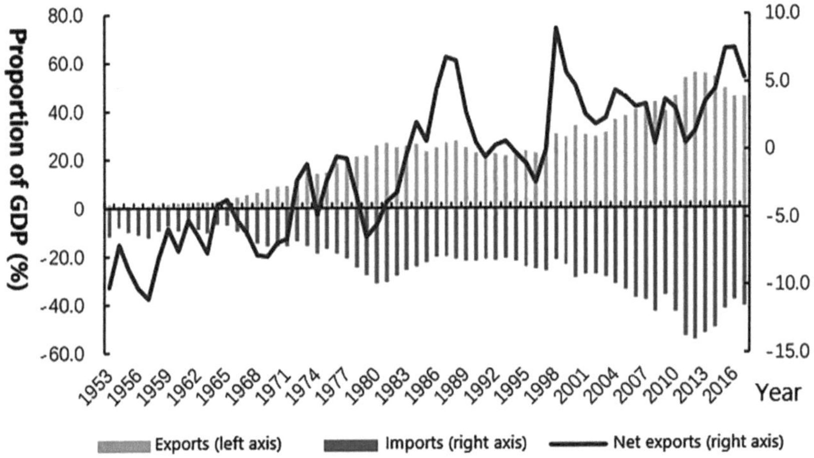

Fig. 11.7 South Korea's imports and exports (1953–2017). *Source*: Penn World Table version 9.1

ton, lower than the US$667/ton of China Steel Corporation in Taiwan and the US$626/ton of Ogishima Steel in Japan (Kim 2014). Posco Steel became the world's second-largest crude steel producer in 1993. The Hyundai Shipyard, built in 1974, achieved profitability in its second year, and the South Korean shipbuilding industry was ranked first in the world in 1999, with a world market share of 33% (Kim 2014). In the 1990s, South Korea's electronic communications industry, represented by Samsung Electronics and LG Electronics, began to flourish and gradually grew into a world-class semiconductor industry enterprise. For example, Samsung Electronics became the world's first company to produce 256 M DRAM semiconductor memory in 1994 (Kim 2014). According to Sanjaya's (2000) classification of the technology type of goods exports, the technological content of South Korea's export goods has been continuously improving since the 1970s, upgraded from mainly low-tech manufacturing exports to a focus on both medium- and high-tech manufacturing exports, as shown Fig. 11.8.

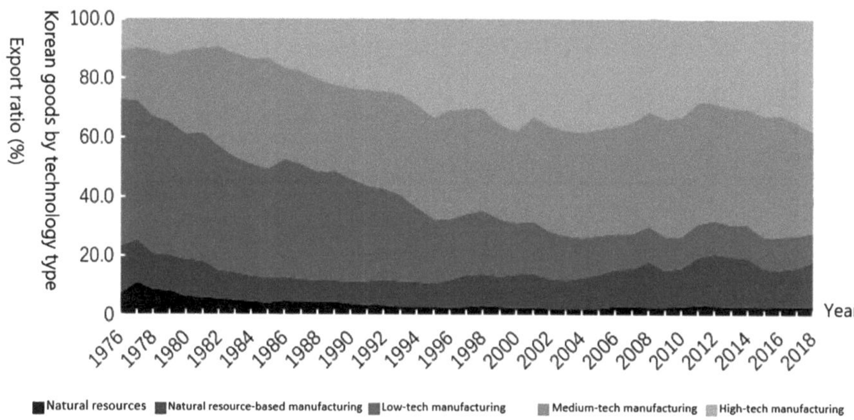

Fig. 11.8 Proportion of South Korea's goods exports by technology type. *Source*: The technology types were classified according to Sanjaya (2000), and the data were from the UN Comtrade database

11.2.3.3 Exchange Rate Undervaluation and Financial Repression

According to the definition of the Central Bank of Korea, South Korea has been implementing a fixed exchange rate system since before 1980 (Bank of Korea 2019). In 1964, the Korean government's strategy to determine the exchange rate changed from overvaluation to undervaluation to expand the cost advantage of the South Korean manufacturing sector in international markets. In order to compensate for the rising costs of the export sector due to the depreciation of the exchange rate, the government also adopted supporting financial repression measures to subsidize it.

Before 1964, under the import substitution strategy, the South Korean government chose to overvalue the exchange rate to promote the substitution of domestic products for foreign imports. With the establishment of the export-oriented strategy, the government continued to devalue the won to stimulate exports. In the 1960s and 1970s, the won experienced several major devaluations: in 1961, the won-dollar exchange rate depreciated from 65:1 to 130:1, in 1964 it depreciated again to 255:1, and in 1975 it further depreciated to 484:1. The continuous currency depreciation reduced the real effective exchange rate of the won by more than 50%. Rodrik (2008) provided a simple method to measure the level of exchange rate overvaluation: using the nominal exchange rate and purchasing power parity in the world table to obtain the real exchange rate (RER = ln (XR/PPP)) and then performing panel data regression on the real exchange rate with respect to the logarithm of real GDP per capita and dummy variables of region and time, the difference between the fitted real exchange rate obtained by regression and the actual real exchange rate is the level of exchange rate overvaluation. A positive value means that the exchange rate of the country's currency is overvalued; a negative value means that the exchange rate of the country's currency is undervalued. The overvaluation of the won in 1953–2017 calculated using this method shows that from 1961 to 1977

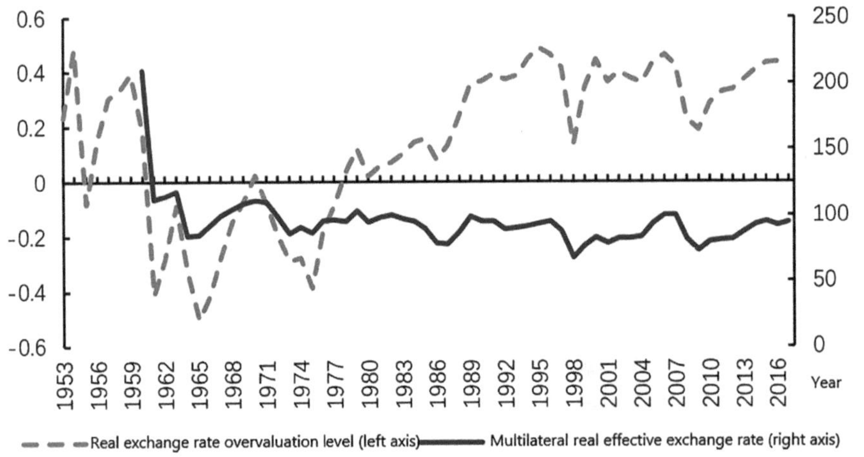

Fig. 11.9 South Korea's exchange rate levels. *Note*: The real exchange rate overvaluation level was calculated based on the Penn World Table version 9.1, and the multilateral real effective exchange rate data were from Bruegel (2021)

(except 1970), South Korea always maintained a policy of an undervalued exchange rate, with an average undervaluation of 23.5%, as shown in Fig. 11.9. In the 1960s and 1970s, when the exchange rate was undervalued, South Korea's exports grew the fastest, reaching 29.0% and 18.7%, respectively.

Although the policy of undervaluing the exchange rate is beneficial to exports, it will inevitably increase the import costs of raw materials and machinery and equipment for enterprises. Relevant data show that the proportion of imported inputs in South Korea from the 1960s to the early 1970s was 25%. Hence, cost increases led the export manufacturing industry, which was more dependent on imported inputs, to oppose the policy during the early stage (Steinberg and Wang 2018). In order to enhance the profitability of the export manufacturing industry, the South Korean government adopted a financial suppression policy, which matched the undervaluation of the exchange rate to reduce the capital cost of this sector in a targeted manner. The South Korean government nationalized the banking industry in 1961 to control the right to appoint bank personnel; in 1962, it revised the Central Bank Act to have direct control over the central bank and established an "official financial" system to completely control the allocation of credit resources. In 1965, the South Korean government strengthened the dual-track loan interest rate system by reducing the loan interest rate for export enterprises from 8% to 6.5% and increasing the loan interest rate for non-export enterprises from 16% to 26% (Steinberg and Wang 2018). The dual-pillar policy of exchange rate undervaluation and financial repression solved the problem of an exchange rate policy that would increase both corporate income and costs, and this greatly benefited South Korean export companies. The attitude towards the policy of undervaluing the exchange rate by the export manufacturing industry changed from opposition to support, and the industry even actively urged the South Korean government to devalue the won during the period of currency appreciation.

11.3 Chapter Summary

In this chapter, the framework of the A-C theory was used to analyze the economic development of South Korea since its founding. First, from the perspective of political and economic history, the political structure and economic policy changes of South Korea since its founding were sorted out, and the economic development difficulties and great achievements of South Korea were reviewed in three stages according to the transformation of the political structure: from multi-peak conflictual governance to the exploration of single-peak governance and to multi-peak reconciliatory governance. Secondly, the experience of South Korea in improving political cohesion and economic accessibility was systematically analyzed. In the process of achieving cohesive political governance, South Korea's centralized leadership system and the universal mobilization of connecting cities and villages reduced social internal friction and brought the national subjects together under the consensus of economic development. In terms of improving economic accessibility and resource allocation, the domestic open market was gradually built up through the implementation of appropriate industrial guidance policies, infrastructure construction, and improvement of labor market quality; externally, the country entered the international open market through docking with the US and Japanese markets, continuously upgraded export-oriented industries, and adopted the policies undervaluing the exchange rate and financial repression. The core strategy was building an internationally competitive tradable manufacturing sector through a set of systematic political and economic policies as a breakthrough to drive the economy to take off. Finally, from the framework of the political cohesion and economic accessibility indicators, the development and the current status of South Korea in terms of political cohesion and economic accessibility since the 1990s were intuitively displayed. The results show that South Korea has a high degree of political cohesion and economic accessibility, especially a high degree of openness represented by external economic accessibility.

References

Bank of Korea (2019) Foreign exchange market: exchange rate system. https://www.bok.or.kr/eng/main/contents.do?menuNo=400186

Bruegel (2021) Real effective exchange rates for 178 countries. https://www.bruegel.org/publications/datasets

Eichengreen B, Perkins DH, Shen KH (2015) In: From miracle to maturity: the growth of the Korean (trans: Ren ZP, Zhang CT). People's Publishing House, Beijing

Gong KY (2014) Evolution and beyond: contemporary Korean politics. Beijing, Intelligence Property Publishing House

Groningen Growth and Development Centre (2014) 10-Sector database. https://www.rug.nl/ggdc/structuralchange/previous-sector-database/10-sector-2014

Jin ZL (1990) A 30-year history of South Korea's economic policy. Korea JoongAng Daily

Ju BH (ed) (1991) Korean economic history. Korea Development Institute

Kim KH (2014) History of the republic of Korea. Social Science Literature Press, Beijing
Korea Economic Development Plan Evaluation Professor Group (1967) Evaluation report on the first five-year economic development plan. Cabinet Planning and Coordination Office of Korea
Mason MTK (1981) Modernization of Korea's economy and society. Korea Development Institute
Ministry of Agriculture, Food and Rural Affairs of Korea (1964) Grain statistics yearbook (1964). Ministry of Agriculture, Food and Rural Affairs of Korea
Political Department of Korea Daily News (1994) The stolen Seoul spring. Korean Literature Institute, Political Department of Korea Daily News
Rodrik D (2008) The real exchange rate and economic growth. Brook Pap Econ Act 39(2):365–412
Sanjaya L (2000) The technological structure and performance of developing country manufactured exports, 1985–98. Oxf Dev Stud 28(3):337–369
Shin KY (2002) Industrialization and democratization in East Asia. Literature and Intelligence Society
Steinberg D, Wang Y (2018) Why did South Korea choose an undervalued exchange rate policy? (part 2). J Financ Dev Res 4:61–63
World Bank (2020) World development indicators 2020. World Bank, Washington, DC
Zhang SY (2005) The growth and structural changes of modern agriculture. The New History of Korean Economy, Ronan
Zhang XC (2018) In Korean capitalism (trans: Xing LJ, Xu M). CITIC Press Group, Beijing
Zhao W (ed) (1995) On modern Korean politics. The Eastern Publishing Co Ltd, Lalbag

Chapter 12
Argentina: From Rapid Growth to Deep Slump

In the early twentieth century, Argentina was one of the richest countries in the world. As shown in Fig. 12.1, Argentina's gross GDP per capita reached 1753 international dollars in 1820, close to that of the United States at 2080 international dollars. In 1913, Argentina's GDP per capita was still 82.3% that of the United States, 105.9% that of Western Europe, 246.1% that of the world, and 280.7% that of Latin America. However, since the 1930s, Argentina's economic growth has entered a period of relative decline, and the gap between it and the United States has continued to widen. In 2016, Argentina's GDP per capita was only 35.6% that of the United States, 48.8% that of Western Europe, 128.5% that of the world, and 136.3% that of Latin America. According to the World Bank's standards of country income level, Argentina still hovers outside the threshold of a high-income country, becoming a typical country caught in the middle-income trap, a turbulent political situation, and frequent economic and financial crises.

Historically, in the course of its development, Argentina has gradually formed five major interest groups: the agricultural and animal husbandry export group, transnational capitalist group, national capitalist group, labor group, and middle-class group. These groups have been in conflict with each other for most of the country's development period, resulting in an impossibility for Argentia to form a highly cohesive society with unimodal and unbiased governance or multimodal and reconciliatory governance. In terms of political governance, Argentina successively experienced the complex evolution of bimodal conflictual governance, multimodal conflictual governance, unimodal biased governance, and a return to multimodal conflictual governance. This clearly shows how the division between the different interest groups in Argentina has led to challenges for cohesive political governance, causing continuous damage to the operation of the economy. In addition, relatively low economic accessibility continues to constrain Argentina's economic growth. According to the A-C theory, there is a significant correlation between a country's political progress and economic development, and an important link behind it is the degree of political cohesion. The degree of political cohesion represents a country's national governance capacity and reflects the degree of consensus and cooperation

C. Chen et al., *From Poverty to Prosperity*, Understanding China,
https://doi.org/10.1007/978-981-95-7171-0_12

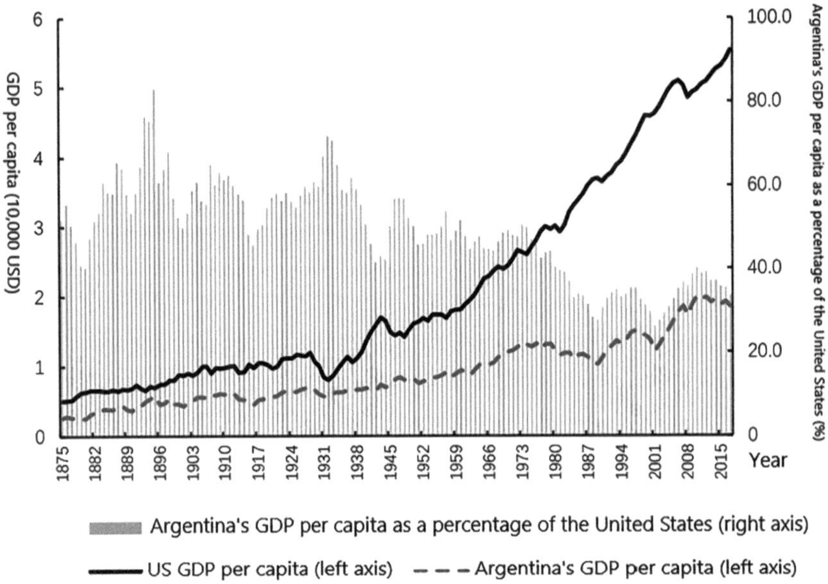

Fig. 12.1 GDP per capita: Argentina vs. United States. *Source*: The Maddison Project Database

among its social interest groups. This chapter starts with a brief history of the political changes in Argentina, and the alliance and division of the social interest groups behind the political changes, and then the interaction between them and economic development is analyzed. Argentina's political and economic development process is a typical negative case—even if a country has high political cohesion and economic accessibility, it still needs to continue to work hard to maintain and improve it. Degradation even in one dimension may have serious consequences for economic and social development.

12.1 Brief History of Argentina's Political Economy

Since Columbus discovered the "New World" in 1492, European colonists began to set foot on the vast land of South America. Argentina, which was originally isolated from Europe, opened a new chapter in its history and experienced the difficult processes of colonial government, independent nation-building, caudillo separatism,[1] and national unification. After national unification, Argentina began its modernization exploration process. Politically, it experienced oligarchic liberalism, populism, and modern representative democracy. Economically, it tried the primary product

[1] The term "caudillo" refers to a military leader who seized local power by force after the collapse of colonial rule in the nineteenth century.

export strategy, import substitution industrialization strategy, and neoliberal development strategy. From the perspective of development achievements, Argentina once achieved brilliant development achievements but later struggled in the middle-income trap for a long time.

12.1.1 Formation and Complexity of Bimodal Conflictual Governance: Early Colonial Period

In the early colonial period (1492–1776), political conflicts were concentrated between the Indian natives and the colonists and became more complex with the diversification of social structure. At this time, the economy of the La Plata River region had two pillars: one was the serf economy under the guardianship system, and the other was the commercial economy driven by the silver transportation trade.

12.1.1.1 Colonizers' Bimodal Conflictual Governance

In 1492, there were about 900,000 Indigenous Indians living in the area that is today's Argentina (Brown 2010).[2] Economically, their production technology was still in the Stone Age, and the main production methods were gathering, hunting, or farming in fertile river valleys. They could not or could only accumulate very few surplus products. Politically, most of these tribes remained in the stage of clans or a village society, with a unified culture formed between tribes. Since there were no gold and silver mines in the area, conquering Indigenous tribes was the main way for colonists to plunder wealth. Bimodal conflictual governance between the colonists and Indigenous Indians was the main political form of this period.

Subsequent economic development promoted the escalation of political conflicts in the region. First, tensions between the colonists and the Indians continued to intensify. The shortage of labor prompted the colonists to adopt a more resolute policy of conquest and suppression against the Indigenous. The technology, economy, and politics of the Indigenous developed during the conflicts, and their war capabilities improved. Throughout the colonial period, the colonists could not establish estates on the Pampas beyond the limit of 60 miles[3] south of Buenos Aires. Second, the development of the Black slave trade made the population structure of the region more complicated. In order to supplement the labor force, the colonists transported about 100,000 Black slaves to Buenos Aires in the 17th and 18th centuries. The arrival of Blacks further complicated racial relations and shaped a future of mixed-race free working class with multi-racial blood. However, compared with

[2] Unless otherwise specified, all data in the section "A Brief History of Argentina's Political Economy" are from this book.

[3] 1 mile is approximately 1.61 km.

Brazil and Cuba, Argentine Black slaves were treated slightly better and did not form a group of escaped slaves.

12.1.1.2 Guardianship System and Silver Trail

In the early colonial period, the La Plata River region implemented a serfdom economy. After the establishment of the "Silver Trail," economic development was mainly driven by trade. The local serfdom was called the "entrusted guardianship system".[4] Under this system, the Spanish royal family enjoyed the ownership of the colonial land, and the colonists, entrusted by the royal family, enjoyed the guardianship, use, and jurisdiction of the land and the Indigenous. The Indigenous were nominally free people and were allocated a small piece of land, but they did not have complete personal freedom and had to pay tribute and perform labor for the guardian. The region lacked endogenous economic power due to its lack of population. In the later period, it mainly relied on the silver industry in Potosí (now in Bolivia) to drive the economy. In 1560, Potosí began to produce a large amount of silver. The silver mining and trade industry gave birth to the "Silver Trail", connecting Potosí and the mouth of the La Plata River, and the region's economic development began to be driven by trade. Every year, about 26,000 mules traveled along the Silver Trail for the transportation of food, silver, and raw materials for silver mining. The Silver Trail and other trade routes led to the rapid growth of Buenos Aires' international trade industry, Salta's mule industry, Cordoba's cattle industry, Mendoza's agriculture, and Paraguay's mate tea planting industry and promoted the development of Buenos Aires's commercial economy and population growth.

In 1580, out of a desire for European trade, the colonists rebuilt Buenos Aires as the main port and trade and commercial center connecting the colony to Spain. In order to prevent Portuguese, Dutch, and British forces from Brazil from interfering in the transportation of silver, Spain stipulated in the early days that Potosí silver could not be exported from Buenos Aires and that direct trade between Europe and the La Plata region was illegal. This made prevalent illegal trade that evaded taxes, and the tradition of tax evasion was formed. During this period, Buenos Aires' foreign trade was monopolized by Portuguese, Dutch, and British merchants, who brought in Black slaves and European goods in exchange for local agricultural and animal husbandry products, such as leather, wine, and wheat, and engaged in illegal silver smuggling. Colonial government officials took the opportunity to use their power to engage in corruption and rent-seeking, further suppressing the interests of the Indigenous. Conflicts between the colonists and the Indigenous became politicized, and the political pattern of bimodal conflictual governance was basically formed.

[4] The guardianship system (*encomienda* in Spanish), also known as the "guardianship system" or "large land grant system", was officially abolished in 1720.

12.1.2 Exploration and Failure of Unimodal and Biased Governance: Viceroyalty and Independence Periods

The complex conflicts in the colonies, combined with the turbulent international political situation, prompted the Spanish royal family to launch the "Bourbon Reform" to strengthen political control over the Rio de la Plata region. However, due to the irreconcilable conflicts, the unimodal politics of the new viceroyalty established by the reform was still biased and eventually collapsed completely due to the independence revolution. As political conflicts intensified, economic development was severely damaged.

12.1.2.1 Bourbon Reform and Exploration of Unimodal and Biased Governance

In the late eighteenth century, the colonies faced multiple conflicts. Politically, conflicts at different levels intensified. In 1740, the Indigenous launched a major uprising; in 1767, the Jesuits, who enjoyed tax exemption and administrative privileges, had their property confiscated and were expelled from the colonies. In addition, the wars between European colonial expansionist countries had an impact on the Argentine region, which involved the division of the colonies and the struggle for trade power. Economically, smuggling and tax evasion hindered the growth of the fiscal revenue of the mother country. The North American War of Independence directly prompted Spain to launch the Bourbon Reform to tighten the autonomy of the Rio de la Plata region and crack down on tax evasion. In 1776, the viceroyalty of La Plata was established, marking the end of Argentina's early colonial period.

The political reform was centered on cracking down on local elites. The political power hierarchy of the new viceroyalty was from high to low, starting from Spanish officials to Spanish-born big business groups to Creoles.[5] Senior officers in the militia could only be white people born in Spain, whereas Creoles could only serve as middle- and lower-level officers and most militias were comprised of mixed-race and people of color. The unimodal and biased political system dominated by Spanish bureaucrats gave rise to the privileged class of Spanish merchants in the economy. The Spanish merchant group controlled the trade between the colonies and Europe by virtue of its connection with European business houses and also controlled the downstream warehouse owners and retail networks. The Spanish merchant group limited the business development space of the Creoles, making them mainly engage in farm and ranch operations on the Pampas Plain. The arrival of Spanish bureaucrats and businessmen impacted the Creoles' autonomy and economic rights, intensified conflicts between different political groups, and fueled the subsequent independence movement.

[5] "Creole" refers to the native white people of Argentina during the colonial period; in the late nineteenth century, it refers to a mixed race with Spanish, Indian, and Black blood.

The core of economic reform was to encourage trade and improve the tax system. In 1778, the number of Spanish ports that could trade directly with the colonies increased from 1 to 10, and the official rule that international trade in the Rio de la Plata region must pass through Lima was abolished. In order to plug tax loopholes, the silver production tax was reduced from 20% to 10%, and other tax rates were also reduced. In 1791, the Spanish royal family also abolished its monopoly on the slave trade. The reduction in trade costs brought huge external demand to the Rio de la Plata region, especially the export of primary products, such as silver, animal skins, and beef jerky, which became the core trade, and increased Spain's trade with its American colonies by 300%. The improvement in economic vitality led to population growth. The urban population of Buenos Aires increased from 37,130 in 1778 to 92,000 in 1809, and the urban population of the two supervisory jurisdictions of Cordoba and Salta del Tucumán almost doubled. In addition, a tax bureaucracy replaced the traditional tax farmers, improving the concentration and efficiency of taxation. The proportion of royal tax revenue from Buenos Aires rose from about 1.5% in the 1770s to about 5% in the early nineteenth century.

12.1.2.2 Independence Revolution and Failure of Single-Peak Biased Governance

The Anglo-French War after the French Revolution also involved Spain, an ally of France, indirectly opening the independence revolution against the viceroyalty of La Plata and the fall of the single-peak viceroyalty rule. The Anglo-French War exposed Spain's two weaknesses. First, Spain's finances were highly dependent on its colonies. The war intensified Spain's exploitation of the colonial economy and aroused strong hatred in the colonies. The war forced Spain to expand the trade opening of Buenos Aires to foreign ships, and the economic strength of Creole merchants was greatly enhanced in the trade with the United Kingdom and the United States. Second, the war exposed the incompetence of the viceroyalty government. In 1806, the United Kingdom invaded Buenos Aires, and the Spanish governor fled without a fight. Creole officers gained military leadership and later led the militia to defeat the British army, and their leader was elected as the new governor.

The spread of European Enlightenment and American revolutionary thought and the improvement of economic and political status led to a surge in Creole nationalism. In 1807, Napoleon overthrew the Spanish royal family, causing Creole elites to no longer recognize Spain's sovereignty over the viceroyalty and to fight for independence. The independence revolution led to the collapse of the political unity of the viceroyalty, and the caudillos, who had their own troops and established their own regimes, ruled various places. The caudillos with Buenos Aires Province as the core were mainly centralists, while the caudillos in other provinces were mainly autonomous federalists, fighting each other endlessly. Most caudillos mainly represented the interests of local landowners and businessmen, so civilian caudillos launched a popular revolution, advocating civilian-based federalism and social reforms, including land redistribution. In 1816, a provincial conference was held and declared the independence of Argentina. The centralists established the United Provinces of the La Plata, while the federalist caudillos continued to implement provincial autonomy. The first Argentine constitution, promulgated in 1819, had almost no practical effect.

With the collapse of the unimodal political form, Argentina's economic openness was no longer dominated by the colonial powers, which objectively increased the openness of the economy. During the Anglo-French War, the United Kingdom blockaded Spanish ports from 1797 to 1802 and from 1805 to 1808, causing the trade volume of Spanish colonies at that time to drop to 10% that in 1790. British merchants took the opportunity to replace Spanish merchants in the dominance of international trade in Buenos Aires. In 1809, the value of goods imported by the United Kingdom to the La Plata River region reached 1.2 million pounds (Szuchman and Jonathan 1994).

12.1.3 From Multi-peak Conflictual to Multi-peak Reconciliatory Governance: Caudillo Period

After the War of Independence, separatist political forces in Argentina began to compete for ruling power, and the country's political governance showed typical characteristics of multi-peak conflictual governance. After experiencing multiple power changes, some powerful caudillos finally stabilized the country's unity through military conquest and economic control, forming a multi-peak reconciliatory pattern under the leadership of powerful forces. The political environment was stabilized, and policies dedicated to improving economic competitiveness could be continuously implemented, laying a solid foundation for Argentina to become a modern country and bringing stable and sustained economic growth. According to the Maddison Project Database, Argentina's average annual GDP growth rate from 1820 to 1870 was 3.25%.

12.1.3.1 Multimodal Conflictual Governance and National Unity Under Leadership of Powerful Caudillos

The constitution, promulgated in 1819, stipulated the country's legislative power, provincial powers, central executive power, and judicial power. However, under this national framework, the central executive power and judicial power were very weak, which made the politics of the United Provinces extremely unstable in the first 10 years of the Caudillo period, full of struggles for political leadership, and manipulation of elections. The emergence of powerful caudillos saw them forming checks and balances with each other, and Argentina's political governance became more stable. From 1829 to 1852, the federalist Juan Manuel de Rosas became the governor of Buenos Aires. With the port status of Buenos Aires, he controlled the inland provinces and enjoyed the exclusive federal diplomatic power, becoming the de facto ruler of Argentina. However, because of his intervention in the political struggles of the East Coast Province and his control over foreign trade, Rosas was overthrown by a caudillo from the neighboring province, Justo José Urquiza, in 1953. In the same year, Urquiza convened the National Congress to approve a new constitution, establish the Argentine Republic, form a national army, declare slavery illegal, and legalize direct international trade on the Paraná and Uruguay rivers. The 1953 Constitution granted the president the right to intervene, allowing future national leaders to reduce the autonomy of provincial governors. Urquiza served as president of Argentina from 1854 to 1860 and strengthened the central government's control over national finances, but he was overthrown by the political forces in Buenos Aires in 1860. Bartolomé Mitre, the governor of Buenos Aires, served as the president of Argentina from 1861 to 1868, and the federalists and the centralists reached a final reconciliation. The 1865 Triple Alliance (Brazil, Argentina, and Uruguay) war with Paraguay helped the Argentine government build a strong national army, which in turn strengthened its control over other provinces. In 1879, the "Desert Expedition" led by General Julio Argentino Roca to the national army completely disintegrated the 400-year resistance of the Indians. At this point, Argentina's national unification process was basically completed, the constitutional system was basically established, the multi-peak conflictual governance evolved into multi-peak reconciliatory governance, and the overall politics tended to be stable.

12.1.3.2 Economic Policies and Growth During Caudillo Period

After Argentina's independence, the economic status of the Spanish merchant group was dominated by foreign merchants, such as British and local Creole merchants. Foreign merchants monopolized Argentina's foreign trade, while local Creoles became compradors and ranchers of foreign trading companies. The economic policy during the Caudillo period, driven by the pursuit of economic interests, showed the dual characteristics of oligarchy and liberalism. In 1826, President Rivadavia instructed the Ministry of Finance to pass the Land Lease Law, declaring that "the state owns the land but authorizes individuals or associations to rent public land within 20 years at a rent of 8% of the land value. And long-term leasing eventually evolved into private land ownership (p. 33)" (Wang 2011). "After Rosas came to power, he abolished the law that prohibited the transfer of state-owned land and allowed free land transactions, which accelerated the process of land concentration. For example, in 1830, 538 landowners in Buenos Aires owned 8.656 million hectares of land; by 1840, 293 landowners owned 8.6 million hectares of land (p. 13)" (Dong 2013a). From 1833 to 1834, the Desert Expedition led by Rosas seized.82 million acres of Indigenous Indian land (Burgin 1946). From 1879 to 1880, the Desert Expedition resulted in 21 million acres of land falling into the hands of only 381 people.

Argentina also implemented a series of open policies and measures, including attracting foreign investment, increasing the construction of railways, encouraging

European immigrants, and strengthening modern education. In 1925, the *Treaty of Friendship, Commerce, and Navigation Between Argentina and the United Kingdom* laid the foundation for Argentina's integration into the British world trade system. In 1860, the Bahrain Company raised a loan of 2.5 million pounds for Argentina to build infrastructure, among the many British capitals that began to flow into Argentina (Bethell 1994). The United Kingdom's investment in Argentina's railways reached 3.76 million pounds and 7.01 million pounds in 1873 and 1877, respectively, and Argentina's railway mileage increased sharply from 47 km in 1861 to 2516 km in 1880 (Dong 2013b). The labor shortage had always been an important factor that troubled Argentina's economic development. The long-standing labor shortage gave ranch workers relatively high bargaining power. The actual wages of workers rose from an average of 7.5 gold pesos per month in 1804 to 12 gold pesos in 1864. The Argentine political theorist Juan Bautista Alberdi and other intellectual elites proposed a new policy to encourage European immigration, such as foreigners in Argentina being exempted from military service and allowed to enjoy the freedom of religious activities and remittance of profits, which resulted in a large number of immigrants pouring into Argentina. In 1854, European immigrants accounted for 10.5% of the rural population in Buenos Aires. After understanding the role of education in economic development and social progress, intellectual elites who had been exiled to Europe spared no effort to promote the secularization and modernization of education and vigorously established schools at different levels.

Following independence, Argentina's inland economy fell into a long-term recession due to the depletion of the Potosí silver mine and the internal caudillo separatism. Only the economy of Buenos Aires and the surrounding areas quickly recovered and grew due to international trade. In the first 40 years after independence, Buenos Aires was blockaded four times, but that did not change its growing economic trend. In the first 10 years of the nineteenth century, only about 100 foreign ships entered the port of Buenos Aires each year; the number increased to an average of 280 ships per year in the 1920s and 1930s, 452 ships per year in the 1940s, and 674 ships per year in the 1950s.

The development of the European industry provided a huge impetus for Argentina's primary product exports. Before the late 1850s, cowhide was the main export commodity of Argentina, before being replaced by coarse wool. Animal fats, horsehide and bones, and salted beef also accounted for a certain share in the trade. Due to the lack of labor, the wheat industry accounted for a small proportion of Argentina's agricultural economy at this time. The booming market for cowhide and cattle by-products greatly stimulated Argentina's cattle industry. In 1825, 70,000 cattle were slaughtered in Buenos Aires; by the mid-nineteenth century, more than 300,000 horses and cattle were slaughtered each year. The development of cattle farming led to a rapid increase in the rural population: from 1820 to 1860, the annual growth rate of urban residents was 1.5% and the annual growth rate of rural residents was 3.4%. The increase in rural population led to the prosperity of the estate economy. The economy of inland provinces also began to revive after 1830, and despite the large number of immigrants going to the coastal provinces, the population of these provinces continued to grow at a rate of 2% per year. Argentina's population grew at an annual rate of 2.5%, from 406,000 in 1810 to one million in 1860. From 1820 to 1870, Argentina's GDP grew at an average annual rate of 3.25%.

12.1.4 Formation and Decline of Single-Peak Biased Governance

This period can be divided into the "peace and management" period from 1880 to 1916 and the development period of new political forces from 1916 to 1930. During these two periods, the National Autonomy Party, which represented the interests of the economic oligarchs, further continued the liberal economic policy after the unification of the country. The cohesive political governance united the entire society, with economic development at the core, and started the fastest modernization process in Argentina's history. During these two periods, Argentina's GDP average annual growth rate was 5.05% and 4.72%, respectively, ranking first and second among the country's seven growth stages.

12.1.4.1 Glory of "Peace and Management" Period

In 1880, Roca took office as the president of Argentina, marking the entry of Argentina into an era of "peace and management". The authority of the Argentine central government was further consolidated, and the cohesion of political governance was improved. Roca and the "Generation of 1880" politicians around him represented the interests of the highest class of Argentine society, including traditional elite families, the rich, and the landlord class. The National Autonomy Party they formed firmly controlled the state power during this period through an indirect election system that restricted the right to vote and provided a list of presidential candidates, providing a stable political environment for Argentina's economic development. The central government weakened the political status of Buenos Aires Province, took back control of tariffs, established Buenos Aires City as the national capital, and forced the province to move its provincial capital; in addition, the government abolished the militia forces of all provinces and took control of the federal army. Because the economic interests and the political class composition were similar, the provinces were unified under the centrally enlightened centralized government. Although caudillo politics in the provinces still remained to a certain extent, the power of the central government was unprecedentedly consolidated, and it had a strong ability to interfere in the affairs of the provinces. Overall, during this period, Argentina's multi-peak reconciliatory political governance gradually turned to single-peak biased governance.

Under the control of the landlord class and political elites, Argentina continued a series of liberal economic policies in the early stage, including opening trade and market, attracting foreign investment and immigration, etc., improving its internal and external economic accessibility, and hence the country's economic development accomplished brilliant achievements. Argentina became a modern country based on exporting agricultural products and importing European technology, capital, management, and labor by using comparative advantages to produce beef, wheat, mutton, and wool for international markets. In the late nineteenth century, coarse wool was Argentina's main export; by 1910, wheat and cereals had replaced it, with wheat growing on one-third of the country's agricultural land, and Argentina surpassed the United States to become the world's most important wheat exporter. During this period, Argentina's manufacturing industry also made great progress. In the 1890s, tanneries, blacksmith shops, wood and metal processing plants, cigarette and match factories, sack factories, and shoe and shirt manufacturers had developed to meet the domestic market demand. Overall, this period was the most glorious period in Argentina's economic growth history: from 1870 to 1916, Argentina's GDP grew at an average annual rate of 5.05%; from 1880 to 1914, Argentina's population grew at an average annual rate of 3.5%, urban population grew at an average annual rate of 5.4%, railway mileage grew at an average annual rate of 10.6%, exports and imports grew at an average annual rate of 6.8%, and manufacturing grew at an average annual rate of 9.3%. In addition, by 1913, the United Kingdom's total investment in Argentina reached £479.8 million (Dong 2013b). From 1880 to 1916, approximately 2.9 million immigrants settled permanently in Argentina, and at least 30% of the population at that time was foreign-born. Another one million immigrants arrived in Argentina in the 1920s.

12.1.4.2 Afterglow of Growth After Failure of Unimodal and Biased Governance

As Argentina's economy developed, new interest groups began to emerge, and the unimodally biased political governance pattern was gradually broken.

The export of primary products, especially agricultural products, greatly increased the value of land. The Argentine elite further expanded its control over the economy from the commercial sector to the agricultural sector, and the difference in land ownership exacerbated the social class division between the rich and the poor. In the fertile Pampas plains, immigrants and native Creoles were mainly landless tenants and farm workers, who had conflicts with farmers from time to time; in inland provinces, immigrants obtained relatively more land and became the rural middle class, while native Argentines remained ranch and farm workers. Within the growing working class, immigrant workers also had serious racial discrimination against Creole workers due to cultural and linguistic differences and refusal to intermarry. However, Creoles became the main source of soldiers for the federal army, and officers of the federal army mainly came from the elites and middle class in remote provinces. The middle and lower-level officers of the federal army represented the interests of the middle class, which laid the groundwork for future conflicts between the military and the elite government.

As the power of the middle class and the working class expanded, the interests of the army and the National Autonomy Party gradually diverged, and the social dissatisfaction caused by the political and economic privileges of the National Autonomy Party became increasingly strong. The party's control over the government was challenged by the opposition Radical Party. Although the core leadership of the Radical Party was composed of dissident oligarchs, it generally received support from farmers, tenants, the urban middle class, and even the working class. In addition, several small-scale rebellions within the army also showed that many officers also supported the Radical Party. Faced with an unfavorable situation, the National Autonomy Party tried to defend its ruling position by expanding the electoral reform of the regime but failed to achieve its goal. In the first election after the reform (the 1916 election), the Radical Party won and controlled the National Congress, and the Socialist Party won the Buenos Aires city election. This was the first time in Argentine history that a power transfer was achieved through elections. The expansion of railways and the rise of the immigrant bourgeoisie also hit the political status of provincial oligarchs.

Due to the complex composition of the Radical Party's supporters, its policies after coming to power were for taking care of the interests of all parties. The core leaders of the Radical Party were landlord oligarchs, so the party's main economic policies did not deviate seriously from the conservative economic policies of the National Autonomy Party; also, in order to give back to the middle-class and working-class supporters, the Radical Party expanded university education to satisfy the middle class who valued education and gave certain support to the working class, especially when workers went on strike to claim their rights from enterprises. However, a series of workers' movements from 1919 to 1922 led to the break between the Radical Party and the Workers' Union, and President Yrigoyen turned to the Argentine Patriotic Union, composed of the right-wing middle class and army officers. The Great Depression in 1929 severely impacted the Argentine economy, and President Yrigoyen's ability to govern was questioned. In 1930, the army launched a coup to overthrow him. This was the first time the army participated in political transformation since it helped Roca usher in the liberal peace period in 1880. This coup marked Argentina's transition from the liberal era to the populist era.

Although the pattern of unimodal political governance was gradually broken from 1916 to 1930, Argentina's economic growth during this period was still very good due to the overall continuity of economic policies. From 1916 to 1930, Argentina's GDP grew at an average annual rate of 4.72%. After the setbacks of World War I, Argentina's economy resumed strong exports in the 1920s. However, it is worth noting that the large-scale expansion of foreign capital caused dissatisfaction among Argentine domestic capitalists. Therefore, the nationalism movement, which advocated the exercise of political rights, restrictions on foreign companies, and the internalizing of the benefits of economic growth, began to rise. Hence, the government steadily increased its power and regulated the economic assets of foreign companies, such as railways, meat processing companies, and oil companies. All foreign companies that were allowed to enter Argentina were subject to state intervention. Objectively speaking, this series of actions led to a decline in the external accessibility of the Argentine economy.

12.1.5 Pursuit and Failure of Unbiased Single-Peak Governance: Period of Populism

As Argentina entered the populist period, its political governance and economic system underwent significant changes. Among them, the most significant one is that during the Perón administration, it once developed towards the pattern of unimodal and unbiased governance. The cohesion of political governance was improved, and the economy achieved relatively significant growth. However, during the two stages before and after Perón came to power, Argentina's political and economic order was relatively chaotic, and the average economic growth rate was the lowest in the 200 years since the country's independence.

12.1.5.1 Multi-peak Conflictual Governance Period

After the military coup in 1930, regardless of whether the government was the military government from 1930 to 1938 or the oligarchic civilian government from 1938 to 1943, Argentina's politics were full of electoral fraud. The Radical Party, which mainly represented the middle class, was excluded from political power, even though it was the largest single political group. Argentina's political governance is in a state of multi-peak conflictual governance. Political conflicts occurred frequently, and the middle class kept taking to the streets to protest.

In addition, after the Great Depression and the outbreak of World War II, European countries turned to war as their focus and their economies fell into a trough, which caused European countries to significantly reduce their imports of Argentine agricultural products. Argentina also had difficulties importing capital goods, raw materials, and industrially manufactured products. In order to cope with the weak export of agricultural products and the shortage of industrial consumer goods, the Argentine government sought to strengthen its export trade with the United Kingdom and to focus on implementing an industrialization strategy, and the Argentine economy began to undergo a major transformation.

In order to strengthen its competition with the United States, Canada, and other countries in agricultural product exports, Argentina negotiated with the United Kingdom: the Roca-Runciman Treaty in 1933 and the Eden-Malbrand Treaty in 1936 preserved Argentina's British export market, at the cost of Argentina's commitment to preferential treatment of imported goods produced in the United Kingdom and to protect British companies in railways and meat processing enterprises, which hurt the development of Argentina's national industry. This enabled Argentina's exports to quickly recover and quickly exceed the level of the 1920s.

However, the rise of nationalism, the outbreak of World War II, and the rise of structuralist theory gradually led to the government's policy of giving priority to the development of the domestic industry. In 1940, Argentina's Finance Minister Federico Pinedo submitted an economic recovery plan, dubbed the Pinedo Plan, to the National Congress, which for the first time clearly proposed industrialization as a long-term strategy for the country. The measures proposed were as follows: first, stabilize agricultural product prices and restrict land rents; second, promote industrial development and industrial exports through export tax rebates and export credits; third, develop the construction industry to create jobs; fourth, strengthen relations with the United States, hoping that the United States would replace the United Kingdom as a capital goods supplier and export market for Argentina's industrial development; and fifth, form a customs union with neighboring countries, such as Brazil, to expand the regional market (Jiang 2018). During the industrialization process, the level of the nationalization of Argentina's economy increased significantly, and the government's influence on and regulation of the economy increased. For example, the Federal Petroleum Reserve Company's production continued to expand, reducing the import share of Argentina's oil consumption from 58% in 1930 to 37% in 10 years. However, due to the turbulent political environment and poor policy implementation, Argentina's GDP grew at an average annual rate of 2.15% from 1930 to 1942, and its GDP per capita grew at an average annual rate of only 0.41%.

12.1.5.2 Pursuit of Single-Peak Unbiased Governance: Perón Period

Amid internal and external troubles, a group of middle-level military officers, including Juan Perón, launched a coup in 1943 to overthrow the civilian government and take over power. Perón was formerly the Minister of Labor in 1943 and the Vice President and Minister of the Army in 1944 before resigning due to political disputes. He was arrested by the military opposition in 1945 and released during a large-scale demonstration by the working class. Perón then organized the Workers' Party (the predecessor of the Justice Party) to run for president and was successfully elected in 1946 and re-elected in 1952.

When he was in power, Perón advocated the construction of Argentina with a third way, different from capitalism and socialism, called "justicialism" (one of the main representative ideas of populism). Politically, Perón advocated a multi-class political alliance composed of the middle class and the military, while incorporating the growing working class into political affairs and ultimately making the oligarchy lose its position. Economically, Perón advocated the implementation of economic nationalism, the import substitution strategy of national industrialization, government control over trade unions, and the improvement of welfare benefits for the working class. Specifically, the Perón government inherited the previous industrialization strategy and strengthened the control of state-owned economy; in addition, it adopted a pro-labor policy to improve workers' welfare. The Perón government issued the Declaration of Economic Independence of Argentina in 1947, nationalized the British-owned railways and the American-owned Argentine Telephone Company through purchase in 1948, and established the National State Industry Bureau and the Trade Promotion Association in 1949 to vigorously promote the industrialization process. The government also restricted the expansion and competitive advantages of foreign companies in Argentina, implemented tariff protection and tax rebates for weak industries, interfered with foreign exchange transactions to promote the import of industrial machinery and raw materials, issued loans to industries through the banking system it controlled, and provided funds for industrial expansion with export tariffs on agricultural products. In addition, out of political needs, Perón increased the wages and welfare benefits of workers in exchange for the support of trade unions. From 1945 to 1948, the wages of skilled workers and unskilled workers increased by 22% and 30%, respectively, and the proportion of domestic income of workers' income increased from 40% to 50%. Most workers enjoyed medical compensation, maternity leave, paid vacations, and freedom from arbitrary dismissal.

In terms of effect, the policies of economic nationalism and national industrialization expanded the interests of the bourgeoisie and the middle class, while the policies of strengthening control over trade unions and increasing workers' welfare took care of the interests of the working class and eased labor-capital relations. In addition, Perón's military background enabled him to coordinate the relationship between the military and the civilian government. Therefore, in the early days of Perón's rule, Argentina experienced a short-lived single-peak unbiased political governance. However, the negative effects of Perón's policy measures soon became apparent. Improving workers' welfare and the resulting demand to balance the interests of the middle class brought huge expenditures to the government. Economic nationalization led to a decline in production efficiency, the expansion of bureaucracy and state-owned enterprises, and rampant corruption. Economic nationalism policies led to a significant decline in the external accessibility of Argentina's economy. Coupled with other factors, such as the surge in domestic consumption and the 1951–1952 drought, which led to a sharp drop in exports and a shortage of foreign exchange, Argentina fell into fiscal deficits, inflation, and economic recession. In just five years, Argentina's inflation rate rose from 4% to 40%, and the average real wage of unskilled workers in Buenos Aires in 1952 was 21% lower than in 1949. Because of the serious fiscal deficit, falling wages, and rising inflation, Perón supporters from the middle class and the working class were severely hit. In 1955, after demonstrations and conflicts between the middle class and the working class, the military launched a coup and forced Perón to resign and flee.

12.1.5.3 Chaos and Long-Term Stagnation During De-perónization Period

For a long time following its establishment, the military government was committed to removing Perón's influence on Argentina, including removing the Justice Party from the government and cracking down on trade unions. The military government's suppression and crackdown on trade unions caused a new generation of trade union workers to call for Perón's return again. University students, who had once contributed to Perón's resignation, began to accept communist revolutionary ideas because of their bleak job prospects and dissatisfaction with social ills and became left-wing guerrillas supporting Perón in the early 1970s. Workers' resistance and guerrilla movements forced the military government to hold elections in 1973. The Justice Party won and Perón returned to the presidency, but he died in 1974 and his widow Isabel succeeded him as president. However, due to the lack of Isabel Perón's government's ability, the country's foreign debt reached US$8 billion in 1975. When the inflation rate reached 600% in March 1976, the military overthrew the government again.

In 1976, the military government formulated a national restructuring process, including purging members of the Justice Party, eliminating guerrillas, and curbing inflation. The government's anti-inflation policy inspired the confidence of foreign investors, and billions of petrodollars flowed into Argentina. The government's arbitrary and unaccountable spending made foreign debt difficult to repay. The military government's debt reached US$18 billion in 1979 and US$40 billion in 1982. In the process of suppressing the guerrillas, the military government's "dirty war" and reign of terror against political dissidents and guerrillas aroused widespread protests from the Argentine people. In 1982, the military government launched the Falklands War against the United Kingdom to divert domestic attention, but the disastrous defeat of the war brought the military government to a complete end and it was forced to announce the holding of a presidential election in 1983. Raúl Alfonsín, who united the many factions in the Republican Party to form the Radical Civic Union, won the election and became president, declaring the complete bankruptcy of populism.

During the period of de-Perónization, Argentina's economy showed a typical stop-start pattern. Each economic growth could only last for 2–3 years. The growth rate in a certain year could reach 4%–5% or higher, but it would fall into recession the next year. This situation was related to Argentina's political and economic structure. Argentina's economy was an agricultural sector that earned foreign exchange through exports and an import-substituting industrial sector that consumed foreign exchange. The measures taken by the government to develop the industrial sector were to increase the proportion of state-owned economies, support the credit sector, and increase workers' wages and benefits, which led to reduced economic efficiency, increased government deficits, and foreign exchange shortages. When the inflation rate rose, deficit reduction was difficult, foreign exchange was scarce, and the agricultural sector could not provide sufficient industrial subsidies, and so the government had to rely on foreign investment to make up for the gap, but the instability of foreign investment exacerbated the fragility of Argentina's economy. The government's economic policies were often more inclined towards short-term policies and more easily captured by interest groups due to the swing between pro-labor and pro-capital, which exacerbated economic volatility. In particular, from 1976 to 1983, Argentina's GDP grew at an average annual rate of only 0.58%, while its GDP per capita grew at an average annual rate of −1.07%.

12.1.6 *Multi-peak Conflictual Governance Under Modern Democracy: Period of Alternating Between Old and New Ideologies*

In 1983, when the military government was forced to step down due to the failure of the Falklands War, Argentina began a multi-peak political pattern of alternating political parties in power. However, there were many political parties in Argentina's political arena, and the important political parties were loosely organized, without a clear program, and often had internal divisions. The alternating of political parties often led to drastic changes in the country's political and economic policies. Behind the alternating of political parties were the political games between different interest groups. In the course of Argentina's political and economic development, interest groups with conflicts in many aspects were formed in Argentina, including the agricultural and animal husbandry export group with the rural association as the core, the multinational capitalist group with the industrial association as the core, the national capitalist group with the General Economic Confederation as the core, the labor group with the General Labor Confederation as the core, and the relatively weak middle-class group (Jiang 2018). Among them, the agricultural and animal husbandry export group and the labor group were at the two extremes of the political spectrum, and the remaining groups were distributed in the middle of the political spectrum. The interests of these political groups were very different and conflicting, which made difficult the realization of cohesive political governance with a ruling party leading the entire society. Argentina's economic policy kept swinging between neoliberalism and populism, which affected Argentina's economic growth. During this period, Argentina's GDP grew at an average annual rate of 2.33%, ranking fifth among its seven growth stages.

12.1.6.1 Alternating Between New and Old Ideologies Under Multi-peak Governance

From 1983 to 2003, Argentina's political situation was turbulent, but it basically pursued neoliberal policies. President Alfonsín, who came to power through the 1983 election, faced mutinies from some middle- and lower-level officers and soldiers in the army many times because he refused to pardon military government personnel and dismiss the military government's anti-human rights behavior. In addition, after the IMF's advice was accepted, Alfonsín's economic reforms did not avoid falling into hyperinflation, which led to his failure in the 1989 election. Workers called for a general strike due to inflation. Mobs looted stores across the country, and Alfonsín was forced to give up the presidency five months ahead of schedule. President Carlos Menem of the Justice Party, who came to power in 1989, vigorously promoted neoliberal reforms centered on privatization and the currency board system, Argentina's economy once experienced significant development. The economic downturn in the later period led the government to expand the fiscal deficit to stimulate the economy, which in turn led to rising foreign debt and inflation, but the measure failed to reduce the unemployment rate. In the 1998 election, Fernando de la Rúa participated in the general election as the presidential candidate of the two-party alliance of the Radical Party and the National Unity Front and was elected president. Faced with a foreign debt of US$132 billion, the Argentine government began to implement an austerity plan. Austerity and unemployment triggered strikes and riots. In 2001, mobs looted stores across the country, forcing de la Rúa to resign. In the following two weeks, Argentina experienced constitutional instability. The National Congress replaced three interim presidents in succession. The fourth interim president, Eduardo Duhalde, presided over the Argentine political situation in 2022 and abandoned the currency board system for issuing the peso, triggering turmoil in the domestic financial market.

In 2003, Néstor Kirchner of the Justice Party was elected as president, and the Argentine social consensus returned to the populist line. Kirchner and his wife served as presidents of Argentina from 2003 to 2015. During their tenures, the government adopted a limited intervention in the market economy, such as strict foreign exchange controls. Benefiting from the continued commodity boom in international markets, Argentina's economy stabilized and achieved good growth, but there were still problems, such as high inflation and continued sovereign debt defaults. In 2015, Mauricio Macri, the leader of the Republican Plan Party, representing the center-right forces, won the election and became president, leading Argentina back to the path of neoliberal economic reform. In 2019, Alberto Fernández, the leader of the National Front Party representing the center-left, won the election and became president, and Argentina's political pendulum swung towards populism again.

12.1.6.2 Continued Economic Dynamic Stagnation

In 1983, faced with high inflation and a high external debt burden, President Alfonsín chose to accept the IMF's fiscal remedy but was unable to promote bureaucratic reform and privatization of state-owned enterprises. Subsequently, the Alfonsín government proposed the "Australis Plan" to stabilize the economy, including issuing new currency, freezing wages and consumer prices, cutting government spending, and developing southern Argentina. However, in the 1980s, public sector employment rose instead of falling, state-owned enterprises continued to lose money, government spending could not be cut, fiscal deficit continued to expand, and inflation was never resolved and never fell below 90%, and so the plan ended in failure.

Although President Menem, who succeeded in 1989, was a Perónist in politics, he went further and more thoroughly than Alfonsín in neoliberal economic reforms. The core content of his reform policy centered on the privatization of state-owned enterprises, the currency board system, and the opening of capital accounts. Within a year of Menem taking office, almost all state-owned enterprises in Argentina were quickly auctioned off and privatized, involving many fields, such as oil, railways, and aviation. In response to high inflation, the Menem government adopted a currency board system that issued pesos in equal amounts with US dollars as reserves. At the cost of giving up monetary policy independence, Argentina's inflation dropped rapidly from 3000% in 1989 to 7% in 1993, but the policy also led to a decline in Argentina's exports and an economic downturn. However, the capital account was fully liberalized, and the currency was allowed to be freely convertible. Nevertheless, the prosperity brought about by neoliberal reforms in the short term once again eroded the fiscal discipline of the Argentine government. From 1993 to 1999, Argentina's debt accounted for 32.9% of GDP, and the fiscal deficit ratio increased from 0.3% to 4.7% (Jiang 2018). When Argentina's export sector was hit by the devaluation of the Brazilian currency in 1998, the economic recession caused international capital to begin to flow out of Argentina on a large scale, Argentina's money supply tightened, and the economy fell into a recession-tightening spiral. In 2000, Argentina promised to implement a fiscal rebalancing policy and asked the IMF for assistance, but it was unable to reverse the trend of foreign capital outflow. In 2001, Argentina had to impose restrictions on its capital account. The IMF also believed that Argentina's reforms did not meet the standards and stopped lending. Argentina defaulted on its external debts, and the economy fell into complete chaos.

From 2003 to 2014, when the Kirchners came to power one after another, their economic policies changed the neoliberal model of the Menem period and chose to strengthen government intervention in the market. In terms of fiscal policy, they moderately expanded government fiscal spending and increased infrastructure investment; in terms of industrial policy, they actively promoted re-industrialization and restored nationalization in the fields of oil, nuclear power, aviation, etc.; in terms of monetary policy, they restricted the freedom of currency exchange, reformed the financial system, and improved the independence of monetary policy; and in terms of trade policy, they strengthened tariffs and non-tariff barriers. Although many of these policies had positive significance, the most important factor that really enabled Argentina's economy to achieve better development during this period was the prosperity of the international commodity market. According to data from the Food and Agriculture Organization of the United Nations, food prices, which were basically stable in the 1990s, experienced a rapid rise in the first decade of the twenty-first century. In 2008, the price indices of food, grains, and oils and fats rose by 121%, 171%, and 227%, respectively. After the 2008 international financial crisis, Argentina's economy fell into a slump again. In 2015, President Macri, who represented the center-right forces, returned to neoliberal reforms and took various measures, including liberalizing exchange rate controls and negotiating with foreign creditors to return to the international capital market. However, during his tenure, Argentina once again experienced a recession with currency depreciation, rising inflation, and debt repayment difficulties. Table 12.1 summarizes the characteristics of Argentina's political cohesion and economic growth from ancient times to the present. Overall, Argentina's economy during this period of alternating ideologies remained in a dynamic stagnation stage. Since 1983, Argentina's economy has experienced continuous positive growth for no more than five years, and most of the time it lasted 2–3 years. Especially since 2011, Argentina's economic growth rate has alternated between positive and negative, and after briefly

Table 12.1 Cohesion of political governance and economic growth in Argentina

<table>
<tr><th colspan="2">Period</th><th>Political status</th><th>Economic growth</th></tr>
<tr><td colspan="2">Pre-Columbian period (50,000 BC–1492)</td><td>Scattered primitive tribes, most of which had not yet formed hereditary and social divisions</td><td>With Stone Age technology, there was no or very little accumulation of surplus products</td></tr>
<tr><td colspan="2">Formation and complication of bimodal conflictual governance: Early colonial period (1492–1776)</td><td>Colonizers gradually established colonial strongholds and were in a bimodal conflictual pattern with the Indigenous. Conflicts between the expanding colonists and the Indigenous intensified, and the Black slave trade complicated the population composition</td><td>The colonizers plundered the wealth and labor development of Indigenous people by delegated guardianship; the silver industry in Potosí drove Buenos Aires's commercial economy and international trade, and the prevalence of illicit trade led to corruption and rent-seeking</td></tr>
<tr><td rowspan="2">Exploration and failure of single-peak biased governance: Period of viceroyalty and independence (1776–1820)</td><td>Dogedistrict period (1776–1810)</td><td>The North American Revolutionary War led to the Bourbon Reform, and the pattern of unimodal and biased governance was initially explored</td><td>Economic reform was centered on free trade and the improvement of the tax system. Spain's trade with its American colonies rose significantly</td></tr>
<tr><td>Independence period (1810–1820)</td><td>Creoles established a united province and promulgated Argentina's first constitution, and the exploration of single-peak biased governance of the former viceroyalty failed</td><td>The Revolution destroyed the commercial networks established by Spain in the heart of South America and interrupted trade from Potosí to Buenos Aires</td></tr>
<tr><td rowspan="2">Formation and development of multimodal reconciliatory governance: Caudillo period (1820–1880)</td><td>Battle of caudillos (1820–1829)</td><td>The government of Buenos Aires was overthrown, the caudillos were divided, and there was a brief pattern of multimodal conflictual governance</td><td rowspan="2">The main export commodities were cowhide and coarse wool. From 1820 to 1870, the average annual GDP growth rate was 3.25%; from 1820 to 1880, GDP per capita grew at an average annual rate of 0.79%</td></tr>
<tr><td>Period of powerful caudillos (1829–1880)</td><td>Promulgation of a new constitution, expansion of the central government's powers, dismantling of Indigenous resistance, and emergence of multimodal reconciliatory governance</td></tr>
</table>

(continued)

Table 12.1 (continued)

Period		Political status	Economic growth
Formation and fading of unimodal and biased governance: Liberal period (1880–1930)	Era of "peace and administration" (1880–1916)	Under the rule of the National Autonomous Party, the central government's power continued to strengthened, and governance reached a single-peak pattern with caudillos from other provinces in exchange for asylum and support	Implementation of liberal economic policies. Average annual GDP growth rate from 1870 to 1916 was 5.05 percent, and average annual growth rate of GDP from 1890 to 1916 was 4.47%. From 1880 to 1916, GDP per capita grew at average annual rate of 1.84%
	Decline of liberalism (1916–1930)	The Radical Party, supported by multiple classes, came to power, and single-peak governance declined	The main economic policy did not seriously deviate from the economic policy of the National Autonomy Party and gave back to both middle- and working-class supporters. The GDP grew at an average annual rate of 4.72% and the GDP per capita grew at an average annual rate of 2.00%
Pursuit and failure of single-peak unbiased governance: Period of populism (1930–1983)	"Infamous decade" (1930–1942)	Election fraud, lack of broad support for the regime	The rise of economic nationalism. GDP grew at average annual rate of 2.15%; GDP per capita grew at an average annual rate of 0.41%
	Military coup d'état and Perón period (1943–1975)	Military coup d'état, Perón's coming to power in 1945, promotion of populism, and existence of unimodal and unbiased governance to realize hope	Under import substitution strategy, economic nationalization greatly increased. GDP grew at average annual rate of 3.90%; GDP per capita grew at an average annual rate of 2.10%
	Failure of de-Perónization (1976–1983)	Military junta's reign of terror, intensification of conflicts between workers and middle class, and the rise of guerrilla movements	Basically, the populist economic policy and the dynamic stagnation economy continued. The GDP grew at an average annual rate of 0.58% and the GDP per capita grew at an average annual rate of 1.07%.

(continued)

Table 12.1 (continued)

Period	Political status	Economic growth
Multimodal conflictual governance under modern democracy (1983–present	Military junta forced to hand over power due to defeat in Falklands War, democracy returned, political parties took turns in power, and crises and turmoil from time to time	The economic policy is dominated by neoliberalism alternating with populism. The GDP grew at an average annual rate of 2.33%, and the GDP per capita grew at an average annual rate of 1.14%

Source: Compiled by authors

becoming a high-income country in 2014, it has returned to the level of upper-middle-income countries. From 1983 to 2016, Argentina's GDP grew at an average annual rate of 2.33%, and its GDP per capita grew at an average annual rate of 1.14%. It can be seen that under a multi-peak conflictual governance pattern between various interest groups and political parties, political governance that is only formally democratic but lacks cohesion cannot guarantee sustained and strong economic growth.

12.2 Reasons for and Lessons from Argentina Falling into Middle-Income Trap

In Argentina's 500-year history, especially in its modernization process of the past 100 years, the country has stumbled and failed to recapture the glory of a hundred years ago. The reasons are as follows. First, it has not completed the deep integration between social ethnic groups and interest groups; second, it has not completed the market cultivation to improve economic accessibility. Except for the natural resource industry, the national industry lacks the necessary international competitiveness and has failed to achieve the improvement of the national industrial value chain.

12.2.1 Cohesion of Political Governance Has Never Been Effectively Improved

In the past 500 years, Argentina successively experienced the difficult processes of colonial rule, independence, caudillo separatism, and national unification. After national unification, Argentina's political model has been experiencing a complex evolution from multi-peak conflictual governance to single-peak biased governance and then back to multi-peak conflictual governance. Although there have been characteristics of occasional short-term multi-peak reconciliatory governance and single-peak unbiased governance, Argentina's political cohesion has never been effectively improved. The many complex factors behind it are worth pondering, which are discussed next.

12.2.1.1 Complex and Diverse History and Culture

Argentina has the typical characteristics of the complex and diverse history and culture of pre-colonial countries in Latin America. First, Argentina has a complex ethnic composition. The local Indigenous people of Argentina and the European colonists had a four-century struggle and conflict. In order to supplement the labor force, the colonists transported about 100,000 Black slaves to Argentina in the 17th and 18th centuries. In the continuous land expansion and colonial conquest, from 1880 to 1916, about 2.9 million immigrants, mainly from European countries, permanently settled in Argentina, making at least 30% of the population at that time foreign-born, and another one million immigrants arrived in Argentina in the 1920s. The complex multi-ethnic population made Argentina's culture extremely diverse. Citizens with Indigenous and Black ancestry were excluded by racial discrimination. European white immigrants had a strong tendency towards anarchist liberalism due to their own culture and their farming and animal husbandry occupations. The economic status differences, which were highly correlated with racial and occupational differences, further deprived the middle and lower classes, discriminated against them, and excluded them from the country's political, economic, and social life. They could not participate in social life and political life normally and could not enjoy the benefits of economic development and social progress for a long time, which aggravated the social rift and was not conducive to the formation of national identity.

Secondly, various social thoughts emerged alternately. The Spanish colonists brought Catholicism to Argentina. According to Weber's point of view, the conservative traditionalism advocated by Catholicism lacks moral emphasis and religious recognition for secular activities, which is not conducive to the establishment of the capitalist spirit and the development of a capitalist economy (Max Weber 2012). At the end of the colonial period, European Enlightenment thought spread to Argentina. Under the catalysis of the French Revolution and the American War of Independence, Argentines launched an independent revolution for democracy and freedom and successfully established their country. After that, liberalism gradually replaced caudilloism and became dominant. After World War II, both left-wing thought and communist thought had an important influence on Argentina. The growth of the working class and the deepening of class contradictions promoted the spread of left-wing ideas, which eventually converged into populism led by Perón and had a long-term impact on Argentina's social culture. Although communist ideas failed to gain a dominant position in Argentina, they indirectly gave rise to bureaucratic authoritarianism in Argentina. Presently, at a time when modern democracy is dominant, different social ideas are still surging in Argentina, making the cohesion of civil society extremely difficult.

12.2.1.2 Political System Full of Problems

Although the Argentine Constitution sought to imitate the US Constitution in a more perfect form, the country's historical inertia or path dependence has left many long-standing problems in its political system unresolved. As a result, Argentina lacks a stable and effective political governance model, which has become an institutional factor that causes continued political turmoil and social instability.

First, its check-and-balance mechanism is unbalanced. The Argentine Constitution stipulates the implementation of the separation of powers. However, there is a lack of checks and balances among the three powers of the Argentine government, where the president's power is too strong, often overriding the legislature and the judiciary without being restrained. Whether it is a military government or an elected government, the first thing the government does when coming to power is often expel judges who are unfriendly to the government in order to control the judiciary. According to statistics, among the 115 Supreme Court judges in Argentina from 1946 to 1998, 17 were expelled, 3 were impeached and had to step down, and 32 were forced to resign, with an unnatural resignation rate of up to 45%.

Second, its political contract lacks guarantees. There is a lack of widely recognized political contracts in Argentine politics, and the color of power politics is obvious. The presidential election system in Argentina has been implemented for more than a hundred years, but the results lack sufficient guarantees. Since 1930, Argentina has had several democratically elected presidents (1930, 1962, 1966, 1976, 1989, and 2001) who were unable to complete their statutory terms. The first five were overthrown by military coups, and the sixth was forced to resign due to domestic riots.

Third, its federal system is loose. Argentina has a federal system of 23 provinces and a federal district, which originated from the separatist autonomy of provinces during the Caudillo period. Under this national system, there is a two-level separation of administrative power. The governors of each province become the real power holders in the power structure. They manage the administration of the province and influence the National Congress and the president through provincial congressmen. The alienation of the power of the governors and the political games between the local governments and the federal government increase the transaction costs. During economic prosperity, the federal government can rely on resource allocation to obtain support from the local governments, but it has been difficult to influence the local governments during recessions.

12.2.1.3 Political Parties Lacking Capabilities

Party politics is the main form of national politics in the world today. As a systematic and institutionalized organization, political parties help and represent different groups to express their interests and demands. However, Argentina's political parties lack the ability to unite most interest groups and have failed to play a bridging role between the government and society. As a result, Argentina's political situation has always been in a state of relative chaos and disorder, with obvious involution.

First, the political parties are insufficiently organized. While most political parties in Argentina have a clear tendency for a certain political movement and a loose organizational structure, the operation of the political parties lacks clear political programs and political goals, relies heavily on the personal relationship between political leaders and party members, and lacks intra-party democratic mechanisms. The lack of programs and goals and the confusion over ideologies have led to internal instability and reduced cohesion within the parties, with frequent splits and alliances and a lack of coherence in ideas and policies after taking power.

Second, the support base of the political parties is weak. There is a significant patronage relationship between the political parties and voters. Voters' support for the political parties is often not based on identification with political programs but on the mutual benefit of material exchange for support. The political parties exchange material benefits, such as food and medicine, for middle- and lower-class voters in exchange for votes, and so they lack stable core support.

Third, the political parties are less independent. "Cambridge History of Latin America" believes that Argentina's political parties "appear to be controlled by corporate activists in society" (Bethel 2001). If a political party lacks an independent support base and funding sources, it can easily become the spokesperson of a particular interest group and lose its representation of the majority group. After 1983, Argentina tried to solve the problem of funding sources of political parties through systematic legislation on political party funding by providing public funds from the government, but the attempt was unsuccessful.

12.2.2 Stagnation of Internal Accessibility of Economy

The stagnation of the internal accessibility of the Argentine economy is a very important reason for the country's unstable economic growth. There are four main factors behind it, namely, the control of the country by economic oligarchs, frequent financial and fiscal turmoil, insufficient infrastructure construction, and a rigid labor market mechanism. The economic oligarchs further control the political economy of the entire country by controlling the core industries of the national economy and restricting the free allocation of resources, the frequent turbulence of the fiscal and financial environment has led to a long-term insufficient level of national investment, the insufficient infrastructure construction has led to the decline and backwardness of the railway and seriously hindered the flow of Argentina's unified commodity and factor market, and the labor market is severely discriminatory, with a large number of workers ending up in informal sectors.

12.2.2.1 Economic Oligarchs Control Country

Before 1880, European colonists had been carrying out large-scale colonial expansion in Argentina and encroaching on the land of Indigenous Indians. In the process, the degree of land concentration continued to increase. The Desert Expedition in 1879 completely disintegrated the Indigenous' 400-year resistance, and 21 million acres of land fell into the hands of only 381 people. In 1914, 8% of landowners control 80% of farmland. In the plantation economic system dominated by agricultural production, these landowners became economic oligarchs and controlled the economic lifeline of Argentina. As a former colony, Argentina's agricultural product export trade to Europe and North America was monopolized by export merchants from the United Kingdom, France, the United States, and other countries, who occupied the top of Argentina's economic system.

Export merchants and farm owner oligarchs sought to maintain this plantation economic model of primary agricultural product exports because of huge profits, resulting in Argentina's low investment rate, low levels of economic and industrial structures, and a price scissors gap between industrial products and agricultural products in industrial countries. In his book *The Enigma of Argentina*, American scholar Will believes that Argentina missed the opportunity to develop an industrial economy three times: in the late nineteenth century, during World War I, and during the Great Depression. The missed development opportunities were not only due to Argentina's agricultural and animal husbandry resource endowment and comparative advantages but also because of the fundamental conflict of interests between the agricultural and animal husbandry groups and the industrial sector. The plantation economy also affected the flow of factors and supply upgrades in the labor market. The differences in land ownership exacerbated the polarization between the rich and the poor. Landless tenants and farm workers could only receive very low wages, were highly dependent on the landowners, and could not move freely to the industrial sector. They also lacked the necessary income to improve their own and their offspring's education level and skills, which further inhibited the expansion of Argentina's domestic demand.

Hence, economic nationalism emerged in the 1940s. Previously, Argentina's main export economic sectors, such as mining, meat packaging, and railway transportation, were mostly controlled by large foreign companies, which made the Argentine working class believe that they were severely exploited by foreign capitalists, stimulating their nationalist sentiments. There were growing calls to remove the oligopoly of foreign companies in the lifeline industries of Argentina's economy. Although economic nationalization achieved results in the short term, in the long run it led to a decline in production efficiency, serious bureaucratization of state-owned enterprises, and rampant corruption. The neoliberal reforms of the 1980s quickly re-privatized sectors related to the lifeline of Argentina's economy, greatly enhancing the economic power of transnational capitalist groups and national capitalist groups.

An important problem brought about by the control of the country by economic oligarchs, such as the agricultural and animal husbandry export groups, transnational capitalist groups, and national capitalist groups is the serious polarization between the rich and the poor in Argentina. According to the World Bank (2020), Argentina's Gini coefficient, which is a measure of wealth inequality, was 0.408 in 1980 in comparison with the United States' Gini coefficient of only 0.346 in 1979; by the beginning of this century, Argentina's Gini coefficient continued to rise to 0.538, while that of the United States was 0.404. Although Argentina's Gini coefficient has declined in recent years, Argentina's serious income inequality is still an unavoidable problem. The combination of high urbanization and the polarization of the rich and the poor has led to the emergence of large-scale slums in Argentina's large cities. According to the World Bank (2020), the proportion of the population living in slums in Argentina's urban population was as high as 30.5% in 1990, rising to 32.9% in 2000, and was still 16.7% in 2014. Slums are distributed in the fringe areas of cities, with low-income levels, poor infrastructure, and chaotic social order, becoming a stubborn disease that is difficult to cure in Argentina's social governance.

12.2.2.2 Turbulent Fiscal and Financial Environment Inhibiting Investment

The rapid accumulation of productive capital is an important factor for a country in achieving industrialization and rapid catch-up. However, one of the distinctive features of the Argentine economy is the turbulent fiscal and financial environment, which significantly inhibits investment in the production sector. Argentina's fiscal turmoil began with the rise of populism. The core of populism is that political leaders rely on economic interests to win over voters. After Perón, Argentina's first populist leader, became president, he significantly increased the wages and welfare levels of his main supporter group of workers. In 1945 and 1948, the wages of skilled workers and unskilled workers increased by 22% and 30%, respectively. The share of workers' income earned domestically increased from 40% to 50%. Most workers enjoyed medical compensation, maternity leave, paid holidays, and protection from arbitrary dismissal. Although Perón and his followers withdrew from the stage of history, Perónism populist policies were continued by administrations who came after them. Excessively high welfare levels have caused the government's actual expenditure to exceed its ability to pay, and Argentina's public debt level remains high.

In addition, lax fiscal discipline has led the Argentine government to continuously monetize national debt, further triggering frequent and severe inflation. Argentina's inflation data from 1914 to 2008 show that, of these 95 years, there were only 23 years when the inflation rate was between 0% and 5%, 26 years when the inflation rate was between 6% and 10%, and 16 years when the inflation rate was between 0% and 5%. The rates of 100% and above were mainly concentrated from 1976 to 1991, as shown in Fig. 12.2.

The reason behind inflation instability is that political turmoil makes politicians more inclined towards short-term behavior, and they regard the primary goal of governing is to as much as possible gain benefits for themselves and their

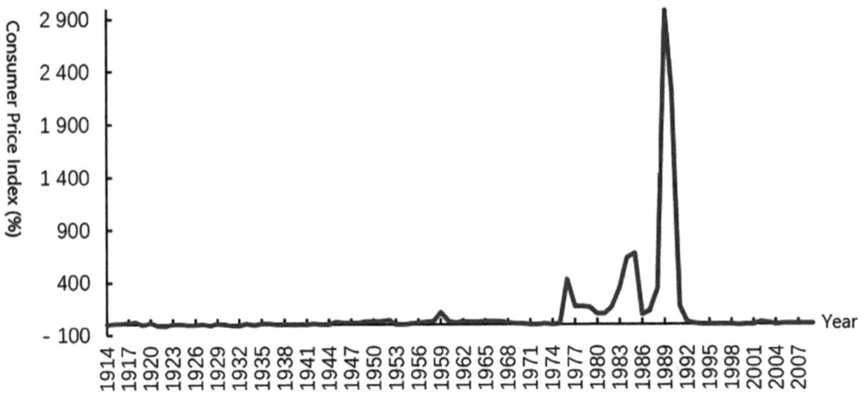

Fig. 12.2 Argentina's consumer price index. *Source*: Palgrave Macmillan (2013)

supporters, which makes a country's economic efficiency low. A stable Argentine currency would mean urban consumers buying substitute commodities, such as Australian wheat and American beef, since domestic products are too expensive, causing farmers to reduce planting and breeding and hence decreasing their income. In contrast, a depreciation of Argentina's currency would mean Argentina's exports regaining competitiveness, which would benefit farmers, while urban residents would have to endure the pain of inflation. When different groups with conflicting interests achieved political changes through the election process, the country's monetary policies shifted accordingly, leading to inflation fluctuations. Inflation puts serious pressure on the value of the peso every two years or so, which is coincidently consistent with the average term of office of Argentina's presidents.

A significant harm of an unstable financial environment to an economy is the suppression of savings and investment. Rapid inflation reduces the real interest rate of savings, making the economy tend to consume rather than obtain fixed asset investment. As shown in Fig. 12.3, when comparing capital formation as a percentage of GDP in Argentina, the United States, and Japan, it can be found that Argentina's investment rate is significantly lower than those of the United States and Japan. Argentina's investment rate has been hovering at a low level of around 15%, and only exceeded 20% in 1997–1998. Even in the 1950s–1980s, when industrialization was the fastest under the import substitution strategy, Argentina's investment rate did not increase significantly and was more than 10 percentage points lower than that of the United States, which had already completed industrialization during the same period. In sharp contrast to Argentina's, Japan's investment rate during its rapid post-war development period rose rapidly from 14.1% in 1950 to 40.6% in 1973.

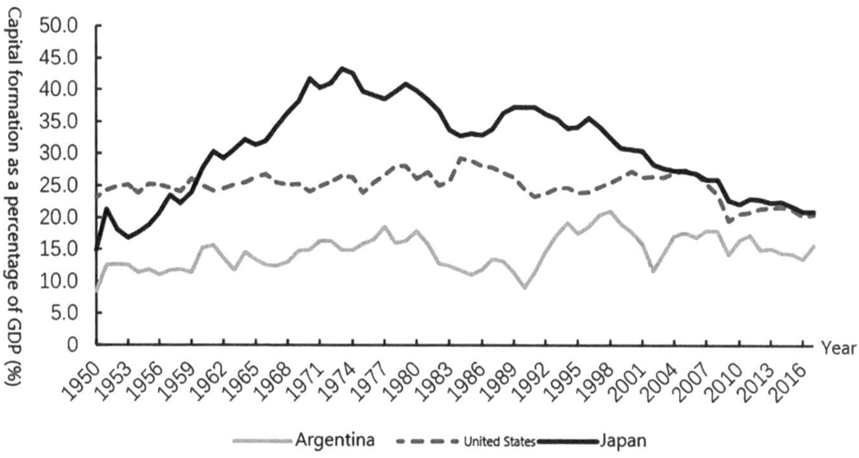

Fig. 12.3 Capital formation as share of GDP in Argentina. *Source*: Feenstra et al. (2019)

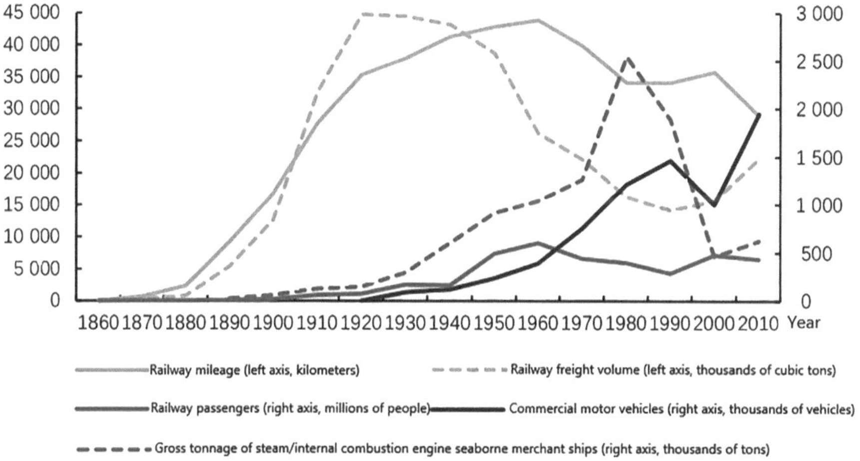

Fig. 12.4 Evolution of Argentina's transport capacity over past 150 years. *Source*: Palgrave Macmillan (2013)

12.2.2.3 Inadequate Infrastructure Construction

Argentina's infrastructure once developed rapidly during the country's economic boom in 1880s–1920s but then showed a serious downward trend. Argentina's primary agricultural products, such as grain and meat, relied heavily on railway transportation. As can be seen in Fig. 12.4, the change in Argentina's railway mileage has been highly correlated with economic growth. The period from the late 1880s to before World War I was the golden period of Argentina's economic growth, and railways played an important role in this process. From 1980 to 1914, Argentina's railway mileage grew at an average annual rate of 10.6%. A large number of farmlands were successfully connected to the Argentine domestic market with the continuous extension of the railway network. Various agricultural products were transported by rail to the port of Buenos Aires and then shipped to European and North American markets by sea. From the 1920s to the 1960s, Argentina's railway construction began to slow down but still maintained a high growth rate, but then it began to decline continuously. In 2010, Argentina's railway mileage was only 28,969 km, a 34% drop from the peak of 43,930 km in 1959. Before the current reconstruction of the Belgrano Freight Railway, an important railway artery in Argentina, only 1400 km of the 7409-km freight section of the entire line in 2014 were barely operational, with frequent accidents and extremely slow transportation speeds, where the average train speed is only more than 30 km/h (Zhang 2018).

The decline in rail mileage does not necessarily mean the decline of transportation infrastructure. It may result from the substitution of rail transportation by other modes of transportation. For example, the data in Fig. 12.4 shows that both sea transportation and road transportation in Argentina achieved rapid development in the later period. But this explanation is not actually valid. Argentina lacks large rivers in the interior, and sea transportation cannot replace railways; for inland transportation, considering the extremely large decline in railway freight volume, there were only about 1.22 million commercial vehicles in 1980. The number of motor vehicles makes it obviously difficult to completely replace railway transportation, and the result is high commodity transportation costs. Therefore, Argentina's transportation infrastructure gradually declined after 1960, significantly hindering the flow of products and factors, as evidenced by the simultaneous drop in railway passenger volume and railway mileage, which indicated the decline in the degree of labor mobility in Argentina in recent decades. Railway freight volume began to decline in the 1830s before railway mileage, and the flow of goods to markets was also hindered. The decline of infrastructure has reduced the accessibility of Argentina's economy internally.

12.2.2.4 Rigid Labor Market Mechanism

Different industrial sectors have different rates of technological progress and different demands for different types of labor. The employment demand structure of the industrial sector and the degree of matching between it and the labor supply structure will affect a country's economic growth rate and per capita income level. Argentina's industrial structure suffers from the problem of premature deindustrialization and a large number of migrant agricultural laborers can only enter low-productivity service sectors. In addition, Argentina's labor force human capital level is low. According to the World Bank (2020), in 2018, Argentina's Human Capital Index ranked 61st among 88 high-income and upper-middle-income countries and 38th among 38 medium- and high-income countries. It also ranked only 14th among countries in terms of income, lower than China and Malaysia. As low-skilled labor moves out of the agricultural sector, most of them enter low-end and low-productivity service sectors. These two factors make Argentina's economic growth rate low and effective demand insufficient.

Figure 12.5 shows the employment proportion of Argentina's primary, secondary, and tertiary industries calculated based on the data of 10 sectors in various countries around the world (Groningen Growth and Development Centre 2014). The data show that the proportion of employment in Argentina's primary industry has continued to decline since 1950 and is now less than 10%, releasing a large amount of surplus labor into cities. According to the World Bank (2020), Argentina's urban population increased rapidly from 73.6% in 1960 to 91.9% in 2018. In addition, the employment share of the secondary industry has been declining since reaching a peak of 35.4% in 1961 and is currently stable at around 20%. According to Rodrik's (2016) calculations, Argentina's manufacturing employment ratio peaked in 1958 when Argentina's per capita income was only about a quarter of what it was when the manufacturing employment ratio peaked in Western European countries. The result of premature deindustrialization was insufficient employment in the manufacturing industry, and high unemployment has become a chronic disease plaguing Argentina after the neoliberal reforms of the 1980s. Figure 12.6 shows that Argentina's unemployment rate has never been below 5% since 1987 and is still at 10%.

A large number of laborers transferring from the primary industry have to enter the urban service sector. Accordingly, the employment proportion of Argentina's tertiary industry has continued to rise and has stabilized at more than 70% in recent years. Because the per capita output level and the growth rate of the service industry are lower than those of the manufacturing industry, this is not conducive to maintaining a faster economic growth rate. In addition, employment within the service industry also shows the phenomenon of being concentrated in low-productivity sectors. Among them, industries with the highest proportion of employment within the

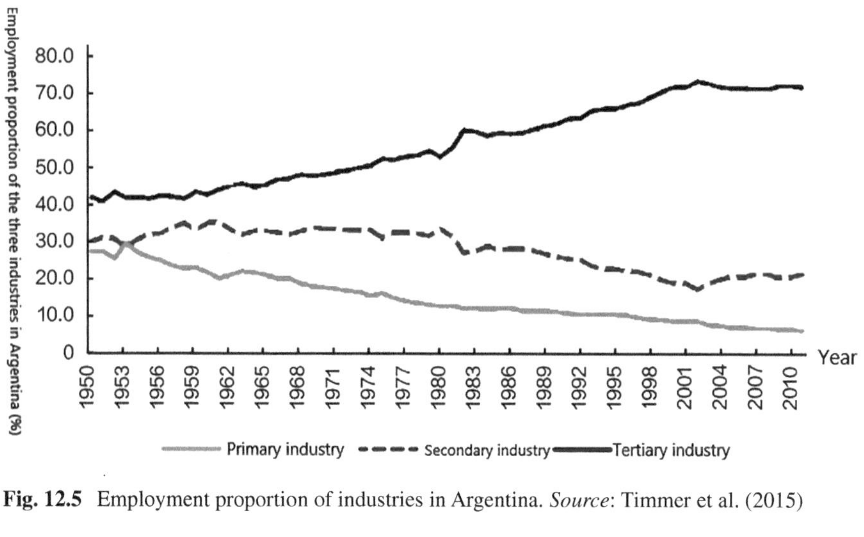

Fig. 12.5 Employment proportion of industries in Argentina. *Source*: Timmer et al. (2015)

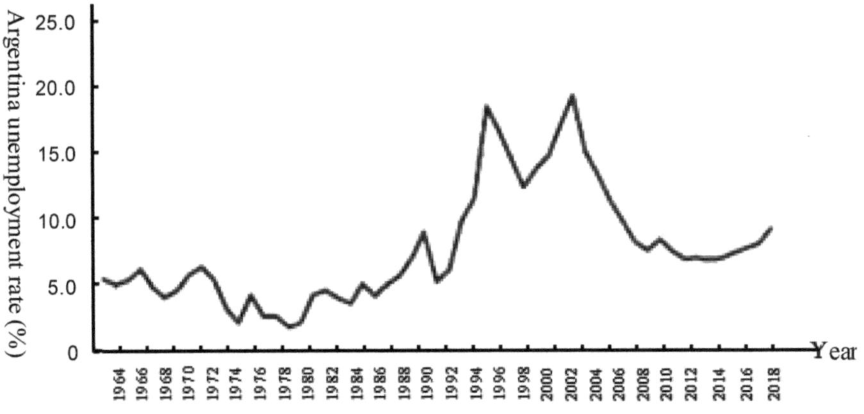

Fig. 12.6 Argentina's unemployment rate. *Source*: International Historical Statistics (2013), World Bank (2020)

service industry in Argentina are trade, accommodation and catering, and government services, accounting for 30%–35%. The employment proportion of industries with higher productivity levels, such as transportation, warehousing, communications industries, finance, insurance, real estate, and commercial services, is relatively low (Timmer et al. 2015). The low income of service industry practitioners has seriously suppressed the growth of Argentina's internal demand.

12.2.3 Degeneration of External Economic Accessibility

The external accessibility barriers of Argentina's economy are mainly reflected in the failure of the import substitution strategy, the low level of international trade, and the radical opening-up policy. The import substitution strategy, which lasted for nearly 50 years, not only hurt Argentina's foreign trade but also caused the Argentine economy to miss the opportunity to undertake international industrial transfer after World War II. There was also an inversion in the import and export product levels in international trade, reflecting that domestic industries could not achieve climbing and forming competitiveness in the global industrial value chain. Furthermore, the overly radical opening-up policy magnified the shortcomings of the weak ability of an emerging economy, such as Argentina, to resist shocks.

12.2.3.1 Failure of Import Substitution Strategy

Under the influence of the Great Depression, World War II, and the structuralist theory, the Argentine government began to actively promote the import substitution strategy in the 1930s. The strategy was centered on industrialization and provided protection and support for high-quality domestic industrial sectors through a series of internal and external institutional arrangements: implementing trade barriers, such as tariffs and quotas for foreign companies; implementing tariff protection and tax rebates for weak industrial sectors; interfering with foreign exchange transactions to promote the import of industrial machinery and raw materials, issuing loans to industries through the government-controlled banking system; and providing funds for industrial expansion with export tariffs on agricultural products. The import substitution strategy rapidly increased the proportion of Argentina's manufacturing industry from 25% in 1940–1944 to 36% in 1970–1974.

However, the trade barriers under the import substitution strategy seriously damaged Argentina's foreign trade scale. Argentina's import tariffs rose rapidly after the Great Depression, and the outbreak of World War II and other factors severely impacted Argentina's import and export trade. As can be seen in Fig. 12.7, Argentina's foreign trade dependence fell by about 60 percentage points in the 1930s. Because international trade barriers after World War II fell rapidly under the guidance of the General Agreement on Tariffs and Trade—WTO framework and Argentina did not officially join the WTO until 1995, Argentina's foreign trade level had always remained at a relatively low level.

Although the import substitution strategy promoted Argentina's economic growth in the short term, it harmed Argentina's economic development in the long term. Argentina's industrial expansion had been "horizontal" or "expansionary" (Guillermo O'Donnell 2008). Its industrial production was mainly concentrated in light industial products and non-durable goods, with little involvement of intermediate goods and capital goods in the upstream of the industry. This situation resulted in the Argentine economy being heavily dependent on externally imported intermediate goods and capital inputs. Bearing high import tariffs, Argentina's domestic industrial product prices were significantly higher than international levels, causing

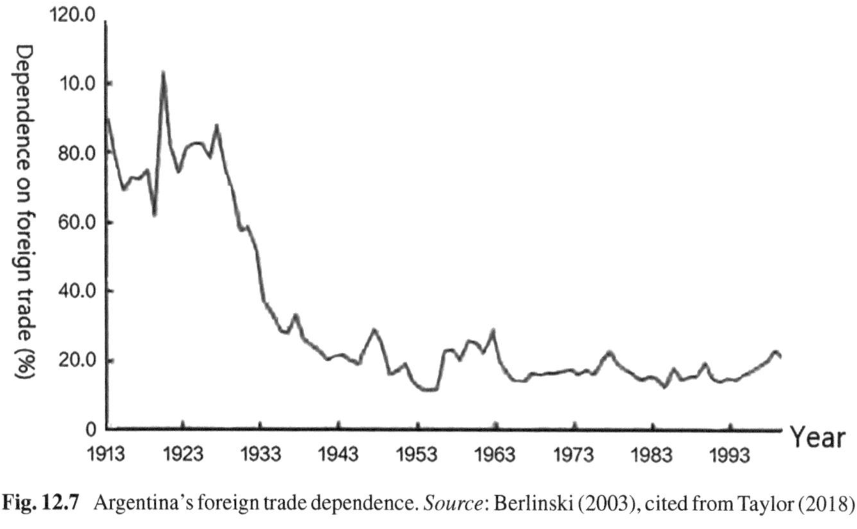

Fig. 12.7 Argentina's foreign trade dependence. *Source*: Berlinski (2003), cited from Taylor (2018)

inflationary pressure to continue to increase. When the import substitution strategy implemented a vertical industrialization policy in the later stages, focusing on large investments in capital-intensive heavy industrial sectors, such as railways and oil, Argentina missed the first wave of large-scale industrial transfers from developed countries to developing countries after World War II and lost a rare development opportunity.

12.2.3.2 Low Level of International Trade

Argentina's exports are mainly agricultural products, while its imports are mainly various industrial products, which reflects that Argentina's international trade level is not high, and the country occupies a low position in the global value chain industrial division of labor. Argentina lacks strong enough competitiveness, which restricts its economic development.

Argentina's export product structure shows that food and live animals have always been its main export products from 1962 to 2017, with a proportion of no less than 31.1%, reaching 75.3% in 1965. If beverages, tobacco, non-edible raw materials, mineral fuels, lubricants and related products, animal and vegetable oils and fats, and other categories of products are taken into account, the proportion of primary products was 62.5%–96.1%. There had been some improvement. The proportion in exports of industrial products, including chemicals, manufactured goods classified by materials, machinery and transport equipment, and other manufactured goods steadily increased from 3.9% in 1962 to 37.4% in 1989 and has since stabilized at around 30% (Taylor 2018). However, compared with the import product structure, Argentina's industrial production and export capacity are still lacking. Argentina's import proportion of industrial products remained at 70%–80% from 1962 to 1990 and further increased to 80%–90% (World Bank 2020) from 1991 to 2017. The obvious inversion of the import and export product levels in international trade highlights the structural contradictions in Argentina's domestic industry. Its low position in the global industrial value chain limits Argentina's ability to accumulate excess profits by meeting international market demand.

The opening up of a country's economy is conducive to its integration into the global economy and obtaining more development opportunities, but the steps and degree of opening up need to match the development stage of the economy, especially the opening up of the capital account. Excessive and advanced opening up of the capital account will bring greater volatility and risks to the domestic economy. After the failure of the import substitution strategy in the 1970s, Argentina carried out two major opening-up measures. Both were aimed at resolving the crisis, but they ended up triggering new crises.

In 1975, Argentina changed the fixed exchange rate system to a crawling peg exchange rate system and lifted most of the restrictions on the capital account; in 1977, it further opened up domestic and foreign financial markets and fully marketized interest rates. The higher rate of return attracted a large amount of foreign capital, and Argentina's foreign debt and inflation rate increased significantly.

Although the Argentine central bank adopted the method of raising interest rates to curb inflation, this further stimulated the influx of foreign capital, increased the demand for the Argentine currency, and pushed up inflationary pressure, forming a vicious circle. The excessive expansion of credit eventually led to a surge in non-performing assets, and the banking industry quickly fell into crisis. The scale of bonds issued by the Argentine central bank for bankrupt liquidation accounted for 3% of GDP. Argentina's banking crisis further triggered a sovereign debt crisis; capital fled Argentina at an accelerated pace and its currency depreciated rapidly, forcing Argentina to take measures to restrict cross-border capital flows. In order to obtain debt relief from creditors, Argentina accepted the reform plan proposed by the IMF in the 1990s, which mainly included trade liberalization, privatization of state-owned enterprises, and financial liberalization, for instance, reducing explicit trade barriers, such as tariffs, and other implicit barriers; privatizing state-owned enterprises through sales, listing, and franchising; implementing a fixed exchange rate system; canceling foreign currency financing restrictions; and achieving full opening of capital accounts. However, the IMF's reform plan did not fundamentally solve the problems faced by Argentina. Instead, underneath the Argentine government's radical opening measures laid hidden dangers for the outbreak of another debt crisis in 2001.

The continuous improvement of an economy's external accessibility plays an important role in a country's economic development. However, it should be pointed out that the pace of opening up should match the development stage of the domestic economy and the government's ability to control risks and also match the need to give full play to the country's comparative advantages and integration into global markets. Overly radical opening up will lead to the transmission and amplification of external risks, increase domestic economic volatility and risks, and even cause an uncontrollable situation.

12.3 Analysis of Argentina's Political Cohesion and Economic Accessibility

In this subchapter, Argentina's political cohesion and economic accessibility indexes from 1996 to 2018 are analyzed by comparing them with the averages of the world and G7 countries, it intuitively shows Argentina's political governance cohesion and economic accessibility to the inside and outside since 1996.

12.3.1 Political Cohesion Index

This section first starts with the political governance cohesion indicators, and the correlation between political cohesion and economic growth from a quantitative perspective is analyzed. As shown in Fig. 12.8, Argentina's cohesion index is in the range of 2.3–2.6 from 1996 to 2018, which is lower than the average levels of the world and G7 countries. From the perspective of fluctuations, Argentina's political cohesion from 1996 to 2015 can be roughly divided into two stages. The first round was the period of large fluctuations before and after the economic crisis and political turmoil from 1996 to 2002, and the second round was the period of small fluctuations from 2003 to 2015 when the political situation stabilized, reflecting the recovery of a social consensus and stability in Argentina after the turmoil. As shown in Fig. 12.9, the comparison of Argentina's GDP per capita growth rate and political cohesion also confirms the positive correlation between political cohesion and economic growth: the increase in political cohesion can promote economic prosperity, while the opposite will lead to economic recession.

Although quantitative indicators have the advantage of being able to more accurately and objectively reflect Argentina's political cohesion, they also have the limitation of a short time series and hence cannot reflect long-term history. In order to make up for this shortcoming, we further analyzed the impact of Argentina's political cohesion on economic growth from a qualitative historical perspective. From a historical perspective, multi-peak reconciliatory governance with unimodal and unbiasedness represents high political cohesion; multi-peak conflictual governance with unimodal and bias represents low political cohesion. According to the Maddison Project Database, the growth rates of Argentina's total economic output in each period since GDP statistics were available are as follows: during the period of unimodal and biased liberalism from 1880 to 1930, the average annual GDP growth

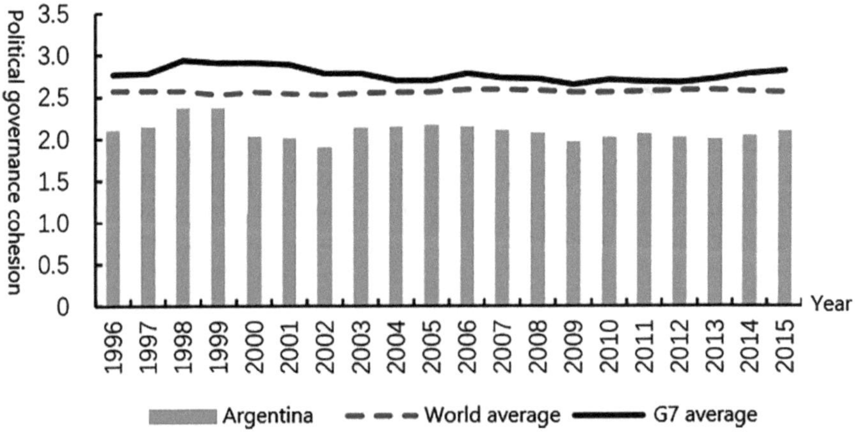

Fig. 12.8 Argentina's political cohesion index. *Source*: Calculation by authors' research team based on data from the Maddison Project Database

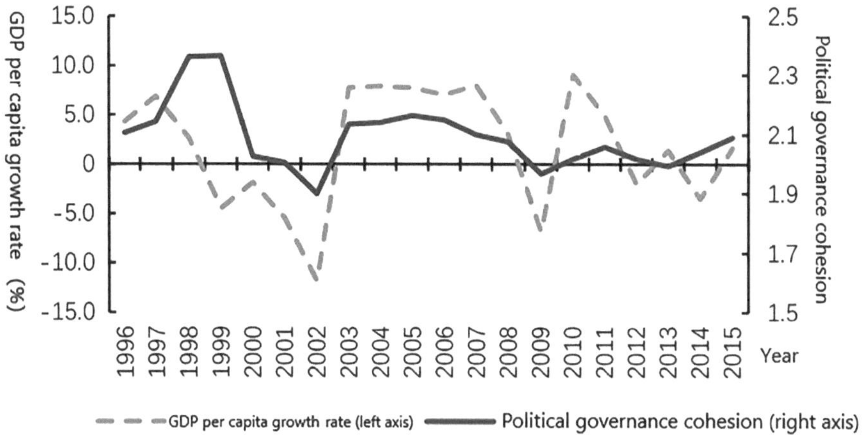

Fig. 12.9 Argentina's GDP per capita growth rate and political cohesion index. *Source*: Calculation by authors' research team based on data from the Maddison Project Database

rate was approximately 4.97%; during the period of Perónism, which pursued unimodal and unbiased governance from 1943 to 1975, the average annual GDP growth rate was 3.90%; during the period of the powerful Caudillo's multimodal conflictual governance from 1820 to 1880, the average annual GDP growth rate was approximately 3.25%; during the period of modern democratic multimodal conflictual governance from 1983 to 2016, the average annual GDP growth rate was 2.33%; during the decade of chaos from 1930 to 1942, the average annual GDP growth rate was 2.15%; during unimodal and biased governance in the period of de-Perónization failure from 1976 to 1983, the average annual GDP growth rate was 0.58%. From the above statistical results, we can see that the positive correlation between political cohesion and economic growth is supported by the data. This is because in a period of high political cohesion, the political structure is stable, government policies and the interests of various groups are incentive compatible, and the enthusiasm of the whole society to engage in economic development can be mobilized to the maximum extent, bringing economic growth and prosperity. On the contrary, during the period of low political cohesion, the interests of all parties are in serious conflict, there are many obstacles in policy formulation and implementation, and the degree of social internal friction increases, causing a negative impact on economic growth.

12.3.2 Economic Accessibility Index

The level of economic accessibility represents the degree of openness and resource allocation efficiency of a country's economy. As can be seen in Fig. 12.10, Argentina's economic accessibility from 1996 to 2015 is far below the average level of G7 countries and only slightly higher than the world's average. This result shows

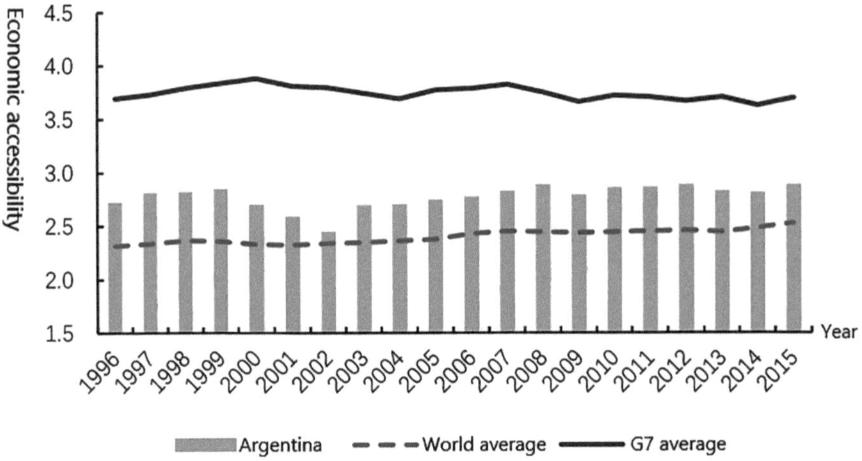

Fig. 12.10 Economic accessibility of Argentina. *Source*: Calculation by authors' research team

that Argentina's economic accessibility is not ranked high in the world, and there is a large gap with major developed countries. The following is an analysis of the two aspects of internal and external accessibility of Argentina's economy.

12.3.2.1 Internal Economic Accessibility Index

Internal economic accessibility measures the extent to which an economy is able to mobilize domestic production factors to participate in economic production activities. High internal economic accessibility means that the economy has a unified, open, competitive, and orderly product and factor market, which can give full play to the decisive role of the market mechanism in resource allocation and effective product circulation and factor flow. Create a good internal market environment for economic development. As shown in Fig. 12.11, from 1996 to 2015, the internal accessibility index of the Argentine economy was generally stable at a level of around 3.4 to 3.5. Although it was significantly higher than the world's average, it was far lower than the average level of G7 countries. The low internal accessibility of the economy indicates that Argentina's domestic market has problems with high industry-entry barriers and poor product and factor mobility, which hinders the improvement of resource allocation efficiency.

12.3.2.2 External Economic Accessibility Index

External economic accessibility measures the extent to which an economy is integrated into global economic activities and the extent to which global production factors and product markets are used to develop the economy. High external

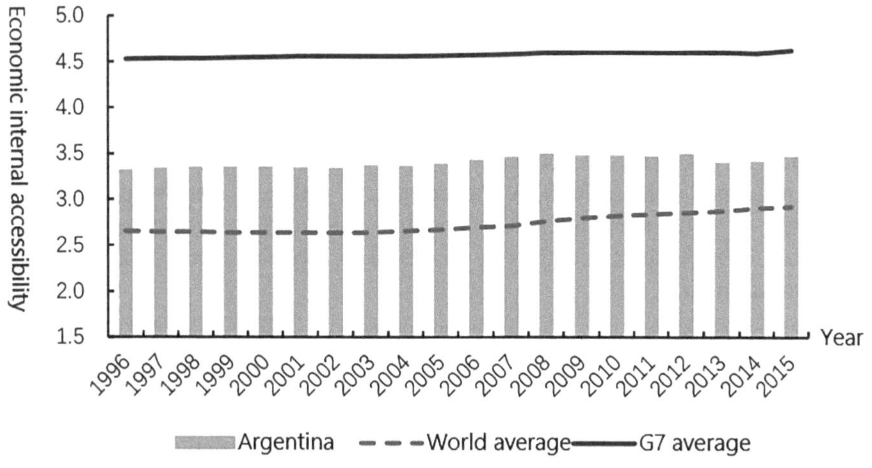

Fig. 12.11 Internal accessibility data of Argentine economy. *Source*: Calculation by authors' research team

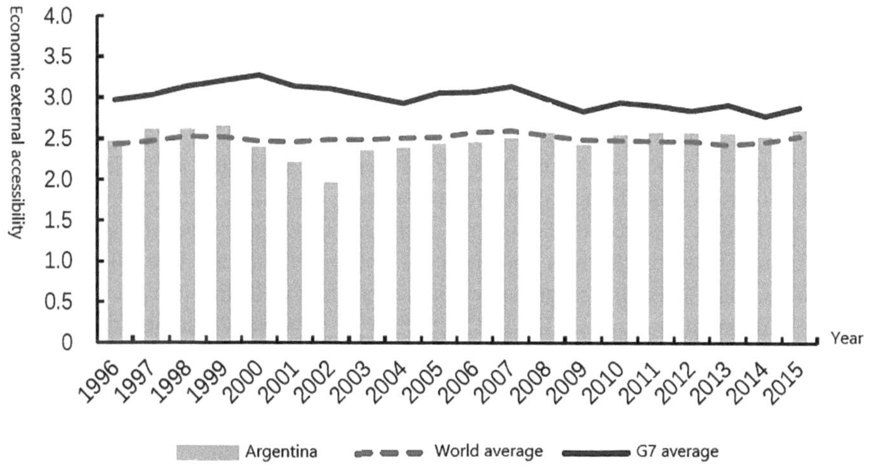

Fig. 12.12 External accessibility data of Argentine economy. *Source*: Calculation by authors' research team

economic accessibility reflects that, when participating in global economic activities, an economy has broken through its own resource endowment limitations and market capacity limitations and has obtained various production factors at the lowest cost on a global scale, while giving full play to its own industrial comparative advantages and production capacity to obtain its global market share. As shown in Fig. 12.12, the external accessibility index of Argentina's economy from 1996 to 2015 is far behind the average level of G7 countries, and roughly equivalent to the world's average, indicating that Argentina's economic openness is relatively low.

12.4 Chapter Summary

In this chapter, the framework of the A-C theory was used to analyze the political and economic history of Argentina since the colonial period. Starting from the two indicators of political cohesion and economic accessibility, Argentina's economic modernization development process over the past 100 years was comprehensively analyzed, revealing the political and economic roots of Argentina's transformation from one of the richest countries in the world to a typical country caught in the middle-income trap.

First, the brief political and economic history of Argentina clearly shows that there is a very strong correlation between Argentina's political cohesion and economic growth. Multi-peak reconciliatory governance with high political cohesion, as well as single-peak unbiased governance, help the whole society form a development synergy and promote economic growth; multi-peak conflictual governance with low political cohesion, as well as single-peak biased governance, lead to serious internal friction in the whole society and inhibits economic growth. The reasons for Argentina's low political cohesion are complex, including the complex and diverse history and culture of the former colony; the interweaving and collision of various ideologies; the serious defects of Argentina's imitation of the separation of powers, democratic elections, and federal system of Western countries; and domestic political parties lacking in organization, support base, and independence.

Secondly, relatively low economic accessibility is also an important factor restricting Argentina's economic growth. In terms of economic accessibility, economic oligarchs rely on their control over the core industries of the national economy to further control the country's political economy, resulting in serious polarization between the rich and the poor and restricting the free allocation of resources. Insufficient infrastructure construction and the decline and backwardness of the railway also seriously hindered the flow of Argentina's unified commodity and factor markets. Frequent turbulence in the fiscal and financial environments has led to a long-term lack of national investment. Furthermore, rigid labor market allocation, high unemployment, and low productivity sectors coexist with each other. In terms of economic accessibility, the import substitution strategy, which lasted for nearly 50 years, not only hurt Argentina's foreign trade but also caused the country to miss the opportunity to undertake international industrial transfer after World War II. In addition, there is an inverted level of import and export products in international trade, reflecting that the domestic industries cannot achieve climbing and forming competitiveness in the global industrial value chain. Moreover, the overly radical opening-up policy has magnified the shortcomings of the weak ability of an emerging economy such as Argentina to resist shocks.

It is the combined effect of the above two factors that has caused Argentina's economy to continue to stagnate for many years and triggered frequent political and economic crises. To overcome these factors, it is necessary for Argentina to reach political reconciliation among its domestic interest groups, improve the efficiency of policy formulation and implementation, carry out economic reforms that are in line with the country's national conditions, and comprehensively improve the internal and external accessibility of the economy.

References

Berlinski J (2003) International trade and commercial policy. In: Paolera G, Taylor AM (eds) A new economic history of Argentina. Cambridge University Press, New York

Bethell L (ed) (1994) Institute of Latin American studies (trans: CASS). The Cambridge history of Latin America, vol 3. Social Science Academic Press, Beijing

Bethell L (ed) (2001) Institute of Latin American studies (trans: CASS). The Cambridge history of Latin America, vol 6 (part 2). Contemporary World Press, Beijing

Brown JC (2010) A brief history of Argentina (trans: Zuo XY). Orient Publishing Center, Beijing

Burgin M (1946) The economic aspects of argentine federalism, 1820–1852. Harvard University Press, Cambridge

Dong GH (2013a) Analysis of the factors of Argentina's economic growth from 1880 to 1914. Hist Teach 6:12–20

Dong GH (2013b) Research on Argentina's path to modernization. Beijing World Publishing Corporation, Beijing

Feenstra RC, Inklaar R, Timmer M (2019) Penn world Table 9.1. University of Groningen, Groningen

Groningen Growth and Development Centre (2014) 10-Sector database. https://www.rug.nl/ggdc/structuralchange/previous-sector-database/10-sector-2014

Jiang H (2018) Institutional choice and pendulum development: the paradox of Argentine development from the perspective of new economic history. Chin Social Science Press, Beijing

O'Donnell GA (2008) Modernization and bureaucratic authoritarianism studies in south American politics (trans: Wang H, Shen MM). Peking University Press, Beijing

Palgrave Macmillan (2013) International history statistics. Palgrave Macmillan, London

Rodrik D (2016) Premature deindustrialization. J Econ Growth 21(1):1–33

Szuchman MD, Jonathan CB (1994) Revolution and restoration: the rearrangement of power in Argentina. 1776–1860. University Nebraska Press, Lincoln

Taylor AM (2018) The Argentina paradox: Microexplanations and macropuzzles. Latin Am Econ Rev 27(1):3

Timmer M, Gaaitzen JV, Klaas V (2015) Patterns of structural change in developing countries. In: Weiss J, Tribe M (eds) Routledge handbook of industry and development. Routledge, London

Wang P (2011) Changes in Argentina's land policy over the past 50 years since independence. J Lat Am Stud 33(1):30-37+80

Weber M (2012) In: The protestant ethic and the spirit of capitalism (trans: Ma QY et al). Peking University Press, Beijing

World Bank (2020) World development indicators 2020. World Bank, Washington, DC

Zhang WZ (2018) The Belgrano freight railway reconstruction project undertaken by Chinese companies is progressing smoothly - Argentina's railway artery is regaining vitality. People's Daily

Chapter 13
Brazil: Industrial Development and Stagnation

Brazil is the largest country in Latin America in terms of both land area and economic scale. Over the past century, Brazil has experienced a long and tortuous development process. At the level of national governance, Brazil has experienced a variety of institutional changes, such as colonial rule, imperial system, military rule, and democratic election system, and there have been struggles, political games, and compromises among various domestic forces. At the economic level, Brazil has experienced continuous exploration of the strategies of single export, import substitution, and export orientation in foreign trade and has also made a series of infrastructure construction, financial reforms, and labor market reforms for the domestic market. From 1930, when Getulio Vargas came to power, to 1960, when the capital was moved to Brasilia, Brazil maintained more than 30 years of rapid growth and quickly grew from an agricultural colonial country with the export of raw materials as the main economic pillar to a middle-income country with great potential. However, in the 1970s, Brazil's rapid growth came to an end, the economy began to decline, and domestic and foreign debts began to soar. For nearly half a century, Brazil has never been able to return to its previous growth track. A series of problems, such as high inflation, imbalance in international payments, serious social conflicts, and slow economic growth, still plague Brazil. In 2015, Brazil's GDP per capita growth rate was only 0.9% and GDP growth per capita was close to zero. To this day, Brazil is still a developing country and there are still many problems to be solved.

From the perspective of the A-C theory, the main reasons for Brazil's slow economic growth come from the following aspects. First, the interests of the ruling party at the federal level and the interests of different groups at the state level are intertwined and difficult to reconcile, forming a fierce competition for administrative power. Under the catalysis of the electoral system, policy goals are distorted and the quality of decision-making is deeply affected. Second, the high degree of autonomy of the local governments has weakened the federal government's power to coordinate decision-making. The independent system of the setting of the fiscal budget and final account, as well as the federal government's fiscal guarantee, make

C. Chen et al., *From Poverty to Prosperity*, Understanding China,
https://doi.org/10.1007/978-981-95-7171-0_13

it difficult to effectively solve the problems faced by Brazil's finance and currency. Third, the construction of market mechanisms is still affected by various factors, such as labor discrimination and capital control, and hence transaction costs are too high and market efficiency is stagnant. Fourth, the absence of macro-control and the random inflow and outflow of international capital have exacerbated the imbalance in the development of the domestic industrial structure, which in turn affect the import and export trade structure and further cause structural problems in Brazil's economic development.

13.1 Evolution of Brazil's Political Governance

Since independence, Brazil's political organization has gone through various forms, including imperial, military dictatorship, and republic. Although there have been repeated changes to different political systems in the short term, the trend has been evolving towards a Western-style democratic system. Brazil was a colonized country before 1809. In 1815, with the improvement of Brazil's economic and international status, the country transformed from a colony to a kingdom and initially formed a state with complete political and economic power. In 1822, Prince Pedro of House Braganza declared Brazil's independence and proclaimed himself emperor, styled as Pedro I, and Brazil entered the imperial era. In 1889, General Manuel Deodoro da Fonseca launched a military coup and deposed Pedro II, the son and successor of Pedro I, overthrowing the empire and establishing a republic. The first federal republic constitution was passed in 1891, naming the country the United States of Brazil.[1] Later, under the impact of the Great Depression, which began in 1929, Brazil's "coffee economy" suffered a severe blow. The frequent coups and dictatorships that followed plunged the country's politics into chaos, and various domestic forces experienced a long period of competition and adjustment. It was not until 1985 that the military government returned power to the people, and the democratic parliamentary system was finally established and has been in operation ever since.

13.1.1 Rise and Fall of Multi-peak Governance Throughout Brazil's Political History

Historically, Brazil's political governance has been carried out under the pattern of multi-peak governance most of the time. Since Brazil became a colony of Portugal in the sixteenth century, large plantation owners and large landowners were the main economic forces domestically. With the rise of the Latin American

[1] "*República dos Estados Unidos do Brasil*" as translated from Portuguese.

independence movement in the early nineteenth century and the improvement of the colonial economy, in order to resist colonial exploitation, the people and the army rebelled against colonial authorities and established the Brazilian Empire in 1822. Only then did Brazil become a country in the modern sense.

However, during the imperial era in the early twentieth century, Brazil was only a loose federation, and the emperor's ability to govern the local areas was very weak, which was closely related to the colonial pattern of governance. During the colonial period, different regions of Brazil produced different cash crops, and production was mainly oriented towards international markets. Domestic economic ties were weak. The state of Sao Paulo in the southeast and the states in the northeast have long maintained a relatively independent mode of production. Even after overthrowing the rule of Portugal and establishing the empire, this system was not fundamentally broken. In 1889, when the Brazilian Empire collapsed and the United States of Brazil was established, this loose political alliance gradually transformed into "state power". At that time, the two most important states in Brazil, Sao Paulo and Minas Gerais, were divided into different factions based on their main economic products (Sao Paulo produced coffee, while Minas Gerais produced milk, etc.). The federal government hoped that the states could achieve economic diversification and shift from their single-export industry. However, most of the political elites in Sao Paulo were coffee plantation owners, and so they strongly demanded policies to support coffee exports and refused to implement the policies of the federal government. In addition, the animal husbandry industry in Minas Gerais was highly dependent on the relevant policies of the Brazilian government. In order to better influence government policies, although the state did not have strong economic strength, it actively participated in the National Congress and gradually gained a majority of seats in the Chamber of Deputies, the National Congress's lower house. Using its control over the government, Minas Gerais vigorously built its infrastructure. In the late 1920s, more than 40% of new railways were built in Minas Gerais. The state also promoted the introduction of relevant policies to protect its products (Burns 2013). Brazil was shrouded in an environment of competition among different political and economic oligarchs. "The adjustments and destruction brought about by the competing oligarchs around the presidential succession dispute have shown a new atmosphere," according to Burns (2013). The problems brought about by the prevalence of state power attracted social attention. The previously oppressed lieutenant class took power through a coup in 1930 and established a new government under the basic framework of centralization. Since then, Brazil entered a period of frequent coups, and one government after another was overthrown with the help of the military. In 1964, Brazil's military coup resulted in a dictatorial and authoritarian military regime. It was not until the military government stepped down in 1985 that the democratic process restarted in Brazil. Brazil's political system gradually took shape. At the federal level, a multi-party legislative system and a presidential executive system were implemented. Each state enjoyed a greater degree of autonomy, with state governors elected by local voters, and each state enjoyed the power to levy taxes and formulate its own budget. Different interest groups competed at the local and federal levels in the form of different political parties. Conflicts and reconciliation under the multi-peak structure continued to recur.

13.1.2 *Gestation, Growth, and Bottleneck of Multi-peak Reconciliatory Governance*

Before independence in 1822, Brazil, as an important colony in South America, undertook a large number of cash crop planting tasks. There was not much economic exchange between plantations distributed throughout different regions. When the Brazilian Empire was established in 1822, it was a very loose organization. The exploitation and oppression of slaves, the friction between church power and secular administrative power, and the confrontation between large landowners in various states and the central government had long existed under the plantation economic system. More importantly, with the widespread planting of coffee in southeastern states, two major interest groups were formed within the Brazilian Empire. One is the large landowner class, represented by the original feudal plantation owners, and the other is the emerging coffee industry interest groups, which were concentrated in southeastern states and cities. "The inevitable struggle between two completely different elements sets the tone for the future," according to Fausto and Fausto (2018). The two different interest groups lacked an effective consultation mechanism, and social contradictions continued to intensify. The emperor, as the representative of the interests of the feudal landowner class, was increasingly disliked by the people. In 1889, the emperor was deposed by the military, the empire was replaced by a republic, and the United States of Brazil was born.

Compared with the Brazilian Empire, the Brazilian Republic made a big step forward on the road to a reconciliatory society. Brazil had long abolished slavery, and the interests of large landowners could no longer compete with the thriving coffee groups and urban middle class after the end of imperial rule. "The control of political rights by the coffee interest class became the most important political feature from 1894 to 1930," as Fausto and Fausto noted (2018). Several major coffee-growing states formed an important political alliance, which managed Brazilian affairs through consultation and mediation, while also firmly holding Brazil's highest administrative power. "With the acquiescence and support of the major states, the incumbent president nominates the next presidential candidate. The selected candidate deals with the main governors and promises to return their favors," according to Fausto and Fausto (2018). Under this circumstance, new national political parties had not yet emerged. Under the reconciliation between the states, the Brazilian Republic rapidly developed an export-oriented industry mainly based on the production and trade of raw materials, such as coffee. Under this governance model, the Brazilian Republic was actually controlled by the localities. The local states elected their own governors, collected taxes, and used the tax proceeds within the state. The localities had great power and even their own local armed forces.

This initial form of reconciliation brought Brazil's first period of rapid growth. In 1889, there were only 626 enterprises in the whole of Brazil; from 1889 to 1914, Brazil added more than 7000 new enterprises. From 1915 to 1919, Brazil added another 5940. In 1920, Brazil's total industrial output value was US$153.06 million, about five times that of 1907 (U.S. Tariff Commission 1949). This was the fastest growth ever in Brazil's history.

In a sense, Brazil at this time had a higher degree of reconciliation than in any previous period, but the social reconciliation was very fragile. First, this was a reconciliation between a few political elites, not a reconciliation among the masses, because the interests of a large number of ordinary people had not improved synchronously and also because, to the same extent, the gap between the rich and the poor had gradually widened. Furthermore, the long-term monopoly of the highest administrative power made its policies have a distinct interest group tendency, which affected the quality of policies in the long run. Hence, when state rights prevailed during the period of the Brazilian Republic, unified actions were difficult to achieve, and national policies were difficult to implement thoroughly in practice. These legacy issues became obstacles that were difficult to bypass in the process of Brazilian governance. Brazil, under the multi-peak governance structure, seemed to have touched the boundary of reconciliation but it has never been able to truly cross the threshold of reconciliation.

13.1.3 Disintegration of Multi-Peak Reconciliatory Governance and Rapid Birth of Single-Peak Unbiased Governance

In fact, the reconciliation of the elites of the Brazilian Republic blocked the possibility of reconciliation with more interest groups. The political rights of Brazil during the Brazilian Republic period had nothing to do with the ordinary people of Brazil. Even for officers who made great contributions in foreign wars, the political system controlled by the big plantation owners was unwilling to share power with them. In addition, after experiencing export dividend during World War I, with the gradual recovery of production in Western countries, a large amount of coffee production capacity was in excess and hence the government borrowed a lot of money to maintain the operation of coffee plantations. The domestic economic performance was in sharp contrast with that during the wartime. At this time, the USA was vigorously promoting the industrialization process and had surpassed the United Kingdom in economic size and international influence, which gave Brazil a great stimulus. More Brazilian people began to feel that the export economy could only guarantee the interests of big plantation owners and that the prosperity and strength of the country required industrialization. It was frustrating that those in power may not stand on the side of the people's interests. "Nationalists … are suspicious of the coffee oligarchy, which seems to have a close connection with the world market … accordingly, their interests are not consistent with the interests of the nation," as noted by Burns (2013, p. 353) The coffee interest group had long held political and economic privileges, and the policy of protecting the interests of plantation owners had caused dissatisfaction among the others, and hence the political system of multi-peak reconciliatory governance began to transform into multi-peak conflictual governance.

In 1930, when Vargas, as a candidate of the Liberal Alliance, failed in the presidential election, he launched a coup with the support of the "Lieutenant Faction" in the army, dismissed the president, and took control of the federal government. After Vargas came to power, he accelerated the weakening of the power of local oligarchs, strengthened centralization, and quickly established a single-peak governance model. He dismissed the governors of each state, who had been elected by local elections, and required that all governors be appointed by the federal government. In addition, he dissolved the National Congress and local government councils and monopolized executive and legislative powers. "The new government initially concentrated its power in every possible way, trying to take control of economic, financial, and political decisions. The oligarchic institutions based on the states and municipalities lost power, and the government began to adjudicate between competing interest groups," according to Burns (2013).

From 1930 to 1945, Vargas ruled Brazil with an iron fist for 15 years,[2] and the country's political governance began to change from multi-peak to single-peak governance. First, Vargas sought a balance between various interest groups and made proper arrangements for new and old politicians, young officers, and people who participated in the coup. Additionally, Vargas disintegrated the long-standing left-wing and right-wing political forces in various ways, enabling him to successfully implement a series of reform policies.

Vargas fully realized the important role of industrialization and hence designed a series of industrialization plans that seemed very necessary at the time through tariff protection to support the development of national industry, as well as implementing an import substitution policy and placing restrictions on foreign capital and nationalization. Furthermore, the government took the lead in vigorously developing industries and infrastructure construction. This series of measures helped Brazil quickly build a modern industrial system. In addition, Vargas did not ignore the agricultural product production that previously dominated Brazil and reduced coffee production in order to control the price of coffee, which was unimaginable in the previous republican period, when each state was independent.

After Vargas' death,[3] Juscelino Kubitschek of the pro-Vargas Social Democratic Party won the presidential election in 1955 and took office on January 31, 1956. During his presidency, Kubitschek implemented an open and enlightened policy in politics, pardoned political prisoners, allowed a multi-party system, and fulfilled Brazil's century-old wish to move its capital. He maintained friendly exchanges with the United States and advocated the "Pan-American Action". In terms of econ-

[2] In October 1945, Brazil launched another military coup and Vargas was forced to give up the presidency. In 1951, Vargas returned to the presidency and won the general election. He was elected president at the age of 68 and died in 1954.

[3] On August 2, 1954, a political murder attempt occurred in Rio de Janeiro, in which a leader of the opposition party was injured and an attendant was killed. Police investigations revealed that the captain of the guard of the Presidential Palace of Vargas was suspected of the attempted murder, and the opposition party made a big fuss about it. On August 24, Vargas wrote his will, shot himself, and died.

omy, he put forward the slogan of "Fifty Years in Five", took measures to achieve rapid industrialization, formulated a development program that included 30 projects, and accelerated the development of food, energy, transportation, education, automobile, shipbuilding, steel, and other industries. In 1961, Kubitschek resigned after completing his term of office. His industrialization goals were basically achieved, but the high inflation during his tenure was widely criticized.

During the Brazilian Republic period, the multi-peak reconciliatory governance quickly pivoted into the pattern of single-peak unbiased governance without major political conflicts, and hence economic policies were effectively implemented, sweeping away economic malaise and opening the "Brazilian miracle" of the industrialization era. In the nearly half a century after 1930, the Brazilian economy maintained an average annual growth rate of 6.5%, of which the average annual GDP growth rate from 1942 to 1962 reached 7.5% (Bethel 1992).

13.1.4 Degeneration of Unimodal and Unbiased Governance During Military Dictatorship

From 1960 to 1964, after a brief turmoil from the end of Kubitschek's term, Brazil began to move further towards the path of industrialization under the rule of the military government. The government's comprehensive intervention in the economy and its open attitude towards foreign capital brought remarkable economic achievements, including rapid growth in infrastructure construction and important technology industries, such as telecommunications. The average annual growth rate from 1969 to 1974 reached 11.2%, while the inflation rate remained at a low level (Fausto and Fausto 2018). The Brazilian miracle attracted global attention.

The long-term rule of the military government led to signs of deviation from the unimodal and unbiased governance model. First, the military government gradually gave up its compromise and integration posture with other interest groups. The military government further weakened the power of the National Congress, established the Police and Military Investigation Bureau, and used its special powers to persecute and suppress opponents. Starting from 1964, the Brazilian political arena was filled with a terrifying atmosphere. Second, the long-term industrialization process caused greater inequality between the rich and the poor. The military government actually represented the interests of the big bourgeoisie and big entrepreneurs. The fruits of economic construction were shared with more people, and government representation was more one-sided. The reason for this biased tendency was largely because the military had long held power and formed a fixed interest group in the process of nationalization. Such interest groups had the natural characteristics of exclusive competition, which led to certain biases in the formulation of economic policies.

During the stage of rapid economic growth, some social contradictions in Brazil could be concealed, but when economic growth slowed down, the domestic situation changed. Due to the long-term inefficiency of state-owned enterprises, as well as the lack of domestic consumption capacity caused by the uneven distribution of social income and the imbalance of the industrial structure brought about by the construction of industry as the core, the pace of Brazil's sustained growth was eventually affected. From 1981 to 1983, the economic recession brought serious consequences, and the military government was forced to hand over power under the pressure of various forces. Thus, the exploration of the single-peak unbiased governance model, which lasted for more than half a century from 1930 to 1984, ended in Brazil. Over the past half century, Brazil had created countless economic miracles, and had leapt from a colonial country that was essentially no different from other Latin American countries to one of the most developed countries in the world. This was due to the people's desire for industrialization, and the demise of this governance model was fundamentally caused by the failure to reasonably distribute the already enlarged pie and by the serious degradation in the model.

13.1.5 Re-formation of Multi-peak Conflictual Governance

The Brazilian Constitution fundamentally cuts off the possibility of a military government continuing to rule in Brazil. A multi-party system via true federalism was re-established in Brazil, and the independence of the federal government and the state governments underwent major changes.

However, since the 1980s, the Brazilian economy has been facing an unstoppable downward trend, and the purchasing power of the working class has fallen by 20%. In 1990, the minimum wage for workers was only 36% that of the previous year (Fausto and Fausto 2018). The new government attributed this problem to the closed political system and the inefficiency of the state's promotion of industrialization. Therefore, starting with President Cazordo, Brazil began a large-scale privatization process. In addition to the privatization of existing sectors, core sectors, such as electricity, oil, and iron ore, also underwent the privatization process. The policy of privatization has re-created a large number of industry oligarchs, some of whom come from the original domestic capitalists and from overseas capitalists. These two groups have gradually become the two most important interest groups in Brazil since the twenty-first century. "The core disputes in Brazilian politics come from two interest groups, one is the domestic interest group and the other is the international capital interest group. The different demands of the two interest groups in ideology, politics, structure, and political representation directly affect the policy-making of the Brazilian government," according to Boito and Saad-Filho (2016). The contradictions between the two sides are difficult to reconcile. This conflict is directly reflected in politics, resulting in a multi-peak structure comprised of various interest groups. The multi-peak characteristics are also obvious. Under the framework of the new democratic political system, many political parties have emerged in Brazil. As of 2017, there are 37 political parties active in Brazilian politics. Candidates from different backgrounds participated in the competition for administrative power, which resulted in many election farces. In 1994, a candidate who announced that he would no longer support local investment in scientific and technological innovation became the Minister of Science and Technology. In 2010, a circus performer was elected as the Speaker of the Sao Paulo State Congress with the slogan of "I don't know what the parliament can do, but if you elect me, I will tell you how to do it" (Vaz de Melo 2015). The large number of political parties have many conflicts in their demands and purposes, which has led to inefficient political consultation.

Under the multi-peak pattern, it has been difficult for Brazil's political governance to return to the level of cohesion in the 1930s. The states have restored their local autonomy, and the regional chief executives and legislatures are elected via local elections. The states still enjoy taxation rights and independently formulate their expenditure budgets. This approach has brought about completely unfavorable results for the domestic economy. Since local debts are covered by federal finances, the investment volume of each state competes with each other, which has caused a lot of duplicate construction across the country and also further aggravated the imbalance of federal fiscal revenue and expenditure. The federal government has not proposed a good solution to this situation because presidents needed the support of the states. After taking office, several presidents, such as Luiz Inácio Lula da Silva (in office from 2003 to 2010), increased the federal government's infrastructure investment expenditure in the states in order to win them over, even if this would further increase the government's fiscal deficit and debt pressure. In addition, two of the four presidents since the 1990s were tried by the judiciary and imprisoned. Candidates from different political parties have different focuses in the policies they promote. Therefore, Brazil faces resistance at different levels in both the formation and implementation of policies. Based on its current situation, Brazil is still in a model of multi-peak conflictual governance.

In order to better understand Brazil's current political governance, we present the indexes of the political concentration and political cohesion of 209 countries in 2018, as shown in Fig. 13.1, where the triangle points represent Brazil's political concentration and political cohesion indexes in 2018, and the diamond points represent the indexes from 1996 to 2018.

It can be seen that, overall, since 1995, Brazil has been a typical democracy with diverse political forces (as its score on the horizontal axis is close to 5). In addition, its political cohesion index has always been below average at 2.78, which puts Brazil generally in the fourth quadrant. The decline in its power concentration index was largely due to the fall of the military government and the emergence of a large number of new political parties. Hence, this shows that the decline in Brazil's political cohesion is closely related to the rise of state power and the irreconcilable contradictions between interest groups.

The decline in political cohesion has two meanings. From the perspective of policy formulation, this means that Brazil's policies do not represent the interests of the majority and that the quality, scientificity, and long-term nature of the policies are challenged; from the perspective of policy implementation, the decline in political cohesion means that the efficiency of policy implementation at all levels of government is poor and the execution is insufficient. Hence, economic growth will definitely be affected, as shown in Fig. 13.2.

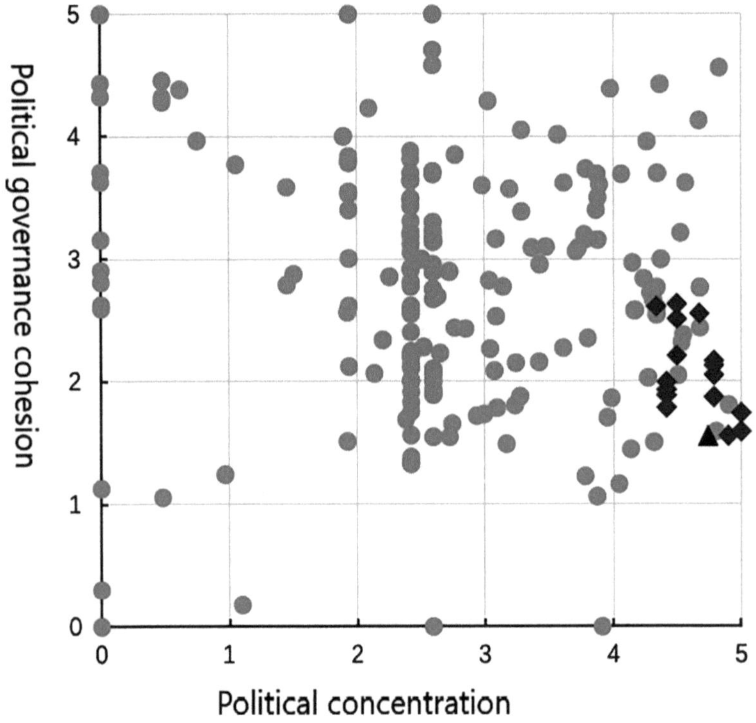

Fig. 13.1 Political concentration and political cohesion indexes in Brazil. Data were compiled by authors

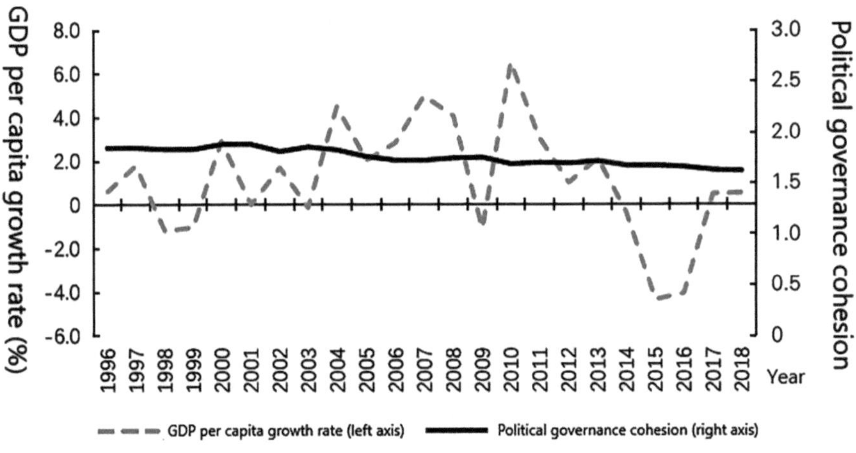

Fig. 13.2 Brazil's GDP per capita growth rate and political cohesion index. *Source*: WDI and authors' compilation

13.2 Slow Internal Opening Process

Brazil has grown from a colonial country to a major power in Latin America after a long process of internal economic opening. From the perspective of labor factors, the slave emancipation movement in 1867 allowed a large number of workers to enter the labor market as equals. The industrialization movement since the 1930s attracted a large number of farmers to the industrial and service sectors. Since the 1970s, more and more women also left their homes and entered the production sector. More people were swept into the process of national development. At the capital level, the monopoly of the economy by large landowners was broken, the oligarchic economy under the framework of state power was severely impacted by centralization, the traditional local capital was challenged by foreign capital due to privatization, and the construction of the financial system was continuously promoted amid twists and turns. From the perspective of market-oriented construction, infrastructure construction is constantly improving and market order is constantly cultivated and established. Nevertheless, today's marketization level in Brazil is incomparable to that half a century ago.

However, it should be pointed out that as a country that has experienced decades of continuous growth of more than 5% and is now in economic stagnation, Brazil's pace of internal opening of its economy has not been smooth and many problems still exist. Compared with those of other BRICS countries, the internal accessibility of the Brazilian economy is not high. From the relative performances of specific sub-indicators, as shown in Fig. 13.3, it can be seen that Brazil does not rank high in any of the indicators. There are still invisible barriers for labor to enter the production link, infrastructure construction is still lagging behind, the inefficiency of the capital market still exists, and the external costs of commodity transactions remain high. These problems cause Brazil to face a more unfavorable position in international competition.

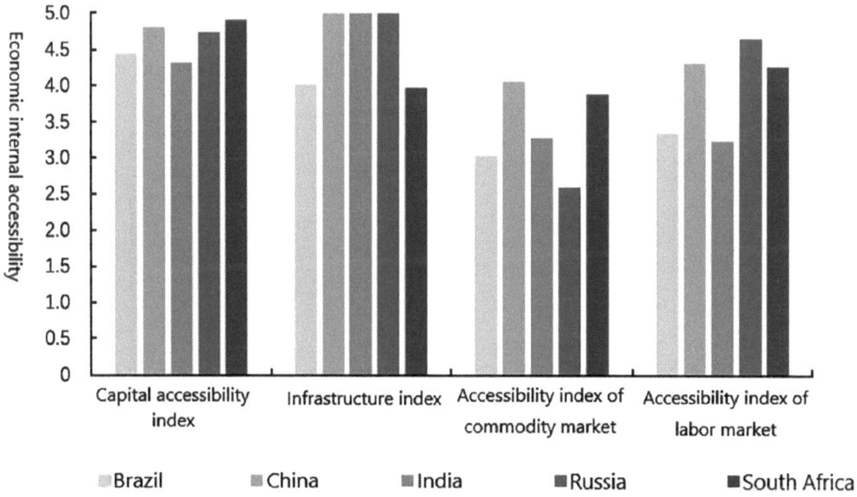

Fig. 13.3 Comparison of BRICS countries' internal economic accessibility indexes in 2015

13.2.1 Invisible Barriers in Labor Market

The labor problem is an important issue for Brazil's economic development. During the industrialization period, a large number of laborers poured into cities, and the speed of influx was higher than the speed of absorption by urban industrial sectors. In addition, due to the generally low quality of the labor force, the possibility of further integration into industrial development was reduced. This led to a series of economic and social problems, which still plague Brazil today, and some of them are still obstacles to Brazil's economic development.

13.2.1.1 Excess Labor Supply

Since the 1930s, with the beginning of industrialization, a large number of farmers have gone to cities to find better jobs. In 1940, less than a third of Brazilians lived in cities; by the 1970s, with the rapid growth of Brazil's economy and the rapid rise of the service industry, the population of major Brazilian cities began to increase rapidly, as shown in Fig. 13.4. In 1980, this proportion reached two-thirds. In addition, with the liberation of women, more and more women joined the production force, which increased the number of Brazilian workers. These workers are concentrated in large numbers in Brazilian cities, forming an important industrial labor force.

However, the influx of a large number of homogeneous laborers into cities in Brazil does not form a truly meaningful labor supply. The concentration rate of labor is significantly higher than the number required for industrial development in cities, resulting in a large number of surplus labor concentrated in cities. These laborers live on the edge of large cities, forming slums. In addition, a large number of Brazilian workers are subject to strict labor access regulations and have to work in informal sectors. Later, with the continuous improvement of industrial concentration and the widespread use of machines, a large number of industrial workers lost

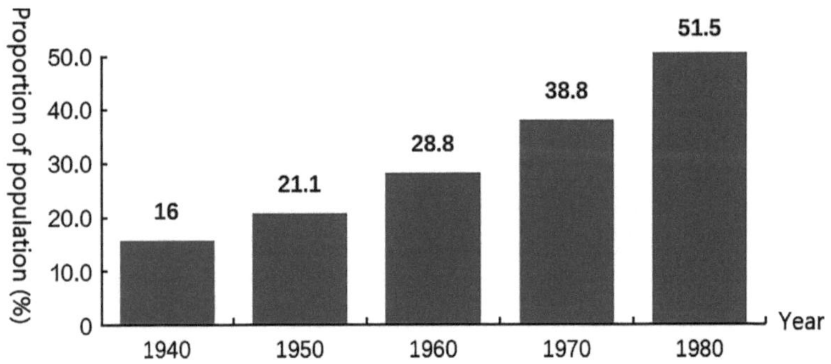

Fig. 13.4 Proportion of population living in cities with population of more than 20,000. *Source*: Bacha and Herbert (1989)

their jobs after being replaced by machines. Although some have been absorbed by the tertiary industry, most are engaged in labor-intensive and low-income service industries.

13.2.1.2 Low-Quality Labor

Among South American countries, the quality of Brazil's labor force is relatively low. As shown in Fig. 13.5, Brazil's average years of education is at a low level. The inevitable result of this situation is a low level of human capital accumulation.

Also, for a long period of time, the adult illiteracy rate in Brazil has remained at a high level. Even in the 1950s, when industrialization had already started, one in two Brazilian adults was illiterate. The labor force that supported Brazil's industrialization and strong economic growth actually received very limited education. In the 1960s and 1970s, cheap labor was still the main industrial force, and the main training it received was on-the-job training. This situation may not have been a big problem at the time, but in the 1980s and later, when technology-intensive industries gradually grew into an important pillar of economic growth, relying solely on a large number of laborers with only low education was doomed to not meet the needs of industrial development.

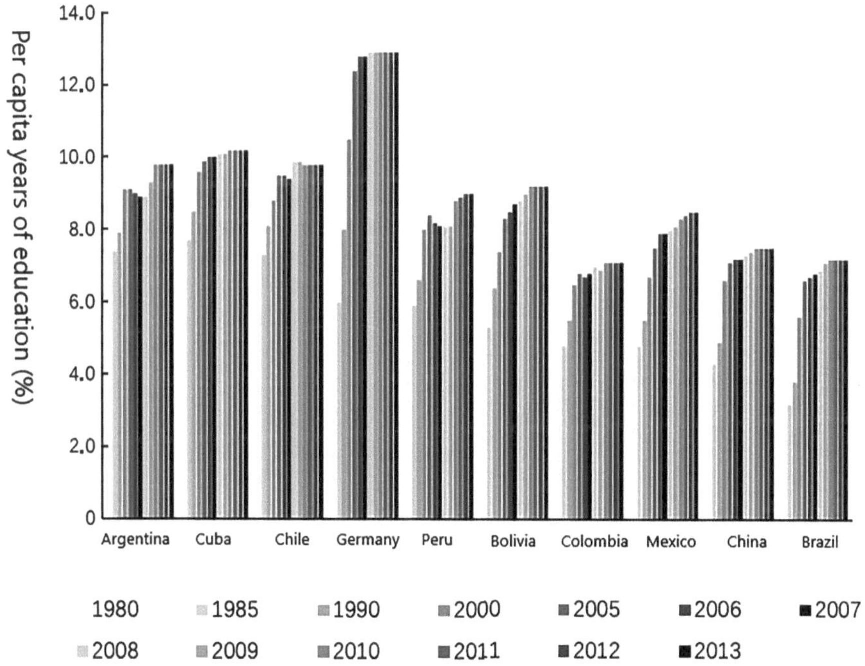

Fig. 13.5 Average years of education per capita in major South American countries and other comparative countries. *Source*: World Bank (2014), International Human Development Indicators

13.2.1.3 Actual Wage Level Continues to Decline and Income Gap Continues to Widen

In the 1950s and 1960s, the secondary industry still had a large absorption capacity for ordinary labor, but after the 1970s, when advanced manufacturing industries put forward new requirements for labor, the labor force could not smoothly enter the secondary industry due to insufficient human capital accumulation and other reasons, which led to two results. Firstly, the labor force, with the lower education level, had to accept the continuous decline of actual income level due to oversupply and fierce competition, as shown in Fig. 13.6. Secondly, with the market demand for skilled labor continuing to increase and yet the supply of skilled labor not changing much, the income gap between skilled workers and those who have not received good training has gradually widened.

From the above analysis, we can see that although Brazil's labor force population is increasing, this total growth shows an obvious imbalance in microstructure. A large number of workers have entered the production force of ordinary labor and poured into labor-intensive sectors, with the industry and construction industries as the main destinations. A large number of new workers have been absorbed by informal sectors and have not been able to enter the wave of advanced industrial development under the influence of employment restrictions and industry thresholds.

13.2.2 Unstable Domestic Financial Environment and Capital Environment

13.2.2.1 Expansion of State-Owned Capital and Economic Inefficiency Under Import Substitution

Brazil experienced a period of rapid expansion of state-owned capital under the import substitution policy. The policy was reflected in raising trade barriers on the one hand and supporting and protecting important domestic industries on the other.

Fig. 13.6 Real value of Brazilian minimum wage (1944–1996). *Source*: Bethel (2013)

But from actual results, this protection measure was inefficient to a large extent. In the process of promoting the import substitution strategy, the government strengthened its control over the national economy by developing state-owned enterprises and increasing the proportion of state-owned enterprises, as shown in Fig. 13.7, and adjusted and regulated the production field through price controls and government borrowing. These practices violated market laws, distorted the allocation of capital factors, and ultimately caused waste of resources and economic inefficiency.

In 1974, a survey of the largest 5113 Brazilian joint stock companies showed that 39% were state-owned, 18% were multinationals, and 56% were domestic private enterprises. In 1985, the net assets of state-owned enterprises rose to 48%, but with sales accounting for only 26% and state-owned enterprises employing only 18.91% of the employees (Melhores e Maiores 1982, 1986). In addition, the return on net assets of state-owned enterprises fell significantly in the 1980s, as shown in Fig. 13.8. By 1990, the return on net assets of state-owned enterprises was only 2.7%, and the largest 50 state-owned enterprises had a total loss of US$6.4 billion (Werneck 1986).

For quite a long time, the Brazilian government used state-owned enterprises as a tool to implement macroeconomic policies. State-owned enterprises often violated the market's optimal goals due to political pressures in their operations, and their profitability continued to decline. A large number of state-owned enterprises (such as Eletrobrás, Brazil's national electricity company, and *Companhia Siderúrgica Nacional* (CSN), Brazil's state-owned steel company) suffered huge losses and their debts continued to rise. Domestic interest rates continued to rise, causing serious damage to the Brazilian economy.

13.2.2.2 Trouble of Inflation

In the 1980s, bank deposits controlled by the federal and state governments accounted for 40% of the total bank deposits. Among the loans issued nationwide, those from the Brazilian Development Bank and local development banks accounted

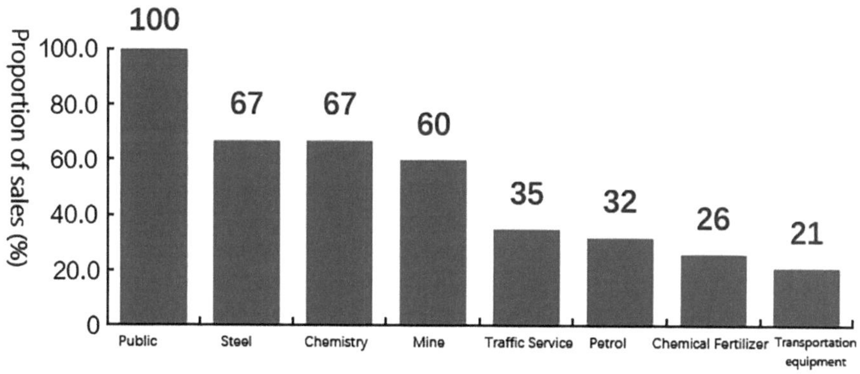

Fig. 13.7 Sales share of Brazilian state-owned enterprises in various sectors (1990). *Source*: Melhores e Maiores (1991)

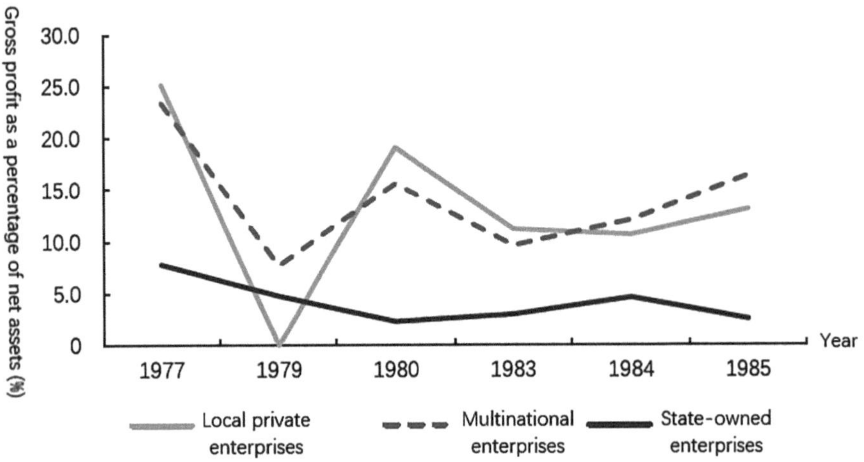

Fig. 13.8 Comparison of return on equity for Brazilian companies of different ownership types. *Source*: Melhores e Maiores (1982, 1986)

for 70% of the national loans (Baer 1969). The government used the Brazilian Development Bank to provide credit loans to promote the development of important departments. However, the efficiency of the use of these loans was very low, resulting in a lot of waste and inefficiency. In many loan contracts, there were even a lot of "gifts". By 1987, gift expenses in related contracts reached 75% of total expenses (Bethel 2013). When a large number of state-owned enterprises began to suffer losses and were unable to repay their debts, the banks faced a large number of bad debts. In addition, the Brazilian government, as an investor in state-owned enterprises, also assumed a large amount of debt, especially debts to foreign creditors.

Furthermore, when economic growth stagnated due to the inefficiency of state-owned enterprises, the Brazilian government chose to expand public spending to stimulate the economy and increase economic growth. The large amount of public sector spending not only further pushed up the government's debt level but also increased the interest rate of the capital market, squeezed the investment of the private sector, and further reduced the efficiency of the economy. Take infrastructure investment as an example. Around the 1970s, Brazil launched a series of state-led grand strategies, many of which were too absurd and ambitious (Bethell 2013), including the Ferrovia do Acon steel plant, the Trans-Amazon Highway in remote areas, the Itaipu Hydropower Station, the over-expanded nuclear industry that did not solve practical problems, etc. Additionally, some obviously high-priced state acquisitions also substantially reduced the efficiency of capital utilization.

As the debt burden became heavier, the Brazilian government chose to monetize the deficit. As a result, the currency began to depreciate rapidly and the inflation rate soared. The basically stable financial order in the 1960s and 1970s was seriously damaged, as shown in Fig. 13.9, which further triggered a series of serious consequences and ultimately triggered multiple rounds of crises.

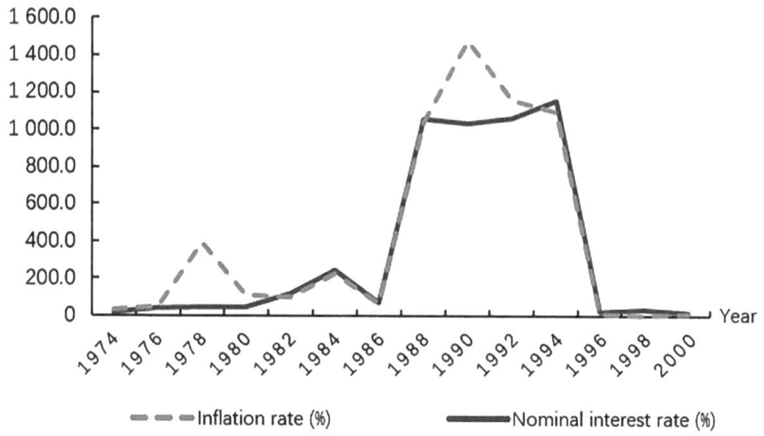

Fig. 13.9 Inflation rate and nominal interest rate in Brazil (1974–2000). *Source*: IBGE (2020), Sistema de Contas Nacionais

13.2.2.3 Capital Market Long Had High Barriers

Capital barriers have long existed within Brazil's financial and economic system. Prior to and during the period of the republic, Brazil had not yet established a complete financial infrastructure, and capital circulation at that time was limited to large plantation owners, large landowners, and other interest groups of the previous era. Since 1930, the process of industrialization promoted the development of the capital market. However, under the dominance of national industrialization, the construction of the capital market was more in line with the needs of state-owned enterprises rather than the needs of private enterprises. In 1965, the Capital Market Reform Law was officially approved. Short-term credit was provided by commercial banks, medium-term credit was provided by newly established financial institutions and investment banks, and long-term loans were provided by the public in the form of shares and bonds in the stock market. However, the largest social investment at this time still came from the government and state-owned enterprises. From 1961 to 1963, government investment accounted for 37.5%, and by 1965, state-owned enterprises accounted for 46.4% (Bethel 1992). Before the privatization process began, the capital market was dominated by the government and large enterprises.

Since 1985, the state-dominated capital market has had to face adjustments and reforms due to its long-term inefficiency. After a series of privatization processes, the capital discrimination between state-owned and private enterprises has gradually disappeared; however, there are still high barriers faced by private enterprises in the Brazilian capital market. Such financial restrictions are not necessarily reflected in clear regulations. A large amount of bureaucratic retention and financial gray areas have brought obstacles to the market-oriented operation of the capital market. These obstacles can be seen from the sensitivity of Brazilian private enterprises to financial assets. From 1995 to 2006, private enterprises had a higher sensitivity to monetary assets, suggesting that private enterprises actually faced higher financial restrictions. This distorted allocation of capital has reduced the innovation ability and performance level of private enterprises and has had an adverse impact on the long-term development of the Brazilian economy (Crisóstomo 2014).

13.2.3 Absence of Infrastructure Construction

Objectively speaking, due to the constraints of the "great cliff" geographical form, Brazil's geographical conditions are not conducive to infrastructure construction. To this day, coastal cities generally face problems, such as too small of a hinterland, loose connections between cities, and inconvenient transportation. But in the medium and long term, Brazil's weak infrastructure has many historical reasons.

The Brazilian economy started with the manor economy. Since the implementation of the manor economy, Brazil has not carried out any thorough land reform in the past few centuries. The original manor economy relied on the land ownership of large manor owners. A few land oligarchs owned a large amount of land. These land oligarchs transformed into industrial oligarchs and service industry oligarchs in modern society. This process of wealth accumulation has never been affected substantially. Brazil's special natural and geographical conditions make it impossible for small- and medium-sized industrial and commercial operators to independently bear the cost of infrastructure construction, let alone lead infrastructure construction. Therefore, before 1930, Brazil's domestic infrastructure construction was mainly concentrated in areas related to the manor economy, and infrastructure in other areas was never built.

With Vargas's coming to power, the call for industrialization continued to grow. In order to promote industrialization, it became even more important to form a unified Brazilian market. At this time, Brazil experienced the first stage of infrastructure construction, with roads, transportation, schools, hospitals, financial institutions, etc., being built continuously. However, after the fall of the military government in 1945, the states paid more attention to local infrastructure construction, and hence the federal government's promotion of infrastructure construction encountered great resistance and the progress of infrastructure construction was sluggish. Take the Dutra government (1945–1950) as an example. In order to promote Brazil's infrastructure construction, the Dutra government ambitiously launched the SALTE plan in 1948, aiming to promote infrastructure construction in the four major areas of health, food, transportation, and energy. However, within the federal government, where state power prevailed, the states were unwilling to pay for projects that benefited other states and instead obstructed the plan in every possible way. "A fatal weakness of the Dutra government, and to some extent its successors, was the inability to ensure sufficient political support in Congress. The SALTE plan was not passed by Congress until the last year of the Dutra government but was abandoned by the new government in 1951.... Political obstruction also prevented the government's new tax bill from being passed," as noted by Bethell (1992).

Since the 1980s, due to the impact of economic recession, Brazil has assumed a large foreign debt burden, and public sector spending has become more stretched. Brazil's series of reforms have mainly focused on solving foreign debt and curbing inflation, and the aging of infrastructure has become more common. As of today, Brazil's coastal roads are still not well developed, and the connection between cities is greatly restricted. Therefore, coastal cities cannot smoothly share infrastructure, and the amount of infrastructure construction is very large. In addition, due to terrain and cost factors, large port cities are unable to transport products from inland cities to foreign countries and the important transit and hub role of port cities cannot be reflected, and so the radiation effect of port cities on the inland economy is weakened. Intuitively, the development of Brazil's port cities is basically the independent development of each independent city, which makes it difficult for Brazil to form economies of scale.

13.3 Unbalanced Development of External Accessibility

Due to its special historical development background, Brazil has always had close ties with external markets in terms of economic accessibility. The main market of the plantation economy in the colonial period was the international markets, with the establishment of the Republic of Brazil seen for a considerable period of time as the coffee industry interest groups controlling the national interests and developing an export-oriented economy. In the "New State" period, Brazil's import substitution policy was a new way of dealing with economic foreign relations. This idea affected the entire Latin America and became an important recipe for promoting economic growth for a period of time. The privatization process since the 1980s and the discussion on foreign investment have all involved Brazil's opening up to the outside world. Although, in terms of total volume, Brazil is still a major country that is often active in international trade. Compared with the 1970s, Brazil's cash crops and agricultural products still appear in international bulk commodity trade, while high-tech industrial products, such as automobiles and aircraft, are no longer in the most competitive first echelon. The reasons and specific economic details are directly related to Brazil's long-term economic environment and economic policies.

13.3.1 Import Substitution Sacrificed External Accessibility of Brazilian Economy

For a long period before World War II, the Brazilian economy was closely connected with international markets and its external dependence remained at a high level. Especially with the continuous expansion of the Industrial Revolution and the change in consumption structure, Brazil imported a large amount of capital goods and consumer goods from abroad and relied on the export of bulk agricultural products to basically achieve a balance of international payments.

During World War II, Brazil's imports of capital goods were restricted by the war. Therefore, after the war, a large amount of import demand, which accumulated during World War II, was released suddenly and foreign exchange reserves, which accumulated during the war, decreased rapidly. In addition, with the gradual stabilization of the post-war international environment, a large number of developing countries emerged as production bases for replacing Brazilian raw materials. Also, with the background of improved technological level, developed countries increased the utilization rate of raw materials and reduced the utilization volume, resulting in a sharp decline in Brazil's export income and foreign exchange reserves. Against this background, the Brazilian government decided to implement an import substitution policy, the core content of which was to use government power to raise trade barriers, thereby protecting the smooth development of national industries for a certain period of time.

As shown in Table 13.1 and Fig. 13.10, after implementing the import substitution policy, Brazil saw a significant import substitution in manufacturing sectors, such as electrical equipment, transport equipment, and mechanical equipment, as well as a reduction in imports in consumer goods sectors, such as textiles, leather manufacturing, clothing, and footwear. Overall, during the period of the import substitution strategy, Brazil's external accessibility declined significantly.

Table 13.1 Changes in Brazil's import structure (1949–1962)

	Share of merchandise imports (%, 1949 dollars)		
Product category	1949	1962	Change
Food, beverages, tobacco	4.58	3.13	−1.45
Textile	3.99	0.13	−3.86
Clothing, footwear	0.05	0	−0.05
Wood products	0.18	0.04	−0.14
Paper and paper products	2.36	2.58	0.22
Printing and printing equipment	0.31	0.47	0.16
Leather goods	0.27	0.01	−0.26
Rubber products	0.12	0.07	−0.05
Chemicals, petroleum, coal products	19.55	18.01	−1.54
Non-metallic mineral products	2.04	1.33	−0.71
Alkali metals and metal products	11.48	11.62	0.14
Mechanical equipment	14.21	12.99	−1.22
Electrical Equipment	6.61	6.27	−0.34
Transport equipment	14.3	10.17	−4.13
Other finished products	1.92	1.95	0.03
Total finished products	81.97	68.78	−13.19
Unprocessed raw materials	18.03	31.22	13.19
Total	100	100	

Source: Statistics from the Economic and Financial Statistics Bureau, the Brazilian Ministry of Foreign Trade, etc.

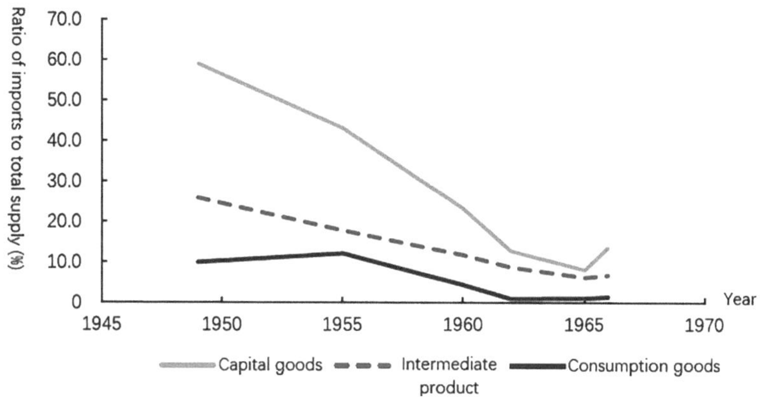

Fig. 13.10 Brazil's imports of various products as percentage of total supply (1949–1966). *Source*: Baer (2014)

13.3.2 Gradual Degeneration of Domestic Industrial Structure Under Import Substitution

Generally speaking, the reasonable idea of implementing the import substitution strategy should be to provide support and assistance to national industries in the early stage of development and to gradually relax the protection policy when the economic scale is basically formed and technology accumulation is competitive so that relevant industries can participate in a wider international competition. Therefore, the accumulation and progress of technology during the import substitution period are very important. The relatively successful experiences of Japan, South Korea, Singapore, and Taiwan show that all of these economies implemented industrial protection policies for a certain period of time. After their core industries had grown and developed, these countries all turned to an export-oriented economy and have maintained a high-level and stable economic development.

However, from the development history of Brazil, its import substitution strategy did not effectively spawn technological progress. Brazil has not only failed to develop a manufacturing industry with high capital intensity but also failed to improve its position in the global industrial chain and reduce the domestic demand for foreign capital goods. On the contrary, it has been importing a large amount of machinery and equipment from abroad; as shown in Fig. 13.11, Brazil's imports of machinery and equipment once accounted for about 40% of all imports during the import substitution period. In addition, since Brazil failed to develop a pillar industry with core competitiveness during the import substitution period, the competitiveness of Brazil's industrial products in international markets began to decline significantly after the 1980s, and the export share decreased year by year and gradually returned to the trade structure that relied on the export of bulk primary products, which has been accompanied by the slow growth of Brazil's economy and society.

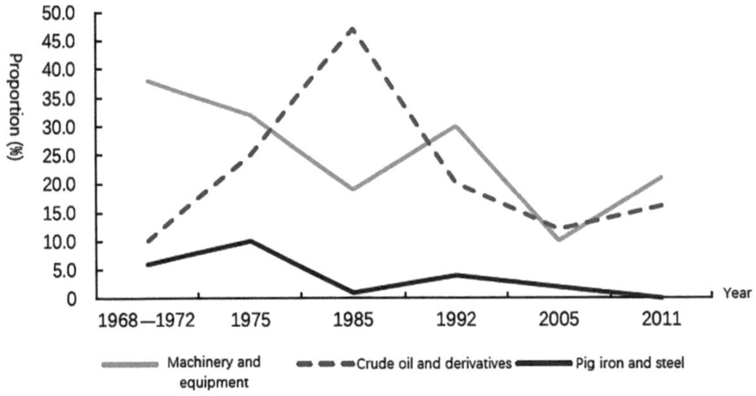

Fig. 13.11 Structure of Brazil's main import products. *Source*: Baer (2014)

On the whole, by sacrificing the external accessibility of its own economy, the import substitution strategy has protected Brazil's national industry to a certain extent, but Brazil has not fully seized the precious strategic opportunity window to cultivate its industries with comparative advantages into pillar industries with international competitiveness. On the contrary, the expansion of inefficient state-owned enterprises has led to the continuous degradation of the industrial structure, and Brazil has not been able to continue to climb up the international industrial chain, hence affecting the leap of Brazil's economy.

13.3.3 Failure of Attempt to Break Through By Improving Cohesion of Political Governance

In order to solve a series of problems facing the Brazilian economy, the federal government chose the path of large-scale privatization in the 1990s. By selling inefficient and highly indebted state-owned assets to private and international capital, as shown in Fig. 13.12, the redundant burden of economic operation was reduced, which not only eased the pressure of government debt but also enhanced market vitality and objectively improved Brazil's production efficiency. From 1986 to 1990, due to the inefficient investment of state-owned assets, the labor productivity of the manufacturing industry only increased by 0.2%; this figure increased to 8.7% after large-scale privatization was officially launched in 1991.

The privatization strategy has indeed increased corporate profits, activated corporate vitality, enhanced the vitality of the Brazilian economy, promoted the improvement of the quality of manufacturing products and the service level of the service industry, and promoted the development of Brazil's advanced manufacturing and high value-added industries. However, due to the lack of sufficient argumentation and top-level design, coupled with the absence of supervision, Brazil did

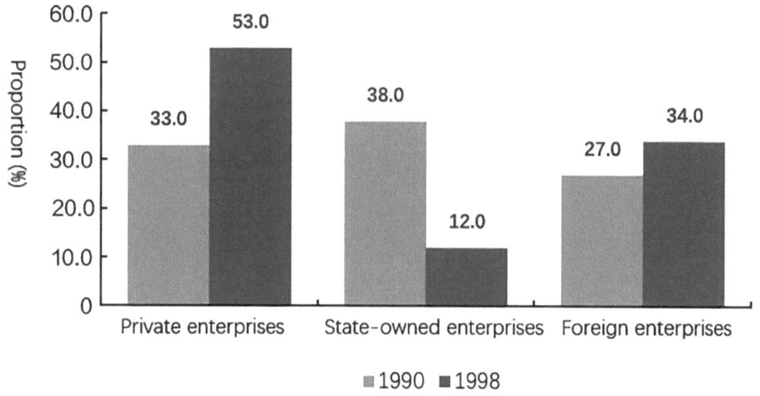

Fig. 13.12 Comparison of proportion of enterprises of different ownership types in Brazil before and after privatization (1990 and 1998). *Source*: Filho and Carla (1999)

not pay enough attention to the welfare of workers and the income distribution of the whole society in promoting the privatization of state-owned enterprises. In particular, a large number of layoffs occurred during the privatization process, while new jobs were not created. This resulted in the majority of workers not benefiting from it, especially the low-income group. The income distribution gap in the whole society has further widened, resulting in a decline in the cohesion of political governance. For example, the Brazilian Federal Railway System had 40,000 employees before privatization, which was reduced to 11,500 after privatization. Steel giants CSN, COSIPA, and USIMINAS also made a large number of layoffs (De Castro 1999). A large number of workers left the reformed enterprises, and since the new enterprises could not provide enough jobs to absorb these laid-off employees, the workers had to flow into the tertiary industry with a lower added value and lower income level. The lack of jobs and the widening income gap have become the main socio-economic problems that have plagued Brazil for a long time. In addition, some critics believe that foreign-funded enterprises are not willing to transfer their R&D departments to the host country. Their basic research departments prefer to be located in the headquarters or places with technology clusters. Even if there are research institutions in overseas branches, their main responsibilities are limited to quality control, etc. As for the competitiveness of core technology enterprises, few enterprises are willing to transfer advanced R&D capabilities and R&D results to the host country. Many people believe that this technological blockade is one of the important reasons why Brazil has had a strong demand for foreign technology for a long time (Baer 2014). Overall, since 1996, the external accessibility index of the Brazilian economy has continued to be low, not only with a large gap with the average level of G7 countries but also significantly lower than the world's average, as shown in Fig. 13.13. This shows that when Brazil participates in global economic activities, it still needs to continuously break through its own resource endowment and market capacity limitations, obtain various factors on a global scale at a lower cost, and give full play to its own industrial comparative advantages and production capacity to gain the global market share.

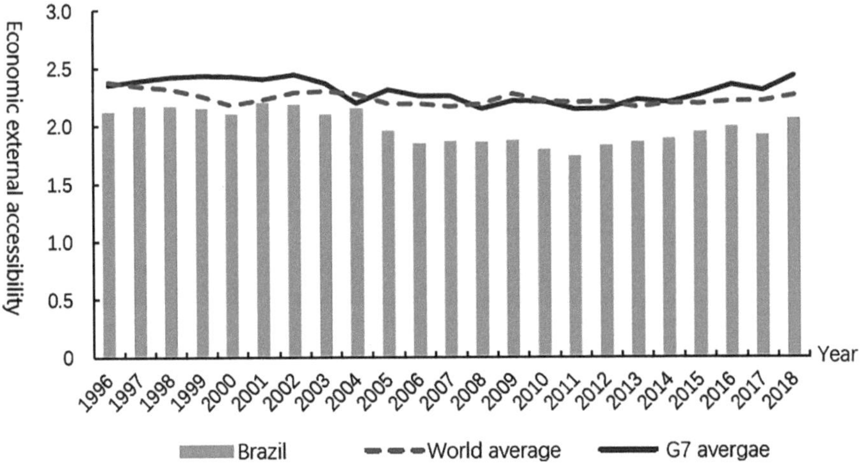

Fig. 13.13 External accessibility index of Brazil's economy

13.4 Chapter Summary

In this chapter, the framework of the A-C theory was used to analyze the problems Brazil has faced in its development, focusing on the process of economic and political development in the country. Firstly, unique causes naturally affect the cohesiveness of Brazil's political governance. The political and economic processes and the political and cultural frameworks led to the prevalence of state power in Brazil, poor political stability for half a century, and numerous domestic interest groups, which had always found it difficult for Brazil to form a good consultation system. Monopolistic economic and political groups had taken turns in taking power, and social policies lacked sustainability and execution. Overall, the cohesiveness of Brazil's political governance is not high. Secondly, in terms of economic accessibility, Brazil's low level of external economic accessibility has been closely related to the import substitution policy. Supporting the development of domestic industries in the form of trade barriers had reduced the relative scale of foreign trade. In the long run, it also caused the domestic industrial structure to gradually deviate from the rules of international markets, further leading to the imbalance and deformation of the foreign trade structure. In addition, the radical privatization process has enabled a large number of opportunities to attract foreign investment to be released quickly and cheaply. The above factors have seriously frustrated the accessibility of the external economy. Thirdly, there are also problems with the internal accessibility of Brazil's economy. Frequent inflation, financial turmoil, and chaotic capital control rules have seriously affected the healthy growth of the capital market. Uncontrolled monopolistic enterprises and state-owned enterprises have slowed the integration of domestic product markets. Brazil's unique natural environment and weak federal government have made large-scale infrastructure construction full of obstacles. The backward education, the deformed industrial structure, and restrictions in the labor market have caused the distortion of labor market resource allocation. The difficulties faced by Brazil in the process of economic development are closely related to its political and economic systems and are also the result of the combined influence of Brazil's natural environment, history, and culture.

References

Bacha EL, Herbert KS (1989) Social change in Brazil, 1945–1985: the incomplete transition. Albuquerque, UNM Press

Baer W (1969) The development of the Brazilian steel industry. Nashville, Vanderbilt UP

Baer W (2014) The Brazilian economy: growth and development (trans: Luo FF). Petroleum Industry Press, Beijing

Bethell L (ed) (1992) The Cambridge history of Latin America (trans: Hu YD et al), vol 5. Social Science Academic Press, Beijing

Bethell L (ed) (2013) The Cambridge history of Latin America (trans: Wu HY et al), vol 9. Contemporary China Publishing House, Beijing

Boito A, Saad-Filho A (2016) State, state institutions, and political power in Brazil. Lat Am Perspect 43(2):190–206

Burns EB (2013) In: A history of Brazil (trans: Wang LX). The Commercial Press, Beijing

Crisóstomo VL (2014) Financial constraints for investment in Brazil. Int J Manag Financ 10(1):73–92

De Castro N (1999) Privatization of the transportation sector in Brazil. In Armando Castelar Pinheiro and Kiichiro Easterly W (2006) Reliving the 1950s: the big push, poverty traps, and takeoffs in economic development. J Econ Growth 11(4):289–318

Fausto B, Fausto S (2018) In: A concise history of Brazil. (trans: Guo CH), Beijing, Oriental Publishing Center

Filho NS, Carla SS (1999) In: Fabio G, Maurício MM (eds) A economic Brasileira nos Anos 90. BNDES, Rio de Janeiro

IBGE (2020) Sistema de contas nacionais. https://www.ibge.gov.br/estatisticas/economicas/contas-nacionais/9052-sistema-de-contas-nacionais-brasil.html

Melhores e Maiores (1982) Exame. Sept 1982

Melhores e Maiores (1986) Exame. Sept 1986

Melhores e Maiores (1991) Exame. Aug 1991

U S Tariff Commission (1949) Mining and manufacturing industries in Brazil. GPO

Vaz de Melo POS (2015) How many political parties should Brazil have? a data-driven method to assess and reduce fragmentation in multi-party political system. PLoS ONE 10(10):e0140217

Werneck R (1986) Poupança estatal, dívida externa e crise financeira do setor público. Pesqui Planej Econ 16(3):566–567

World Bank (2014) International human development indicators. World Bank, Washington, DC

Chapter 14
International Experiences in Avoiding Middle-Income Trap

The process of a country's transition from poverty to prosperity does not reach the end smoothly once it is started. Since 1960, 101 economies in the world have entered the ranks of middle-income countries, but only 13 of them successfully entered the ranks of high-income countries. The vast majority of countries have not successfully completed the process of moving from the ranks of middle-income countries to the ranks of high-income countries. In the middle of catching up, economic growth can stagnate or even regress for various reasons. In many cases, it is not difficult for a country's economy to achieve temporary high growth. What is rare is maintaining sustained rapid growth over a long period of time. This chapter presents an analysis of countries and regions that grew rapidly to enter the ranks of middle-income countries through both positive and negative historical facts, and why they fell into the middle-income trap and could not eventually succeed, as well as important conditions for avoiding to fall into the middle-income trap.

14.1 Two Different Types of Declines Following Rapid Growth

Looking at the growth history of various countries' economies since the Industrial Revolution, there are takeoffs and declines, and no country can maintain high growth forever. The distribution of growth speed and path patterns can be roughly divided into the following categories.

The first category is advanced economies. For example, the United Kingdom and the United States have been pioneers in the global technological frontier for a long time and are the main sources of technological revolution. Their growth often relies on supply (technological) breakthroughs to drive demand upgrade growth and the formation of new industries. The typical feature of their growth pattern is to maintain a low and relatively stable speed for a long period of time (the dotted line in

C. Chen et al., *From Poverty to Prosperity*, Understanding China,
https://doi.org/10.1007/978-981-95-7171-0_14

Fig. 14.1). Of course, the United States was also a follower, especially before the end of the nineteenth century. In a sense, the United States can also be classified as the third category of countries, to be discussed below.

The second category is countries whose growth cannot take off. For example, some African countries south of the Sahara Desert have not gotten rid of the "Malthusian cycle"[1] for a long time, have not started the industrialization process in the modern sense, and their economies have generally remained at a low level and low growth.

The third category is countries with catch-up-squeezing growth. These countries often used advanced countries as benchmarks and used ready-made experience in technology, management, market, and system, as well as giving full play to their latecomer advantages and their own resource endowment advantages to catch up with advanced countries, but the time they took to reach a certain level of development was significantly short. For example, it took the advanced economies hundreds of years to increase their GDP per capita from 1800 international dollars to 11,000 international dollars. It took the UK 141 years, the US 109 years, and Germany 103 years. The time taken by latecomer economies is significantly shortened, such as Japan taking 54 years, Singapore taking 37 years, Hong Kong taking 31 years, and South Korea and Taiwan only taking 27 years. The lower the level of GDP per capita of these economies when they took off, the higher their economic growth rate in the subsequent catch-up process; the later the takeoff time, the shorter the time it took for them to reach a certain level of development. Most of the economies that achieved rapid growth since World War II belong to this category, where China also belongs.

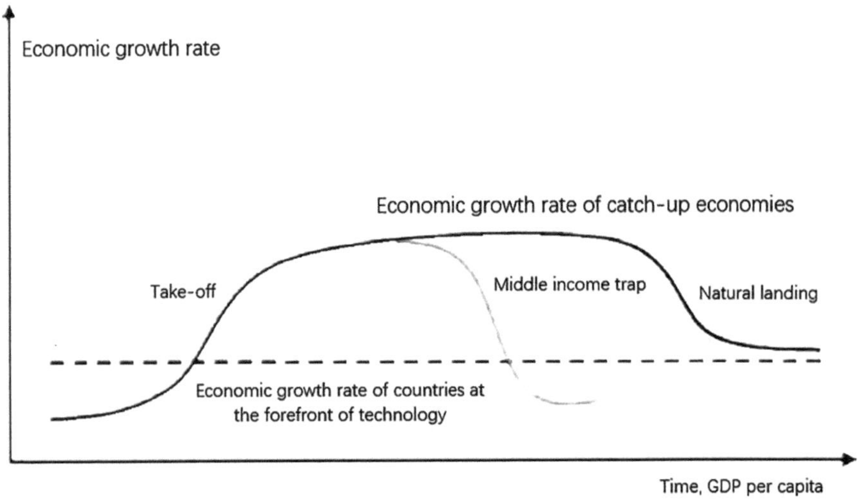

Fig. 14.1 Types of economic growth paths

[1] A series of cyclical changes caused by the interaction between population growth and limited resources.

The above three categories mainly focus on the two characteristics of "economic takeoff" and "growth rate" but do not pay attention to the landing problem after the takeoff. The traditional mainstream economic thought believes that once economic growth takes off, it will be self-sustaining and achieve sustained growth. But history shows that this is not the case. Not every economy that takes off can successfully complete the entire process of industrialization and achieve a smooth landing.

As shown in Fig. 14.2, the research conducted by the Development Research Center of the State Council and the World Bank shows that since 1960, 101 economies in the world have entered the ranks of middle-income economies. However, by 2010, only 13 of these economies, such as Japan, South Korea, Taiwan, Hong Kong, Puerto Rico, Mauritius, Singapore, Israel, etc., successfully entered the ranks of high-income economies, completed the basic catching-up task, and successfully landed at the high-income level (their economic growth rate is shown as the black solid line in Fig. 14.1. However, the vast majority of countries did not successfully complete this process. In the middle of the catching-up process, the economic growth of these countries, such as Latin American countries and Eastern European countries, stagnated or even regressed due to various reasons, and they fell into the middle-income trap (their economic growth rate is shown as the gray line in Fig. 14.1).

0-=There is no clear and recognized definition of the middle-income trap in the academic and policy fields. It roughly describes the following phenomenon. After a country's economy escapes the "Malthusian cycle", economic growth starts in the

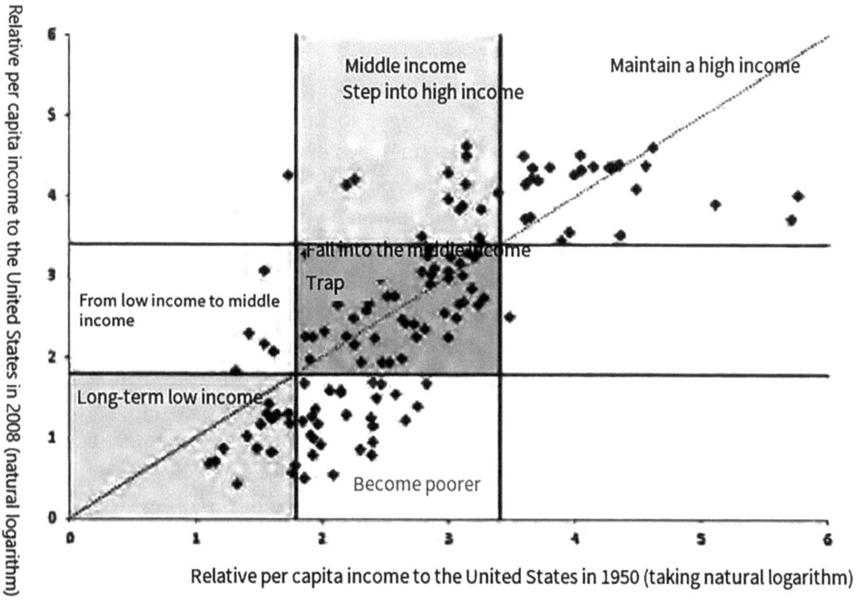

Fig. 14.2 Development of 101 middle-income economies since 1960. *Source*: Joint Research team of the World Bank and the Development Research Center of the State Council (2013)

modern sense with industrialization as its characteristic. For a period of time, the country's per capita income level is greatly improved, and it ranks among the middle-income countries. However, in the process of moving from middle-income to high-income, due to the influence or impact of certain internal and external factors, economic growth stagnates or even regresses for a long period of time, and it cannot truly become a high-income country for a long time.

There may be two prospects following high-speed growth. As shown in Fig. 14.1, there are two completely different situations at the end of the high-speed growth period in the process of economic catch-up. One is the slowdown of growth after successful industrialization and the basic completion of the catch-up process. The peak of the output (or the growth rate) of representative industrial products, such as steel, cement, and automobiles, appears roughly in the same period, followed by a natural decline. The decline usually occurs when the GDP per capita reaches 11,000–12,000 international dollars. For example, Germany, Japan, and South Korea are all countries that successfully caught up economically after World War II, and their economies basically conformed to this trend. Germany's GDP per capita growth rate from 1947 to 1969 was 7.9%. After its GDP per capita reached 10,440 international yuan in 1969, Germany's GDP per capita growth rate began to decline significantly, with an average annual growth rate from 1970 to 1979 of 3.1%. Japan's GDP growth rate from 1946 to 1973 was 9.4%. After its GDP per capita reached 11,434 international yuan in 1973, Japan's economic growth rate gradually declined, and its average annual GDP per capita growth rate from 1973 to 1983 dropped to 3.2%. South Korea's GDP per capita growth rate from 1953 to 1995 was 7.9% per year. After its GDP per capita reached 11,850 international yuan in 1995, South Korea's economic growth rate also declined significantly. From 1996 to 2008, its economic growth rate was 4.6% per year.

The other is that the catch-up process has not been completed, but due to a country's economic system, development strategy, social differentiation, or other reasons, the is interrupted, and the economy stagnates or even regresses for a long time, which is an unnatural decline. The decline point often occurs when the country's GDP per capita reaches 4000 to 6500 international yuan. At this time, industrialization has not been completed, and the economic growth rate declines more, mostly by more than 5 percentage points or more than 50%, and economic development falls into the middle-income trap. For example, the economies of Brazil, Argentina, and Mexico fell into a period of relative stagnation from 1981 to 2000, and their average annual GDP growth rates were 67.6%, 50%, and 58.5% lower than those of their high-growth period (1950–1980), respectively. For another example, the average annual GDP growth rates of the Soviet Union, Hungary, Romania, and Poland were 4.8%, 4.1%, 6.5%, and 4.6%, respectively, from 1950 to 1975, while from 1976 to 2000, the average annual growth rates of these countries dropped to −0.6%,[2] 0.7%, −0.6%, and 1.5%, respectively.

[2] The data after the disintegration of the Soviet Union are the total of all member states.

14.2 Some International Experiences in Avoiding Middle-Income Trap

From a historical perspective, the essence of a country falling into the middle-income trap is that its industrialization has not been successfully promoted and completed. To prevent falling into the trap, it is necessary to maintain the dynamic adaptability of the development strategy, and the key to ensuring strategic adaptability is to continuously increase the national participation rate. The main way internally to increase the national participation rate is to break down barriers and unify the market, and the main way externally is to actively participate in the global division of labor in accordance with the principle of dynamic comparative advantage. In addition, maintaining the openness of the industrial system, promoting agricultural modernization, controlling the income distribution gap within a reasonable range, and giving full play to the role of the government are also several important conditions.

There are different views and disputes on which countries fall into the middle-income trap. From an economic history perspective, Latin American countries and former Soviet and Eastern European countries are often considered to have typical characteristics in this regard. However, industrialization pioneers, such as the United Kingdom, the United States, Germany, Japan, and South Korea, which quickly caught up after World War II, did not have similar situations. Why did some countries successfully avoid the middle-income trap while others have not? Through systematic comparative analysis, we believe that there are some important facts and international experiences that are worth learning from.

14.2.1 Completion of Industrialization Process

Industrialization is the basic feature of modern economic growth. The essence of the middle-income trap problem is that industrialization has not been successfully completed. From the historical experience of economic development in various countries.

In the process of climbing from low to high per capita income levels, there will always be various challenges, constraints, or bottlenecks, and economic growth can be relatively stagnant for a period of time or even stagnant for a long time. Although the specific conditions of various countries vary greatly, whether the middle-income trap can be successfully avoided depends on whether industrialization can be smoothly promoted. If the low-income trap and the poverty trap highlight the problem that industrialization is difficult to start, then the middle-income trap emphasizes the problem that industrialization cannot be continuously promoted nor finally completed.

Latin American countries and former Eastern European countries are typical representatives of economies falling into the middle-income trap. Their biggest commonality is that they have all experienced obvious stagnation, regression, and even interruption of their industrialization process. The biggest difference for the United States, Japan, Europe, and other countries that successfully entered the high-income level is that, except for the factor of global war, they successfully completed the industrialization process without interruption.

14.2.2 Maintaining Dynamic Adaptability of Growth Strategy

The main reason for the stagnation of industrialization is that an unbalanced growth strategy does not transform into a balanced growth strategy in a timely manner. The development experience of countries around the world shows that, whether for an advanced country or a latecomer, industrialization often requires a certain market scale and a sector (or region) with new technological breakthroughs (or availability) to take the lead in starting the development. Rapid economic growth is often driven by a few sectors (or regions), which have typical unbalanced growth characteristics. Almost no country can take the path of balanced development from the beginning. With the deepening of the industrialization process, it is necessary for developing sectors (or regions) to take the lead through the forward and backward links between the market and industries, gradually driving the growth of other sectors (or regions) and transforming unbalanced growth into a balanced development. Successful industrialization is a process from unbalanced development to balanced development. The unbalanced strategy can achieve obvious success for a period of time (especially in the early stage), but the economic development of a country, especially a large country, cannot always rely on the development of a few individual sectors (or regions) throughout the whole process. An extremely single, unbalanced strategy will lead to serious structural imbalances and affect the smooth progress of industrialization.

Latin American countries over-rely on the import substitution strategy and have long isolated domestic industrial production from international markets. Due to the dual effects of a small domestic market and declining international competitiveness, their international balance of payments and domestic economic structure have continued to deteriorate, ultimately leading to stagnant growth. Similarly, Eastern European countries used their government's high mobilization capabilities to adopt a development strategy of "focusing on accumulation, ignoring consumption, focusing on heavy industry, and ignoring light industry", which rapidly increased the industrialization rate in the short term but distorted the inherent economic connection between the industrial sector and other sectors. As the implementation time of this strategy extended, the imbalance of the internal economic structure gradually worsened, ultimately leading to stagnation and regression of economic development.

At a specific stage of development, the adoption of import substitution and the emphasis on the role of the government in mobilizing resources are not unique to Latin American and Eastern European countries. They were adopted in most industrialized countries, including the United Kingdom, the United States, and Japan.

The key is whether adaptive adjustments are made. The "under-industrialization" of Latin American countries and the "over-industrialization" of Eastern European countries are essentially the results of long-term rigid reliance on unbalanced development strategies without timely promoting the transformation of the economy to a balanced development according to changes in economic and social development conditions. In essence, it is the failure of adaptive adjustment of development strategies. The basic evolution of economic development comprises moving through the following stages: from imbalanced to balanced development, then from balanced development to a new level of imbalanced development, and then to a higher level of balanced development. National economic strategies need to make timely adaptive adjustments according to different stages.

14.2.3 *Continuous Improvement of National Participation Rate*

Continuously improving the national participation rate in industrialization is an important basis for judging the adaptability of a development strategy and a key condition for continuously promoting industrialization. The process of industrialization is also a process of transforming traditional sectors. A large number of labor forces in traditional sectors are gradually transferred to modern sectors, and income growth is achieved through more adequate employment and improved labor productivity; furthermore, the demand for traditional sectors is expanded through industrial connections, and income growth is promoted by expanding the overall production scale. In addition, through technology diffusion, traditional sectors can be transformed, the combination of factors can be improved, and the overall economic efficiency can be improved. International experiences show that the process of deepening industrialization is the process of a country's residents continuously integrating into a modern economic system. Successful industrialization has the element of extensive participation, and the adjustment of industrialization strategy should take improving the national participation rate as an important goal.

As industrialization continues to advance to a higher stage, various resources should be mobilized and attracted to participate in industrialization to the maximum extent, so that more and more people can directly or indirectly participate in the modern industrial chain through employment and can transfer from traditional sectors to modern sectors, and hence a wider range of people can share the fruits of industrialization. If only a limited number of people participate in a country's industrialization process, while others are excluded from industrialization for a long time, the country's income growth will be significantly limited, the space for the expansion of the internal and external markets will be unsustainable, social stability will decline, and ultimately industrialization will lack stamina.

Latin American countries are typical examples of falling into the middle-income trap, and their biggest problem is the insufficient national participation rate. Due to the long-term implementation of the import substitution strategy, the method of isolation from international markets has been adopted to protect the development of industrial products that meet the needs of the domestic market. However, due to the small domestic market space, the advantages of economies of scale cannot be brought into play, the prices of industrial products are high, and the economy lacks international competitiveness. The protected industries are unable to absorb traditional sectors due to the difficulty in expanding their scale, and a large number of working people are not integrated into the modern economic system. In addition, due to the limitations of the incompatible internal industrial system, the implementation of import substitution still requires a large amount of imported intermediate capital goods and machinery and equipment, and the foreign exchange required for imports is mainly obtained from the export of primary products. The small trade surplus of traditional sectors is then used to support the development of modern sectors, making the international balance of payments inherently fragile. Moreover, against the backdrop of highly concentrated land, a large number of landless people have poured into cities, but they have no direct connection with industrialization, which makes urbanization and industrialization incompatible, causing a series of social problems. The core of the problem of the lack of industrialization in Latin American countries is the insufficient national participation rate. The adjustment of the development strategy of Latin American countries not only failed to increase the national participation rate but also made more people stay out of industrialization, making them lose the channel for income growth, which inevitably led to growth stagnation.

A key reason for the major setback in the growth of Eastern European countries is the problem of insufficient national participation rate under artificial division. Influenced by Stalin's "two parallel world markets" theory, the Soviet economy was in a semi-closed state. Foreign economic and trade cooperation was mainly carried out between member countries of the Council of Mutual Economic Assistance, and this cooperation was actually an extension of the Soviet Union's domestic command economic system. Therefore, without real incentives and pressure from international market competition, enterprises and products lacked real competitiveness. The economy developed under this situation was basically based on domestic demand and had little to do with the development of the entire world economy, changes in international markets, and the progress of science and technology. This resulted in insufficient participation of human capital and serious distortion of the economic structure. A large number of laborers could not transfer normally to non-agricultural industries due to administrative restrictions and the collective farm system. Although the proportion of industrial output value in total output value continued to increase, under the strategy of advanced military industrial development, the resources and limited surplus of the agricultural and light industrial sectors were forcibly occupied, the light industry was underdeveloped, and the heavy industry was overdeveloped, resulting in the continued intensification of the contradiction of unbalanced employment. The growth of modern sectors forced the take-over of surplus labor from traditional sectors, and a large number of laborers were restricted to outside high-growth industrial sectors. The growth momentum was ultimately unsustainable.

14.2.4 Breaking Down of Domestic Barriers and Exertion of Dynamic Comparative Advantages

Breaking down barriers to unify the domestic market and actively participating in the global division of labor in accordance with the principle of dynamic comparative advantage are fundamental ways to increase the national participation rate. Compared with agricultural civilizations, a major change in the industrialization era is that demand constrains and dominates supply. The problem of effective demand constraints in low-income countries is more prominent. Due to low income, effective demand is insufficient, the market space is small, a large number of resource factors are idle and cannot be effectively organized to participate in production, and the limited surplus of traditional sectors cannot be mobilized and utilized. Once industrialization is launched, in order to ensure that the per capita income level continues to rise, the core task is to break through demand constraints and continuously expand the market space. With a larger market, a deeper division of labor, and a stronger capacity of factor absorption capacity, more people can be guaranteed to effectively integrate into modern economic growth, which promotes sustained income growth, hence forming a virtuous cycle of market expansion, increased participation rate, income growth, and further market expansion.

For the internal market, the focus is to break the constraints and barriers of geographical boundaries, regional markets, society, and systems; give priority to the development of advanced social capital, such as infrastructure; promote the free and unimpeded flow of population and factors; and improve the property rights system and contract protection, so as to shorten the distance, expand the boundaries, promote concentration, deepen the division of labor, and form an effective and unified domestic market. For the external market, the focus is to actively participate in the international division of labor in accordance with the principle of dynamic comparative advantage so that the country's superior resources can play a role in global markets and participate in the global factor combination; in terms of the international division of labor, the focus is produce and serve as many people as possible in the world (scale expansion), while constantly improving the country's position in the international division of labor (value chain improvement). Countries that successfully avoided the middle-income trap, whether the United Kingdom, the United States, Germany, Japan, or South Korea, which developed rapidly after World War II, generally conformed to this basic trend. However, since the beginning of industrialization, Latin American countries always incurred historical debts in breaking down domestic barriers and unifying the market, and their investment in advanced social capital, such as infrastructure, was obviously insufficient. Their rapid development in the late nineteenth century and early twentieth century was mainly driven by the export of primary products, but this was strictly controlled by large landowners and external capital, and the dual structure characteristics were not broken but strengthened. When the countries turned to the import substitution strategy after the 1940s, they further violated the principle of comparative advantage, affected the breadth and depth of their participation in the international division of labor, and limited the improvement of industrial competitiveness and the expansion of market space. The defects of the starting point of industrialization and the artificial market isolation sowed the seeds for the subsequent long-term economic stagnation.

14.2.5 Expansion of Scale of Industries and Promotion of Technology Entry

Actively expanding the scale of industries, improving the industrial system, and maintaining openness are important driving forces for promoting technological progress and industrial upgrading and are also basic conditions for promoting the transition of a growth model from "factor-driven" to "innovation-driven". For a latecomer country, since the technical constraints it faces are not as strong as those of developed countries, and the system can also be imitated and learned, it has the conditions to achieve extraordinarily compressed rapid growth and the possibility of catching up with advanced countries quickly. However, practice has proved that latecomers cannot make arbitrary choices of existing technologies. Demand constraints and insufficient scale will limit the selection and application of technologies. Demand constraints will not only limit the choice of technology but will also strengthen or transform into technological constraints to a certain extent. The application of existing technologies and the growth of demand interact with each other. When the market scale is very small, many existing technologies cannot be adopted or are economically undesirable. Expanding the scale is the basis for standardized production, which is conducive to the selection and application of advanced technologies, reducing unit costs, and improving overall economic efficiency. Expanding the scale of industries, expanding the forward and backward connections between the market and industries, promoting the aggregation of industrial chains, and forming a relatively complete industrial system are conducive to promoting innovation. From an economic perspective, there is a clear difference between innovation and invention. Innovation is the commercialization process of invention and creation, and it has obvious clustering and systematic characteristics. With wider forward and backward connections, higher industrial agglomeration, a more complete industrial system, and a more suitable supporting institutional environment, the more likely it is for an economy to form an industrial system that is conducive to innovation and remains open to the outside world, as well as a greater possibility of innovation and a more significant contribution of innovation to development.

The problems faced by Latin American countries are mainly small markets, insufficient scale, and incomplete industrial systems, which seriously constrain the space for technology selection, limit the application of technology, and hinder technological progress. The problems faced by Eastern European countries are the lack of system openness, self-circulation in a closed system, and the hardening defects of the internal structure. Due to the obstruction of technological progress and industrial upgrading in the process of industrialization, the market space cannot be effectively expanded, which in turn limits the development and growth of the growth model based on factor input, not to mention limiting the gradual formation of an innovation-driven growth model. Therefore, countries that fall into the middle-income trap often show that the stage of factor-driven (investment-driven) growth has not been successfully completed.

14.2.6 Utilization of Foreign Capital Based on Giving Full Play to One's Own Advantages

Utilizing foreign capital based on giving full play to one's own advantages, improving competitiveness, and avoiding serious dependence on external funds and technology are important factors in ensuring the internal stability of economic growth. Using external funds can not only solve the problem of insufficient funds in the early stages of development, but more importantly, it can directly connect with the external market, expand the space for external demand, and give full play to the role of one's own comparative advantages; in addition, through cooperation and industrial connections, the spillover effect of foreign capital in technology and management can be used to improve the technical level and management capabilities of relevant domestic industrial sectors and enterprises. However, in the process of utilizing foreign capital, it is necessary to give full play to one's own advantages, emphasize close connection with the development of local industrialization and industrial systems, promote the development and growth of domestic enterprises, continuously improve the competitiveness of domestic industries, prevent foreign capital from excessively controlling the domestic economy, and prevent the domestic economy from over-relying on external funds and technologies, so as to avoid the transfer of foreign capital or external market fluctuations from causing major impacts on domestic development.

An important lesson for Latin American countries is the over-reliance on external funds and technologies. The investment of multinational companies is only borrowing cheap production factors and labor in Latin America, and the spillover effect of technology and management has been obviously insufficient. Moreover, due to improper investment attraction policies, foreign capital has formed too much control over the countries' primary product exports during the early stage and their high-tech industrial product production during the later stage and has no close connection with local industrial development and upgrading. Attracting foreign investment at the cost of a large number of preferential policies has aggravated the disadvantageous position of domestic enterprises in competition and artificially squeezed their development space, affecting and restricting their development and growth, and hence their own products lack competitiveness in international markets.

14.2.7 *Promotion of Development of Agricultural Sector and Agricultural Modernization*

The basic characteristics of industrialization are that relatively the status of agriculture has declined and that of manufacturing has risen, but the advancement of industrialization does not mean the weakening or abandonment of the agricultural sector. The development of agriculture itself is both the starting point of industrialization and an important driving force for the continuous advancement of industrialization. The surplus of traditional sectors is an important basis for the rapid development of modern sectors. For most industrialized countries, the starting point of the industrialization process often starts with agricultural development, followed by the gradual promotion of the development of light industries, and then moving on to heavy industries and advanced manufacturing. The significant contribution of agriculture to industrialization is not only reflected in the provision of early capital investment, sufficient labor, and basic raw materials but also in the important market for industrial product consumption demand.

There are two aspects of international experiences that should be paid special attention to. First, a relatively fair rural land system is not only conducive to promoting the development of agriculture itself and providing strong support for subsequent industrial development but also an important means to adjust the initial income distribution gap. Rural land reform and farmers' independence and freedom are important conditions for promoting the rapid transfer of agricultural population to higher-productivity sectors. The United States and Germany in the nineteenth century, as well as Japan, South Korea, and Taiwan in the twentieth century, are all examples of the successful implementation of land policies to promote the sustainable development of industrialization.

Second, in the process of industrialization, we must always attach great importance to the development of agriculture and implement agricultural modernization. This is an important guarantee for breaking the dual structure, narrowing the urban-rural gap, and promoting the smooth progress of industrialization. Actively adopting a variety of policies to support agricultural development, implementing industrial feedback to agriculture, and using modern technology to transform traditional agriculture are among common characteristics of countries that successfully avoided the middle-income trap.

The long-term neglect of agriculture has led to a serious lag in rural reform, which is an important reason for the stagnation of development in Latin American countries in the later period of industrialization. After Latin American countries broke away from colonial rule and gained independence, they did not carry out fundamental transformations of traditional agriculture and land systems, and traditional sectors lacked internal demand and motivation for industrialization. The development of capitalism and the start of modern industry were almost entirely driven by the export of primary products, and the development of agriculture itself did not receive basic attention. In addition, serious land concentration prevented the vast number of landless farmers from gaining more benefits from the prosperity brought about by the export of primary products. In the later period, the development of industrialization in a few sectors has not improved the dual characteristics but has become more prominent. The gap between the rich and the poor has widened rapidly, a large number of unemployed people have poured into cities, the degree of urbanization has been artificially high, and social problems have become prominent.

14.2.8 Maintaining of Social Class Mobility

Regulating the income distribution gap and improving the mobility of social classes are important conditions for ensuring the smooth advancement of industrialization and the coordinated development of the economy and society. Absolute equality of results (egalitarianism) and excessive income gaps are not conducive to the sustained and stable development of the economy and society. A reasonable income distribution structure is generally more conducive to long-term economic growth. A fair income distribution is conducive to the pursuit of common ground and can resolve the differences among various interest groups on various economic policies and the timely implementation of the policies; in addition, a fairer income distribution will result in more people with the same consumption capacity and preferences and in greater demand for standardized products and is more conducive to the deepening of industrial standardized production and specialized division of labor.

International experiences show that during the period of rapid economic growth, the income distribution gap often widens, but as the economy continues to grow, the income distribution gap will gradually narrow, which basically conforms to the "inverted U-shaped" characteristics summarized by Kuznets. However, it should be noted that this change in income distribution does not necessarily occur naturally but is accompanied by conflicts and compromises among different social groups, hence requiring active intervention by the government. In addition, it should be noted that an income distribution gap does not necessarily lead to serious social problems and economic growth stagnation. The widening of the income distribution gap over a period of time is not the most terrible thing. The most terrible thing is that the income distribution gap is locked between people and generations and that the unreasonable income distribution relationship is solidified. If there is mobility between people and between classes, members of all classes of society will have the hope and motivation to change their status quo, and the economy and society will remain vibrant. On the contrary, the lack of social mobility will cause social unrest and disharmony between classes, which will result in economic and social development to lose the necessary social cohesion and economic development to inevitably fall into stagnation or even regression.

14.2.9 Maintaining of Strong Governance

The government plays an irreplaceable and important role in ensuring the smooth progress of industrialization and avoiding from falling into the middle-income trap. Whether it is a federal government or a unitary government, whether it believes in liberalism or authoritarianism, in the process of a country's continuous industrialization, although the degree and focus are different, the government plays a very important and irreplaceable role, which is mainly reflected in providing property rights protection, maintaining political and social stability, mobilizing social resources (through taxation, incentive policies, or direct participation) for advanced social capital investment, providing public services and adjusting income distribution gaps, breaking the bottleneck of insufficient supply of public products, and maintaining the stability and continuity of macroeconomic policies.

With the development of industrialization, a larger market scale, a finer division of labor, and a more complex transaction, the public domain will also expand rapidly, which will make the externality problem more prominent; the public services required by society will constantly increase; and the demand for government functions will not be weakened but strengthened. However, the government cannot replace the market. The government and the market are mutually reinforcing and complementary. Since the 1930s, an important feature of the global economy has been the reduction of growth volatility and the increase of stability, which is closely related to the general emphasis by governments on macroeconomic regulation.

In avoiding the middle-income trap, there are important differences between successful countries and failed countries. First, successful governments have managed to maintain strong governance, not be swayed by interest groups, not be confused by short-term interests, maintain the dynamic adaptability of development strategies, and adhere to long-term development goals. Second, to adhere to the fundamental role of the market mechanism in resource allocation, these governments have been able to focus on overcoming obstacles and bottlenecks in the public sector, focus on promoting institutional reforms, and create a good environment for market development, industrial upgrading, and technological innovation. Third, successful governments have managed to handle the coordination between economic and social development, establish a social public safety net, promote the majority of citizens to actively participate in the industrialization process, share the fruits of economic and social progress, avoid serious polarization and confrontation among social classes, and maintain sustained social stability.

14.3 A–C Theory's Perspective on Avoiding Middle-Income Trap

The progress of an economy from low-income to middle-income depends on the start of the industrialization process; after reaching middle-income status, if the sustainable advancement of industrialization can be guaranteed, the country may smoothly enter the ranks of high-income, while if industrialization is terminated prematurely, the country will fall into the middle-income trap. The factors of success are inherently consistent with the A–C theory's dual-pillar framework of political cohesion and economic accessibility.

The A–C theory asserts that the necessary condition for sustained economic growth is the integration of a stable political and social environment and an open and orderly market environment. A stable political and social environment requires the realization of cohesive political governance so as to coordinate various interest groups to reach a social consensus, form a unified collective action, and promote efficient policy implementation; an open and orderly market environment requires an open and inclusive economic system so that various economic entities can voluntarily and relatively conveniently participate in various economic opportunities. Both pillars are indispensable for an economy to start industrialization, develop steadily in the process of industrialization, and eventually enter the ranks of high-income countries.

Without cohesive political governance, society will fall into a state of conflict between various interest groups and classes. Under this conflictual governance model, the government is coerced by a few interest groups and classes and is not sufficiently representative, resulting in frequent political turmoil, and the resulting policies cannot balance the interests of all parties well. The government also lacks representativeness and authority, and the policy implementation is inefficient and sluggish, with especially an inability to make rapid and appropriate adjustments according to changes in the social and economic situation. Excessive internal friction in society leads to a lack of a basic stability guarantee for economic development, resulting in the economy being unable to take off or falling back quickly after taking off.

Limited economic accessibility represents a loss of resource allocation efficiency because production factors cannot flow efficiently and smoothly within and outside the economy. An economy with limited internal accessibility does not have a unified, open, and orderly internal market due to defects in the economic system, business environment, infrastructure, and other factors. The market mechanism cannot play its decisive role in the resource allocation process, such as enterprise entry, product trading, capital and labor pricing, and flow, resulting in waste or mismatch of its own resource endowment. An economy with limited external accessibility cannot deeply integrate into global economic activities due to development strategies, economic models, trade structures, and other reasons and thus cannot use international industrial division of labor to improve production efficiency. The economy cannot break through its own resource endowment limitations and obtain various production factors at the lowest cost on a global scale; in addition, the economy cannot break through its own market capacity limitations and give full play to its own industrial comparative advantages and production capacity to gain its international market share. The lack of international division of labor specialization based on dynamic comparative advantages and the pull of international market demand will also lead to the economy failing to take off or landing soon after taking off and failing to achieve high growth for a long period of time.

Economies that have successfully avoided the middle-income trap generally have successfully established political cohesion and economic opening up to the outside world, thus ensuring the start and smooth progress of industrialization. Take Singapore and South Korea, two of the "Four Asian Tigers" after World War II, for example. Both countries relied on the authoritarian system led by political strongmen to complete the construction of national consensus and a strong government, formulated development strategies that could balance the interests of various interest groups and classes, established a professional and efficient technical bureaucracy and a national economic mobilization system, and achieved a relatively cohesive social structure, all of which provided a stable political guarantee for the takeoff of industrialization. In addition, both countries established an orderly and open economic system, actively participated in the global industrial division of labor, started with the introduction of foreign capital to establish export-oriented industries, and used international market demand as the initial engine of industrialization. Then, with the improvement of economic strength and the maturity of the market environment, they continued to expand the scale of industries, gradually extended capital-intensive and technology-intensive industries, and finally realized the opening of the financial system to form a complete industrial system. Compared with the small city-state of Singapore, South Korea, as a medium-sized country, not only achieved an orderly opening up of its economy to the outside world but also focused on opening up the economy internally. By increasing the input of agricultural and rural infrastructure, production equipment, and chemical fertilizers, the productivity of the agricultural sector has been greatly improved, enabling the agricultural sector to generate a large amount of surplus labor, which has effectively flowed to industrial sectors with strong demand. In addition, both countries have enhanced the internal and external connectivity of their economies through large-scale construction of transportation infrastructure, such as ports and/or highways, and by breaking down domestic and foreign barriers to entry and exit, integrating into international markets, and building a unified domestic market. It is particularly important that Singapore and South Korea achieved dynamic adjustments in political and economic policies relatively smoothly during their industrialization process, thus ensuring the cohesion of political governance, rather than entering the form of single-peak biased governance or multi-peak conflictual governance, and ensuring a high political and economic participation rate of the people. For example, Singapore has always adhered to the policy of ethnic integration and joint participation and has continued to implement the policy of homeownership to protect citizens' basic housing rights, such that the ruling People's Action Party has maintained a model of single-peak unbiased political governance. Although South Korea experienced some twists and turns in the process of disintegration of the military authoritarian system, it eventually smoothly transitioned to a multi-peak reconciliatory governance model with the change of social situation, ensuring the completion of the industrialization process.

Countries that once achieved excellent high-speed growth but then fell into stagnation often failed to continue the model of single-peak unbiased governance or multi-peak reconciliatory governance during the high-speed growth period, and the government lost its representativeness and national economic mobilization capabilities; the economic development strategy also failed to achieve dynamic adjustment of inclusive and balanced growth, and the large income distribution gap caused class confrontation and a large number of economic entities not getting equal economic opportunities. Take Argentina and Brazil as examples. Both are countries whose economies stagnated after high-speed growth. Both experienced the takeoff stage but have not yet entered the ranks of high-income countries. Argentina and Brazil were born out of the livestock or plantation economic system of the colonial period. There are important interest groups, such as powerful agricultural product production groups and export trade monopoly groups. The ethnic composition is complex, with many differences in cultural traditions among ethnic groups, and there are discrimination and conflicts between them. In addition, both countries are federal countries, and even during the military dictatorship or empire period, they were unable to completely solve the problem of state power's influence over the central government. Their special economic system and inherent deficiencies in state construction have led to the lack of stability in the political governance of Argentine and Brazilian societies. Their political governance structure is easily in chaos, the political games of interest groups are out of control, the central government lacks the ability to implement policies, and the national political and economic participation rate is low. Their central government's lack of mobilization capacity has led to insufficient investment in domestic infrastructure, a wide income distribution gap, and an inability to effectively connect a fragmented and narrow domestic market. Their unbalanced growth strategy has not been transformed into a balanced growth strategy in a timely manner. Their long-term import substitution strategy and the over-correction economic liberalization policy under the Washington Consensus have caused their economy's external accessibility to swing violently between excessive restriction and excessive openness, making it impossible for them to achieve orderly economic opening and orderly industrial upgrading, leading to stagnation in industrialization.

Reference

Joint Research Team of the World Bank and the Development Research Center of the State Council (2013) China in 2030: building a modern, harmonious and creative society. China Financial & Economic Publishing House, Beijing

Chapter 15
Relative Growth Rate and Continuous Economic Catch-Up

The process of a country's transformation from poverty to wealth is not only a process of surpassing itself but also a process of surpassing other economies. To a certain extent, it reflects the competition and mutual catch-up of growth rates among countries. Therefore, for a catching-up economy, the significance of relative growth is greater than growth itself. This paper constructed the concept and indicators of relative growth rate, identified the characteristics of national economic takeoff and deceleration under the same framework, and obtained characteristic facts different from existing studies. Based on the GDP per capita and growth rate data of more than 180 countries and regions from 1900 to 2018 and with the world economic benchmark growth rate as a reference, the high-speed growth interval of typical economies and the takeoff and landing nodes of the high-speed growth interval are identified in this chapter. Based on the factors of the duration of high-speed growth of typical economies and the level of GDP per capita at the time of landing, the current economic development stages of 41 typical economies were divided into five groups, including suspension after takeoff, industrialization process, economic transformation period, transformation stagnation, and developed countries, and then a group empirical analysis was conducted. In addition, the A-C theory was incorporated, and the impact of political governance and economic accessibility on the development process of various countries was combined for analysis and discussion on the reasons for economic takeoff and landing.

15.1 Economic Catch-Up: Absolute Growth Vs. Relative Growth

For a country to go from poor to rich, it usually needs to go through the complete stage of economic takeoff to deceleration and experience a sufficiently long period of high growth before it can achieve a significant improvement in relative national

C. Chen et al., *From Poverty to Prosperity*, Understanding China,
https://doi.org/10.1007/978-981-95-7171-0_15

strength. Since the Industrial Revolution, latecomer countries have embarked on the road of catching up by accepting technology diffusion and taking advantage of the dividends of globalization. A few of them successfully achieved the transformation from poor to rich and leaped into the ranks of middle- and high-income countries, while other catching-up economies suffered failures and even fell into the quagmire of political turmoil and economic recession.

Since mercantilism, economists have continued to look for the driving force of rapid economic growth. From the Harrod-Domar growth model to the Solow model, from the institutional growth theory of Kornai and others to the new growth theory of Romer and others, economists have continuously deepened their understanding of economic growth, while De Soto and others have personally prescribed various prescriptions for latecomer countries, in order to understand economic takeoff and deceleration from multiple perspectives, such as political economy. How to achieve high economic growth is the core issue in development economics. To analyze economic catch-up, it is necessary to first reasonably identify the criteria of high economic growth. In the pioneering study by Hausmann et al. (2005), three criteria were used to identify economic takeoff, which are rapid growth, rising growth rate, and upward shift of the growth rate axis, and corresponding threshold conditions were given. Studies that followed have tried various factors, such as economic growth acceleration, deceleration, and sustainability, and used factor models to find the reasons behind high economic growth. In recent years, more and more studies have focused on high growth intervals and growth sustainability.

There are two things worth noting in studying economic catch-up. One is the time points of economic takeoff and landing (takeoff point and turning point), and the other is the duration of the high growth interval. If the starting point and end point of the high growth interval and the duration of high growth can be identified by setting appropriate and simple threshold conditions, the development process of catching-up economies can be better understood.

Regarding economic takeoff and deceleration, Berg et al. (2012) discussed the conditions for economic takeoff, deceleration, and stability and found that there are three main influencing factors: the degree of income distribution equality and democratic institutions, export orientation, and macroeconomic stability. Eichengreen et al. (2012) provided a relatively detailed data description and cause analysis of the slowdown in the growth of major economies in the world. Jones and Olken (2008) put forward three main conclusions: economic growth acceleration and collapse are asymmetric phenomena; the typical characteristics of collapse are increased price fluctuations and reduced investment, while the takeoff of growth is mainly related to the expansion of international trade; and sustained growth is difficult. For a country to go from poor to rich, it usually needs to go through the complete stage of economic takeoff to deceleration, and its growth rate needs to exceed that of other countries during the same period. Becker et al. (2011) mainly described the story of how countries such as France and Germany accepted the diffusion of British technology and developed rapidly during the Industrial Revolution. This story of economic takeoff has been played out frequently in the history of the world economy. Yang and Yao (2008) examined the relationship between a country's foreign trade pattern and economic development performance in its economic development on the basis of Hausmann et al. (2005). The paper proposed the concept of limited catch-up and identified the impact of industrial upgrading on economic development.

Unlike the above-mentioned studies, many studies believe that economic takeoff and landing are actually difficult to predict and there is no stable pattern. Hausmann et al. (2008) defined the conditions for a sharp economic downturn and analyzed economies that suffered economic crises and they found that most of the variables would not help predict the duration of the crisis. Easterly (2006) identified the conditions for economic takeoff and found that the idea of achieving takeoff through specific factors or external help was not supported by data, and there were few successful cases. Economic takeoff is not related to aid, investment, or necessarily education spending.

Some studies examined the impact of political institutions on the economy. Acemoglu et al. (2003) studied the impact of political institutions and conflicts on economic performance and believed that countries that pursue distorted macroeconomic policies, including high inflation, large budget deficits, and exchange rate fluctuations, will have slower economic growth. Ineffective political institutions will limit the economic vitality of a country, such as political corruption, political instability, and deprivation of property. Countries that adopt extractive institutions are more likely to experience economic crises, causing the country to fall into a low-income quagmire. Sen (2013) proposed through national case studies and cross-national econometrics that understanding the political driving force of economic growth requires explaining the political dynamics of the transition from one growth stage to another. The political driving factors for early growth acceleration are different from those for sustained growth. Informal institutions may play a role in accelerating growth, while having formal and reliable commitment institutions, providing public goods, and overcoming coordination failures are more important in maintaining growth.

Poor and rich countries are relative concepts. Given a long enough period of development, most countries can always reach a certain level of wealth. However, only countries with significantly higher economic growth rates than other countries, or at least countries with the same level of development, can improve their status and ranking in the world and change the relative status of their economic development level. Moreover, economic development and technological progress are often not uniform. Wars, technological breakthroughs, or economic crises will significantly change the world's average growth rate, causing the world economy to show rapid growth or continued downturn in a certain period of time. Therefore, the use of a new relative growth indicator can not only reflect the dynamics of the world's technological advancement frontier but also reflect the development trends of major economies in the world, reduce the impact of the global economic cycle on the examination of economic growth, and better portray the process of latecomer countries' economic status in catching up and their economic performance changes.

In this study, existing literature review and conclusions were mostly based on the identification and analysis of the absolute growth rate. The main analysis was carried out based on the construction and measurement of the relative growth rate. The identification conditions based on relative growth were set up to identify the high-growth economic interval. The concept of the relative growth rate was constructed using the idea of the world's technological frontier. There are several important considerations for using the relative growth rate. First, the relative growth rate can reflect whether a country is doing better or worse than other countries during the same period, highlighting the meaning of "catching up". Second, an indicator system based on the relative growth rate can show how long a country is better than the control group. Third, the relative growth rate can well reflect the inherent factors of takeoff and landing. Fourth, the approach via the relative growth rate can well smooth the economic boom cycle. Based on the identification of high-growth economic intervals, combined with the impact of political landscape evolution on the development process of various countries, the new analytical framework of the A-C theory was then used to analyze the reasons for economic takeoff and landing.

15.2 Construction of Relative Economic Growth Rate and Reference Benchmark

This paper first sorted out the GDP per capita growth rate data of more than 180 countries and regions from 1900 to 2018. For long-term data, we used the 2013 version of the Maddison Project Database. The database contains the GDP per capita data of more than 180 countries and regions from 1900 to 2010, as well as their annual GDP per capita growth rate. Considering that most studies on post-war economic growth used data from the World Bank database, this paper matched the data from the World Bank database with those from the Maddison Project Database for the GDP per capita and GDP growth rate from 1960 to 2018. The GDP per capita growth rates before 1960 were obtained from calculations based on the Maddison database, while the economic growth rates after 1960 came from the World Bank database.

The core of constructing a relative growth rate is to construct a benchmark growth rate. The construction of indicators needs to consider both cyclical factors and the factors of the world's technological frontier and technological diffusion.

We used the average growth rate of G7 countries from 1900 to 2018 as a benchmark. This benchmark setting was based on the idea of the evolution of the world economy and technological frontier. In the first Industrial Revolution, the world's technological frontier was the United Kingdom. Since 1860, the world's growth frontier has been jointly driven by the United States, the United Kingdom, France, Germany, and Japan. The average growth rate of these countries represents the technological frontier of the world economy and is also the reference for major countries to catch up. After World War II, the G7, which includes Canada and Italy, began to become the leader of the world's economic frontier, representing the development of advanced countries. The economic growth rate of G7 countries can well reflect the main development of the world economy after World War II. In addition, adding Japan, Canada, and Italy to the benchmark growth rate can reduce the sharp fluctuations in data caused by various factors, such as the world wars, economic crises, and economic fluctuations in a single country, making the benchmark growth rate more representative. Considering the different status and weights of G7 countries in the world economy in different periods, this article used the weighted average growth rate of GDP per capita to better reflect the average level of G7 countries.

Figure 15.1 shows the weighted average growth rate of GDP per capita of G7 countries since 1900. The benchmark growth rate shows obvious cyclicality, with two major booms: after the Great Depression and after World War II. However, the economic growth rate of major developed countries has been declining for a long time since the 1970s, and negative growth occurred during the world economic crisis.

Compared with the growth rate benchmark commonly used in current research, the construction of this indicator has several characteristics. First, it avoids using the US economic growth rate as the benchmark. Many studies use the US economic growth rate as the speed of progress at the world's technological frontier and as a reference for the growth rates of various countries. This approach is too subjective because the calculated relative growth rate does not reflect the world's economic cycle and technological progress cycle at the time and also fluctuates violently when the economic growth of a single country is used as the standard. Second, it avoids using the world's average growth rate as a benchmark. It is difficult to include the concept of the world's technological frontier and, furthermore, the world's average growth rate also includes late-developing catching-up countries, making it difficult to fully reflect a country's catching-up effect. Third, it avoids using the growth rate comparison between countries with the same income level. Catching up is the process of low- and middle-income countries catching up with high-income countries. Hence, it is difficult to reflect a country's process of catching up with developed countries by comparing with countries with the same income level.

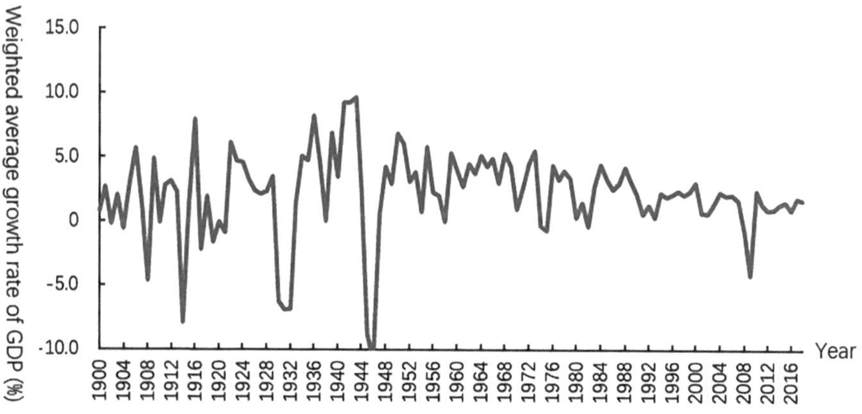

Fig. 15.1 Weighted average growth rate of GDP per capita of G7 countries (1900–2018)

To further eliminate the impact of economic fluctuations, we performed a nine-year moving average on the economic growth rate.[1] This is because the moving average of a short time series would leave too many short-term economic fluctuations. If we were to use the moving average of a long time series, the start and end years of economic takeoff and slowdown would change a lot, and data fluctuations would have a lag effect, affecting our judgment of the economic turning point. Therefore, the time span of the moving average should not be too long. The study tried the moving average of HP filtering and other parameters, and the conclusion was not sensitive to the parameters.

15.3 Identification Conditions and Results of High-Speed Economic Growth Intervals

By comparing a country's growth rate and technological frontier, the country's position and status can be better reflected. Only when the economic growth rate is faster than the benchmark growth rate can it be said that the country is in a catching-up state, and its economic operation and economic performance are worth an in-depth study. Based on data processing, we analyzed the difference between the relative growth rate and absolute growth rate and set threshold conditions to identify relatively high-speed economic growth intervals.

15.3.1 Comparison of Relative Growth Rate and Absolute Growth Rate

Figure 15.2 is a schematic diagram of the relative growth rate and absolute growth rate. It can be seen that the world's economic growth rate after the war was very high and lasted for more than 20 years in the 2%–4% range, but its relative growth rate did not turn positive until the mid-to-late 1990s. This reflects the huge postwar advantages of developed countries. Japan, France, Germany, and other countries maintained high growth for more than 20 years during post-war reconstruction, driving the benchmark growth rate to remain high, and the gap in economic status between developed countries and latecomers widened rapidly.

Taking South Korea as an example, the results of analysis using the relative growth rate in judging high economic growth are obviously different from those of using the absolute growth rate. Figure 15.3 shows the data of the absolute growth rate and relative growth rate of South Korea from 1900 to the present. After the war, there has always been a gap between the absolute growth rate and the relative growth rate of South Korea. Taking the absolute growth rate as an example, South Korea

[1] We tried various smoothing methods and a threshold period of nine years seemed reasonable.

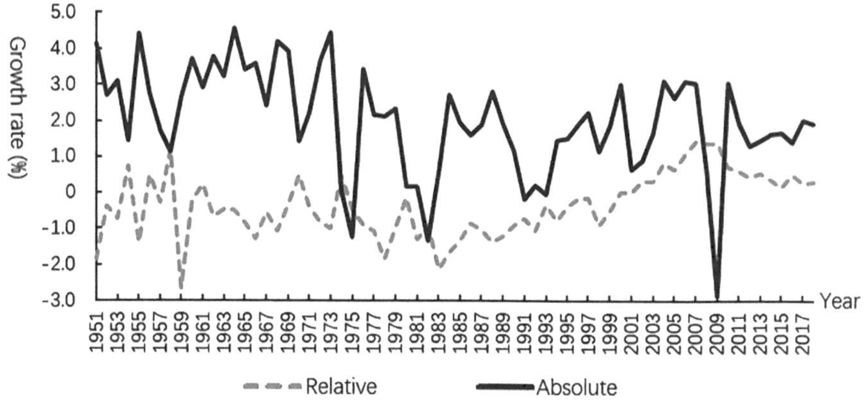

Fig. 15.2 Absolute growth rate of world economy, and relative growth rate of world economy compared with that of G7 countries

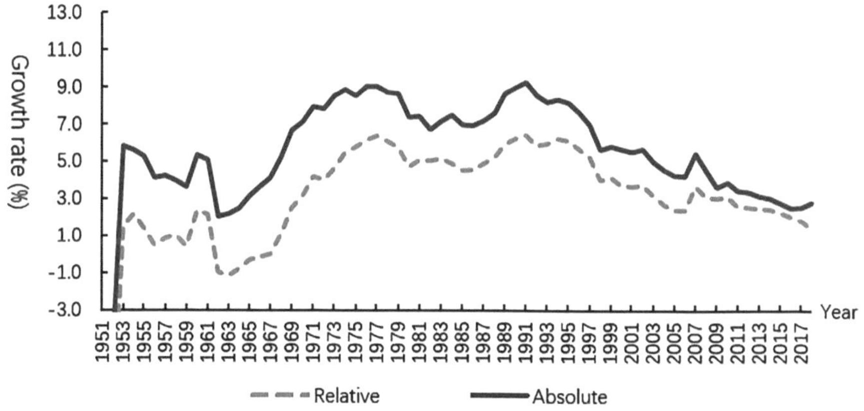

Fig. 15.3 South Korea's absolute growth rate and relative growth rate compared with that of G7 countries

can be said to have positive growth continuously since after the war. After 1950, its economic growth rate has always remained above 2% and there has been a prosperous trend of sustained high economic growth. However, based on its relative growth rate, South Korea did not show positive growth relative to the benchmark growth rate until around 1965, and its relative national strength and international status increased. The two standards differ by 15 years in judging economic takeoff. This shows that from the post-war period to 1965, South Korea's economic recovery relied on the background of the world's post-war prosperity, and there was nothing outstanding. After 1965, its economic performance was more outstanding.

15.3.2 Identification of Conditions for High-Speed Economic Growth Intervals

By setting relative growth rates and identification conditions, this paper hoped to characterize high-speed economic growth intervals, thereby identifying the entire process from economic takeoff to landing, using two principles.

The first is that economic growth should be defined as a country doing better than other countries, not just having a high absolute value of growth. There have been many studies on the absolute value of economic growth, but there is limited research on relative growth.

Second, the high-speed economic growth interval should be long enough to change a country's relative position in the world. We believe that an economic cycle is usually about eight years, so if a country's growth rate is higher than the benchmark growth rate for nine consecutive years, this period is considered to be a high-growth interval. Too short a time window will lead to too much noise in short-term fluctuations, and too long a time window will make the standard too harsh. If a longer window is required, the economy will take off, but too few results will be identified, which will lose its meaning.

Regarding the criteria for judging high growth, this paper did not require the growth rate of an economy to be higher than a certain threshold of the benchmark growth rate. This is because, first, the setting of the threshold is subjective and, second, the benchmark growth rate has been at 2%–3% for a long time, which is higher than the high growth threshold of many studies in the literature. A growth rate higher than the benchmark is already showing that the country's economic performance is excellent.

15.3.3 Results of Identifying High-Growth Economic Intervals

Based on the standard of a relative growth rate greater than 0% for nine consecutive years, 92 countries or regions were identified to have high growth intervals. To identify catch-up high-growth intervals, various factors, such as GDP level per capita, population size, and cumulative growth rate, needed to be considered.

Table 15.1 lists the most recent high-growth intervals of 41 countries with a GDP per capita of more than US$1000, a population of more than ten million (except Singapore and Mauritius), and a cumulative growth rate of more than 20 percentage points higher than that of the benchmark country. It lists the takeoff year and the GDP level per capita at that time, the landing year and the GDP level per capita at that time, the GDP level per capita in 2018, the time span of high growth, and the average relative growth rate.

The takeoff-time judgment standard is that the average relative growth rate in the 10 years after the takeoff point is 3 percentage points higher than that in the previous 10 years, and the landing time judgment standard is that the average relative growth

Table 15.1 Takeoff and landing years of typical high-growth countries and their GDP per capita

Country	Takeoff year	Landing year	GDP per capita in takeoff year (2010 USD)	GDP per capita in landing year (2010 USD)	GDP per capita in 2018 (2010 USD)	Span (years)	Average relative growth rate (%)
China	1977	2013	280.0	5710.6	7752.6	37	6.9
Mauritius	1985	2018	2762.8	10,578.6	89.5	34	2.6
South Korea	1966	1995	1277.5	12,055.2	26,761.9	30	5.6
Vietnam	1992	2018	478.4	1964.5	1964.5	27	4.3
Poland	1993	2018	5827.6	16,659.3	16,659.3	26	3.0
Japan	1946	1969	3065.7	18,837.2	48,919.8	24	5.0
Myanmar	1992	2013	205.9	1174.1	1571.9	22	7.4
Cambodia	1999	2018	398.3	1205.0	1205.0	20	5.1
Canada	1900	1917	5514.9	9093.9	51,391.7	18	2.0
Turkey	2002	2018	8003.5	15,069.0	15,069.0	17	3.1
India	2003	2018	2335.6	2100.8	2100.8	16	4.6
Singapore	1960	1974	3503.4	9440.2	58,247.9	15	7.3
France	1919	1933	5323.4	8026.9	43,663.6	15	3.7
Spain	1961	1975	8172.6	16,626.4	32,949.6	15	2.3
Saudi Arabia	1961	1974	12,909.7	39,152.1	20,819.7	14	9.2
Islamic Republic of Iran	1957	1970	2980.6	7015.0	6952.4	14	5.1
Bangladesh	2005	2018	617.5	1203.2	1203.2	14	4.3
Dominican Republic	2005	2018	4472.7	7697.7	7697.7	14	3.6
Uzbekistan	2004	2016	1131.8	2229.8	2366.3	13	4.9
Germany	1947	1958	4913.8	13,588.6	47,477.8	12	6.6
Peru	2002	2013	3359.2	5919.2	6453.6	12	4.4
Indonesia	2007	2018	2757.9	4284.7	4284.7	12	3.4
The Philippines	2007	2018	1968.8	3022.0	3022.0	12	3.3
Bolivarian Republic of Venezuela	1920	1930	1641.9	4822.7	14,025.4	11	10.4
Cuba	1999	2009	3298.8	5596.1	6816.9	11	4.5
Russian Federation	1999	2008	5876.2	11,087.8	11,729.1	10	5.8
Sri Lanka	2003	2012	1933.2	3286.0	3936.5	10	5.1
Greece	1963	1972	7815.9	15,738.3	23,558.1	10	4.6
Malaysia	1988	1997	4042.1	7041.7	12,120.1	10	4.4
Ukraine	2000	2008	1818.0	3322.0	3110.2	9	6.4
Thailand	1987	1995	1857.9	3531.7	6361.6	9	6.2
Brazil	1968	1976	4147.4	7296.3	11,026.2	9	4.6
Argentina	2003	2011	7380.5	10,883.3	10,043.5	9	4.5

(continued)

Table 15.1 (continued)

Country	Takeoff year	Landing year	GDP per capita in takeoff year (2010 USD)	GDP per capita in landing year (2010 USD)	GDP per capita in 2018 (2010 USD)	Span (years)	Average relative growth rate (%)
Portugal	1965	1973	6029.6	11,281.3	23,994.7	9	4.3
Iraq	1992	1999	1846.0	4393.8	5477.7	8	13.8
Kazakhstan	2000	2007	4491.6	8523.8	11,165.5	8	8.0
Romanian	2001	2008	5224.6	8914.0	11,532.1	8	6.6
Angola	2002	2009	2433.8	3549.6	3229.6	8	5.6
Sudan	2005	2012	1206.5	1787.0	1855.6	8	5.0
Zambia	2003	2010	1033.3	1489.5	1672.3	8	4.4
Chile	1991	1997	6291.7	8932.1	15,130.2	7	4.5

rate in the 10 years after the turning point is 3 percentage points lower than that in the previous 10 years.

15.4 Study on High-Speed Growth Grouping at Different Stages of Development

The 41 typical countries identified have distinct characteristics in the stage of high-speed growth and are at different stages of economic development from poor to rich. The data show that the GDP levels per capita in the declining growth stage of high-speed growth vary greatly, and the GDP levels per capita in 2018 also vary greatly. Based on this, these countries can be divided into five groups according to the stage of economic development: suspension after takeoff, in the process of industrialization, transition period after high-speed growth, stagnation after high-speed growth, and developed countries. In this chapter, the main characteristics, deep-seated reasons, and development trends of economic growth in different groups are analyzed.

15.4.1 Countries with Suspended Growth After Economic Takeoff

Based on the standard that a relative growth rate greater than 0% for nine consecutive years is recorded as high-speed growth, countries whose high-speed growth ended as of 2018 and whose GDP per capita in 2018 was less than US$6000 (in 2010 US dollars) were included in the grouping of countries with growth stopping after economic takeoff. This group includes Myanmar, Zambia, Sudan, Uzbekistan, Sri Lanka, Ukraine, Angola, Iraq, and other countries, as shown in Table 15.2.

Table 15.2 Typical countries with post-takeoff aborts

Country	Takeoff year	Landing year	GDP per capita in takeoff year (2010 USD)	GDP per capita in landing year (2010 USD)	2018 GDP per capita (2010 USD)	Span (years)	Average relative growth rate (%)
Myanmar	1992	2013	205.9	1174.1	1571.9	22	7.4
Zambia	2003	2010	1033.3	1489.5	1672.3	8	4.4
Sudan	2005	2012	1206.5	1787.0	1855.6	8	5.0
Uzbekistan	2004	2016	1131.8	2229.8	2366.3	13	4.9
Sri Lanka	2003	2012	1933.2	3286.0	3936.5	10	5.1
Ukraine	2000	2008	1818.0	3322.0	3110.2	9	6.4
Angola	2002	2009	2433.8	3549.6	3229.6	8	5.6
Iraq	1992	1999	1846.0	4393.8	5477.7	8	13.8

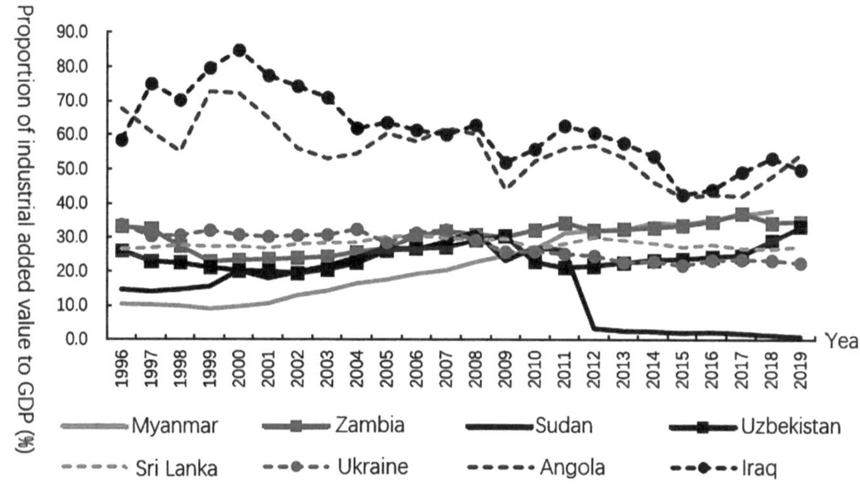

Fig. 15.4 Industrial value added as percentage of GDP for typical countries that stopped taking off

This group has the following main characteristics. First, the high-speed growth phase has a short time span, generally about 10 years, or although the time span is long, the GDP level per capita is low at the beginning and still low at the end, such as in Myanmar. Second, the GDP per capita level is relatively low at the end of high-speed growth. Except for Iraq, the GDP level per capita of other countries in this group is less than US$4000. Third, the economic growth in the later period is relatively slow. After the end of high-speed growth, the economic growth of these countries is weak, and the GDP per capita of some countries has even declined. Fourth, the level of industrialization is generally low. As shown in Fig. 15.4, except for Iraq and Angola, the industrialization level of the countries in this group has been around 30% for a long time.

The empirical analysis results show that significant variables mainly include indicators comprising internal economic openness, political cohesion, and GDP level per capita.

The degree of political cohesion is significantly positive. Based on the A-C theory, political cohesion has a positive impact on economic growth. The more cohesive the political governance, the more conducive it is to sustainable economic growth. The empirical analysis results also show that political cohesion is very important for economic takeoff, and only by reaching a social consensus can economic and social reforms be promoted. The economic takeoff of these countries was halted after taking off because the cohesion of political governance was damaged and declined significantly.

The impact of economic accessibility is negative. Based on the A-C theory, economic accessibility helps drive economic growth. However, the degree of openness of this group to the outside world is not significant, indicating that its opening to the outside world policy has not had a substantial effect on economic development, and the degree of internal openness is significantly negative, which also indicates to a certain extent that there are more prominent problems in domestic economic policies. The problem resulted in the short duration of rapid economic growth in this group of countries.

The impact of GDP level per capita is positive. During the economic takeoff stage, as the GDP level per capita increased, the economic growth rate also accelerated, indicating that early accumulation is necessary to promote further growth.

15.4.2 Countries in Process of Industrialization

Based on the criterion that a relative growth rate greater than 0% for nine consecutive years is recorded as high-speed growth, countries that are still in high-speed growth as of 2018 were selected into the grouping of countries that are in the industrialization process. This group includes Bangladesh, Cambodia, Vietnam, India, the Philippines, Indonesia, Thailand, Dominican Republic, Mauritius, and other countries, as shown in Table 15.3.

This group has the following main characteristics. First, the high-speed growth lasts for a long time, generally about 20 years. Some countries have been growing rapidly for more than 10 years but are still in the process of rapid growth. Vietnam has maintained high-speed growth for 27 years, with an average relative growth rate of 4.3%. Mauritius has maintained continuous growth for a longer time, but its average relative growth rate is only 2.6%. Second, the GDP level per capita has increased rapidly. In 2018, Thailand's GDP per capita rose to US$6361.6, the Dominican Republic's GDP per capita rose to US$7697.7, and Mauritius's GDP per capita rose to US$10,578.6. Third, the level of industrialization has increased significantly, as shown in Fig. 15.5; especially in Asian countries, such as Cambodia, Vietnam, and Indonesia, the proportion of industrial added value to GDP is still in an upward trend.

Table 15.3 Typical countries in process of industrialization

Country	Takeoff year	Landing year	GDP per capita in takeoff year (2010 USD)	GDP per capita in landing year (2010 USD)	2018 GDP per capita (2010 USD)	Span (years).	Average relative growth rate (%)
Bangladesh	2005	2018	617.5	1203.2	1203.2	14	4.3
Cambodia	1999	2018	398.3	1205.0	1205.0	20	5.1
Vietnam	1992	2018	478.4	1964.5	1964.5	27	4.3
India	2003	2018	2335.6	2100.8	2100.8	16	4.6
Philippines	2007	2018	1968.8	3022.0	3022.0	12	3.3
Indonesia	2007	2018	2757.9	4284.7	4284.7	12	3.4
Thailand	2002	2018	3731.3	6361.6	6361.6	17	2.5
Dominican Republic	2005	2018	4472.7	7697.7	7697.7	14	3.6
Mauritius	1985	2018	2762.8	10578.6	10578.6	34	2.6

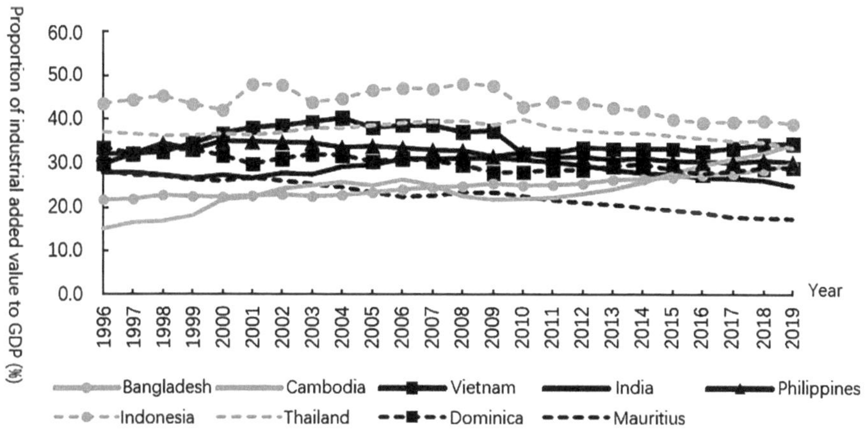

Fig. 15.5 Industrial value added as percentage of GDP in typical countries undergoing industrialization process

The results of the empirical analysis show that the significant variables mainly include indicators comprising external openness, internal openness, political form, total factor productivity, and GDP level per capita.

Both external openness and internal openness are significantly positive. Economic openness helps promote economic growth. To achieve economic takeoff and rapidly advance the industrialization process, a country needs to increase the degree of economic openness externally and internally and better establish a unified domestic and foreign market. An important reason why these countries can continue to promote the industrialization process is their expansion and maintaining of a high level of economic openness externally and internally.

The political governance status is significantly positive. Based on the A-C theory, the coefficients corresponding to the multi-peak and unimodal indexes are not significant, but the coefficient of the political form of this group is significantly positive, indicating that political stability at this stage is of certain help in effectively grasping the direction of economic development.

The impact on total factor productivity is positive. Technological progress is an important driving force for economic growth. The higher the increase in total factor productivity, the faster the economic growth. Late-developing economies have gained obvious technological catch-up effects from technological frontier economies.

The impact on GDP per capita level is negative. As the industrialization process gradually deepens and the GDP level per capita increases, the economic growth rate will transition from accelerated growth to growth slowdown. The higher the GDP level per capita, the potential economic growth rate will decrease.

15.4.3 Countries in Transition Period of Rapid Growth

Based on the standard that a relative growth rate greater than 0% for nine consecutive years is recorded as high-speed growth, countries whose high-speed growth ended as of 2018 and whose GDP per capita in 2018 exceeded US$6000 (in 2010 US dollars) were selected. This is a group of countries that have entered a post-transition period of rapid growth and includes Cuba, China, Peru, Malaysia, Kazakhstan, Romania, Chile, Turkey, Poland, and other countries, as shown in Table 15.4.

This group has the following main characteristics. First, some countries show the characteristics of secondary high-speed growth, with a high average growth rate but for a short duration. For example, Peru's economic growth rate continued to be higher than the benchmark growth rate from 1900 to 1938 in the early twentieth

Table 15.4 Typical countries in transition period after high growth

Country	Takeoff year	Landing year	GDP per capita in takeoff year (2010 USD)	GDP per capita in landing year (2010 USD)	2018 GDP per capita (2010 USD)	Span (years)	Average relative growth rate (%)
Cuba	1999	2009	3298.8	5596.1	6816.9	11	4.5
China	1977	2013	280.0	5710.6	7752.6	37	6.9
Peru	2002	2013	3359.2	5919.2	6453.6	12	4.4
Malaysia	1988	1997	4042.1	7041.7	12120.1	10	4.4
Kazakhstan	2000	2007	4491.6	8523.8	11165.5	8	8.0
Romanian	2001	2008	5224.6	8914.0	11532.1	8	6.6
Chile	1991	1997	6291.7	8932.1	15130.2	7	4.5
Turkey	2002	2018	8003.5	15069.0	15069.0	17	3.1
Poland	1993	2018	5827.6	16659.3	16659.3	26	3.0

century. Although the average relative growth rate was only 1.9%, it laid a good foundation for accumulation. Second, some countries have maintained a stable transition, with a low average growth rate but for a long duration. For example, Poland's GDP per capita reached US$5827.6 in 1993, and on this basis, it continued to grow at an average relative growth rate of 3.0% for 26 years. In fact, countries in transition, such as China, have only ended high-speed growth and are still in medium-high growth, entering a stable transition stage similar to that of Poland. Third, the GDP level per capita is relatively high at the end of high-speed growth, and the general GDP level per capita reaches US$6000 or even US$9000. Fourth, after the end of high-speed growth, economic growth enters medium-high growth, which is a critical period to determine the success of economic transformation. Fifth, the industrialization process has entered the middle and late stages, or it has been basically completed. As shown in Fig. 15.6, the proportion of industrial added value in GDP in China and Malaysia is close to 50%. Kazakhstan, Peru, Romania, Chile, and other countries have also seen obvious peaks in their industrialization levels.

The results of the empirical analysis show that the significant variables mainly include indicators comprising external openness, internal openness, political form, total factor productivity, and GDP level per capita.

External openness and internal openness are still significantly positive. The economies are in a post-transformation period of rapid growth, and the degree of economic openness externally and internally is still very important. The continuous expansion of the degree of economic openness externally and internally and the constant improvement of the unified domestic and foreign markets will contribute to economic transformation and upgrading.

Multimodal political governance is significantly negative. Different from the economic takeoff stage, the multi-peak pattern during the economic transition period may have a certain negative effect on economic development. This may be

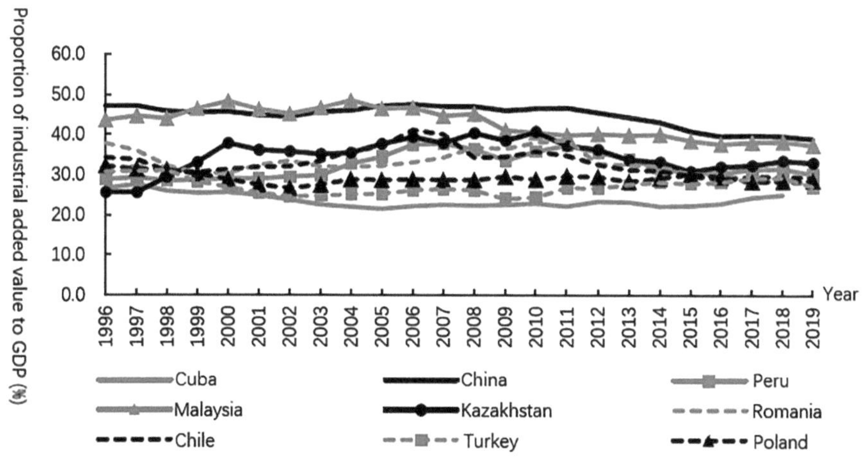

Fig. 15.6 Industrial value added as share of GDP in typical countries in transition period after high growth

because there are large differences in the direction of economic development and corresponding policy orientations during the economic transition period, making it more difficult to form a consensus, which in turn affects economic growth.

The impact on total factor productivity remains positive. Technological progress is also an important driving force for economic transformation. The faster total factor productivity increases, the faster the economic transformation process. At this time, the technological catch-up effect obtained by late-developing economies from technological frontier economies is getting smaller and smaller, and the requirements for independent innovation are increasing.

The impact on GDP per capita level is negative. The higher the GDP level per capita, the more the economic growth will slow down, especially during the economic transition period, which is often accompanied by the economy moving from high-speed growth to medium-speed or medium-high-speed growth.

15.4.4 Countries Stagnating After Rapid Growth

Based on the standard that a relative growth rate greater than 0% for nine consecutive years is recorded as high-speed growth, countries whose high-speed growth ended as of 2018 and whose GDP growth per capita had slowed or even declined by the end of high-speed growth in 2018 were selected into the grouping of countries that stagnated after rapid growth. This group includes Iran, Brazil, Argentina, Russia, Saudi Arabia, Venezuela, and other countries, as shown in Table 15.5.

This group has the following main characteristics. First, the GDP level per capita was relatively high at the end of the high-speed growth. After the high-speed growth, Iran's GDP per capita reached US$7015.0 in 1970, Brazil's GDP per capita reached US$7296.3 in 1976, Argentina's GDP per capita reached US$10,883.3 in 2011,

Table 15.5 Typical countries that experienced stagnation after rapid growth

Country	Takeoff year	Landing year	GDP per capita in takeoff year (2010 USD)	GDP per capita in landing year (2010 USD)	2018 GDP per capita (2010 USD)	Span (years)	Average relative growth rate (%)
Islamic Republic of Iran	1957	1970	2980.6	7015.0	6952.4	14	5.1
Brazil	1968	1976	4147.4	7296.3	11026.2	9	4.6
Argentina	2003	2011	7380.5	10883.3	10043.5	9	4.5
Russian Federation	1999	2008	5876.2	11087.8	11729.1	10	5.8
Saudi Arabia	1961	1974		39152.1	20819.7	14	9.2
Bolivarian Republic of Venezuela	1920	1930			14025.4	11	10.4

Russia's GDP per capita reached US$11,087.8 in 2008, and Saudi Arabia's GDP per capita reached US$39,152.1 in 1974. Second, the transformation was unsuccessful and economic growth stagnated for a long time. Iran's GDP per capita in 2018 was equivalent to that in 1970; Brazil's average growth rate from 1976 to 2018 was only 1.3%; Argentina's average growth rate from 2011 to 2018 was −1.1%; Russia's average growth rate from 2008 to 2018 was 0.6%; and Saudi Arabia's GDP per capita in 2018 was only 53.2% of that in 1974. Third, the level of industrialization is not high. As shown in Fig. 15.7, although Saudi Arabia, Venezuela, Iran, and other countries have experienced a relatively high level of industrialization, their industries are overly dependent on a single industry, such as oil, and the subsequent driving force of economic growth is insufficient. Russia, Argentina, and Brazil have a low level of industrialization; in 2019, the proportion of industrial added value in GDP was 32.2%, 23.4%, and 17.9%, respectively, which is difficult to support a higher level of economic growth.

The empirical analysis results show that significant variables mainly include indicators comprising external openness, internal openness, political cohesion, political form, and total factor productivity.

Keeping the economy open remains important. Among them, the degree of external openness is significantly positive, indicating that opening up to the outside world has played an important role in the economic growth of these countries, but the degree of internal openness is significantly negative, indicating that there are major problems in the internal economic policies of these countries, which has led to economic stagnation.

The degree of political cohesion is significantly positive. During this period, it is very important to maintain a high degree of political cohesion. The inability or difficulty in reaching a social consensus is also an important reason for the stagnation of economic growth in these countries.

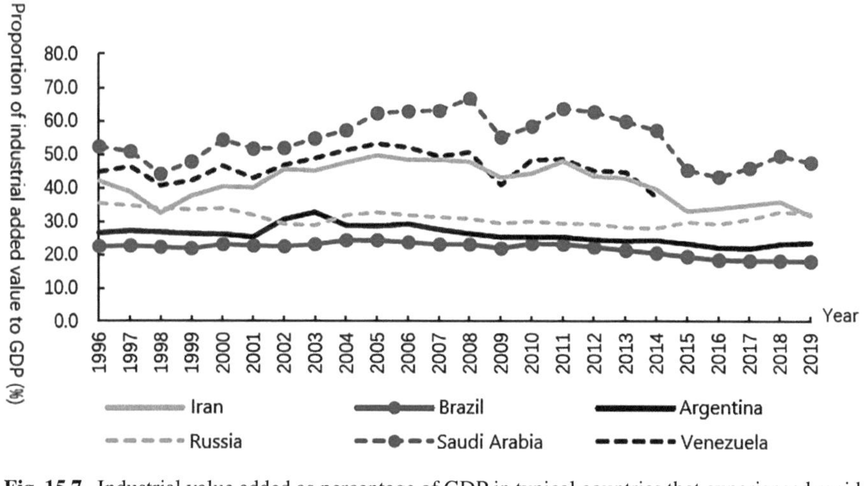

Fig. 15.7 Industrial value added as percentage of GDP in typical countries that experienced rapid growth followed by stagnation

The intersection term between multimodal political form and political cohesion is significantly negative. Since the degree of political cohesion is significantly positive and the coefficient of the intersection term with political form is negative, this shows that the multimodal form at this stage has certain constraints on reaching a social consensus.

The impact on total factor productivity remains positive. After achieving rapid economic growth, the role of population and capital factors in driving economic growth has declined and technological progress has become more difficult. Slow technological progress is also an important reason for the stagnation of economic growth in these countries.

15.4.5 Countries That Entered Ranks of Developed Countries

Based on the standard that a relative growth rate greater than 0% for nine consecutive years indicates high-speed growth, we selected countries whose high-speed growth ended by 2018 and whose GDP per capita continued to grow steadily from the end of high-speed growth to 2018, and these countries were included in the grouping of countries that entered the ranks of developed countries. This group includes Singapore, Portugal, South Korea, Greece, Spain, Japan, Germany, Canada, France, and other countries, as shown in Table 15.6.

This group has the following main characteristics. First, the economic transformation period can last for 10–20 years, during which the economy can maintain medium-to-high growth. For example, Spain's GDP per capita rose from US$8172.6 to US$16,626.4 from 1961 to 1975, with an average relative growth rate of 2.3% over 15 years. Second, after the successful economic transformation, steady growth can be maintained. For example, Japan's average GDP per capita growth rate from

Table 15.6 Typical countries that entered ranks of developed countries

Country	Takeoff year	Landing year	GDP per capita in takeoff year (2010 USD)	GDP per capita in landing year (2010 USD)	2018 GDP per capita (2010 USD)	Span (years)	Average relative growth rate (%).
Singapore	1960	1974	3503.4	9440.2	58247.9	15	7.3
Portugal	1965	1973	6029.6	11,281.3	23,994.7	9	4.3
South Korea	1966	1995	1277.5	12,055.2	26,761.9	30	5.6
Greece	1963	1972	7815.9	15,738.3	23,558.1	10	4.6
Spain	1961	1975	8172.6	16,626.4	32,949.6	15	2.3
Japan	1946	1969		18,837.2	48,919.8	24	5.0
Germany	1947	1958			47,477.8	12	6.6
Canada	1900	1917			51,391.7	18	2.0
France	1919	1933			43,663.6	15	3.7

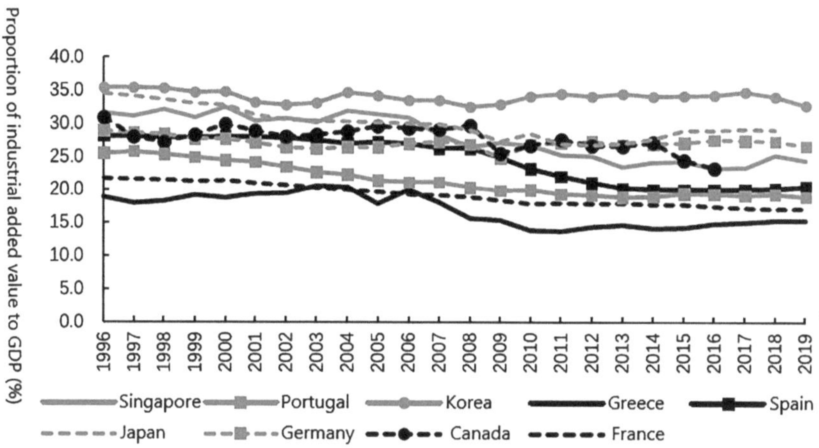

Fig. 15.8 Industrial value added as percentage of GDP in typical countries that entered ranks of developed countries

1969 to 2018 was 2%. Third, the GDP level per capita is relatively high at the end of the economic transformation. Generally, the GDP level per capita will exceed US$10,000 or even US$15,000. Fourth, the industrialization process is basically complete. As shown in Fig. 15.8, the proportion of industrial added value remains relatively stable according to the characteristics of the industrial structure. South Korea, Japan, and Germany continue to maintain a high level, which was 32.8%, 29.1%, and 26.7%, respectively, in 2019.

The empirical analysis results show that significant variables mainly include indicators comprising external openness, internal openness, political cohesion, political form, and total factor productivity.

Both external openness and internal openness are significantly positive. After the economy entered the ranks of developed countries, it is still very important to continue to open up to the outside world and build a unified domestic market, which is an important reason for maintaining sustained economic development.

The degree of political cohesion is significantly positive. During this period, it is still important to maintain a high degree of political cohesion, and maintaining social consensus is an important factor in ensuring sustainable economic development.

The impact on total factor productivity continues to be positive. Total factor productivity is the intrinsic driving factor for economic growth in developed countries.

15.5 Chapter Summary

It can be seen that whether it is to achieve rapid economic growth or to catch up with developed economies, political stability and economic openness are indispensable. In particular, to achieve economic catch-up, the requirements for economic growth are higher, which requires higher political cohesion and economic accessibility.

15.5.1 Economic Takeoff and Sustained Growth Require Political Cohesion

The analysis results show that political cohesion is very important for economic takeoff. Only when social consensus is reached can economic and social reforms be initiated. At present, there are still many countries that have not achieved economic takeoff. Some countries have stopped their economic takeoff again. Some countries have fallen into long-term stagnation after experiencing rapid growth. One of the important reasons is that political cohesion has been destroyed and it is impossible or difficult to reach social consensus. In the analysis, most countries that failed to catch up experienced political turmoil, which affected their economic performance. Therefore, maintaining political cohesion is crucial for economic takeoff, maintaining rapid growth, and achieving catch-up.

15.5.2 Economic Takeoff and Continuous Catch-Up Require Continuous Improvement of Economic Accessibility

The process of a country going from poor to rich is a process of competition and catch-up among countries. For a country to go from poor to rich, it usually needs to go through the complete stage of economic takeoff to deceleration and go through a high-growth stage for a long enough time. Since the Industrial Revolution, latecomer countries have embarked on the road of catching up by accepting technological diffusion and taking advantage of the dividends of globalization. A few of them successfully achieved economic transformation from poor to rich and leaped into the ranks of middle- and high-income countries, while some catching-up economies encountered failures and even fell into the quagmire of political turmoil and economic recession. Whether a successful catch-up can be achieved depends on whether a high level of economic accessibility can be maintained at all stages of economic development. Continuous improvement of the external and internal openness of the economy will help to make full use of the large international and domestic markets, optimize resource allocation, gather advantageous factors, continuously improve production efficiency, and continuously improve the position of the country's economy in the global industrial division of labor.

15.5.3 Single-Peak Governance and Multi-peak Governance Have No Significant Impact on Economic Growth in General, But There Are Stage Differences

Political forms with single-peak governance and multi-peak governance have no significant impact on economic growth in general but have a certain positive impact in the early stage of economic takeoff and have a certain negative impact in the period of economic transformation and in the period after an economy enters the ranks of developed countries. In terms of stages, in the stage of economic takeoff, the coefficient of political form is significantly positive, indicating that the multi-peak form in this stage has a certain help in effectively grasping the direction of economic development. Unlike the stage of economic takeoff, the political form in the economic transformation period is significantly negative. The multi-peak form in this stage may have a certain negative effect on economic development. It may be because there are large differences in the direction of economic development and the corresponding policy orientation during the economic transformation period, which makes it more difficult to reach a consensus, thereby affecting the pace of economic growth. After an economy enters the ranks of developed countries, the cross-terms of political form, economic openness, and political cohesion are all significantly negative. Excessive multi-peak forms will also have a certain negative impact on economic development.

15.5.4 Improving Total Factor Productivity Is Continuous Driving Force for Economic Growth

At different stages of economic development, total factor productivity has always been an important source of economic growth. In the early stages of economic development, by integrating into the global economy and obtaining technology diffusion dividends from developed countries, a country's total factor productivity can be rapidly improved. As the level of economic development and technology approaches those of the world's leading countries, the improvement of total factor productivity will gradually slow down. As the economy enters a period of transition, the technology catch-up effect obtained by late-developing economies from technologically advanced economies becomes smaller and smaller, and the requirements for independent innovation become higher and higher. Economic growth mainly depends on the speed of technological progress.

15.5.5 Economic Growth Rate and GDP Per Capita Show Inverted U-Shaped Correlation

In the stage of economic takeoff, the GDP level per capita has a positive impact on the economic growth rate. At this time, when the GDP level per capita is low, the economic growth rate accelerates as the GDP level per capita increases. When the GDP level per capita reaches a certain level, the impact of the GDP level per capita on the economic growth rate weakens. After the economy has experienced a long period of high-speed growth, especially during the economic transition period when the economy enters a medium-speed or medium-high-speed growth from high-speed growth, the GDP level per capita has a negative impact on the economic growth rate. The higher the GDP level per capita, the slower the economic growth rate. Overall, the economic growth rate and the GDP level per capita show an inverted U-shaped correlation.

References

Acemoglu D, Johnson S, Robinson J et al (2003) Institutional causes, macroeconomic symptoms: volatility, crises and growth. J Monet Econ 50(1):49–123
Becker SO, Hornung E, Woessmann L (2011) Education and catch-up in the industrial revolution. Am Econ J Macroecon 3(3):92–126
Berg A, Ostry JD, Zettelmeyer J (2012) What makes growth sustained. J Dev Econ 98(2):149–166
Eichengreen B, Park D, Shin K (2012) When fast-growing economies slow down: international evidence and implications for China. Asian Econ Pap 11(1):42–87
Hausmann R, Pritchett L, Rodrik D (2005) Growth accelerations. J Econ Growth 10(4):303–329
Hausmann R, Rodriguez FR, Wagner RA (2008) Growth collapses. CID working papers 136. Center for International Development at Harvard University
Jones BF, Olken BA (2008) The anatomy of start-stop growth. Rev Econ Stat 90(3):582–587
Sen K (2013) The political dynamics of economic growth. World Dev 47:71–86
Yang RD, Yao Y (2008) Limited catch-up and economic growth. Econ Res J 8:29-2s+64

Appendices

Appendix A: Construction of Key Indicators and Data Description

In this book, we not only proposed the core framework of the A-C theory, which is a political economics framework that explains economic development based on the two dimensions of economic accessibility and political cohesion, but also tested and demonstrated the main conclusion of the A-C theory and its universality based on multiple case studies and a series of statistical econometric analyses. A lot of analysis and discussion here depended on the construction of two key indicators: economic accessibility and political cohesion. In this appendix, we will introduce in detail how these two key indicators were constructed.

Construction of Political Governance Indicators

As mentioned above, political governance in the A–C theory mainly measures the structure of political power distribution within an economy. Next, we characterized the overall characteristics of a country's political governance from two dimensions, namely political cohesion and political centralization.

Political cohesion considers whether the government can represent the interests of the majority rather than the interests of some groups in the policy-making process and whether the policy can be implemented and executed efficiently. Based on this, we mainly used the following three sub-indicators to construct the cohesion index. The first sub-indicator was an indicator to measure government efficiency, that is, the quality and implementation of policies, which was used to characterize whether a country's policies can be well implemented, whether the service group of a policy was broadly representative, and whether a policy could be smoothly implemented. The second sub-indicator was the social resistance when a policy was implemented, focusing on whether the formulation of a policy was affected by public opinion

C. Chen et al., *From Poverty to Prosperity*, Understanding China,
https://doi.org/10.1007/978-981-95-7171-0

discussions and the accountability of the policy. We believe that the more complex the public opinion discussions on a policy are, the greater the constraints it will be subject to and the greater the impact on the rapid implementation of the policy. The third sub-indicator was the government's social mobilization and execution capabilities. Here, we used the government's taxation capacity to measure it—generally speaking, the stronger the taxation capacity of a government, to some extent this means that the government has higher social mobilization and execution capabilities. By standardizing these three sub-indicators within the range of [0, 5] and weighted averaging the standardized results, we could get the political cohesion index of each country.

In comparison, the construction of the political concentration index was relatively simple because it mainly examines whether public power is concentrated in a specific economic and social interest group or political group. In this book, we constructed the power concentration index based on the World Bank's classification standards and quantitative indicators for a country's electoral system (such as Table A.1) and the Herfindahl index of political parties. The reason why the electoral system index was selected as a sub-indicator is that the electoral system can represent the distribution of a country's social forces from a mechanism perspective, thus well describing the single-peak and multi-peak morphological indicators mentioned above. According to the World Bank's score for a country's government and head of state system, the higher the score, the higher the degree of multipolarity in the country's political governance. Another sub-indicator is the Herfindahl index of political parties, which measures the concentration of seats held by a country's political parties in parliament. We standardized these two sub-indicators, which were in the intervals of [1, 7, 0, 1], respectively, in the interval of [0, 5], and obtained the political concentration index after taking the weighted average.

Construction of Economic Accessibility Indicators

Economic accessibility measures the openness, inclusiveness, and diversity of an economy, including whether an economy can allow various production factors to participate in production activities in a non-discriminatory manner and whether the

Table A.1 World Bank standards for scoring different electoral systems

Condition	Level
There are no rules	1
There are no election rules	2
The way of election, there is a candidate	3
One party, multiple candidates	4
Multiple political parties, and the party that wins the election gets all parliamentary seats	5
Multiple political parties, the largest party that won the election got more than 75% of the seats	6
The largest party that won the election received less than 75% of the seats	7

economy can participate in the international economic division of labor in a deep, comprehensive, and diversified manner. Based on this, we constructed economic accessibility indicators from two aspects, namely internal accessibility and external accessibility.

Internal accessibility mainly refers to whether the domestic economic system arrangement provides convenience for economic factors to participate in social production and economic development, mainly including whether the labor force can migrate freely and be employed in the labor market without discrimination, whether capital can enter a certain field smoothly, and whether the transportation and logistics conditions are good to keep transaction costs within a reasonable range. Specifically, we mainly selected sub-indicators in three dimensions: capital, labor, and commodity markets. We measured capital accessibility by the cost of starting a business (such as the ratio of startup cost to per capita GNI), labor market accessibility by the percentage of regularly paid labor in the total employed population and the number of passengers carried per kilometer of railway per year, and commodity market accessibility by the logistics performance index. By standardizing these four sub-indicators and taking a weighted average, we could get the internal accessibility index.

External accessibility measures whether a country is well integrated into the global economic system. We measured a country's external accessibility level from three dimensions: the size of a country's external market, the scale of foreign capital entering domestic investment or domestic capital leaving, and the richness of a country's trade structure. Regarding the size of the external market, we measured the size of a country's external market from a global perspective based on the ratio of the country's total export value/domestic GDP to the global export value/global GDP; the larger the index, the larger the country's external market size. Similarly, we constructed the openness scale of a country's capital market based on the average of two indicators: the ratio of the country's outward FDI/domestic GDP to the global outward FDI/global GDP and the ratio of the country's received FDI/domestic GDP to the global received FDI/global GDP; the larger the indicator, the higher the activity and openness of the country's capital market. In addition, openness to the outside world is not only reflected in the scale, but whether a diversified and systematic open pattern is formed is also an important criterion for measuring the degree of openness of a country.

External accessibility based on trade, as described above, consists of two parts. One is the ratio of a country's total commodity exports to the country's GDP in the year, divided by the ratio of the total exports of the countries entering the world to the total global GDP in the year, and the ratio is taken as the cube root. Then the largest 2.5% of the samples and the smallest 2.5% of the samples are set to 5 and 0, respectively, and the 95% of the samples in the middle are standardized from 0 to 5. The second is the ratio of the country's total external imports and exports to its GDP in that year, divided by the ratio of the total external imports and exports of all countries in the world to the total global GDP in that year, and then taking the cube root of the ratio, and then setting the largest 2.5% of the samples and the smallest 2.5% of the samples to 5 and 0, respectively, and standardizing the 95% of the samples in the middle to 0–5. The weighted average of the two is the external accessibility index based on trade.

An external accessibility index based on FDI consists of two parts. The first is the ratio of the total FDI entering the country in the year to the country's GDP in the year, divided by the ratio of the total FDI inflows into all countries in the world to the total global GDP in the year. The cube root of the ratio is taken, then the largest 2.5% of the samples and the smallest 2.5% of the samples are set to 5 and 0, respectively, and 95% of the samples in the middle are standardized to 0–5. The second is the ratio of the total FDI outwards of the country in the year to the country's GDP in the year, divided by the ratio of the total FDI outwards of all countries in the world to the total global GDP in the year. The cube root of the ratio is taken, then the largest 2.5% of the samples and the smallest 2.5% of the samples are set to 5 and 0, respectively, and 95% of the samples in the middle are standardized to 0–5. The average of the two is the external accessibility index based on FDI.

An external accessibility index based on the export structure represents the sum of the percentage of agricultural products, minerals, and fuel exports in a country's total exports in a certain year. After standardizing it from 0 to 5, this value is subtracted from 5 to get the openness measured by trade structure:

5 – ((sample to be standardized – minimum value of total sample) / (maximum value of total sample – minimum value of total sample) × 5)

By standardizing the above three sub-indicators and taking the weighted average, we could get the external accessibility index. By taking the weighted average of the internal accessibility index and the external accessibility index and standardizing them, we could get the economic accessibility index of each country each year.

Other Notes on Data

Except for a few case studies that required a longer time span, the data used in this book's econometric analysis were relevant data from 209 countries from 1996 to 2018.

As mentioned above, the political governance index has three main sub-indicators. To measure these three sub-indicators, we selected the government effectiveness index, voice and accountability index, and the proportion of tax revenue in GDP of each country in the World Development Index (WDI) of the World Bank.

For economic data, in addition to the indicators used in the construction of the above indicators, we also compiled the following data from the World Bank database:

- GDP per capita (in constant 2010 US dollars)
- GDP per capita (in terms of international purchasing power parity in 2011 US dollars)
- GDP per capita (in current prices of local currencies)
- GDP per capita growth rate (in constant local currency prices)

On this basis, we classified the development stages of countries based on GDP per capita (constant 2010 prices, US dollars). If the GDP per capita was within US$0–US$4000, it was in Stage 1; within US$4000–US$8000, it was in Stage 2; within US$8000–US$12000, it was in Stage 3; within US$12000–US$16000, it was in Stage 4; and if the GDP per capita exceeded US$16,000, it belonged to Stage 5.

For other questions about the data, please contact the authors.

Appendix B: Explanation of Chinese Historical Data Used in the Book

In Chap. 2 of this book, we reviewed the changes in China's political governance and economic system since the Xinhai Revolution based on the A-C theory, using a large amount of relevant data. Considering that the data used involve multiple sources, in addition to the explanation of the construction of relevant indicators in Appendix A, we will make some additional explanations in this appendix.

As we explained in Appendix A, with a few exceptions, the data used in this book mostly span from 1996 to 2018. However, the data cited in the analysis and discussion of the changes in China's political governance and economic system since the Xinhai Revolution span from 1911 to 2019. All monetary units are 1990 international dollars.

The related variables involved in the empirical study are as follows:

Land area:	Obtained and cross-validated from the World Bank database and Chinese historical records.
Purchasing power parity (PPP) GDP (1990 international dollars, millions):	Data were from the World Bank database and Maddison Project Database.
Population:	Data were from the World Bank database and Maddison Project Database.
PPP GDP per capita:	Obtained by dividing PPP GDP by population data.
GDP per capita growth rate:	Calculated based on PPP GDP per capita.
China's outward direct investment:	Data on China's outward direct investment since 1950 were from the World Bank. According to the research by Xu et al. (2017), China's outward direct investment before 1950 was very small and negligible, which was very common in many developing countries during the same period.

Foreign direct investment in China:	For data before 1936, refer to Cambridge History of the Republic of China (Volume 1), page 117. The data were compiled based on Hou Jiming's Foreign Investment and Economic Development in China from 1840 to 1937, pages 13 and 17. Among them, the proportion of China's investment in global investment was calculated in two steps: first, calculate the proportion of British investment in China in 1914 and 1931 to the total British investment, then calculate the proportion of the total British investment in China in the total global investment in China in those years. An estimate based on these. After 1949, the Soviet Union provided a large amount of assistance to China. The specific direct investment amount and the global direct investment total cannot be calculated in detail. Therefore, the corresponding index of China's FDI in 1949 was used as the indicator before the Soviet Union withdrew its experts from 1949 to 1960.
The proportion of exports to GDP and the proportion of imports and exports to GDP:	Data were from Xiao Lianglin's "China's Foreign Trade Statistics, 1864–1949," pp. 23–24, 274–275; Zheng Youkui's "China's Foreign Trade and Industrial Development," p. 259; and the World Bank WDI database. However, there were still missing data in the middle after the three data sources were spliced together. Considering that the economic activities of China's important export destinations, including Northeast China, Beijing-Tianjin, and Jianghuai, were basically stagnant and foreign trade activities were bleak before and after the three major battles of the Liberation War, we assumed that the proportion of China's exports to GDP and the proportion of imports and

	exports to GDP during this period were both 0. In addition, we assumed that the proportion of exports and total imports and exports to GDP changed at a uniform rate within a certain time range, so as to fill in the missing years.
The proportion of primary agricultural products, fuels, and primary metals in exports:	Data since 1962 were from the World Bank WDI-related export structure data, and data before 1962 were from Zheng Youkui's "China's Foreign Trade and Industrial Development," pages 32 and 34, in which tea and raw cotton were classified as primary agricultural products, and the rest of the caliber were the same. For years that were not counted, the data were estimated and supplemented, assuming that the rate of change was stable.
Railway passenger turnover (million people/kilometer):	Data from 1912 to 1947 were from Yan Zhongping's "Selected Statistical Data on China's Modern Economic History"; data from 1996 to 2019 were from the World Bank WDI Railway Passenger Capacity Index, and the data during the period were calculated through equal speed transformation. Refer to Ma Qianli's "A Brief History of China's Railway Construction" to organize the railway construction process during the period as a reference.
Market logistics level:	Data from 1912 to 1947 were from Yan Zhongping's "Selected Statistical Data on China's Modern Economic History" and data from 1996 to 2019 were from the World Bank WDI Railway Freight Capacity Index.
The proportion of labor with monthly and weekly wages to total labor:	The data for 1912 were from the "First Agricultural and Industrial Statistics Table of the First Year of the Republic of China," and the machinery manufacturing industry, ship and vehicle manufacturing industry, appliance manufacturing

industry, pharmaceutical industry, electrical industry, metal refining, and other industries were selected as industries with fixed wages to obtain the proportion of their labor force to the total labor force. The data for 1933 were from Liu Dajun's "National Economic Statistics in 1933", where among the industries belonging to this category were heavy industries, such as ships, internal combustion engines, electricity, railways, metallurgy, and machinery. It is worth noting that although the textile industry had a large number of employees, they were largely temporary workers, and the number of employees was adjusted at any time according to the quality of the industry. Many other low-threshold light industries had such characteristics, so they were not included. The total number of workers was 58,148,360, of which 807,875 were classified as having fixed monthly and weekly salaries. In order to make up for the data from 1912 to 1933, we assumed that the number of people with fixed monthly and weekly salaries increased at a uniform rate year by year during these 22 years. The proportion of employees in state-owned enterprises and collective enterprises in the total population from 1949 to before the Three Major Reforms was also made up according to this logic. In addition, before the reform and opening up, the development of private enterprises was restricted, and their scale was relatively limited. Therefore, the labor force with fixed income mainly came from government departments, state-owned enterprises, and collective enterprises. We used the number of employees in government departments, state-owned enterprises, and collective enterprises as the number of labor forces with fixed

	income. The relevant data came from the Ministry of Human Resources and Social Security.
Policy accountability and policy implementation:	Data were from the World Bank WGI database.
The proportion of tax revenue to GDP:	The relevant tax types and tax information from the 2nd to 24th year of the Republic of China were obtained through the fourth chapter of the Fiscal Yearbook and the Fiscal Yearbook Supplement edited by Kong Xiangxi, and the currency was converted into 1990 international yuan. In Xu et al. (2017), the industrial output value in 1911 was estimated to be 21.095 billion international yuan (1990 prices) based on the same data.
Government head election system:	According to the specific mechanism for the generation of heads of state and heads of government in China, the specific standards of the World Bank were matched.
Parliamentary seats via the Herfindahl index:	These were calculated based on the specific situation in China since the Xinhai Revolution. The main time nodes considered include the North-South peace talks, the assassination of Song Jiaoren, multiple parliamentary elections, the Northern Expedition, the Ninghan River, and several stages of Chiang Kai-shek's dictatorship. Intra-party struggles were not taken into account here, but if different warlords controlled and influenced parliament, the number of seats in parliament was reflected in the index (History of the Republic of China, The Cambridge History of the Republic of China (Volumes I and II)).

Reference

Xu Y, Shi Z, Leeuwen VB, Yuping N, Zhang Z, Ma Y (2017) Chinese national income, ca. 1661–1933. Aust Econ Hist Rev 57(3):368–393

MIX
Papier aus verantwortungsvollen Quellen
Paper from responsible sources
FSC® C105338

If you have any concerns about our products,
you can contact us on
ProductSafety@springernature.com

In case Publisher is established outside the EU,
the EU authorized representative is:
Springer Nature Customer Service Center GmbH
Europaplatz 3, 69115 Heidelberg, Germany

Printed by Libri Plureos GmbH
in Hamburg, Germany